W9-COA-524

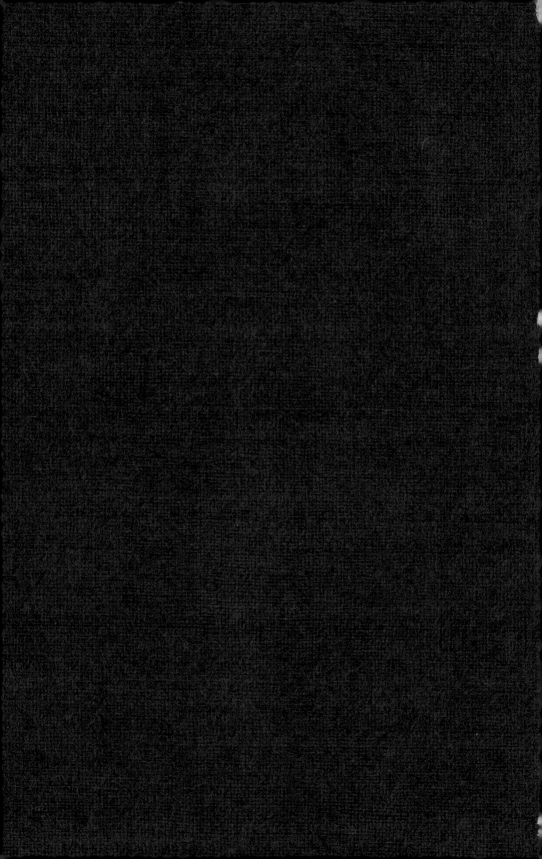

CLINICAL AND DIAGNOSTIC INTERVIEWING

Clinical and Diagnostic Interviewing

Edited by Robert J. Craig, Ph.D.

JASON ARONSON INC.
Northvale, New Jersey
London

10 9 8 7 6 5 4 3 2 1

Library of Congress Cataloging-in-Publication Data

Clinical and diagnostic interviewing / edited by Robert J. Craig.
p. cm.
Includes index.
ISBN 0-87668-848-2
1. Interviewing in psychiatry. I. Craig, Robert J., 1941- .
[DNLM: 1. Interview, Psychological—methods. WM 141 C6407]
RC480.7.C55 1989
616.89—dc 19
DNLM/DLC 89-29
for Library of Congress CIP

Manufactured in the United States of America. Jason Aronson Inc. offers books and cassettes. For information and catalog write to Jason Aronson Inc., 230 Livingston Street, Northvale, New Jersey 07647.

This book is dedicated to:
Kevin Gerard
Kathleen Terese
Daniel Robert

Contents

Contributors

DANIEL A. BEACH, Ph.D.
Department of Psychology
Rosary College
River Forest, Illinois

ROBERT J. CRAIG, Ph.D.
Illinois School of Professional Psychology and
Director, Drug Abuse Program
West Side VA Medical Center and
School of Public Health
University of Illinois at Chicago
Chicago, Illinois

JOESPH A. FLAHERTY, M.D.
Professor and Director of Education and Training
Department of Psychiatry
University of Illinois at Chicago
Chicago, Illinois

ALLEN J. FRANCES, M.D.
Professor of Psychiatry
Cornell University Medical College
Payne Whitney Clinic
New York, New York

ELIZABETH FRICK, Psy.D.
Private Practice
Department of Psychiatry and Behavioral Sciences
Northwestern University Medical School
Chicago, Illinois

F. MOISES GAVIRIA, M.D.
Professor and Director, Affective Disorders Clinic
Department of Psychiatry
University of Illinois at Chicago
Chicago, Illinois

DAVID GOODMAN, Ph.D.
Private Practice
St. Charles, Illinois

SALVATORE R. MADDI, Ph.D.
Professor and Director, Social Ecology Program
University of California, Irvine
Irvine, California

FRANK GRUBA-McCALLISTER, Ph.D.
Faculty
Illinois School of Professional Psychology
Chicago, Illinois

RALPH S. IENNARELLA, Ph.D.
Faculty
Department of Psychiatry and Behavioral Sciences
Northwestern University Medical School
Chicago, Illinois

PIERRE-EMMANUEL LACOCQUE, Ph.D.
Staff Psychologist
Department of Psychiatry
Luthern General Hospital
Park Ridge, Illinois

NELL LOGAN, Ph.D. (A.B.P.P.)
Faculty
Illinois School of Professional Psychology
Chicago, Illinois

CHERYL MARSHALL, Psy.D.
Coordinator, Eating Disorders Program
Luthern General Hospital
Park Ridge, Illinois

J. REID MELOY, Ph.D.
Chief, Forensic Mental Health Services
San Diego County
San Diego, California

THOMAS W. PHELAN, Ph.D.
Private Practice
Carol Stream, Illinois

ELIEZER SCHWARTZ, Ph.D.
Faculty
Illinois School of Professional Psychology
Chicago, Illinois

TIMOTHY S. TRULL, M.A.
Department of Psychology
Cornell University Medical College
White Plains, New York

J. SCOTT VERINIS, Ph.D.
West Side VA Medical Center and Department of Psychiatry
University of Illinois at Chicago
Chicago, Illinois

THOMAS A. WIDIGER, Ph.D.
Associate Professor of Psychology
University of Kentucky
Lexington, Kentucky

TIMOTHY J. WOLF, Ph.D.
Private Practice
San Diego, California

ROBERT J. YUFIT, Ph.D. (A.B.P.P.)
Northwestern University
Institute for Psychiatry and
President, American Association of Suicidology
Chicago, Illinois

Preface and Acknowledgments

The idea for this book derived from my experiences in conducting yearlong seminars in clinical interviewing for graduate students in clinical psychology. Along with several of my colleagues at the Illinois School of Professional Psychology, who were also conducting these intense, small group seminars, I experienced a sense of frustration in locating texts to use for this purpose. Although interviewing is essential to the role tasks of all mental health professions, it is surprising to find so few resources devoted to this topic. Our course evaluations consistently requested a pragmatic textbook as an aid in training in clinical interviewing. Recently, a few books on interviewing have been published but most have been tied to interviewing for DSM-III-R disorders. This is too narrow a focus for the kinds of knowledge and information needed by clinicians when faced with certain interviewing situations.

In discussing this dilemma with practicing clinicians, I found that they too had a need for source material on clinical interviewing. This was particularly true when they were faced with patients or problem areas in which they had limited training or experience. For these situations they said they would prefer a sourcebook that provided a summary of the main issues or factors to be assessed, as well as guidelines that provided a systematic and comprehensive approach to the diagnostic and clinical interviewing process. Based on these evaluations and recommendations I decided to undertake the endeavor.

Having edited a book before, I was fully cognizant of the difficulties that lay ahead. Once the idea took shape and the book's organization had been decided, the most crucial task was selecting clinicians who understood the nature of patients' and their problems, who stayed abreast of contemporary developments in their fields of specialization, wrote well but pragmatically, and had the ability to put their expertise into writing against a deadline.

Assembled here are the clinicians who did meet these criteria and who truly deserve to be called "outstanding." This volume attests to the enthusiasm with which they approached their work.

Many editors of contributed books provide their authors with a basic structure to follow to ensure that the book has a certain degree of coherence and organization. I feel, however, that such structuring may result in a loss of clinical richness. Therefore, each of my contributors was given the following directions: (1) Assume your audience knows nothing about your topic. If they were faced with a patient suspected of having this particular problem, what would they need to know to make a competent assessment? (2) Whenever possible, cite relevant research to substantiate your material so that clinical interviewing may be placed on a more empirical basis, and (3) cite case examples illustrating your concepts.

I felt that this structure would allow the reader to see how abstract concepts are dynamically expressed in actual clinical contexts. These directives provided organization while allowing each contributor to develop the kind of chapter he or she felt represented the "state-of-the-art" in their particular area. The result, I think, is a readable and pragmatic contribution to the field of clinical interviewing.

This volume was not produced in a vacuum. Indeed, I received the assistance and cooperation of many people during this project. I want to particularly acknowledge the contributions of Patricia Bernbom, Psy.D., who facilitated the acquisition of several of the contributors, who gave me continued verbal support and encouragement during the entire process, and whose boundless energy, enthusiasm and dedication to ethical practice is a model for us all. Eli Coleman, Ph.D., suggested one of the contributors. I am also deeply appreciative to the individual contributors who met deadline requirements, and to their secretaries and typists for delivering a quality product to me in the requested format. Thanks to Joan Langs, consulting editor, who made many valuable suggestions that improved the quality of the manuscript, to Nancy Morgan Andreola, whose superb copyediting immeasurably improved this manuscript, to Dorothy Erstling who kept the project moving along at a timely pace, and to Jason Aronson, M.D., for his faith in this volume. Finally, I thank my graduate students, colleagues and professional friends for suggesting and supporting this work.

All of the material in this volume is original material except for my chapter on drug abuse, which is an expanded version of a paper that originally appeared in *Professional Psychology: Research and Practice* (1988), vol. 19, pp. 14–20, entitled "Diagnostic Interviewing with Drug Abusers," copyright 1988 by the American Psychological Association and reprinted and adapted by permission of the publisher.

Introduction

This book is divided into four parts. Introductory chapters on clinical interviewing are presented in Part I. In Chapter 1, Craig introduces the process of clinical interviewing. He reviews methods of obtaining information, compares structured and unstructured interviews, discusses the physical setting as an ingredient in interview preparation, and reviews the different kinds of interviews. He then presents and contrasts the way patients and clinicians approach the interview process. He reviews basic interviewing techniques, notes the interpersonal qualities of a clinician thought to be influencing variables towards an effective interview, and presents the phases of a clinical interview that include the introduction, exploration, hypothesis testing, client feedback, and termination. The dynamic nature of the clinical process and the interaction between client and clinician is noted throughout. Craig stresses the nostrum that the clinician is in control of the process during all phases of the interview.

In Chapter 2, Gruba-McCallister argues that the success of the interview—a relationship characterized by reciprocity and sharing—rests upon a particular stance and set of attributes in the clinician. In particular, it depends on the quality of the relationship that the clinician is able to establish with the client. The interviewer tries to learn enough about the client to make an accurate diagnosis and appropriate recommendations, and at the same time is being therapeutic. This relationship is the key to the interviewing process. By paying attention to feelings created in himself by the client, the clinician can more accurately assess the way the client interacts in life. Gruba-McCallister uses the word "dialectic" to convey the mutuality that exists at multiple levels in the interview. Clinicians need to understand how their own presuppositions, attitudes, and beliefs can influence the nature and direction of the interview. The process of "bracketing" is recommended to reduce these biases. A receptive, participatory, observational approach is recommended to arrive at an assessment. From a phenomenological viewpoint, it is the perceptions and experiences of the client that the clinician needs to understand.

Part II presents the most contemporary theoretical orientations extant in the field of mental health. These chapters demonstrate that interviews are not aimless but rather stem from philosophical and theoretical positions concerning the nature of human behavior and that these orientations *per se* influence the interview itself.

In Chapter 3, Iennarella and Frick stress that a psychoanalytically-oriented interview rests on the assumption that unconscious psychological processes play a critical role in determining behavior. Psychoanalytic interviews are of two types, those which focus on psychodynamics and intrapsychic structures, and those which concentrate on object relations and interpersonal functions. Kernberg's Structural Interview is presented as a prototype of the interview that focuses on psychodynamics and intrapsychic structures, while Sullivan's approach is presented as a prototype of an interview that concentrates on object relations and interpersonal functioning. The chapter highlights Kohut's method for dealing with narcissistic issues, Gill's approach to analyzing transference, and Langs' development of a framework for understanding unconscious communications. An initial session is presented, followed by a discussion of the clinical material, which helps the reader understand some of the more abstract concepts used by the psychoanalytic orientation. The authors conclude that the differences among the various psychoanalytic approaches is more a matter of emphasis than substance.

Maddi, in Chapter 4, indicates that the humanistic branch of psychology, with its roots in Rogerian philosophy and a nondirective approach to treatment, has traditionally eschewed diagnosis, as "insufficiently appreciative of human subjectivity and unnecessary as a guide to psychotherapy." According to Maddi, however, within the existential and humanistic tradition there are assessment goals and techniques that do have relevance to the assessment process. He sees the concepts of psychological maturity, premorbidity, and psychopathology as the concepts that are most relevant in theorizing about human behavior. Humanists view psychopathology as a violation of what it means to be human, while existentialists see it as a chronic sense of meaninglessness. Psychological maturity is defined by the construct of "authenticity." Premorbidity, or what Maddi calls "conformism," stems from a relative lack of symbolization, imagination, judgment and decision making (what the analysts would call "ego"). Stress undermines adjustment and results in psychopathology. Maturity, from this perspective, is referred to as "fully functioning." Premorbidity and psychopathology result from receiving conditional positive regard. Symptom formation is the incongruence between the sense of self and the ideal self. Maddi describes the process of interviewing from a humanistic/existential framework that emphasizes current experiences, processes, and content, and he provides examples via client statements that illustrate the concepts developed in the paper. There are questionnaires that present assessment from the humanistic/existential viewpoint. Differences between these two orientations are presented and Maddi details interviewing concepts from both perspectives. The chapter concludes with the assertion that there is a significant conceptual and technical material in the existential/humanistic orientation that has relevance to the clinical process of interviewing.

A behavioral orientation is unique among the major approaches in that it does not include intervening variables or reified entities. The approach requires neither an id, ego, superego, nor empathic stance from the therapist (unless that *is* the response designated for reinforcement and modeling), nor does it deal in hypothetical constructs, such as role boundary disturbances, enmeshment, and the like. Behaviorists deal directly with overt behavior. Behavioral assessment assumes that all behavior is lawful and controlled by the general principles of learning. In Chapter 5, Beach explains classical and operant conditioning and provides examples of each. The topics of modeling, learned emotional responses, and verbal conditioning are addressed as they apply to the clinical interview. A behavioral epistemology assumes behavior is determined largely through differential rewards and punishments within the individual's learning history. The chapter concludes with the structure and content of a behavioral interview.

A family systems orientation, both for interviewing and for interventions, requires a different kind of thinking. Whereas all of the other orientations presume a linear causality between symptom and pathology, a family systems approach assumes a circular causality. Individual psychopathology plays a role in the homeostasis functioning of the family as a system. In Chapter 6, Goodman traces the roots of the family systems orientation, beginning with the seminal contributions of the "communication school." Much of current systems practice strikes a middle ground, integrating the Structural approach of Minuchin and the Strategic approach of Jay Haley. The major tenet in this approach is that every symptom or sign of psychopathology is, at its source, a sign of a dysfunctional family system. A family systems orientation diverges from other approaches in that the interviewer is expected to begin interventions to change the family system at the onset of the initial interview.

Part III presents chapters dealing with interviewing the basic kinds of populations that are frequently encountered by mental health clinicians.

Depression is one of the most ubiquitous psychological disturbances, with psychological, social and biological factors playing roles in the development of depressive symptoms. In Chapter 7, Flaherty and Gavaria provide a list of common symptoms of depressive syndromes. DSM-III-R categories of affective disorders are presented, with a brief description of their clinical course and epidemiology. Also discussed is the role of personality in the development of affective disorders. The authors recommend that personality should be readdressed after the affect disorder has been resolved, since the manifestations of personality style may be a reaction to the affective state. Other disorders (adjustment disorders, organic affective disorder, schizophrenia, schizoaffective disorder) that often present with depressive symptoms are discussed for the purpose of differential diagnosis. A format for interviewing for affective disorders is presented, along with promising laboratory tests that may provide more definitive diagnostic categorization and prescriptive response to pharmacotherapy. Also presented are the common rating scales (Hamilton, Beck), SADS, and psychological tests that are useful in these assessments.

Substance abuse has become endemic in our society and mental health clinicians are faced with the increasing responsibility of assessing substance abuse. In Chapter 8, Craig presents principles of interviewing adult drug abusers and covers diagnostic classification, categories of abuse, changing concepts of addiction and dependence, determination of abuse liability, reliability of patient self-reports, structured and unstructured clinical interview formats, available diagnostic instruments, dual diagnosis, confidentiality, and countertransference. A case example and a list of interview suggestions is included.

Defining alcoholism is a major issue since the syndrome is multivariate with many manifestations. In Chapter 9, Verinis addresses the different diagnostic criteria that have been proposed to define alcoholism, including Jellinek's "species," the World Health Organization and the National Council on Alcoholism's criteria, Feighner, Pattison, and DSM-III-R criteria. Verinis reviews the manifestations of alcoholism in females, the elderly, Blacks, Hispanics, American Indians, and Asians. Alcoholism can coexist with affective disorders, schizophrenia, sociopathy/psychopathy, drug abuse, anxiety, and various organic brain syndromes. The issue of suicidal risk in these populations is also addressed. The concept of the "alcoholic personality" is discussed and case history material is interspersed to illustrate applications of these issues. Finally, Verinis offers some suggestions on how to interview a person suspected of or presenting with problematic drinking and/or alcoholism.

Eating disorders are increasingly common. Within this spectrum of disorders, anorexia and bulimia have become the most prevalent. Marshall presents the DSM-III-R classifications and criteria for anorexia and bulimia, discusses differential diagnosis, and concurrent psychiatric conditions that have been linked with these two disorders. She details the medical, nutritional, and psychological aspects, and presents the factors that should be considered in an initial evaluation. She stresses the need for a medical exam and nutritional assessment, a weight history, social history, and a mental status exam. Specialized inventories are available to assess eating disorders, but the traditional mental health clinical interview remains the most popular method. The chapter concludes with a consideration of treatment recommendations.

In Chapter 11, Lacocque covers the psychodiagnostic interviewing of obese patients. He presents the different types of obesities and their etiologies, and focuses on diagnosis and assessment devices. Specific guidelines are provided to assess patient's motivation for treatment, perfectionistic strivings, psychosocial adaptation, insight and denial level, eating habits, body image, and capacity to mourn. Tables and an interviewing guide are also presented.

No aspect of mental health has captured the attention of clinicians like the issue of personality. Discussions of personality seem to dominate case conferences, presentations, and reviews. Personality disorders are defined as patterns of inflexible, maladaptive personality traits that result in significant impairment in social or occupational functioning, and/or subjective distress. They are receiving more attention since the inclusion of a separate diagnostic axis in DSM-III and the development of more objective criteria. Widiger and coauthors (Chapter 12) contend that many clinicians do not follow DSM-III-R criteria and instead form subjective impressions that they have found clinically useful. However, unless each clinician diagnoses on the basis of a systematic standard of criteria sets, the reliability of personality diagnosis will remain low.

Various structured personality instruments are available. The authors advise to assess traits with behavioral referents, rather than from opinion, since patients will vary on the degree of meaning they infer to any request for trait information. Functional impairment and subjective distress are two key factors to address when evaluating for personality disorders. Thus authors advise us to assess traits, not situational reactions to temporary conditions. Controversies and issues in the area of personality diagnosis are presented, including trait versus state issues, traits versus situations, traits versus roles, clinical judgment, and categorical versus dimensional thinking.

The field of child abuse is becoming highly sophisticated and specialized. In Chapter 13 Wolf discusses the specialized skills needed by the clinician who initially evaluates a child or adolescent suspected of child abuse or neglect. Methods to establish goals and rapport are initially presented, procedures for recognition and evaluation are outlined and special techniques and aids for interviewing, such as anatomically correct dolls, are presented and debated.

Phelan, in Chapter 14, provides an historical review of the diagnosis of Attention Deficit Disorder (ADD), and then details the basic symptoms of the condition. He stresses the notion that children with ADD tend to have pervasive problems that affect performance in school, at home, and socially. Therefore, these three spheres must be specifically addressed in the evaluation. Misconceptions about the disorder are clarified so that the clinical interviewer can avoid these pitfalls during the assessment. The evaluation of ADD is unique in that direct observation of the patient in the clinician's office is the least useful part of the diagnosis. The initial work-up must include a great deal of information from outside sources such as the parents, school personnel (especially the primary teacher), and pediatrician. Phelan suggests that the ADD evaluation process involve a parent interview, a behavior rating scale, home and school questionnaires, collection of school information, and psychological testing, particularly for a learning disability. He details what areas must be specifically addressed in each of these components. The premise of the chapter is that a competent evaluation of ADD cannot be made without a thorough approach.

Part IV presents special focused exams. Some, such as the mental status exam and the assessment of suicidal risk, become part of the clinical interview when indicated by material elicited during the interview process. Others, such as the assessment of suspected child abuse victims, or the forensic interview are not part of a regular clinical interview.

Schwartz (Chapter 15) traces the development of the contemporary mental status exam (MSE) to the systematic observations of Emil Kraepelin, which led to a psychiatric nosology based on observations and descriptions, culminating in DSM-III-R. The author then provides guidelines for the general content categories one needs to assess when describing a patient's mental status and highlights the major systems in each. These categories include general appearance, behavior, affect and mood, speech and thought, perceptions, orientation, attention and concentration, memory, and intellectual functioning. Schwartz considers the MSE versatile because of its adaptability to different theoretical perspectives.

Research has not yet established a definitive indicator of suicide in patients at risk, but empirical studies and clinical observations have demonstrated that certain factors increase the probability of its occurrence. In Chapter 16, Yufit discusses the thorny problem of differentiating between an intent to die versus an attempt to communicate. He presents a Quantified Focused Interview that explores specific areas considered to be associated with high suicidal potential, and provides quantification of these variables, deriving an index of suicidal potential. Included in the chapter is a Suicide Screening Checklist that helps the clinician organize the interview. Thus, Yufit recommends both a structured, quantified approach and a clinical interview, as an aid to making these difficult judgments.

Logan's assessment of children (Chapter 17) shows that childhood behavior problems differ from adults, but the purpose of assessment remains the same. While DSM-III-R classification system is the most frequently used nosological system for childhood disorders, there are other systems to consider. The interviewer's task is to understand the roles played by the parents and the child, within the context of the child's age and life circumstances. Childhood problems may be age-appropriate developmental issues, transitory reactions to specific life circumstances, or more severe disorders. Clinicians are urged to inspect their own reactions, which provide important clues to specific characteristics of the child as well as the parents' reactions to the child. A recommended assessment outline is offered. Material on interviewing parents and preparing the child for evaluation are presented. Logan makes recommendations on how to deal with the issue of confidentiality vis-a-vis the parents. Different types of children's interviews (traditional mental health, play, conversation, direct behavioral observation) are discussed and a case example is presented to illustrate chapter contents.

Many clinicians are now being trained in forensic issues such as fitness to stand trial, insanity pleas, and custody evaluations. These new roles provide exciting opportunities for the clinician and challenges clinical skills. Meloy (Chapter 18) elaborates on the basic characteristics of the forensic interview. These include the coercive context of the interview, the absence of confidentiality and privileged status of the interview, use of findings by laymen, the possible presence of distortion, and the probability of disagreement and challenge to the basic findings.

The art of clinical interviewing is a dynamic process that incorporates the material presented in these chapters. For example, to assess depression, one needs to do a mental status exam, assess for suicidal risk, and evaluate possible alcohol or drug abuse problems. The material necessarily requires separation for didactic purposes, with the realization that there is no such separation in actual clinical practice.

PART I

Basic Elements in a Clinical Interview

1 The Clinical Process of Interviewing

ROBERT J. CRAIG, Ph.D.

The clinical interview is endemic to all mental health disciplines, yet it has received surprisingly little attention in the literature. Most classic psychiatry and psychology texts include a chapter on the topic (Stevenson 1959, Wiens 1976); research has been conducted and summarized on the anatomy of a clinical interview (Matarazzo 1965, 1978, Wiens and Matarazzo 1983); and, more recently, literature has appeared on interviewing, but the latter has been tied rather specifically to DSM-III-(R) (Endicott and Spitzer 1978, Hersen and Turner 1985). The purpose of this chapter is to provide a basic introduction to the clinical process of interviewing. Topics include the ways in which patients and clinicians approach an interview, techniques, phases, and a discussion of the last minutes of an initial interview.

SOCIAL VERSUS CLINICAL INTERACTIONS

A clinical interview has much in common with social interaction and contains elements of group and dyadic dynamics; however, there are fundamental differences between a clinical interview and other types of relationships. In a clinical interview, most rules of social etiquette do not apply. The conversation is focused on the patient and is mostly unidirectional. The relationship is nonintimate and professional, with the expectation that communication between the parties is relevant to the task at hand. There are limits of time, place, and frequency of interaction imposed by both parties. The clinician's statements have a larger purpose than mere mutual dialogue, and the specific goals and expected outcomes are established as a result of the clinical interaction (Kanfer and Seheft 1988).

METHODS OF OBTAINING INFORMATION

Most of the information obtained in a clinical interview is based on patient self-report, combined with the interviewer's clinical observation. This is not to discount other sources of information, such as collateral reports from significant others, case records, psychological testing, or supplemental structured interviews. However, we will focus in this book on the direct interview of an individual patient because it is both the most common and the most clinically rich source of information.

STRUCTURED VERSUS UNSTRUCTURED INTERVIEWS

Interviews can be either structured or unstructured. Structured interviews prescribe a set of questions over defined content areas. (Several references to various structured interviews are provided in Section III of this volume, so they will not be elaborated upon here.) Unstructured interviews are the more common type in clinical settings. They usually lack a rigid format, but they are not without structure. The interview follows a sequence, as described in this chapter, and covers key content areas, as detailed in Section III of this book. Thus there is a structure to even an unstructured interview.

THE PHYSICAL SETTING

The physical setting of a clinical interview and its effect on the interviewing process is a subject that is often neglected in training, yet the *physical surround* is an important element in any clinical interview. The ideal physical setting is comfortable for both patient and clinician. The interview office should be attractively furnished, should be maintained at a comfortable temperature, and should contain all the elements required to properly conduct the interview (such as pen, pencil, notepad, or tape recorder).

The therapist should *schedule enough time* to devote full attention to the patient and to complete the interview in one sitting. Whenever possible, *interruptions are to be avoided*. Telephone calls should be transferred, a "do not disturb" sign should be placed on the door, or colleagues should be otherwise instructed not to interrupt during an interview. If the therapist cannot ensure that the interview will not be interrupted, the patient should be informed in advance that interruption is likely, but it should be kept to a minimum. *Privacy and confidentiality* should be maintained. This is sometimes difficult, such as when an interview must be conducted at a patient's bedside, but every effort must be made to respect the patient's privacy.

KINDS OF INTERVIEWS

There are different kinds of interviews, distinguished by the purpose for which they are being conducted.

Intake Interview

The purpose of the intake interview is to obtain preliminary information about a prospective patient. This type of interview usually occurs in agencies whose purposes may include the determination of the patient's eligibility in terms of the agency's mission. Other purposes of intake interviews are (1) to obtain sufficient information to present the case at a clinical conference, (2) to clarify the nature of the services that the agency provides or the nature of the treatment that the patient will receive, (3) to communicate agency rules, regulations, and policies to a prospective patient, (4) to determine the type of treatment that would most benefit the patient and the therapist that would be best for the patient, (5) to obtain general information for agency records, and (6) to determine referral to a more appropriate resource, if necessary.

Case History Interview

The case history is a part of most clinical interviews. When more elaborate and detailed sequencing of this history is needed, an interview is conducted for the sole purpose of reviewing the nature of the patient's conflicts in historical sequence, with a focus on critical periods, antecedents, and precipitants. Case history interviews can be one of the richest sources of information about a patient. Case histories can also be obtained from the patient's family or friends.

Mental Status Exam

A mental status exam is conducted to determine the degree of mental impairment associated with the clinical condition under investigation. Among the content areas assessed are reasoning, thinking, judgment, memory, concentration, speech, hearing, and perception. This type of information is most often required when the symptoms suggest a major psychiatric disorder, neurological involvement, or substance abuse. Chapter 15 presents a detailed description of a mental status exam.

Pre- and Post-testing Interviews

Psychological tests are often a part of the clinical work-up. However, it is a basic misunderstanding of the nature of clinical tests to assume that a clinical report is based solely on test results. To simply administer a test and report the results is a kind of psychometric mentality that may miss important aspects of patient behavior. Modern psychological evaluations include reviews of a patient's record, consultation with relevant staff, and a clinical interview with the patient. Some psychologists prefer to interview the patient prior to testing in order to explain the reasons for testing and its benefits to the client, and to cover certain administrative arrangements, such as the time and place of testing and the payment of fees. When the interview is conducted after the completion of testing, the psychologist usually has developed certain hypotheses as a result of testing and wishes to explore these ideas further with the patient as a kind of "testing-the-limits" approach, in order to assess the patient's insight with respect to the information presented.

Brief Screening Interview

The brief screening interview is distinguished by a time-limited, focused format. The clinician is interested only in a specific area and is willing to forego other elements of the interview in order to screen for the desired information in a brief time period. This type of interview is conducted for the following purposes, among others: (1) to assess immediate suicidal risk in a depressed patient who is presenting in crisis, (2) to determine whether a patient needs to be involuntarily committed to a psychiatric hospital, (3) to determine whether medical referral is needed, (4) to determine whether a patient can be managed in an outpatient setting, and (5) to determine fitness to stand trial. The brief screening interview is followed by referral, and the patient is likely to participate in a more traditional clinical interview at a later date.

Discharge Interview

Some therapists conduct formal discharge interviews with patients who are about to leave an inpatient or outpatient program. The purpose of this type of interview is to learn from the patient's perspective what she/he has gained from treatment, to review aftercare plans, or to work through any unresolved problems the patient may have prior to termination or discharge.

Research Interview

As clinical research becomes increasingly valued, the research interview will be used more frequently in clinical settings. This kind of interview is specific to the nature of the research being conducted. It is usually part of a rigid protocol that has been approved by an institutional review committee. Such an interview is conducted with the patient's permission, which she/he grants by signing a document attesting to informed consent.

THE PATIENT'S APPROACH TO THE INTERVIEW

A clinical interview will be influenced by the patient's immediate reason for seeking the interview, which in turn depends on whether or not the patient has voluntarily sought help or has been referred by a third party. A voluntary patient presumably has noticed a problem, has made failed attempts at resolution, perhaps by discussing the problem with friends or using other self-help approaches, and then seeks professional direction. Most voluntary patients come with an expectation that their problem will be ameliorated through this professional assistance. Thus it is usually easier to elicit information and to establish a therapeutic alliance when the patient is self-referred. When a patient has been referred by a third party, the level of resistance generally tends to be higher, and it is therefore more difficult to form a working alliance. It is the therapist's task to attempt to work through this resistance and at the same time conduct the interview so that the clinical task is accomplished despite this resistance.

Whether self- or other-referred, the patient's *purpose or motive* for coming to the session will also influence the clinical process. Even when a patient appears to be self-referred, there may be hidden agendas that serve to compromise the purity of the clinical interview. For example, a man who has committed incest may ask for treatment, but his true motive may be to present a remorseful facade to a judge at an upcoming court hearing. A woman may come to an interview obtensibly seeking relief from anxiety and depression resulting from back pain following an injury at work, but her true purpose may be to improve her chances of receiving workers' compensation by demonstrating the intractability of her condition and the psychological suffering it has caused. A drug abuser may seek treatment to hide from people to whom he owes money. A chronic schizophrenic may seek hospitalization, reporting hallucinations, delusions, and suicidal ideation, merely to get off the street and be housed and fed. I once conducted an interview with a patient who complained of marital dissatisfaction. As the interview ended, the patient asked me if I thought she was crazy. When pressed for the reason for this question, she said that her husband had told her that she was crazy, so she wanted a letter from a professional attesting to the fact that she was sane. This was her real purpose for scheduling the interview. Thus it is the therapist's responsibility to determine the person's genuine purpose for seeking professional assistance, since this will affect not only the interview in progress but also future attempts at intervention.

The *patient's expectations* will also affect the interview. One family came to a therapist's office complaining about their daughter's behavior and demanding that the therapist give her an injection to make her behave. The family expected that medicine would be given and that obedience would be the result. All patients come to an interview with certain expectations about the role behaviors of the therapist, the interview process, and the potential outcome. It is a good idea early in the initial interview to clarify any misunderstanding about the nature and purpose of the session. Simply asking the patient "What do you think we are going to do here?" or "Have you been told the reason for this interview?" is a good way to begin such clarification.

The patient's *perception of the therapist* can also affect the direction of the interview process, the information that is revealed in the session, and the therapist's response to the patient. The relationship between patient and therapist can be construed as one of parent to child, teacher to pupil, judge to accused, or lover to love object. These perceptions may be transferences, or they may be veridical assessments of the therapist's behavior. The patient's view of the therapist can affect the entire clinical process. There is no easy way to assess such perceptions in an initial interview. They often remain unsaid and unchallenged, and they may be outside the patient's awareness. However, it is important for the therapist to realize that such perceptions and misperceptions exist and affect the dynamic interaction between patient and therapist during the interview process.

In summary, voluntary or involuntary status of the patient, the purpose of the interview (manifest and latent), the patient's expectations, and the patient's perceptions of the therapist are the salient factors that affect the patient's approach to an interview.

THE THERAPIST'S APPROACH TO THE INTERVIEW

Just as patients come to an interview with their own set of predispositions, so too do therapists. The first factor that influences a therapist's approach to an interview is his *philosophical orientation.* Rarely does a therapist enter an interview as a blank slate. Therapists have a theoretical framework that dictates the areas of inquiry, the method of inquiry, their assessments and evaluations, and their goals. An interview from a family systems perspective is quite different from an interview with a behavioral orientation. A therapist whose philosophy is psychodynamic and a therapist whose orientation is humanistic and nondirective are likely to offer different assessments of a clinical situation. (The nature of these differences is more fully explicated in Section II of this book.)

Personal values and beliefs are a second factor that determines a therapist's approach to an interview. The therapist will select from the patient's material that which is most important. This selection is formed in part by the therapist's orientation but also by his values and beliefs as they relate to the content of inquiry. Research has repeatedly shown that patients improve in psychotherapy to the extent that they come to share or adopt the values and beliefs of their therapists. While one therapist may place a high value on expression of feeling, another may value a commitment to introspection or a willingness to look for antecedents and consequences of behavior. These areas will thus be given more attention by the therapist because he believes that they are more important.

A therapist eventually attempts to *understand the patient and the problem* in a way that is consistent with his theoretical orientation. Thus most therapists make a diagnosis, but the frame of this assessment differs among the major theoretical philosophies. One therapist may describe the problem as "preoedipal," while to another the problem may be "faulty communication within a dysfunctional dyad designed to maintain a dominant-submissive relationship pattern," or "inadequate reinforcement when he tries to be assertive," or a "bipolar affective disorder." Similarly, the patient may be construed as narcissistic, or as overadaptive, or as needing unconditional positive regard. By the end of every clinical interview, the therapist has made some evaluation or assessment of both the problem and the patient. On the basis of this assessment, goals are set and treatment methods are determined (Perry et al. 1987).

To summarize, the therapist approaches the interview with a philosophical orientation and a set of personal values and beliefs, and then attempts to understand the patient and the problem. Goal setting and treatment planning, variously labeled as assessment, evaluation, or diagnosis, are then based on that understanding.

INTERVIEW TECHNIQUES

Therapists have an array of techniques that they use in an interview. Irrespective of theoretical orientation, all therapists use some of these approaches. Their philosophical orientation often dictates which ones they will use the most and the degree of emphasis they place on any one technique, but these techniques form the basis of the interview process. No single technique should be used to the exclusion of the others. Rather, they are used in combination to form a dynamic interview. These techniques include direct questioning, reflection, restating (paraphrasing), clarification, confrontation, self-disclosure, silence, explanation, reframing (cognitive restructuring), interpretation, and humor (Table 1–1).

Questioning

This is the technique most often used by clinical interviewers. The patient is asked direct questions in areas determined by the interviewer. Questioning may be either *direct* or *open-ended*. A direct question may begin with words such as *now*, *what*, and *why*, but it invites a closed response when it is framed to elicit a yes–no response. Questions that are closed (for example, How old are you?) evoke a brief answer from the respondent, who then merely waits for the interviewer to ask another question. Too many closed questions become regressive. It is more desirable to ask open-ended questions (such as, How does your spouse's behavior make you feel?). While neophyte therapists predominantly use the technique of direct questioning, it actually takes a skilled therapist to receive the maximum return from the question asked, while still maintaining free-flowing communication.

Reflection

This technique requires the interviewer to skillfully restate the patient's cognitive or emotional material so as to demonstrate to the patient that his feelings or statements have been understood. Therapists who sub-

Table 1-1. Interviewing Techniques

Technique	Patient's statement	Therapist's response
Questioning	As a kid I was always in trouble.	What kind of trouble were you in?
Reflection	I just can't seem to get anywhere in life.	Your lack of progress frustrates you.
Restatement	Thoughts are racing in my mind. I just can't concentrate. I'm so confused.	These strange things in your head are disturbing to you.
Clarification	My mother is out most of the night, leaving me alone. She comes home at all hours. Sometimes she doesn't come home at all.	What is your mother doing when she is out like this?
Confrontation	I only drink a couple of times a day.	Let's be honest! You drink every morning and every night after work. Face it! You're dependent on alcohol.
Self-disclosure	People don't understand what it's like not to be able to learn. I can't get good grades in school. I'm stupid.	When I was in school, I was dyslexic too. But you can still do well in life despite this problem. You're not stupid. You have special needs.
Silence	I get so angry that I feel like kicking him where it hurts.	(No response)
Exploration	My father used to beat me.	I need more information. How often did he beat you? How did he do it? Was he drunk at the time?
Reframing	I realize now he'll never change. I have to accept that.	How could you take advantage of the situation so that it can benefit you?
Interpretation	I got so mad at my father that I flushed his tranquilizers down the toilet.	You play a role with your mother that you feel your father should play. You want your father to stand up to your mother—that's why you did it. If he were more assertive with her, then maybe you wouldn't have to be.
Humor	Sometimes I feel like I'm two persons walking around in one body.	Well, at least you'll never be lonely. You'll always have each other.

scribe to the client-centered/Rogerian approach tend to rely quite heavily on reflection as a therapeutic tool and have made seminal clinical and research contributions toward our understanding of its usefulness and effectiveness. Once again, clinical skill is required if this technique is to be used effectively. The overuse of reflection in an interview is counterproductive because important areas are left unaddressed.

Restatement (Paraphrasing)

Restatement simply rephrases what a patient has said in a clearer or more articulate manner. This technique is also known as paraphrasing, and it lets the patient know that the therapist is paying attention. It differs from reflection in purpose. Restatement is most often used to facilitate understanding or for clarification, while reflection is used as a therapeutic intervention.

Clarification

Clarification is usually done by using one of the other techniques (questioning, paraphrasing, or restating), but the purpose is to provide understanding of the client in the interview. This technique rarely evokes defensiveness in the patient because most patients want the therapist to understand their problems or their perspective. By seeking clarification, the therapist gives the patient an additional opportunity to tell his story so that it is fully understood.

Confrontation

Confrontation is a technique whereby the therapist points out discrepancies between what is observed and what is stated. It is sometimes used when a patient says something different from what the therapist perceives that the patient is experiencing, or when the patient's statements are inconsistent with his usual behavior. Confrontation is most often employed with substance abusers and other patients with character disorders to break through their denial and their rigid defenses. It usually has the effect of increasing anxiety and precipitating the avoidance and denial that it was meant to address. Confrontation has evolved into a pejorative approach because of the negative reports that emanated from therapeutic communities, where the technique has been used to the near exclusion of other approaches. While the technique has benefited many patients in such settings, others merely erect a defensive barrier so that the approach never reaches them.

Confrontation can be constructive or destructive. It is most beneficial when it is based on factual content, devoid of hostile reference, and focused on material that the patient should be addressing but isn't because of conscious or unconscious avoidance. Inexperienced therapists often have difficulty using confrontation because of their own insecurities and because of their lack of skill in managing the patient's response if the technique is mishandled.

Self-Disclosure

In using self-disclosure, the therapist conveys personal experiences or feelings to the patient. Self-disclosure is intended to facilitate increments of patient self-disclosure within the interview to benefit the patient. Research has shown that self-disclosure by the therapist facilitates self-disclosure by the patient (Cozby 1973). This technique should be used only sparingly, however, or it may set up a false expectation in the patient. The therapist must be judicious in determining what information will be disclosed and its probable effect on the patient.

Silence

Neophyte therapists see silence as a dreadful experience, a product of their own inadequacy as interviewers. When silence occurs because of the interviewer's failure to lead the session along a determined course, these feelings are valid. However, silence can be an interviewing technique as well as a therapeutic device. Silence provides the patient with an opportunity to process and understand what has been said, and it can thus move the interview in a positive direction. Silence must be timed appropriately and in such a way that the patient understands that the therapist is using the silence for a reason. The reason is usually to promote introspection, or to allow the patient to reassimilate his emotions after release.

Exploration

Exploration is a technique whereby the therapist covers areas in a patient's life that require more in-depth review. It may also be used in a "testing-the-limits" approach, whereby the therapist tries to determine how much insight a patient has, or how much pressure it takes before a patient experiences a given feeling. Most patients expect to be questioned about certain areas and activities and might wonder (usually to themselves) why these areas were not considered in the interview. Therapists should not be afraid to explore certain areas, even if they might be viewed as sensitive.

Reframing (Cognitive Restructuring)

This technique, referred to as reframing or cognitive restructuring, has either the patient or the therapist restate their beliefs, attitudes, or feelings in a manner more closely tied to reality. It provides a fresh perspective on a situation and serves to undercut negative self-statements and irrational thoughts that often accompany maladaptive behavior. It can promote new ways of thinking and new insights that can lead to behavior change.

While a powerful technique, it does require practice and skill development before it will produce its full impact.

Interpretation

This technique has been considered the *sine qua non* of clinical interviewers. Here, the therapist provides information in such a manner that behavior is explored and its motivation is understood by the patient. It derives historically from the psychoanalytic method, which is aimed at "making the unconscious, conscious." It is the most difficult of all techniques to grasp because its use necessitates a comprehensive mastery of theory of personality and motivation, followed by supervised experience. Most therapists, regardless of persuasion, (client-centered therapists may be an exception), use interpretation in one form or another. Some rely on it more exclusively than others. Therapists in training should use this technique with great care, and only when they are certain that the formulation fits the facts and after consultation with their supervisors. Some patients merely accept clinician pronouncements, believing in the expertise, knowledge, and authority of the therapist. Therefore, we must be judicious and careful when offering interpretations.

Humor

We are only beginning to understand the role of humor in clinical evaluations. Freud considered humor the highest form of defense but proffered no role for it in therapeutic work, other than to psychoanalyze it. However, humor can reduce anxiety, facilitate therapeutic movement, and enhance the interview. As with any technique, overreliance on this approach will convey to the patient that the therapist is not taking the interview seriously. This is inappropriate and unprofessional. Timing is critical in the use of this technique. Humor should be delivered with the ultimate purpose of benefiting the patient.

THE THERAPIST'S INTERPERSONAL QUALITIES

Therapists bring with them more than a theoretical orientation, a set of personal values and beliefs, and a history of training that establishes a minimal level of competence that is enhanced by subsequent experience. They also bring to the interview a set of personal characteristics that some have argued are more important than any theoretical method or technique. Table 1-2 lists these traits.

INTERVIEW PHASES

A good clinical interview develops in phase progression along predictable stages *that are controlled by the therapist*. Various authors have at-

TABLE 1-2. Interpersonal Characteristics of the Therapist

Trait	Definition
Empathy	The ability to understand the patient from the patient's perspective.
Genuineness	The freedom to be oneself; a lack of phoniness.
Warmth	The quality of being open, responsive, and positive toward a patient.
Respect	The ability to convey to patients that they have the power to change and to participate in that process.
Positive regard	The ability to accept patients despite their negative behavior, attitudes, or demeanor.

tempted to capture and label these phases, but Sullivan (1954), operating from the perspective of a social psychiatrist, was among the first to conceptualize the interview as phase-sequenced. He characterized these stages as the formal inception, the reconnaissance, the detailed inquiry, and termination. According to Sullivan, by the end of the *formal inception*, the therapist knows why the patient has come to the interview. The *reconnaissance*, the second stage, is the period in the interview during which the therapist obtains a brief sketch of the patient. Sullivan believes that this should take about 20 minutes. At the end of this stage, Sullivan recommends that the therapist tell the patient what he believes to be the nature of the problem. It is not presumed that the initial problem identified is the major problem in the patient's life; this may actually emerge much later, in subsequent sessions. According to Sullivan, however, identification of a problem gives both patient and therapist a direct path to follow and something concrete to work on. The *detailed inquiry* is the third stage, and it is the point in the interview when the initial impressions gained during the second stage are developed more thoroughly. The *termination* phase follows, during which the therapist makes a final statement summarizing what has been learned in the interview, giving the patient a behavioral prescription, making a final assessment (prognosis), and initiating formal leave-taking.

Benjamin (1969), operating from a psychosocial perspective, divides the interview into three main stages, defined by the *initiation* or statement of the problem, followed by *development*, wherein both patient and therapist agree on the nature of the problem, and then followed by *closing*.

Kanfer and Scheft (1988), writing from a behavioral epistemology, subdivided the interview into *role structuring, creating a therapeutic alliance, developing a commitment for change, analyzing behavior, negotiating treatment objectives, and planning or implementing*.

From a patient-centered perspective, Rogers (1942) described the characteristic steps in a clinical interview as follows: the patient *comes for help*; the *situation is defined*; and through acceptance, clarification, and the expression of positive feelings, there is *development of insight*.

While most distinguished therapists from a variety of disciplines have attempted to capture the phases of the clinical interview, each has done so from a unique theoretical framework. Each then frames the analysis of the problem according to the assumptions and theorems provided by this philosophical orientation.

Irrespective of these philosophical differences, there are stages in an interview that most therapists would agree are the major points in the process. First, there is the *introduction*, which roughly corresponds to Sullivan's formal inception. The primary task during this phase is to understand the patient's reason for seeking the interview; the major tasks in this stage are the development of rapport and the establishment of trust.

Second, there is an *exploration* phase, corresponding to Sullivan's reconnaissance and detailed-inquiry stages. Here the therapist has formed an initial impression, and the primary task is to develop a hypothesis, consistent with the therapist's theoretical orientation, that accounts for the presenting problem and explains the psychological adaptation to the precipitating stress in the light of historical and developmental issues. This could be described as "fixations," as "unbalanced family hierarchy," as "negative reinforcements." The crucial step is to form a hypothesis accounting for the main facts in the case.

The third stage represents *hypothesis testing*. After the hypothesis has been formulated, the therapist develops a series of further inquiries to test the hypothesis within the interview by delving into other areas or situations in the patient's life. If the initial hypothesis is accurate, the material elicited should be consistent with and should elaborate upon the central hypothesis. The second and third stages are the most difficult for novice therapists, due to their lack of experience both with the process and with the breadth of qualitative analyses required.

During the fourth stage, *feedback* is offered. Here the therapist tells the patient the highlights of the assessment or evaluation. This stage, which corresponds to Sullivan's termination phase, is too often ignored even by seasoned therapists who, after asking a series of questions in the interview, leave the session without ever telling the patient anything. Note that this usually does not occur in medical interviews. There, a patient presents complaints or symptoms to the physician, who then tells the patient what is wrong (diagnosis). Perhaps more tests are needed to rule out several competing etiologies, but the patient usually leaves the physician's office with some idea about the direction that the physician is taking to address the problem. All too often, a mental health interview does not include this important step. Many patients no doubt fail to return for subsequent sessions (Baekeland and Lundwall 1975) because they do not believe that the therapist understands them or their problem, or both; thus the patient believes that the therapist cannot be of help. This problem is easily solved by the therapist's simply telling the patient, in language the patient can understand, what he thinks is causing the difficulties. This will allow the therapist to determine the accuracy of the assessment and the level of the patient's resistance to the notion.

The final phase is *termination*. The task in this stage is to develop a treatment plan that is geared toward the attainment of mutually agreeable goals.

DYNAMIC INTERACTION

An interview is a dynamic interaction between patient and therapist. The nature of this interaction has been stressed by adherents of some orientations (such as psychoanalysts) and minimized by others (including nondirective and behavioral therapists), yet these transferential processes must be attended to before the therapist can decide whether or not they should be addressed. Even Rogerians admit that transference occurs; they just don't believe that it is important in the therapy. Behaviorists agree that the relationship between patient and therapist is important in order to facilitate the implementation of the behavioral strategies. Thus all schools recognize that there are processes occurring between patient and therapist that must be considered and that may become a focal point in the process.

THE LAST FIVE MINUTES

We noted earlier that *termination* is the last stage of a clinical interview. This phase deserves to be discussed in greater detail.

In listening to interview tapes made by therapists in training, I have been horrified at the way some have decided to close their interviews. This phase tends to be anxiety-producing for students, especially when they realize that they have mishandled it. Interviews too often end abruptly, without closure and without consideration of the important clinical information that can be obtained in the last few minutes. Just as a surgeon, after completing an operation, spends the last few minutes suturing the wound, so too must a clinical interviewer spend the last few minutes of a session ensuring that there is closure, by paying attention to important processes that may occur here, while simultaneously engaging in the final tasks that will complete the interview.

There are certain tasks that should be accomplished at this stage of the interview. By this time, the analysis has been made, goals have been established, and a treatment plan has been developed upon which the patient has agreed. The last part of the interview should be spent in decathecting from the patient's emotional intensity, and in ensuring that all relevant information has been addressed. The therapist should ask the following questions at this point: Is there anything else you want to tell me that you feel is important? Have we left anything out? Do you have any questions you want to ask me? This last question may be the most important, because it allows the patient to ask important questions that may be lingering. During this time, the therapist should be *observing* how the *patient* handles the process of separation from the interview, because it may provide clues to how the patient handles these issues in actual life.

Finally, some type of closing is appropriate. The therapist might want to thank the patient for participating in the interview or for sharing personal information. Or, the therapist might address how he feels about the interview, now that it is over, or might use the time to remind the patient of certain administrative issues, such as the date and time of the next appointment.

My goal in this chapter has been to acquaint the reader with some of the basic elements of a clinical interview. My hope is that the reader will have learned something from this chapter and will be motivated to read the remainder of this volume. So too with patients. As therapists, we hope that our patients will learn something from the initial interview that will motivate them to seek further understanding of their problems.

REFERENCES

Baekeland, F., and Lundwall, L. (1975). Dropping out of treatment: a critical review. *Psychological Bulletin* 82:738–783.

Benjamin, A. (1969). *The Helping Interview* (2nd ed.). Boston: Houghton Mifflin.

Cozby, P. C. (1973). Self-disclosure: a literature review. *Psychological Bulletin* 79:73–91.

Endicott, J., and Spitzer, R. L. (1978). A diagnostic interview: the schedule for affective disorders and schizophrenia. *Archives of General Psychiatry* 35:837–844.

Hersen, M. L., and Turner, S. M., eds. (1985). *Diagnostic Interviewing*. New York: Plenum.

Kanfer, F. H., and Scheft, B. K. (1988). *Guiding the Process of Therapeutic Change*. Champaign, IL: Research Press.

Matarazzo, J. D. (1965). The interview. In *Handbook of Clinical Psychology*, ed. B. Wolman, pp. 403–450. New York: McGraw-Hill.

——— (1978). The interview: its reliability and validity in psychiatric diagnosis. In *Clinical Diagnosis of Mental Disorders*, ed. B. Wolman, pp. 47–96. New York: Plenum.

Perry, S., Cooper, A. M., and Michels, R. (1987). The psychodynamic formulation: its purpose, structure, and clinical application. *American Journal of Psychiatry* 144:543–550.

Rogers, C. R. (1942). *Counseling and Psychotherapy*. Cambridge: Houghton Mifflin.

Stevenson, I. (1959). The psychiatric interview. In *American Handbook of Psychiatry*, vol. 1, ed. S. Arieti, pp. 197–214. New York: Basic Books.

Sullivan, H. S. (1954). *The Psychiatric Interview*. New York: W. W. Norton.

Wiens, A. N. (1976). The assessment interview. In *Clinical Methods in Psychology*, ed. B. Wiener, pp. 3–60. New York: Wiley.

Wiens, A. N., and Matarazzo, J. D. (1983). Diagnostic interviewing. In *The Clinical Psychology Handbook*, ed. M. Hersen, A. Kazdin, and A. Bellak, pp. 309–328. Elmsford, NY: Pergamon.

2 Phenomenological Orientation to the Interview

FRANK GRUBA-MCCALLISTER, Ph.D.

Psychological instruments and test batteries proliferate, but the interview remains among the most important tools employed by therapists in the assessment of patients. It calls upon most, if not all, of the therapist's skills, diagnostic as well as therapeutic. The success of the interview rests upon a particular stance and set of attitudes on the part of the therapist.

RECIPROCITY AND RAPPORT IN THE INTERVIEW

First we must define the word *interview* itself. *Inter-* means "between," "reciprocal," and "shared." This prefix points to the first essential feature of the interview. It is a relationship between two persons and is characterized by reciprocity and sharing. The success of the interview depends upon the quality of the relationship that the interviewer is able to establish with the patient. What needs to be shared is a feeling of understanding and mutual trust. There is a giving and taking that occurs throughout the course of the interview, around which a sense of mutuality evolves. Likewise, the degree of mutuality achieved in the interview influences the level of sharing that occurs.

This matter of mutuality refers to an issue often regarded as important not only to the interview situation, but also to other types of helping relationships: rapport. Rapport is characterized by a sense of being "on the same wavelength." As such, it implies a feeling shared by the participants in a relationship that allows for an open, easy sharing of information.

The manner in which this process occurs has been variously described. Sundberg and Tyler (1962) describe it as a working out of common purposes. Sullivan (1954) calls it an integration of reciprocal motivation. Other terms used are "working relationship" or "therapeutic alliance." By any name, the relationship requires the achievement of some agreement between the interviewer and interviewee regarding the purpose for and goals of their relationship. Matarazzo (1978) points out that this goal is "usually ill-defined and inadequately stipulated" (p. 47); herein a good part of the difficulty in establishing and maintaining rapport can be found.

Negotiation

Thus, negotiation of a set of common purposes or goals is part of the task of both therapist and patient in the interview process. As a result, some of these goals are made explicit, while others may remain implicit and unexpressed. The negotiation is based upon the different roles of interviewer and interviewee and the expectations, motivations, and needs that go along with these roles. As Sullivan (1954) notes, the interview, as an interpersonal situation, offers the opportunity for complementary needs to be resolved or aggravated, which will then affect the establishment of rapport.

THE PATIENT'S EXPECTATIONS

The patient comes to the interview with a number of expectations and needs. Principal among these is the expectation of being helped. This expectation is often expressed as the desire for a remedy, a cure, a definitive answer to one's problems. This unrealistic attitude is prompted in part by the patient's keen distress and by the desire to be rid of this distress with the greatest expedience. It is also related to the authoritative role into which patients tend to place therapists, endowing them with omnipotence or special powers.

While this belief in the therapist's omnipotence represents an extreme attitude, when expressed in its more moderate form it becomes the patient's expectation that he will derive some benefit from the interview. The therapist must take this expectation seriously; over the course of the interview the patient should indeed come to some greater understanding of self that may then lead to an increased capacity for positive change. Correspondingly, the therapist must be careful not to be pulled into accepting the omnipotent role and becoming a rescuer. Steiner (1974, pp. 280–289) provides an excellent discussion of rescue and its hazards.

Learning

The need for the patient to learn something useful was stressed by Sullivan (1954) in his classic work on the interview, and yet it is still frequently neglected. Since the interview is most often seen as a diagnostic tool and a form of psychological assessment, the patient is often regarded as responsible for providing information in response to a series of questions posed by the interviewer. That is, it is the therapist who is trying to learn something about the patient in order to make an accurate diagnosis and offer appropriate recommendations. However, the interview can no more be separated from therapeutic intervention than it can be from psychodiagnostics. Questions posed by the therapist must be designed to promote greater understanding for the patient as well. The skill with which the therapist is able to frame questions has a substantial influence on the establishment of a good relationship with the patient. Questions must reflect a respect for the patient and his feelings, sensitivities, and strengths. They should be framed tactfully and with acknowledgement of the patient's defenses. Questions also perform a therapeutic function in that they can convey implicit suggestions designed to encourage the patient to consider alternative behaviors or to regard a problem from a different perspective. Finally, the patient is likely to be preoccupied with many questions from the very start of the interview, and it is good practice to allow the patient to ask some of these questions toward the end of the session.

Ambivalence

Although the patient expects to learn something useful, there is an essential ambivalence characteristic of the patient seeking help. On the one hand, patients are experiencing distress and are motivated to share information and to reveal themselves in order to find relief. However, the very issues that patients need to share are often painful and embarrassing, so there is an opposing need to keep them hidden and unexpressed. The need to maintain one's self-esteem and the fear of losing the therapist's respect are two very powerful forces that operate throughout the course of the interview and interfere with the free expression of information and feelings. Here again, the therapist's understanding, interest, respect, and tolerance are crucial to diminish this reluctance. The importance of building trust is likewise evident. The therapist's questions must enable the patient to maintain a sense of self-respect and dignity while also facilitating the sharing of information that may be painful and distasteful.

Thus, patients can learn something valuable in an interview from the way they are treated by the therapist. Patients expect to be treated with compassion and understanding, but as we have noted, they also come into the interview with unrealistic expectations born out of distortion and lack of information. The manner in which the therapist interacts teaches the patient something that works to correct not only misconceptions about the therapist and the nature of clinical work, but also misconceptions that the patient may have about himself. The hope is that the patient will increasingly see himself as a worthwhile person who possesses the resources and abilities necessary to deal effectively with problems and to experience life as meaningful and enriching.

The Patient's Interpersonal Style

The relationship that the therapist establishes with the patient provides some valuable learning experiences for the patient, but the reverse is also true. Therapists must be sensitive to the sort of relationship that patients establish with them. As Sundberg and Tyler (1962) point out, "Each individual person has his own revealing way of entering the situation" (p. 105). They note that from the very start of the interview, patients convey to the therapist how they want and expect to be responded to. By picking up on these expectations and attitudes, the therapist develops a sense of how the patient will approach similar interpersonal situations.

One of the key areas that must be assessed during the interview is the way in which patients tend to interact with others and the basic beliefs and assumptions that guide how they approach interpersonal relationships. The relationship between the therapist and the patient is a microcosm of this broader sphere of relationships. The interview offers the distinct advantage of possessing a stronger interpersonal component than other forms of psychological assessment. The various dynamics that unfold as the relationship between therapist and patient evolves during the interview is thus a fertile source of information. The therapist must be alert to feelings that the patient arouses as well as to feelings that the patient displays (or does not display) in response to the therapist's interventions.

The latter point is made by psychoanalytic theorists who speak of development of transference during the interview. In this case, the patient's responses to the interview provide insights into unconscious feelings and behaviors based in relationships with significant figures from the past. However, this notion can be extended. An entire nexus of relationships—past, present, and future—converge and play themselves out in the interview for both patient and therapist. Thus there are any number of "ghosts" present in the room at the time of the interview. Sensitivity to this facet of the interview enables the therapist to formulate a clearer sense of the patient's interpersonal sphere.

Interviews offer the patient a chance to experience a relationship that has the potential to encourage greater personal development and health. The mutuality and reciprocity so central to good therapeutic rapport are also the cornerstones of good relationships in general. This relationship between therapist and patient can be regarded as a dialectical one. The dialectic has many meanings (see Rychlak 1976). Here it refers to an interaction in which the uniqueness and individuality of each person is respected while a deeper underlying bond that transcends such differences is also recognized. Laing (1960) talks of a dialectical relationship as one "mutual enrichment and exchange of give-and-take between two beings 'congenial' to each other" (p. 92). Buber's (1970) description of the I–thou relationship is another example. Existentialists call it "encounter."

THE THERAPIST'S EXPECTATIONS

The therapist also brings certain expectations to the interview. These include expectations of being able to ask questions, make inquiries, and receive significant and relevant information. Expectations such as these are based on the role of the therapist as expert. Schafer (1954) points out the potential pitfalls of certain aspects of the therapist's role that can diminish the effectiveness of the interview. Therapists must be aware of the needs and motives that they bring to the interaction so that they can be carefully monitored and thus not interfere with the goal of achieving an objective, unbiased assessment of the patient.

Attention

This brings us to the second part of the word *interview*. One of the meanings of the word *view* is "to look at attentively." In the interview, the principal instrument of assessment and observation is the therapist. So we must look at factors that influence the therapist's ability to attend effectively to all facets of the interview and to gather the data needed to formulate a valid assessment.

The key word is *attention*. In order to describe the kind of attention needed by the therapist, we can again turn to the dialectic. One meaning of the dialectic is the bipolarity of meanings, or how meanings implicitly suggest their reverse. This is reflected in how human thought is structured around two poles that, while different, mutually define each other and are thus necessary to each other's existence. This is the dialectic of self versus other, subject versus object, knower versus known. Frankl (1967) noted:

> There is yet another polarity to be considered. This is the rift between the subject and object of cognition. This rift is also ineradicable though many an author speaks of having 'overcome' it. Such a statement is questionable, for such an achievement would be tantamount to overcoming *la condition humaine*—the insurmountable finitude of being human. [p. 48]

Human thought constantly fluctuates in focus. At times we are outer-directed and absorbed in the object of our attention. At other times our awareness is reflected back upon ourselves as the knower and center of experience. When our attention is focused upon one of these poles, the other is always implicitly there and can emerge and come to the fore in the next instant. The shift from one pole to the other can be thought of as a figure–ground relationship.

The Therapist as Participant-Observer

The attention of the therapist conducting the interview is likewise organized around these poles. Sullivan (1954) describes the role of the interviewer as that of participant-observer. In using this term, Sullivan stresses the interpersonal aspect of the interview. The therapist's personality inevitably enters into the process, particularly since the therapist is the principal instrument for assessing the patient in the interview.

The role of participant-observer can be understood in terms of the dialectical structure of human thought. As participant, the therapist is absorbed in the process of the interview itself. This requires a receptive, open orientation that is basic to an empathic relationship. In such a state, the therapist loses the sense of being a separate individual and instead becomes absorbed in the patient. In so doing, the therapist conveys to the patient a sense of being understood and accepted.

As observers, therapists must be able to remove themselves from this process and analyze it from a more objective, third-person perspective. At these times, the therapist views the patient from a more detached stance that enables him to bring to bear clinical experience and theory in order to discern problematic patterns, conflicts, strengths, and supports that will eventually be integrated into a case conceptualization. From this perspective, the interviewer employs active listening, questioning, and probing in order to gather data needed to formulate hypotheses.

This represents the first dialectic that characterizes the interview process. It is well expressed in this quote from Frankl (1967):

> The therapeutic relationship develops in a polar field of tension in which the poles are represented by the extremes of *human closeness* on the one hand and *scientific detachment* on the other. Therefore, the therapist must beware lest he be beguiled into falling prey to the extreme of considering only one of these. This means that the therapist must neither be guided by mere sympathy, by his desire to help his patient, nor conversely repress his human interest in the other human being by dealing with him merely in terms of technique. [p. 144]

What has been described thus far is related to what Sullivan (1954) calls alertness to the patient. However, as he actually points out, the therapist must also maintain alertness regarding his own behavior within the interview. In addition to the constant fluctuation between an active versus passive attitude that occurs when the interviewer focuses attention on the patient, a second ever-present dialectic in the interview is alertness toward the patient versus alertness toward the self.

Therapists first need to be aware of what they do in the interview in order to monitor how this might impact upon the patient's behavior and the quality of the relationship that will be established. The key is to avoid any behavior or attitude that might prove to be disruptive to the interview process or might distort the therapist's construction of the world view of the patient. The danger is that the interviewer's prejudices, beliefs, and preconceptions will so color his perceptions that all sense of the patient will be lost. This process is described by Dass and Gorman (1985), who write:

> So we jump between listening and judging. But in our own consciousness, we find ourselves primarily in our own thoughts, not *with* another person. Not only are we listening less, but the concepts our mind is coming up with start to act as a screen that preselects information. One thought rules out another. [p. 99]

To avoid this pitfall, therapists must be aware of their needs, motives, values, and prejudices and must not permit them to intrude upon the listening process. Maintaining this sort of awareness and control is a great challenge. How can we hope to achieve a view of the patient that is generally free of bias? While there is no definitive answer to this question, several valuable means can be proposed.

The mind of the therapist is the most important instrument that is employed in the interview, as in all clinical work. This instrument must be sharpened, focused, and carefully tuned. The resulting mental discipline enables the therapist to better screen out distractions, biases, and other intrusive attitudes in order to more accurately listen to what the client really has to say. A much deeper and more intense level of communication is made available to both the interviewer and the patient as a result. An additional benefit to the therapist is that mental discipline broadens self-awareness. As one's sense of self is expanded, new insights into oneself become possible. Again turning to Dass and Gorman (1985):

> Our ability to remain alert to our own thoughts as they come and go serves us in our relations with others. We hear into their pain . . . they feel heard . . . we meet together inside the confusion. And yet we ourselves are able to note, perhaps even to *anticipate*, that moment when another's entrapment of mind might be starting to suck us in. We are as alert to what is happening within *us* as we are to what is happening in *them*. [p. 114]

Learning to concentrate, to quiet the mind sufficiently to enable oneself to focus accurately on what is being communicated by the patient and what is being communicated within, is thus the first means that can be proposed to achieve the awareness necessary for successful interviewing. Numerous methods and techniques have been proposed to develop the powers of mental concentration. Most are akin to meditation. The particulars of such methods lie outside the scope of this chapter, but the interested reader can consult the previously mentioned work by Dass and Gorman (1985), as well as the books by Le Shan (1974), Humphreys (1968), and Carrington (1977), for further information.

The Phenomenological Stance

A second method, which is related in many respects to the discipline of meditation, is offered by the philosophical school known as phenomenology. Phenomenology as a philosophy seeks to study how human experience is influenced by various presuppositions or pre-existing biases that the mind brings to bear in structuring experience and giving it meaning. The philosopher whose name has been most closely associated with phenomenology is Edmund Husserl (1962). He hoped to develop philosophy as a rigorous science. By this he meant that he wanted to achieve an absolutely valid knowledge. Such knowledge would have to be free of prejudice or presupposition. The quest for this knowledge might also lead to primary presuppositions that do not require clarification because they are immediately evident.

While the scope of phenomenology is much broader than the tasks involved in interviewing, the therapist can gain some insight and wisdom from phenomenology and its method. The therapist's task, like the phenomenologist's, is to come to a clearer understanding of his own basic or primary presuppositions. These presuppositions consist of attitudes, beliefs, and values that one regards as unquestionable and self-evident. They form a personal philosophy from which one regards and interprets all of one's own experiences. These assumptions often operate subtly and outside of awareness, which increases the risk of bias and distortion.

To rid oneself completely of these assumptions is a requirement that few, if any, can achieve. However, a method in phenomenology called "bracketing" provides an alternative approach. While the application of this method as proposed here departs in certain respects from the manner in which it is used in phenomenology, it does not depart from its spirit and intent. The idea behind bracketing is to temporarily suspend or put out of action one's presuppositions so that they do not interfere with the formation of an unbiased understanding of the patient's experience as it is revealed within the interview. In a sense, one's biases and presuppositions are placed within brackets and thus rendered inoperative. The interviewer who can succeed in performing this operation of bracketing is likely to be more successful in differentiating the reality of the patient that is being constructed from the interview data from what is contributed to that data based on the interviewer's own interests, values, and biases.

In order to bracket these presuppositions, the interviewer must be aware of what they are. As previously noted, this self-knowledge can be achieved through the heightened awareness that comes with mental discipline. In many ways, what is being stressed here is the need for the therapist to make a careful study of experience, the structure in which it occurs, and the process through which experience develops and grows.

The resulting awareness of the patient that one achieves by suspending one's biases has been variously described. Maslow (1971) calls it Taoistic objectivity. In this state we are noninterfering spectators. We allow patients to just be, and to unfold in all their various facets before our eyes. The goal of Taoistic objectivity is not to try to interfere, control, or improve. Instead, it is characterized by loving perception in which the patient is regarded with intense interest and even fascination.

Staying within an Eastern-philosophy framework, Goldstein (1976) describes this awareness from a Zen perspective as "bare attention." We observe things and persons as they are, without choosing, comparing, or evaluating. It is awareness that is focused in the present moment and that is open, passive, and receptive.

This open, receptive attitude goes a long way toward enabling the therapist to enter the world view of the patient. It also conveys to the patient an acceptance and understanding that are conducive to positive changes within the helping relationship. Within the dialectical framework that we have been following, however, we need to remember that we must also direct this sort of awareness back toward ourselves. In so doing, we make available still more sources of valuable information. There is first a greater willingness on the part of the therapist to accept these deeper-level responses and feelings that have been stirred in the interaction with the patient. More trust is placed in this intuitive sense. Second, the feelings that are experienced in response to what the patient says and does during the interview, if not colored by the therapist's own prejudices, lead to a clearer sense of the ways in which others experience the patient and the type of interpersonal relations the patient typically develops. From this assessment, the patient's basic beliefs and assumptions can be inferred.

Thus a passive and receptive attitude is essential to the success of the interview. Nevertheless, such an attitude alone is not enough. Returning to the therapist's participant-observer role, the need to detach oneself from the interview process and critically appraise and evaluate it is equally necessary. The passive, receptive attitude enables the therapist to gather the necessary information to capture the patient's world view. These data must then be submitted to the therapist's clinical experience and knowledge of theory if he is to look beyond this information and discover within it deeper levels of meaning and significance.

The interview process thus represents an ongoing balancing act for the therapist. Attention may be directed outward toward the patient or reflected back upon the interviewer. This attention may take the form of being passive, receptive, and noninterfering, or it may be more detached, critical, and evaluative. The process is a dynamic, ever-changing one, taking one form and then another from moment to moment. It is not surprising, therefore, that interviewing is hard, demanding work requiring flexibility and the constant attention of the therapist.

Clinical Judgment

The need to critically analyze the interview data brings us to a second meaning of the word *view*, which is "judgment." Interviewing involves the exercise of judgment by the therapist in order to arrive at an assessment based on a theoretical perspective. As data from what the patient says together with what the therapist observes are gathered, hypotheses are generated to make sense of and to order these data. These hypotheses are the product of a critical, analytic attitude.

The hypotheses, or educated guesses, made by the interviewer are a means whereby what appear to be discrete pieces of information become related and interwoven in a meaningful fashion. The therapist's task is to use hypotheses in order to make connections and to discern patterns. The patient is often unaware of these patterns or is aware of them but feels locked into them and unable to break free. The therapist's ability to introduce order by identifying patterns and relationships helps the patient to become more aware of them. The therapist's ability to see beyond these patterns and to creatively reorganize them into new ones helps the patient to change them.

Hypotheses are tentative and must be tested. While this idea seems self-evident, the tendency to forget this tenet is perhaps one of the most common problems to which clinicians fall prey. The same tendency of the mind that leads us to introduce order and stability into our experience can also, if unchecked, lead us to come to premature closure regarding a belief or assumption and can make us unwilling to challenge or alter a position that we have settled upon. One of the most common reasons that patients seek help is that they have become frozen in distressing patterns for which they see no alternatives. A therapist who does likewise is of little value to the patient.

Multiple Hypotheses

For this reason, the therapist must engage in still another balancing act while conducting the interview. The therapist should try to entertain more than one hypothesis at all times. The process of the interview becomes one of testing these hypotheses, rejecting some, supporting others, and generating new ones. At no point should only one hypothesis be entertained. Even at the end of the interview, one may settle upon a number of hypotheses in which one can place considerable confidence, but there should still be enough room for doubt that further exploration and inquiry would either strengthen these hypotheses or suggest others.

Hypotheses play an important role in guiding assessment. They tell the interviewer what additional information should be acquired either during the interview or at a later time. They point the interviewer in the direction of other areas of the patient's life that should be discussed. If the interviewer has a firm hold on the hypotheses he wishes to test, the task of developing a systematic line of inquiry becomes simpler. However, this line of inquiry need not be rigid and ritualized, as is the case when one follows some preordained or prescribed outline of questions. Rather, by being guided by the data provided by the patient, and by constantly challenging and modifying one's hypotheses, one can accommodate any patient's individuality.

The goal of the interview is to arrive at a case conceptualization. Here again the therapist's judgment and command of theory is critical to success. It is theory that guides the creation of hypotheses used to explain the data. Large amounts of information can be condensed and integrated within the framework provided by one's theory of human behavior. Again this is frequently expressed in terms of basic themes or patterns that seem to prevail in the patient's life. The value of a good theory is that it provides the therapist with a sense of the critical issues, themes, and problems with which humans must come to terms through the course of their lives. Indeed, the case conceptualization must ultimately come to reflect the patient's personal philosophy and the basic premises and beliefs that guide his thoughts, feelings, and behavior.

A dialectical relationship must exist between the data provided by the patient and the theoretical perspective applied by the clinician to these data if the resulting case conceptualization is to be valid. Again, one must avoid imposing one's world view on the patient while at the same time not accepting uncritically the data that he provides.

SHARING THE PATIENT'S WORLD VIEW

The patient's world of experience is made pre-eminent in the establishment of a case conceptualization. It is this world of experience that the therapist seeks to capture. The role of theory and the hypotheses it generates is to provide the means whereby the patient's world view can be described in a manner that makes sense (not only to the therapist and the patient but to others as well), lends meaning (by the relationships it draws from the data), and offers new insights (by making new relationships possible).

The value of arriving at the fullest possible appreciation of the patient's world view is that it makes the patient's thoughts, feelings, and behavior more understandable. There is nothing that a patient says or does that is "crazy" in the sense that it has no meaning or is illogical. Its meaning and logic can be understood only once the case conceptualization we develop captures the experience of the patient. This approach is exemplified by the work done by Laing (1960, 1967). From the perspective of what he calls a social-phenomenological approach, Laing maintains that the bizarre and crazy behavior of the schizophrenic can be made socially intelligible when viewed within the patient's original family context and ongoing life situation. Laing (1960) writes:

> The therapist must have the plasticity to transpose himself into another strange and even alien view of the world. In this act, he draws upon his own psychotic possibilities, without foregoing his sanity. Only thus can he arrive at an understanding of the patient's existential position [p. 34].

A similar position is articulated by Boss (1963). He notes that the therapist's attitude should be concerned not so much with whether the patient's behavior or thinking is accurate, correct, or real. Instead, the clinician must bracket or suspend the issue of the "reality" of the client's experience and accept it as having validity and meaning in light of the patient's existential situation.

Thus the exercise of judgment by the interviewer in applying theory to the data acquired from the interview is not intended to be the imposition of the interviewer's world view upon the patient's. There can be little hope of rapport in an interview in which such a process occurs. The result will be the patient's feeling misunderstood and perceiving the therapist as coming from another world. In this sort of situation, the therapist can likewise feel irritated because the patient is "not catching on"; the therapist may ascribe failure to the patient who does not embrace his world view.

A situation in which therapist and patient agree on many basic assumptions and beliefs likewise poses problems. The interview becomes an exercise of mutual confirmation of views, and a critical part of the therapist's capacity to help the patient to change is lost. Some challenge to the patient's dearly held beliefs and expectations is required in order to generate the alternatives that make change possible.

Respect for the patient's experience must therefore be central to the therapist's attitude. The invalidating of one's experience is one of the most potent factors contributing to psychopathology. It would thus be a serious disservice to the patient for the therapist to engage in a similar pathogenic process. The recognition of the validity of the patient's experience communicates the sense of acceptance that is needed in the interview situation. The therapist must not hide behind theory to transform the patient into a diagnosis, a syndrome, or some other set of abstractions. The purpose of theory is to provide the means whereby we can appreciate the patient as alive, real, dynamic, and unique. Laing (1967) summarizes this point: "[A]ny theory not founded on the nature of being human is a lie and a betrayal of man. An inhuman theory will inevitably lead to inhuman consequences—if the therapist is consistent" (p. 53).

In this chapter, I have described a particular stance and related attitudes important to the success of the interview. This stance requires an understanding of certain basic facets of the human condition, including the structure of human thought and the dilemmas with which all humans must struggle. The human condition provides the common base upon which the interview rests, for both the therapist and the patient are joined in the endeavor of making sense of their experience—experience that is grounded for both in the human condition they share. Thus the interview holds promise for growth in self-awareness and understanding not only for the patient, but for the therapist as well.

REFERENCES

Buber, M. (1970). *I and Thou*, trans. W. Kaufmann. New York: Charles Scribner's Sons.

Boss, M. (1963). *Psychoanalysis Daseinanalysis*, trans. L. Lefebre. New York: Basic Books.

Carrington, P. (1977). *Freedom in Meditation*. New York: Doubleday.

Dass, R., and Gorman, P. (1985). *How Can I Help?* New York: Knopf.

Frankl, V. (1967). *Psychotherapy and Existentialism*. New York: Simon and Schuster.

Goldstein, J. (1976). *The Experience of Insight*. Boulder: Shambhala Press.

Humphreys, C. (1968). *Concentration and Meditation*. Baltimore: Penguin.

Husserl, E. (1962). *Ideas*, trans. W. R. Boyce Gibson. New York: Collier.

Laing, R. D. (1960). *The Divided Self*. Baltimore: Penguin.

——— (1967). *The Politics of Experience*. New York: Ballantine.

Le Shan, L. (1974). *How to Meditate*. New York: Bantam.

MacKinnon, R. A. (1980). Psychiatric interview. In *Comprehensive Textbook of Psychiatry* vol. 1, ed. H. Kaplan, A. Freedman, and B. Sadock, 3rd ed., pp. 895–905. Baltimore: Williams & Wilkins.

MacKinnon, R. A., and Michels, R. (1971). *The Psychiatric Interview in Clinical Practice*. Philadelphia: W. B. Saunders.

Maslow, A. H. (1971). *The Farther Reaches of Human Nature*. New York: Viking.

Matarazzo, J. D. (1978). The interview: its reliability and validity in psychiatric diagnosis. In *Clinical Diagnosis of Mental Disorders*, ed. B. B. Wolman, pp. 47–96. New York: Plenum.

Ripley, H. S. (1975). Psychiatric interview. In *Comprehensive Textbook of Psychiatry*, vol. 1, ed. A. Freedman, H. Kaplan, and B. Sadock, 2nd ed., pp. 715–723. Baltimore: Williams & Wilkins.

Rychlak, J. F., ed. (1976). *Dialectic: Humanistic Rationale for Behavior and Development*. Basel, Switzerland: S. Karger.

Schafer, R. (1954). *Psychoanalytic Interpretation in Rorschach Testing*. New York: Grune & Stratton.

Steiner, C. (1974). *Scripts People Live*. New York: Bantam.

Sullivan, H. S. (1954). *The Psychiatric Interview*. New York: W. W. Norton.

Sundberg, N. D., and Tyler, L. (1962). *Clinical Psychology*. New York: Appleton-Century-Crofts.

PART II

Approaches to Interviewing

3 Psychoanalytic Interviewing

RALPH S. IENNARELLA, Ph.D. and ELIZABETH FRICK, Psy.D.

The discipline of psychoanalysis rests upon the fundamental tenet that unconscious psychological processes play an important role in determining human behavior. The main objectives of psychoanalytic treatment are the description, understanding, and modification of disruptive unconscious processes. Psychoanalytic inquiry has typically relied upon diagnostic interviewing as the principal method for assessing unconscious motivation, psychic functioning, and personality organization. This chapter will provide detailed reviews of the major diagnostic interviewing approaches that serve psychoanalytic investigations. An extended clinical vignette will be presented to illustrate the more basic features of the various approaches.

The interviewing approaches are grouped into two general categories: those that focus on psychodynamics and intrapsychic structure, and those that concentrate on object relations and interpersonal functioning. The former approaches attempt to assess psychological functioning primarily through an evaluation of intrapsychic processes and configurations (including psychodynamics, ego functions, and structural organization). The latter groups attend principally to an assessment of interpersonal transactions and patterns (such as interpersonal relationships, narcissistic transferences, the patient's experience of the therapeutic relationship, and transference and nontransference) in assessing overall psychological functioning. It is important to note that facets of most of these diagnostic approaches are included in any comprehensive psychoanalytic evaluation. However, certain psychoanalytic schools and traditions typically emphasize the diagnostic importance of one approach more than the others. It is in this respect that the approaches are distinct and separate.

PSYCHODYNAMICS AND INTRAPSYCHIC STRUCTURE

Freud (1923) introduced the term *psychodynamics* to describe the interplay of motivational drives and the psychological processes that regulate, inhibit, and channel them in the production of human behavior. The psychodynamic interview examines the patient's predominant wishes or motives, unconscious fears, goals and standards, characteristic defenses, and perception of external reality. The aim is to assess the ways in which these facets of psychological functioning are integrated, underlie the individual's symptoms or character traits, and interfere with adaptation. Saul (1977, 1980) has suggested one outline for a psychodynamic diagnostic interview and, for convenience, divides clinical material into three main groups: anamnestic data, conscious emotional attitudes, and unconscious associative data.

The anamnestic data provide a historical review, past and present, of major life events. A thorough grasp of the patient's current reality situation is vital for understanding how his basic dynamics and present emotional problems interact with the environment. The patient's current situation is examined both as the patient's own creation and as a source of pressure and stimuli to which he reacts. The history seeks to determine how much of the problem is internally based and how much is a reaction to environmental stressors.

Included in the history is a description of the development of the patient's symptoms, the circumstances of their onset, and their course. The circumstances surrounding the onset of symptoms, in particular, may reveal specific emotional vulnerabilities. Similarly, factors leading the patient to seek treatment at a particular time may also point to such vulnerabilities.

Gathering a history of significant emotional relationships is also crucial. As a rule, relationships experienced during the first 6 years of life are of utmost importance. It is during this period that the basic patterns of emotional reaction, the individual's core motivations, are formed. Early emotional influences are examined with respect to their intensity, consistency, duration, and relationship to developmental phase. The patient's emotional investments in the past, particularly in early childhood, are seen as providing the key to the present psychodynamics.

The second main grouping of clinical material concerns conscious emotional attitudes. This area includes the patient's principal feelings about himself and others, currently and during early childhood. It is also important to obtain the patient's own understanding of himself and the principal complaints. Related to such self-perception is an exploration of the patient's view of the future, expectations, fears, and ambitions.

Additional focus is given to the patient's delineation of major motivational forces. The patient generally has some conscious awareness of these forces and their influence. The patient is asked to recount his sexual development, the interplay between wishes for dependence and independence, feelings of inferiority, and aggressive motivations. In conjunction with this analysis, the individual's strengths, talents, and skills are assessed.

The third main grouping of clinical data, unconscious associative data, is an indirect and rich indicator of the patient's deepest patterns of motivation. Both earliest memories and dreams are considered to be quite revealing. In particular, the individual's first or earliest childhood dreams, repetitive dreams, and current dreams are noteworthy. The dream of the night preceding the interview may be particularly informative. A parallel analysis is made of conscious fantasies. Finally, the patient's explicit and implicit attitudes toward the interviewer are also examined, since these are particularly important in understanding the patient's current motivations.

As a brief illustration, a psychodynamic interview might reveal that the overtly cocky and aggressive bully is actually a timid and doubt-ridden individual who was continually berated and criticized by his father during childhood. Having repressed his feelings of inadequacy and fearfulness, he attempts to overcompensate for his underlying insecurity through belligerence and hostility. He might physically provoke men of greater physical stature as a way of simultaneously denying and affirming his sense of psychological weakness.

Ego Functioning

Bellak and his colleagues (Bellak and Hurvich 1969, Bellak et al. 1973, Bellak and Fielding 1978) have emphasized that the assessment of individual ego functions is central to differential evaluation of the degree and type of psychopathology. Bellak believes that the concept of the ego, as part of the tripartite model of the ego, id, and superego, can be operationally defined by its functions—specifically, in terms of an individual's adaptive strengths and weaknesses. Along with his associates, Bellak has devoted a great deal of attention to the identification of 12 ego functions, the specification of their component factors, and the development of criteria for assessing their adaptive adequacy. The backdrop of the assessment is an anamnesis, with particular attention paid to clarifying chief complaint, precipitating events, and current life situation (Bellak and Faithorn 1981). The history is aimed at permitting a visualization of the settings, significant people, events, their interactions at various times of life, and the degrees of impact of these circumstances, people, and events.

A careful assessment of ego functions critical in negotiating the vicissitudes of life is particularly important. A profile of an individual's assets and liabilities, demonstrating the level of functioning in various areas, provides a basis for understanding and predicting behavior. Bellak and his co-workers have identified 12 specific ego functions: reality testing; judgment; sense of reality; regulation and control of drives, affects, and impulses; object relations; thought processes; adaptive regression in the service of the ego; defensive functioning; stimulus barrier; autonomous functioning; synthetic-integrative functioning; and mastery-competence. By way of illustrating how these functions are operationalized in terms of clinical material, the main clinical components of each function will be briefly outlined.

REALITY TESTING

Reality testing includes an individual's ability to distinguish between inner and outer stimuli—that is, the ability to make a distinction between ideas and perceptions. The ego function of reality testing also concerns the accuracy of one's perception, including one's orientation to time and place and the ability to interpret external events accurately. A final component is the accuracy of inner-reality testing, which pertains to the level of reflective awareness of inner states and psychological mindedness.

JUDGMENT

Judgment is assessed in terms of anticipation of the consequences of intended behaviors (such as legal culpabilities and social disapproval) and the extent to which behavior reflects the awareness of these consequences. Also included is the extent to which the individual's affect is appropriate to (congruent with) the anticipation of a behavior's consequences (for example, anxiety in relation to legal ramifications).

SENSE OF REALITY

Sense of reality means the extent to which external events are experienced as real and includes the degree to which the body, its functioning, and the patient's behavior are experienced as familiar and unobtrusive and as belonging to (emanating from) the self. In addition, the assessment of this ego function includes the level of self-esteem and the feeling of separateness from the external world and from other individuals.

REGULATION AND CONTROL OF DRIVES, AFFECTS, AND IMPULSES

The regulation and control of drives, affects, and impulses refers to the directness of impulse expression and the effectiveness of delay and control mechanisms. The strength of drives, affects, and impulses is evidenced in dreams, fantasies, conscious experience, and overt motor behavior. This ego function also concerns the degree of frustration tolerance and the extent to which drives are channeled through ideation, affective expression, or manifest behavior.

OBJECT RELATIONS

Object relations takes into account the manner and degree of relatedness to others. Also important is the extent to which present relationships are adaptively or maladaptively patterned upon older ones. The extent of object constancy is another consideration, in terms of the individual's ability to summon up gratifying images of others in the face of frustration.

THOUGHT PROCESSES

Thought processes concerns the adequacy of those functions that adaptively guide and sustain thought, such as attention, concentration, anticipation, concept formation, memory, and language. Included are the relative primary- and secondary-process influences on thought—namely, the degree to which thinking is organized and oriented in accordance with reality considerations. This addresses the extent to which thinking is delusional or autistic and the degree of looseness of associational processes.

ADAPTIVE REGRESSION

Adaptive regression in the service of the ego reflects the ability to relax perceptual and conceptual acuity with a concomitant increase in awareness of previously preconscious material. This process is followed by the induction of new organizations of this material, thereby increasing adaptive potential as a result of such creative integration.

DEFENSIVE FUNCTIONING

Defensive functioning considers the degree to which defensive operations adaptively or maladaptively influence ideation, affect, and behavior. It entails evaluation of the efficiency of the defensive repertoire under various stressors and is evidenced by the degree of emergence of anxiety, depression, or other dysphoric affects.

STIMULUS BARRIER

Stimulus barrier indicates the subject's threshold for, sensitivity to, and awareness of stimuli impinging upon various sensory modalities. The assessment of stimulus-barrier functioning also applies to the nature of reactions to various levels of sensory stimulation in terms of the extent of disorganization or withdrawal provoked and the active coping mechanisms and defenses elicited.

AUTONOMOUS FUNCTIONING

Autonomous functioning is assessed according to the degree of impairment of primary-autonomy apparatuses, such as functional disturbances of sight, hearing, intention, language, memory, learning, or motor functioning. Also evaluated is the degree of impairment of secondary autonomy, including disturbances in habit patterns, learned complex skills, work routines, hobbies, and interests.

SYNTHETIC-INTEGRATIVE

Synthetic-integrative functioning includes the elimination of contradictions within the ego—that is, the capacity to reconcile or integrate discrepancies in attitudes, values, affects, behaviors, and self-representations. It also refers to the degree of maintenance of continuity in behavior, as in the ability to carry out planned activity. Another component is the active relating and integrating of different aspects of psychic and behavioral events, not necessarily in conflict, in order to increase adaptation. Lastly, synthetic-integrative functioning refers to the degree of maintenance of stability and level of organization when external conditions change suddenly or stressfully.

MASTERY-COMPETENCE

Mastery-competence is based on the individual's overt, conscious statement of feelings of adequacy. Also reflected here is the individual's expectation of success and the subjective experience of actual performance. In other words, an assessment is made of how the individual feels about *how* he does and *what* he can do with efficacy.

The Structural Interview

Kernberg (1975, 1976) believes that understanding the patient's intrapsychic structural characteristics can vastly improve diagnostic precision. The id, ego, and superego are structures that dynamically integrate the mental processes of defensive operations and internalized object relations. Kernberg applies structural concepts to the analysis of the patient's predominant intrapsychic organizations and instinctual conflicts, and proposes the existence of three broad structural organizations: neurotic, borderline, and psychotic. Kernberg asserts that, in addition to the biological, familial, psychodynamic, or psychosocial factors that contribute to the development of a particular disorder, the interactive effects of all these factors are reflected in the individual's overall psychic structure.

Kernberg (1984) has outlined an approach for using a "structural interview" as a diagnostic method. The assumption is that the interviewer's focus on the patient's main conflicts will create enough tension that the structural organization of mental functioning will emerge. The interview combines the traditional mental status examination with a psychoanalytically oriented assessment focusing on patient–therapist interactions. The aim of the interview is to tactfully elicit patients' pathology while demonstrating respect and concern for their emotional reality.

The assessment of structural organization is based primarily on the degree of identity integration (the integration of self- and object-representations), the types of defenses predominating (primitive versus advanced), and the capacity for reality testing (impaired versus intact). The structural interview centers on the clarification, confrontation, and interpretation of the identity conflicts, defense mechanisms, and reality distortions that the patient reveals in interaction with the interviewer. Kernberg defines clarification as a nonchallenging, cognitive exploration of the limits of patients' awareness of their productions. Through confrontation, the interviewer describes to the patient those aspects of the material that indicate the presence of conflictual functioning, defensive operations, contradictory self- and object-representations, and decreased awareness of reality. The interviewer uses interpretation in an attempt to resolve the conflictual nature of the material by proposing unconscious motives and defenses that make the previously contradictory appear logical. Transference interpretation is also employed in confronting and clarifying the current interaction between patient and interviewer.

Kernberg has devoted much attention to the clinical and diagnostic characteristics of principal structural criteria. Identity integration refers to two qualities of self- and object-representations. First, there is a differentiation of self-representations from object-representations, thereby providing a maintenance of ego boundaries and a sharp delineation between the self and others. Second, all self-images and object-images, both "good" and "bad," have been integrated into a comprehensive concept of both self and others. The structural interview constitutes an experimental situation in which the extent of integration of self and the perception of objects can be explored and tested. The lack of identity integration, or identity diffusion, is clinically represented by a poorly integrated concept of the self and of significant others. As an illustration, Kernberg (1984) describes a woman who was disgusted with men who were "only out to use women as sex objects." She had escaped from the sexual advances of a previous boss and had avoided social contacts because of men's predatory sexual approaches, but had also worked for some time as a Playboy "bunny." When confronted with the contradiction between her assertions and her choice of employment, the woman reacted with surprise.

A closely related structural issue concerns the quality of object relations. Of importance here are the stability and depth of the individual's relationships with others as manifested by warmth, concern, empathy, understanding, and the ability to maintain a relationship when it is subjected to conflict or frustration. The quality of object relations is largely dependent on identity integration, and dysfunctions may become immediately apparent in the patient's interaction with the interviewer. Kernberg states that such interactions are typically brief and highly diagnostic, permitting further assessment of structural organization.

As previously mentioned, an additional criterion of structural organization is the nature of an individual's defensive repertoire. High-level defensive operations center on repression and related mechanisms of reaction formation, isolation, undoing, intellectualization, and rationalization. These mechanisms operate to protect the ego from intrapsychic conflicts by the disavowal of an impulse, its ideational representation, or both, by the conscious ego. Primitive defensive operations center on splitting and other related mechanisms, such as primitive idealization, projective identification, denial, omnipotence, and devaluation. These defensive operations protect the ego from conflicts by means of dissociation. That is, contradictory experiences of the self and significant others are actively kept apart in an effort to reduce the anxiety related to these conflicted states.

The third major structural criterion identified by Kernberg is reality testing, defined by the capacity to differentiate self from nonself, to distinguish intrapsychic from external origins of perceptions and stimuli, and to realistically evaluate one's own affect, behavior, and thought content in terms of ordinary social norms. Reality testing is clinically represented by the absence of hallucinations and delusions; the absence of grossly inappropriate or bizarre affect, thought content, or behavior; and the capacity to empathize with and clarify another person's impressions of the self. Kernberg states that the structural interview provides an ideal opportunity for evaluating reality testing. For example, if the therapist's interpretation of a primitive defense mechanism results in an improvement in the patient's immediate functioning, then this reflects the maintenance of reality testing. If such intervention leads to a deterioration in the patient's immediate functioning, then this indicates the loss of reality testing.

Kernberg (1984) has summarized the differentiation of structural organization (neurotic, borderline, and psychotic) in terms of the principal structural criteria (identity integration, defensive operations, and reality testing). Neurotics display an integrated identity, rely on repression and other high-level defenses, and demonstrate the capacity to evaluate self and others realistically and in depth. Borderlines are characterized by identity diffusion, a predominance of splitting and other low-level defense mechanisms, and variability in accurate reality testing. Psychotics have self- and object-representations that are poorly delimited, and there may be a delusional identity. In addition, they tend to employ primitive defense mechanisms, and their capacity to test reality is severely impaired.

OBJECT RELATIONS AND INTERACTIONAL FUNCTIONING

Sullivan (1953, 1954) saw the interview process as a dialogue between patient and therapist, aimed at understanding patients through an awareness of their interpersonal relationships and their relevant thoughts and feelings. The interviewer was not conceptualized as a detached examiner, but rather as a "participant-observer." The patient and interviewer examine and clarify the fundamental interpersonal events in the patient's life. Based upon this exploration, general formulations of the patient's interpersonal relationships and emotional functioning are developed. These formulations are then tested and validated by further examination of the patient's experiences from various points of view and in diverse kinds of interpersonal relationships (Chapman 1978).

Sullivan concentrated his theoretical system and clinical techniques on interpersonal relationships. He proposed that people carry into their interpersonal relationships unhealthy tendencies which derive from close relationships during childhood and adolescence. Parataxic distortions occur such that an individual deals with another person as if that person were someone from the individual's past. Thus, we tend to repeat patterns of feelings and behaviors that were gradually developed over our formative years.

Sullivan believed that each interview should have an underlying format of four general components: inception, reconnaissance, detailed inquiry, and termination. The four stages are not employed rigidly, but serve as ways of observing and organizing interpersonal events and relationships and of formulating the patient's general approach to interpersonal problems. The inception often begins with inquiry into the difficulty that has caused the patient to seek help. This initial entree is broad and essentially no more than a general invitation to talk. The aim here is to begin to establish the interview as an interpersonal process wherein the patient's feelings of self-esteem and self-worth are supported.

In the reconnaissance, the interviewer and the patient take a broad look at the patient's life. The main purpose is to establish a basic understanding of the patient as an individual and of the experiences that shaped his personality and problems. A broad inventory of the patient's life history and current adjustment is elicited. Sullivan suggests an examination of childhood relationships, school adjustments, adolescent experiences, vocational history, sexual adjustment, social activities, and personal habits. For all of these areas, the emphasis is on interpersonal relationships and their emotional coloration. During the reconnaissance, the interviewer also observes the patient's reactions to the interview process, including the patient's emotional response to areas discussed and the kind of interpersonal relationship established with the interviewer. The latter would consider, for example, the patient's rigidity versus flexibility in dealing with the interviewer, and the patient's tendencies to be controlling, suspicious, passive, evasive, and so on.

The detailed inquiry is an in-depth exploration of the patient's life and problems. In effect, Sullivan sees the detailed inquiry as an extensive exploratory course of psychotherapy. The patient and the interviewer examine how current interpersonal problems are continuations of maladaptive ways of interacting that began in earlier relationships. In general, questions are believed to be more useful than statements, because questions focus the patient's attention on the issue at hand and also open new areas for discussion. Sullivan believed that many interviewers allow much important material to go by unexamined, and that such material may be lost permanently.

The termination of an interview consists of a brief summary or recapitulation of what has been accomplished. Sullivan held that the patient should carry away something beneficial from each interview and should feel that something was accomplished, however small. The summary is not a lecture by the interviewer, but a dialogue in which both the interviewer and the patient participate. Thus the patient is offered the opportunity to amend the interviewer's statements, and both interviewer and patient discuss the patient's comments and views.

Narcissism and the Self

Kohut (1971, 1977) has offered a unique theoretical and clinical approach to the diagnosis and treatment of narcissistic pathology, and this approach has been summarized by Basch (1980) and Doroff (1979) among others. According to Kohut, the nuclear disturbance in such pathology is the absence of psychological structure that normally maintains a unitary, stable self-concept and an adequate sense of self-esteem. Narcissistic patients are seen as having failed to progress through the developmental steps necessary for the formation of self-cohesion and self-esteem. The interpersonal relationships, or object relations, of such patients are characterized by the use of others (objects) as *selfobjects.* That is, objects function as a substitute for the missing psychological structure in regulating self-cohesion and self-esteem. Within the context of the therapeutic situation, these patients transfer demands onto the therapist that are in the service of such selfobject needs. Kohut spoke of these transferences as *selfobject transferences* and saw them as the patient's unconscious attempt to reactivate and complete previously thwarted developmental tasks.

Kohut identified two parallel developmental lines that together determine self-esteem. He referred to these aspects of the cohesive self as the "archaic grandiose self" and the "idealized parent imago." The grandiose self is manifested by the expectation that one is the center of the universe and that everyone and everything exists only to serve one's needs. Kohut called this type of selfobject transference the *mirror transference* and delineated three subtransferences. The merger transference represents the most primitive stage of narcissism. Here the therapist is experienced as physically separate but not psychologically distinct. The patient has no sense of the therapist as a person with separate psychological boundaries. The patient attempts to maintain a sense of self by treating the therapist as an object to be controlled and used as it suits the patient. This subtransference is characteristic of patients who regard it as their fundamental right to call their therapists whenever and as often as they wish.

The alter-ego, or twinship, transference manifests a higher level of narcissistic development. The therapist's psychological separateness is acknowledged, but not his individuality. The patient safeguards his self-concept by implicitly assuming that his opinions, beliefs, and goals are identical to the therapist's. This would be conveyed, for example, by the patient who becomes extremely disillusioned with the therapist because of the therapist's failure to appreciate a particular literary style that the patient values.

In the mirror transference proper, the therapist's separateness and individuality are acknowledged. However, the patient feels worthwhile and functional only when he experiences the therapist as approving. The therapist is important only to the extent that he mirrors or reflects the patient's sense of worth. Thus, the therapist who fails to react appreciatively to the patient's new wardrobe may be experienced as demonstrating an inability to care.

In summary, the various forms of the mirror transference recapitulate those needs that were apparently not met when the patient was younger. The patient, lacking a sense of identity, looks to the therapist to impart a sense of the patient as a worthwhile, appreciated, and appropriately functioning individual. If the treatment proceeds well, the grandiose conceptualization of the self is modified, and grandiosity is transformed into a healthy sense of self-esteem.

The idealizing transference represents the patient's need to fuse with the therapist in order to possess the therapist's omniscience and omnipotence. Parallel to the grandiose concept of the self as all-powerful is the experience of being cared for by the therapist, who is looked up to as an ideal, thus providing the patient with an encompassing sense of well-being. The patient experiences the therapist as the source of well-being and expects that the therapist will provide everything the patient wants. An illustration would be the patient who, at the initial session, emphatically declares that he "knows" the therapist is able to "understand everything" about him. The patient's identity and self-esteem can be ensured through union with the admired therapist. The therapeutic process transforms the unquestioning idealization of childhood and fosters the development of a mature ability to devote oneself to individuals and causes that transcend the narrower interests of the self. The patient's idealization is funneled into identifications with others that are not consuming and destructive.

Kohut's approach to the diagnosis of narcissistic character pathology is through the trial analysis—more generally, through a trial course of psychotherapeutic treatment. Since patients with narcissistic disturbances are seen as manifesting arrests in the development of the grandiose self or the idealized parent imago, or both, the therapeutic process would progressively demonstrate the failure of these primitive psychological organizations to become integrated with the rest of the personality. That is, the spontaneous establishment of one of the stable narcissistic transferences is the best and most reliable diagnostic sign of narcissistic pathology, whereby the therapist is relied upon as a mirroring or idealized selfobject rather than as a separate and whole object. The therapist comes to understand these needs from the clues the patient provides in his associations and behaviors.

Goldberg (1978) has elaborated upon this type of "wait-and-see" diagnostic approach. In essence, the therapist uses the initial sessions as a test for transference readiness and for an evaluation of the type of relationship that will emerge. An assessment of the patient's identity integration is also important. For example, do the patient's regressive swings toward fragmentation become wider and less easily reversible (manifesting the identity diffusion of the borderline), or do they become increasingly shallow, manageable, and absorbed into the emerging, stable narcissistic transference (representing the more integrated identity of the narcissistic individual)? Perhaps the most common sign of a beginning narcissistic transference is the patient's report of disconcerting symptoms, such as sexual acting out, hypochondriacal episodes, irritably arrogant behavior, painfully depressive moods, and feelings of emptiness and depletion during weekends and other times of interruption in the treatment. This symptomatic picture is understood as reflecting a partial fragmentation of the self as a consequence of a disruption in the narcissistic transference.

Analysis of the Transference

In a series of papers on the concept of transference, Gill (1979, 1982, 1984, 1985) argues that the bulk of analytic work should focus on the interpretation of the "patient's experience of the relationship with the therapist" (PERT) in the here-and-now. Gill contends that this type of intervention creates the opportunity for a special kind of new interpersonal experience with the therapist—one that interrupts repetitive, maladaptive, interactional patterns and thereby promotes insight and adaptive change. At the heart of Gill's theoretical system and technical approach is a consistent and concentrated evaluation and conceptualization of the PERT.

Hoffman and Gill (1986) have delineated six major propositions of this approach: (1) The understanding and interpretation of the PERT is a critical aspect of the psychoanalytic process and the distinguishing feature of the analytic method. (2) Both the diagnostic and therapeutic processes are enhanced by good interpretations of the PERT. (3) The patient and therapist's collaborative exploration of the PERT is fundamentally important and encompasses explication of how their current relationship reflects the patient's earlier conflictual patterns. (4) The therapist continually interacts with the patient and always makes a contribution to the PERT. Thus, the PERT, while having its origins in the patient's past, is relevant to the present situation with the therapist and is not defined as solely the patient's "distortion" of the therapist's behavior. (5) Much of the PERT is conflictual, with the patient wanting both to expose and to hide many of its aspects. The patient's communications, therefore, are essentially compromise formations that result in the PERT's being communicated in disguised form. (6) The therapist's basic task is to help uncover the latent meanings of such disguised communications. The therapist fosters the exploration of these meanings either through their active interpretation or by directly encouraging the patient to elaborate upon them.

Gill (1983) has offered three general principles relevant to the assessment of the PERT within the context of face-to-face interactions with the patient. First, since the patient's core psychopathology is manifested in the immediate interpersonal interaction with the therapist, the therapist should be continually ready to inquire into the PERT. Therapists cannot assume that their view of the here-and-now interaction with the patient is the same as the patient's experience of it. Gill sees the interpretive process—that is, the attribution of meaning to behavior—as a highly arbitrary enterprise. All the more reason, he contends, that therapists should do more inquiring and less interpreting.

Second, the therapist should always be ready to consider associations not explicitly about the relationship as disguised allusions to it. Gill talks chiefly of two mechanisms here. Displacement refers to the patient's allusions to the PERT via discussion of particular issues with a third party. As a simple illustration, a patient's commentary on her father's intrusiveness might be an indirect expression of her experience of the therapist as intrusive. Identification also comes into play when the patient attributes to himself attitudes that he believes the therapist has toward him. For example, a patient expressing contempt for his wife might be communicating his impression of the therapist as being contemptuous of him. Gill is quick to point out that to focus on the implications of external relationships for the therapeutic relationship is not to deny the independent significance of these other relationships. Rather, the emphasis on the therapeutic relationship is based on the assumption that the PERT is parallel to the patient's experiences in other relationships.

Third, the therapist will inevitably, to a greater or lesser degree, fall in with the patient's prior expectations. The patient is continually exerting pressure upon the therapist, in one form or another, to conform to the patient's characteristic modes of relating. Therapists must therefore be ever cognizant of their behavior and how it may be affecting the patient. More specifically, Gill maintains that every aspect of the PERT has some connection to an actual stimulus within the therapeutic situation. Each interpretation of the PERT must therefore be made in a spirit of recognizing and respecting the plausibility of the patient's experience, given the information the patient has.

Unconscious Communication

Langs (1973, 1983, 1985) has offered a comprehensive framework for the initial interview, based upon his study of unconscious derivative communication, and attempts to integrate major aspects of the analytic approaches discussed thus far. Specific areas of assessment include the nature of the patient's presenting problem, the precipitating factors for seeking treatment, the developmental history, current dynamic issues, level of ego functioning, and the nature of intrapsychic conflict. Within this context, issues of narcissism, depression, anxiety, and any acute symptoms such as suicidal or homicidal ideation are also evaluated. The goals of the interview are (1) to establish the nature of the patient's emotional problems, (2) to convey a sense of the therapist's competence to help the patient insightfully resolve these problems, (3) to manage early resistances that might interfere with treatment, (4) to establish the therapeutic contract, and (5) to evaluate the patient's style of communication and capacity to work in therapy.

It is the process within which the initial interview unfolds, rather than the specific content areas recommended for evaluation, that most distinguishes Langs's approach from other analytic perspectives. This position is perhaps best known for its emphasis on the importance of unconscious communication. The major premise of Langs's approach is that unconscious conflict, the basis of all emotional problems, is so threatening that it is blocked from direct awareness and expression (Lubin 1984). For this reason, during the interviewing process, patients cannot directly verbalize the full genetic and dynamic basis of their problems; rather, they express indirectly important latent clues to its specific nature through associations and symptoms.

As Langs (1973) began to listen to patients' associations from this frame of reference, he observed how acutely perceptive patients are of the therapist's interventions and the therapeutic setting and how powerfully patients respond to specific stimuli emanating from these sources. These reactions and perceptions are, for the most part, outside of the patient's awareness and communicated in disguised form. In the initial interview, therefore, therapists must continuously search for potential triggers within the therapeutic relationship that might help them to decode, organize, and understand the meaning of the patient's symptoms, complaints, and associations. The communicative approach makes an active effort to introduce some objectivity into the therapeutic interaction by distinguishing patient responses that are primarily distorted and function as clearer expressions of underlying neuroses (transference) from those that are for the most part valid perceptions of the therapist and the setting and are therefore nonneurotic (nontransference). For example, a therapist is late to the interview, and the patient proceeds to talk about feeling slighted in relationships with others who can't manage their lives and maintain commitments. Here the therapist must take into account the real stimulus impact of the lateness on the patient's associations before any interpretation of possible transference implications can be considered.

Langs has described two basic phases in the initial consultation hour. The first phase is unstructured and proceeds at the patient's pace. The therapist opens the interview by inviting the patient to talk about the problem that he is experiencing. The process unfolds with the patient free associating and the therapist maintaining a basic attitude of receptivity, attentively listening and observing on both manifest and latent levels. Detailed history taking, recording of the session (Frick 1985), active questioning, and probing are all discouraged as stimulating resistance and promoting communication on a superficial, manifest level. This position maintains that a richer and more dynamic understanding of the patient's problems is gained by allowing free association to unfold.

The patient who remains relatively silent presents specific difficulties, and it is recommended that the therapist always first attempt to understand and interpret the unconscious basis for such resistance. As with all other resistances, the therapist first makes mental note of what has transpired since the beginning of the relationship, in an attempt to determine what might be stimulating the patient's inability to talk. When the patient does not provide adequate information for the therapist to interpret the underlying basis for the silence, a careful playback of prior associations or a minimum of well-chosen questions is recommended.

In the second phase of the interview, approximately two-thirds of the way through the session, the therapist makes recommendations to the patient based on the ongoing assessment developed earlier. The therapist makes a summary statement to the patient, indicating an ability to assist the patient in resolving his emotional problems, and the therapist then describes how the therapy will proceed by outlining the framework for treatment. The basic treatment ground rules, which establish the core relationship between patient and therapist, include the following: (1) working in a stable, consistent, and relatively neutral setting; (2) establishing a single, fixed fee; (3) determining a set time and length for each session; (4) establishing responsibility for attendance at all scheduled sessions; (5) emphasizing the importance of the patient's free association along with the therapist's maintenance of free-floating attention and relative silence. Implicit ground rules also include the therapist's capacity to contain the patient's projective identifications, the therapist's relative anonymity and neutrality, the therapist's use of appropriate silence and valid interventions, an exclusive one-to-one relationship with total privacy and confidentiality and the essential absence of physical contact.

Langs's approach maintains that this set of basic conditions for treatment offers the patient an optimal therapeutic holding environment. Such an environment helps to isolate the patient's illness for exploration, facilitates expression of primarily transference-based conflicts, and elicits anxieties that reflect the patient's fears of entrapment and death based on the anticipated loss of giving up old and familiar, but basically pathological, modes of relatedness (Keene 1984). The therapist's ability to manage this therapeutic framework, and to analyze pressures from the patient to deviate from it, are critical.

CASE HISTORY

The following is a detailed summary of an initial psychotherapy session. The session does not serve as an illustration of how each of the interviewing approaches previously discussed might actually be enacted in a face-to-face encounter with a patient. Rather, the session material will be used to demonstrate how the clinical data could be conceptualized from each of the approaches. Suggestions on how the various approaches might further pursue their respective diagnostic aims will also be provided.

> The patient is a 16-year-old white female whose mother initially contacted the therapist, having been given the therapist's name by a physician. The mother described her daughter as immature, clingy, and troubled by superstitions. The daughter had recently seen other therapists, but refused to continue with them. Both mother and father had attended the daughter's initial sessions with the previous therapists. The present therapist asked the mother to have her daughter contact the therapist directly to schedule the initial appointment. The daughter called the therapist the next day, and an appointment was scheduled. The session was held in a small clinic where both the referring physician and the therapist maintained offices. The patient waited with a girlfriend but was interviewed alone.
>
> *Patient: I look pretty tonight. I look weird. I don't know what to say. Where do we begin?*
> *Therapist: Why don't you just begin by telling me a little bit about the problem that you are having.*
> *Patient: Well, this really sounds crazy, but I have these fits and they have really gotten worse. I have to keep doing things over and over and I can't stop it. I have*

this thing with shoes. If they aren't all lined up a certain way, I freak out. And all of the toothbrushes in the bathroom, they can't be touching one another. Maybe they represent family members. I was riding in a car with a friend and she had some things on the dashboard. I had to keep straightening and arranging them and she looked at me and said, "Stop it!" But I have to do it. And when I'm alone in the car, like if my umbrella is in the back seat, I'm afraid it will jump up and attack and kill me. I lock myself in my room. I'm afraid that the telephone will rise and chase me around the room. I sleep with my mother. I've never slept in my own bed. I saw another therapist and he didn't say anything except "Are you going to be OK?" as I was leaving and gave me pills.

And my mother expects me to be a mother to her. She's always competing. Three days of the week she wears my clothes. She divorced my dad and married my stepdad, but now she's dating men closer to my age than hers. I want a mom who is really a mom and there for me. She doesn't want me to leave for college. She says one thing, but really means something else.

I brought a friend with me instead of her tonight. I brought the check, too. I just need to know how to make it out. I just got back from Italy with my real father. He got jealous if I wanted to flirt with any other boys and he walked around in his underpants in front of me. Now is that any way for a father to act? My boyfriend is hooked on drugs. I'd like for him to be able to use again some day. I'm the only one who takes care of him. Will you be talking to my mother?

Therapist: You've talked about feeling extremely anxious and compelled to keep things straight and separate. When they aren't, you feel like you might be attacked and killed. You feel like your mom and dad want to be more like you than separate from you, which feels seductive and wrong. And now you're asking me if I'm going to talk to your mom. First, I talked with her on the phone and then I said it would be best for you to call me directly. In a way, I did one thing and said to do something else. I think that what you're really telling me here is that in order for me to help you, for you to feel safe here with me, I need to establish some clear boundaries and talk just to you and keep your parents totally out of it.

Patient: My mother would probably die if she heard me talking about her this way. It's like she'd want me to tell her side, too. [silence] And she will probably ask, "Well, what did you tell her?" Should I come back? I think I should. Sometimes I just feel so down. I'm always trying to make other people happy.

Therapist: [The therapist expressed to the patient that she felt that she could help her begin to resolve her problems and outlined the basic therapeutic framework with the patient including the fee, face-to-face mode, time, frequency of sessions, method of payment, confidentiality of the sessions, and the way in which the therapy would unfold.]

Patient: I wanted to see a man, not a woman, but you've said more tonight than those other therapists said all together. Seeing you will be kind of like talking to God. I can say anything I want in here to you. It really freaks me out . . . you know, my stepfather is the only one who really understands and cares about me. Tonight, before I left, he said, "You know, Emily, I never asked you about your therapist and therapy before, not because I don't care, but because I just don't think it would be appropriate."

Discussion of Clinical Material

An interviewer who was primarily interested in establishing a psychodynamic diagnosis would take special note of the patient's symptomatology, such as her compulsion to straighten and arrange objects so that they line up without touching and her fears of being attacked. The compulsive arranging could be understood as a symbolic attempt to regulate the parents' overinvolvement with the daughter. The patient's fear of attack could be seen as the projection of her own angry, hostile impulses toward her parents, while simultaneously representing her guilt and need to be punished for wanting to separate. The psychodynamic interviewer could corroborate these formulations by soliciting the patient's recollections of her earliest memories, childhood dreams, and current fantasies. Particularly instructive might be an examination of the onset of the patient's symptoms in relation to what specifically characterized her relationship with her parents at that time.

With specific attention to ego functioning, the interviewer would particularly focus on the girl's adaptive strengths and weaknesses. For example, there is clinical data to indicate impaired reality testing. She demonstrates a limited ability to distinguish between inner and outer stimuli when she speaks of her fear that the phone will rise and chase her around the room. There is no awareness on her part that this fear derives from inner feelings of suffocation and hostility related to her parents. At the same time, she does show some signs of insight when she comments on her mother's dependency needs ("She expects me to be a mother to her") and insists that she wants "a mom who is really a mom." With respect to the regulation and control of drives, affects, and impulses, the patient channels these psychological forces into obsessive-compulsive behaviors, at the expense of productive affective expression. Overall, the interviewer attempts to develop a profile of the patient's various ego functions, the stability and pervasiveness of which is evaluated across contact with various people, events, and settings.

In developing a structural diagnosis, the interviewer assesses the patient's associations from three basic perspectives: degree of identity integration, types of defenses, and capacity for reality testing. For example, the patient begins the hour with contradictory statements, "I look pretty tonight. I look weird." She also reports feeling terrified when alone, and boundaries between family members are notably blurred. All this points to a fragile identity integration. Defense mechanisms show a failure of rationalization and a reliance on projection, externalization, and concretization. Efforts to structure the world through obsessive-compulsive rituals are failing. Impaired reality testing is evident from the presence of bizarre affect and content. The structural approach would focus on the patient's main conflicts and attempt to create an optimal level of tension in the interview. Thus, the patient's defenses would be interpreted by the interviewer to determine whether reality testing improved, suggesting a borderline personality organization, or deteriorated to a psychotic level of functioning.

The interviewer who focuses on the diagnostic significance of interpersonal relationships would quickly take note of the similarities in the girl's relationships with her mother, father, and boyfriend. In all three relationships, her needs are ignored while she takes care of, satisfies, and accommodates to the others. An additional relationship that must also be considered is that with the girlfriend who accompanies the patient to the session. The interviewer would carefully explore all of these and other relationships in great detail. A broad inventory of the patient's life would be sought, looking to the connection between early interpersonal experiences and current interpersonal relationships. The interviewer would tentatively explore the patient's parataxic distortions of the girlfriend and boyfriend vis-á-vis the parents and other significant relationships. Also deserving careful consideration are the possible parallels between the stepfather and therapist, both of whom were described in a relatively positive fashion.

When evaluating the presence of narcissistic pathology, the interviewer would concentrate on the patient's presenting complaints and object relationships. This patient's poor self-concept and use of others, such as her mother and girlfriend, to regulate self-cohesion and self-esteem would be viewed as diagnostic of impairment of the self. The initial interview would be considered the beginning of a trial analysis. In effect, this first session would represent a test evaluation of the type of transference relationship that might develop. After the therapist intervenes, there are hints of the development of an idealizing transference in the patient's comparison of the therapist to God and in her statement about how helpful she anticipates the therapist will be. This would be silently noted and allowed to develop across sessions, thus providing a medium conducive to the development of a stable narcissistic transference.

To illustrate the evaluation of the patient's experience of the therapeutic relationship, we can discuss the patient's closing remarks. The girl praises the therapist for having said more than her previous therapists combined, likens the therapist to God, and psychologically connects the therapist to her stepfather, who is "the only one who really understands and cares" about the patient. What immediately precedes this is the therapist's comments that expressed her felt ability to help the patient resolve her emotional problems and outlined the basic therapeutic framework. Thus the therapist's comments as a whole can be taken as the stimulus precipitating the patient's experience of the therapist as an idealized figure. The patient's experience of the therapist is plausible given the therapist's expression of confidence in being able to help, organization in outlining the treatment framework, and caring through the description of how therapy would unfold. An interviewer focusing on the diagnostic significance of the PERT might propose such an interpretation to the patient, encouraging her to elaborate on her experience of what is going on between them. The interviewer would essentially attempt to assess what in the patient's past led her to organize the interpersonal field as she did, attributing to it an idiosyncratic significance, and whether this interpersonal attitude is rigid (pathological transference) or flexible (nonpathological transference).

The interviewer who focuses on the importance of unconscious communication would first attempt to organize the derivative meanings of the patient's associations as responses to specific stimuli emanating from the interviewer and the treatment framework that she establishes. For example, this patient manifestly raises the issue of the therapist's further contact with the mother and the therapist's relationships with both the referring physician and the clinic, the latter through her query about to whom she should address the check. Given these stimuli, the associational content would first be understood as an unconscious perception of the therapist, who, like the patient, is "afraid of being alone" and may experience difficulty maintaining appropriate boundaries. These perceptions derive from the therapist's affiliations with the referring physician and the clinic, as opposed to an ideal of a completely confidential and private treatment framework. The patient's pathological reaction to such perceptions is evidenced through her severe symptomatology. Based upon the intensity of the patient's reactions to her perceptions of the therapist and the therapeutic setting, the interviewer would anticipate that maintaining an optimal, exclusive, confidential relationship would also be intensely threatening to this patient. Furthermore, it would be likely to stimulate her efforts to alter the conditions of treatment and seek symptomatic relief through behavioral discharge rather than through insight and working through.

The diagnostic interview has long been the principal data-gathering instrument for psychiatry and psychology. As the foregoing illustrations have demonstrated, psychoanalytic approaches to diagnostic interviewing offer a rich, in-depth, and truly unique perspective on psychological functioning. The general diagnostic focus is on the interplay and organization of psychological processes, as well as on the complex and often subtle patterning of interpersonal interactions. No other discipline provides such a comprehensive analysis and synthesis of the structural and object-relational aspects of human behavior. Each of the approaches reviewed addresses both intrapsychic structure and interpersonal functioning. The difference between the approaches is a matter of emphasis, with one approach stressing the importance of its particular diagnostic focus more than the others. Together, these approaches convey the vitality and rigor of psychoanalytic inquiry and constitute a powerful diagnostic tool.

The authors wish to gratefully acknowledge the assistance of Cynthia Keene, Psy.D., who critically reviewed each version of this chapter and offered valuable suggestions.

REFERENCES

Basch, M. D. (1980). *Doing Psychotherapy*. New York: Basic Books.

Bellak, L., and Faithorn, P. (1981). *Crises and Special Problems in Psychoanalysis and Psychotherapy*. New York: Brunner/Mazel.

Bellak, L., and Fielding, C. (1978). Diagnosing schizophrenia. In *Clinical Diagnosis of Mental Disorders*, ed. B. J. Wolman, pp. 757–774. New York: Plenum.

Bellak, L., and Hurvich, M. (1969). A systematic study of ego functions. *Journal of Nervous and Mental Diseases* 148:569–585.

Bellak, L., Hurvich, M., and Gediman, H. (1973). *Ego Functions in Schizophrenics, Neurotics, and Normals.* New York: Wiley.

Chapman, A. H. (1978). *The Treatment Techniques of Harry Stack Sullivan.* New York: Brunner/Mazel.

Doroff, D. R. (1979). Treatment of the narcissistic personality disorder. In *Object Relations and the Developing Ego in Therapy*, ed. A. J. Horner, pp. 227–271. New York: Jason Aronson.

Freud, S. (1923). The ego and the id. *Standard Edition* 19:3–59.

Frick, E. M. (1985). Latent and manifest effects of audiorecording in psychoanalytic psychotherapy. In *The Yearbook of Psychoanalysis and Psychotherapy*, ed. R. Langs, pp. 151–176. Emerson, NJ: New Concept Press.

Gill, M. M. (1979). The analysis of the transference. *Journal of the American Psychoanalytic Association* (suppl.) 27:263–288.

——— (1982). *Analysis of Transference: Theory and Technique.* Vol. 1. New York: International Universities Press.

——— (1983). The interpersonal paradigm and the degree of the therapist's involvement. *Contemporary Psychoanalysis* 19:200–237.

——— (1984). Robert Langs and technique: a critique. In *Listening and Interpreting: The Challenge of the Work of Robert Langs*, ed. J. Raney, pp. 177–187. New York: Jason Aronson.

——— (1985). A critique of Robert Langs' conceptions of transference, evidence by indirection, and the role of the frame. In *The Yearbook of Psychoanalysis and Psychotherapy*, ed. R. Langs, pp. 177–187. Emerson, NJ: New Concept Press.

Goldberg, A. (1978). *The Psychology of the Self.* New York: International Universities Press.

Hoffman, I. Z., and Gill, M. M. (1986). A scheme for coding the patient's experience of the relationship with the therapist (PERT): some applications and extensions. Unpublished manuscript.

Keene, C. (1984). Framework rectification and transient negative effects. In *Listening and Interpreting: The Challenge of the Work of Robert Langs*, ed. J. Raney, pp. 267–300. New York: Jason Aronson.

Kernberg, O. F. (1975). *Borderline Conditions and Pathological Narcissism.* New York: Jason Aronson.

——— (1976). *Object Relations Theory and Clinical Psychoanalysis.* New York: Jason Aronson.

——— (1984). *Severe Personality Disorders: Psychotherapeutic Strategies.* New Haven: Yale University Press.

Kohut, H. (1971). *The Analysis of the Self.* New York: International Universities Press.

——— (1977). *The Restoration of the Self.* New York: International Universities Press.

Langs, R. (1973). *The Technique of Psychoanalytic Psychotherapy.* Vols. 1 and 2. New York: Jason Aronson.

——— (1983). *Psychotherapy: A Basic Text.* New York: Jason Aronson.

—— (1985). The first session. In *The Yearbook of Psychoanalysis and Psychotherapy*, ed. R. Langs, pp. 125–150. Emerson, NJ: New Concept Press.

Lubin, M. (1984). Views on neurosis, listening, and cure: a discussion of Gill's comment on Langs. In *Listening and Interpreting: The Challenge of the Work of Robert Langs*, ed. J. Raney, pp. 415–430. New York: Jason Aronson.

Saul, L. J. (1977). *The Childhood Emotional Pattern.* New York: Van Nostrand Reinhold.

—— (1980). *The Childhood Emotional Pattern and Psychodynamic Therapy.* New York: Van Nostrand Reinhold.

Sullivan, H. S. (1953). *The Interpersonal Theory of Psychiatry.* New York: W. W. Norton.

—— (1954). *The Psychiatric Interview.* New York: W. W. Norton.

4
The Existential/ Humanistic Interview

SALVATORE R. MADDI, Ph.D.

It may seem odd to be writing about assessment interviewing from an existential/humanistic perspective, as this position has eschewed diagnosis as insufficiently appreciative of human subjectivity, and as unneccessary as a guide to psychotherapy. This deemphasis of assessment has been coextensive with an unwillingness to theorize elaborately, for fear of rendering human experience as static and complete rather than pulsating and becoming, and as predictable and conventional rather than free and individualistic. Despite what might be called this deconstructionist bias, there is in the existential/humanistic position some bona fide personality theorizing, and some screening or intake interviewing. Scrutinizing these efforts permits explication of assessment goals and techniques that are existential/humanistic in spirit and that can serve as a guide to those interested in applying this position.

In the pages that follow, I will first consider existential/humanistic theorizing, and then proceed to how these thoughts are expressed in interviewing practice. As in any clinical position on human behavior, the most relevant theorizing concerns the assumptions framing the views of psychopathology, premorbidity, and maturity (Maddi 1988a). It is how the patient is doing with regard to these three evaluative criteria that gives direction to assessment interviewing.

EXISTENTIAL THEORY

It must be said at the outset that terms like *psychopathology, premorbidity,* and even *maturity* sound foreign to existential psychologists. The connotations of these terms are objectionable to them for reasons already mentioned. I will use these terms nonetheless, in order to facilitate comparisons with other approaches more accepting of them.

In order to define psychopathology, we must have a sense of normal behavior, and of what constitutes deviations from normal that are so contradictory as to appear sick. There is little resembling objectivity in this matter of defining psychopathology, and different positions arrive at different conclusions. When we are dealing with adults, normalcy is usually described in the language of maturity. Psychological maturity is the result of sound development. One whose development has not been ideal may be vulnerable to psychopathology. Not themselves actual illnesses, these vulnerabilities, or premorbidity, only result in psychopathology when certain precipitating factors or stressors are encountered. As you can see, my introduction to the terms *psychopathology, premorbidity*, and *maturity* is deceptively simple. Actually, these terms are so embedded in and critical to any approach that they must be completely explicated. So let us get on with the task, as the existential approach is no exception.

Psychopathology

A behavior is regarded as psychopathological by any well-developed approach when it violates assumptions about what it means to be human (Maddi 1988b). Sometimes these inhuman actions are deviations from social convention. Often, however, they are common, everyday behaviors. It is an important function of the various approaches to alert us to actions that may be damaging to ourselves and others even though they are accepted by society (Maddi 1988b). Indeed, when an approach appears to define psychopathology as social deviance, you can expect that it is not conceptually well developed, because it substitutes socially conventional views of what is acceptable for considered assumptions about maturity and failures to reach it.

The existential approach has a very definite position on what constitutes psychopathology. The common denominator is that psychopathology involves a strong, chronic sense of meaninglessness. Underlying this view is the belief that humans are unique among living beings because of the ability to construct meaning through self-reflective thought and through decision making (Binswanger 1963, Boss 1963, Frankl 1965, Kobasa and Maddi, 1977, May et al. 1959). Thus, to feel a chronic, desperate sense of meaninglessness is to fail to be human, and this is serious enough to be regarded as psychopathological.

Various existentialists have depicted states of meaninglessness. The philosopher Sören Kierkegaard (1954) spoke of "the sickness unto death," by which he meant a kind of psychological death in which persons feel that their lives have been wasted and there is nothing of value left. Among psychologists, Frankl (1965) delineated the noogenic neurosis, a state of emptiness similar to that described by Kierkegaard. Incorporating much in other existential positions, my position (Maddi 1967, 1970) attempts to be both comprehensive and detailed by distinguishing three forms of existential sickness, or meaninglessness. In order of decreasing severity, they are *vegetativeness, nihilism,* and *adventurousness*. Each has cognitive, affective, and behavioral components.

In *vegetativeness*, the cognitive element is that the person cannot find anything in whatever is being done or can be imagined that seems interesting or worthwhile; the emotional element is apathy and boredom, punctuated by bouts of depression that become less frequent as the disorder is prolonged; and the behavioral element is indolence and aimlessness. Vegetativeness is the most severe existential pathology because there is little or no sense of meaningfulness left. Persons suffering vegetativeness go through their days in a lost, aimless, empty way, doing only what they have to, and often not even that. The disorder can become severe enough to render sufferers incapable of caring for themselves. Much in what is called burnout, depression, and simple schizophrenia is covered by the vegetative syndrome.

In contrast, *nihilism* is a less severe sickness because some sense of meaning persists. But it is paradoxical meaning, or antimeaning. In nihilism, the cognitive element is the cynical conviction that nothing purporting to have meaning is really meaningful, that nothing is what it seems. This belief is accompanied at the emotional level by frequent feelings of disgust and anger, and at the behavioral level by competitiveness and ungenerosity. Sufferers of this syndrome are quick to expose whatever appears to have face validity, and they revel in the angry, competitive exposure of the naivete in others whose beliefs are more straightforward. They are often quite skilled in developing diabolically effective negativistic accounts of experience. But have them encounter something manifestly meaningless and they will be equally agile in insisting on its meaningfulness. Episodes like these show the nihilistic process at the heart of this disorder. The nihilism syndrome bears some similarity to paranoid, obssessive-compulsive, and aggressive states.

Finally, the *adventurousness* syndrome involves the least severe form of pathology because those suffering from it retain a partial sense of meaning (in contrast to vegetativeness), and that meaning is positive rather than paradoxical (in contrast to nihilism). In adventurousness, it is common, everyday life that has lost meaning, and the sufferer is forced to every greater risk and deviancy in order to experience satisfaction and vitality. At the cognitive level, adventurers are attracted to that which is dangerous, believing the rest to be banal. At the emotional level, there are mood swings between the poles of boredom or apathy, and exhilaration or anxiety, depending on whether it is everyday life or risk that is being encountered. Similarly, at the action level, adventurers are indolent or decisive, depending on whether the circumstances of the moment are challenging or routine. Sufferers of this syndrome can be soldiers of fortune and perennial joiners of causes, on the one hand, or addicted gamblers and substance abusers, on the other hand. Traditionally defined mood disorders have much in common with adventurousness. Many respected industrialists and professionals fall into this category, regardless of the socially acceptable nature of their activity.

Maturity

The existential viewpoint on maturity is in many ways the opposite of the viewpoint on psychopathology. If it is the nature of humans to construct meaning, then to qualify as mature, one must be able to do this regularly and effectively. The mature life-style is called *authenticity* by existentialists. Summarizing the thinking of several relevant philosophers and psychologists, I have elsewhere (Maddi 1967, 1970) delineated the characteristics of authenticity as including (1) the tendency to choose the future rather than the past in decision-making situations, (2) self-definition as a person who can influence social and biological experience through use of wits, (3) the belief that society is the creation of humans and is therefore best considered in their service, (4) vigorous expression of symbolization, imagination, and judgment, (5) the belief that life is best when there is continual growth through learning, (6) the knack for finding something interesting and worth while in whatever one is doing, (7) the willingness to tolerate the anxiety normally surrounding new experience in order to choose the future, (8) a minimum of guilt over missed opportunities, (9) decisiveness of actions, and (10) a tendency to conduct interpersonal relationships intimately rather than contractually.

As you can tell from the foregoing characteristics, the authentic life-style involves persons in vigorous interaction with their social, physical, and biological surroundings; a rather continual growth process; and a cognitive, emotional, and behavioral definiteness that is aptly called *individuality* (Maddi 1970).

In order to appreciate why authenticity is the epitome of maturity for existentialists, it is important to reflect on the associated assumptions concerning human nature, or the core of personality (Maddi 1988). Existentialists assume that humans are by their nature not only *social* and *biological*, but also *psychological*. Their psychological side is expressed in an active propensity for *symbolizing* (generalizing specific experiences into abstract categories, such as words), *imagining* (combining and recombining symbols without the requirement of external experience), and *judging* (taking a preferential or ethical stance toward the fruits of symbolizing and imagining). This symbolizing, imagining, and judging lends the character of *decision making* to experiencing that has extensity in time.

Persons who symbolize, imagine, and judge vigorously are proficient at differentiating experiences from one another (have many categories or symbols), at formulating ideas about change (have a rich imagination), and at developing preferences and ideals (form definite judgments). This certainly makes them individualistic (Maddi 1988b), but it also gives them heightened awareness that they formulate the meaning in their lives by the decisions they make. In decision-making circumstances, they recognize that they can launch themselves into the future or stay with what is already familiar. Choosing the future is the way of growing through learning, whereas choosing the familiar (the past) teaches one little or nothing. Concomitantly, choosing the future is anxiety provoking, because the unknown is unpredictable. However safe choosing the past may seem, it brings with it the guilt of missed opportunity.

To achieve the life-style of authenticity, one must learn to tolerate anxiety sufficiently so that one can choose the future regularly and thereby continue to grow and have a sense of vitality, control, and satisfaction. What one needs to do this is *courage*, and this is learned by youngsters in interaction with parents who reward them the largest proportion of the time, encourage them to try tasks that exceed their capacities just a little, and expose them to a wide variety of experiences interpreted as richness rather than chaos (Kobasa and Maddi 1977).

Premorbidity

Persons not fortunate enough to experience the ideal developmental conditions just summarized will develop a premorbid life-style instead. If parents punish more than reward, set tasks that are either too difficult or too easy, and protect their offspring from variety and change, the result is a life-style aptly characterized as *conformism* (Maddi 1970).

The dimensions of *conformism* are (1) definition of self as a player of social roles in which it is important to be pragmatic and acceptable in a conventional sense, (2) a belief in the paramount importance of biological needs, in the sense of physical comfort, materialism, and survival, (3) a sense of powerlessness to influence events, (4) chronic feelings of alienation and a sense of missed opportunity, (5) an inability to tolerate the uncertainty of change, preferring the status quo, and (6) a tendency to conduct interpersonal relationships on a contractual rather than intimate basis (Maddi 1970).

The premorbidity, or vulnerability, to psychopathology constituted by conformism stems from a relative lack of symbolization, imagination, and judgment, and a concomitant choice of the familiar rather than the new in decision-making circumstances. Conformists consequently feel that life has passed them by, and that they are frail and inadequate.

Certain stressors can undermine the conformist adjustment (Maddi 1967), precipitating the psychopathologies of meaning mentioned earlier. These stressors include (1) social upheavals (such as economic depression, war, political changes, job loss), (2) threats to physical well-being (such as illness or physical attack), and (3) confrontations with one's own superficiality (this is usually forced by some significant other who is suffering because of this superficiality). Social upheavals can undermine adjustment because the conformist's underlying assumption is that it is the social system (institutions, norms, reference groups) that lends meaning to life. In effect, the conformist is treating society as if it were perfect enough never to change, so when it does, trouble ensues. Similarly, threats to physical well-being undermine adjustment because the conformist's underlying assumption is that physical well-being is the most important thing lending meaning to life. Forced recognition of superficiality undermines adjustment because it confirms the conformist's worst fears, fears carefully guarded against.

HUMANISTIC THEORY

As in the existential approach, humanistic theory does not accept the traditional emphasis on psychopathology and assessment. Indeed, there is even less basis in humanistic approaches for discerning implicit assumptions about psychopathology, maturity, and premorbidity. Nonetheless, let us plunge in.

Maturity

A rather clear position on maturity is contained in the theories of Rogers and Maslow. According to Rogers (1959, 1961), ideal or *fully functioning persons* are (1) open to experience (rather than defensive), (2) spontaneous rather than rigidly planful (flexible, adaptive, and inductive), (3) organismically trusting (tend to listen to cues from their bodies rather than subscribing to conventional values), (4) experientially free (have a subjective sense of free will), and (5) creative (productive of new ideas and things). Theorizing similarly, Maslow (1955, 1962) describes ideal or *self-actualized persons* as having (1) realistic orientation, (2) acceptance of self, others, and the natural world, (3) spontaneity, (4) task-orientation (rather than self-preoccupation), (5) a sense of privacy, (6) independence, (7) appreciativeness, (8) spirituality (not necessarily in a formal religious sense), (9) identity with humankind, (10) feelings of intimacy with a few loved ones, (11) democratic values, (12) recognition of the difference between means and ends, (13) humor (that is philosophical rather than hostile), (14) creativeness, and (15) nonconformism.

In general, Maslow's characteristics of maturity emphasize cognitive functioning (such as democratic values, identity with humankind, recognition of the difference between means and ends) more than do those of Rogers. Further, the characteristics developed by Rogers emphasize process, emotionality, and intuition more than is true for Maslow. Nonetheless, both depictions are humanistic in that they render maturity as a rich, sensitive, intuitive openness to experience and a nondefensive ability to reflect on this experience.

In all conceptions of personality, maturity is considered a joint product of expressions of the core or basic innate tendency that defines humanness and an ideal reaction to such expressions on the part of significant others. Humanistic positions are no exception. According to Rogers and Maslow, the core tendency is *to actualize inherent potential.* This tendency underlies all human behavior. If youngsters are to become mature, their natural efforts to express their potential must receive *unconditional regard* (uncritical appreciation and support) from significant others. If they have this, they will have no need to modify their natural behavioral tendencies to conform to values imposed by significant others. Thus they will grow by ever-greater expression of their inherent potential and will accept themselves readily, without imposing on themselves conventional conditions of worth.

Premorbidity and Psychopathology

It is particularly difficult to discern humanistic distinctions between premorbid and psychopathological states. Both Rogers (1959) and Maslow (1962) are clear that if youngsters encounter *conditional* (rather than unconditional) *positive regard* from significant others (that is, if these others impose their own or conventional standards of evaluation on the youngsters' behavior), then maturity is jeopardized. The resulting life-style, called *maladjustment* by Rogers (1959), includes:

1. conditions of worth
2. incongruence between the subjective self and the inherent potential
3. defensiveness, rather than openness to experience
4. living according to an inflexible plan rather than existentially
5. disregarding organismic messages rather than trusting them
6. feeling manipulated rather than free
7. behaving conventionally rather than creatively.

Maslow (1962) appears to endorse such theorizing, adding notions of cognitive ridigity and authoritarian values.

From these theorists' views on how the maladjusted life-style develops, one would conclude that it expresses premorbidity. But there is no formal humanistic theorizing about additional factors, such as stressors, that can undermine this life-style and lead to frank psychopathology. Nor do Rogers and Maslow detail conceptions of psychopathology per se. There are only three possible meanings to this state of affairs: (1) the maladjusted life-style is regarded as psychopathology; (2) some different viewpoint on psychopathology (for example, that contained in DSM-III) is endorsed in understanding mental illness; or (3) there is disbelief in the existence of psychopathology altogether.

Rogerians appear to reject number 2 and endorse either 1 or 3 with some inconsistency. When they endorse number 1, they are operating as if psychopathology inheres in life-styles rather than in breakdowns in the face of pressures (this is like using Axis II rather than Axis I of DSM-III-R). When they endorse 3, they join forces with other critics of the idea of mental illness as a form of victimization imposed by conventional society on persons having nothing more than problems in living. On the whole, Maslovians also tend to endorse 1 and 3, rather than 2. Early in his career, however, Maslow did appear to regard traditional bases for considering psychopathology (of the sort that have culminated in DSM-III-R) rather useful. So it is possible that he and others like him might also find alternative 2 congenial, although their writings are not at all clear on this.

DIAGNOSTIC ASSESSMENT

Now we have the theoretical underpinnings of diagnostic interviewing in existential and humanistic approaches. On the one hand, there is more specificity than might have been expected from the general deemphasis on systematization of human behavior that exists in these approaches. On the other hand, there are certain obstacles to heavy reliance on diagnostic assessment.

Existential Psychology: Overview

As is the case in assessment generally, the existential approach focuses on psychopathological states, premorbidity, stressors, and maturity. Regarding psychopathology, the emphasis is on determining degrees and qualities of meaninglessness. With premorbidity, what is searched for are various characteristics of a conforming life-style that express (1) a reliance on conventional society and organismic biology as that which defines living, (2) a sense of powerlessness and threat in coping with complexity and change, and (3) feelings of boredom and sadness about missed opportunities. As to stressors that might have precipitated psychopathology, one looks for social and interpersonal upheavals, threats to physical survival, and confrontations with one's own superficiality. Determining maturity, or authenticity or individuality, involves the search for life-style characteristics that are in many ways the opposites of those defining premorbidity.

Needless to say, premorbidity and maturity are life-styles that are rooted in developmental experience. But existential psychology does not emphasize identification of these developmental experiences as a key to sound diagnostic assessment.

Existential Psychology: Diagnostic Interviewing

It is typical for the therapist to ask patients to talk about their problems or themselves, and to probe as needed. In this regard, the therapist is not particularly passive, and can be confrontational as needed, giving feedback to patients on how they sound to another person. The emphasis is on current experiences and problems rather than the past, unless the interviewee's insistence suggests that something in the past is of paramount importance. Further, there is no special focus on dreams; in existential psychology, these nighttime experiences have no greater validity as a diagnostic guide than do daytime experiences.

The therapist is after both experiential process and content. As to process, the therapist listens carefully to patients in order to determine how they make the inevitable decisions that mark human life. The interviewer is trying to determine (1) the level of awareness in the patient that personal experience is constructed by the decisions we make, and (2) whether decisions tend to be made for the future or the past. Thus, a patient who says "My life is like a treadmill. I'd like to get off, but you can't do that, what with all the obligations and responsibilities you have. For once in my life, I'd like to be able to plan something, or just to take it easy" expresses little awareness of the personal decisions that must have been made, however implicitly, that lead to the trouble. In contrast is the high level of awareness in the following statement: "As I think about my divorce, I realize all the little things I did, and failed to do, that contributed to the problem that finally did us in. I wish I could blame it all on my spouse, but I know that's not true."

Whether decisions are made for the future or the past depends on what, in any particular circumstance, is new and what is familiar for the patient. A patient who is choosing the past might make the following statement:

> As the time of the cocktail party approached, I began to wonder whether I wanted to go. Even though I was feeling lonely and bored, I wasn't sure I'd have a good time. The thought of meeting all those new people seemed daunting. What would I have to say to people like that? It began to seem more and more attractive to stay home and watch a movie. I felt like I was finking out on my friend, who was nice enough to try to help me meet new people, but finally I stayed home anyway. I felt a little inadequate, but it was so comfortable to be warm and cozy in bed watching that movie.

This statement also contains the anxiety that attends thinking about choosing the future, and the guilt resulting from shrinking from it by choosing the past. Contrast that with a clear choice of the future:

> I couldn't decide whether to take the job or not. Taking it meant leaving my friends and relatives, and the city I knew so well. I even began to think that the old job wasn't so bad after all, even though I had done so much complaining about it. But I always came back to thinking about how exciting this new job opportunity was—just the kind of thing I had been preparing for. And I kind of knew that I had been in a rut for quite a while, not learning anything, seeing the same people, doing the same things. Finally I screwed up my courage and decided to take the new job. After all, the worst that could happen is that I wouldn't like it.

This person also experiences anxiety in facing the future, but finds that path developmentally valuable enough to take it. Understandably, there is no sign of the guilt of missed opportunity. What is important diagnostically is not whether any one decision is made for the future or the past, but whether the pattern or regularity over time favors one or the other direction.

Diagnostically, a low level of decisional awareness and a tendency to choose the past are characteristic of the premorbid life-style, of conformism, and of the various psychopathological states of meaninglessness. In contrast, high decisional awareness and regular choices of the future suggest the mature or authentic life-style.

The content of experience, as shown in beliefs about self and world, in actions, and in continuing moods, also aid in diagnosing mature and premorbid life-styles and psychopathological states.

The following are examples of relevant expressions of conformism:

PLAYER OF SOCIAL ROLES

"Whenever I go to a party, I always try to find out what everyone will be wearing, because I always want to fit in."

"At work meetings, I take my cue from my superiors and the older workers, so that I can give them what they want."

EMBODIMENT OF BIOLOGICAL NEEDS

"I read everything I can about diet and exercise, because the most important thing you have is your health."

"As I get older, I live in fear of having a stroke or a heart attack."

"I love my wife, but I'd take every opportunity for a little free sex, if there were no strings attached."

MATERIALISM

"When I graduated from college, I took the job offer that made me the most money, even though the other one might have been more interesting."

"I admit that it made me feel lower than low when Joe showed up in his white Rolls-Royce."

PRAGMATISM

"As a lawyer, my sense of ethics is to help my client get off rather than to worry about what might or might not be just."

"There's no point in worrying about abstract problems that you can't do anything about anyway. It's enough to do what you can."

CONTRACTUAL RELATIONSHIPS

"I spend my time with my customers and the others in the office, and although we usually talk about work-related matters, we sometimes talk about other things—you know, the weather, sports—but never controversial things like politics or religion."

"I don't like to meet with people unless I know what they want from me and how that fits into my goals."

POWERLESSNESS

"What's the sense of trying hard at work—someone else always gets the glory anyway."

"It's one of the more foolish ideas we humans have that we can influence what's going on around us."

ALIENATION AND MISSED OPPORTUNITY

"I'm half way through my life, and nothing has happened. The days just come and go, and all that's happened is that I get older and more bored."

"I could have become an artist, but somehow it just didn't happen, and now what do I have to show for all these years of life?"

FEAR OF CHANGE

"Every day I feel like I'd like to stop the world and get off."

"This crazy technological race is leading us to chaos. Soon we're going to blow ourselves up or something."

The following are examples of expressions of the authentic life-style:

SELF-DEFINITION AS INFLUENCER

"I find that when I try to take a part in town meetings, people generally listen to me as long as I am not all tied up in my own little problems."

"I've noticed that I enjoy sex more when it's with someone who excites my imagination."

SOCIETY AS HUMAN INSTRUMENT

"After all, where did society come from, if not from our own efforts to cooperate or compete together?"

"Society isn't some monolithic, God-given thing out there. It's up to us to make it work for us."

INTIMATE RELATIONSHIPS

"I really like meeting someone and trying to get to know them on a real, personal basis."

"I like to know all sorts of things about people, not in order to control them, but because it's more fun sharing secrets than just talking about the weather or politics."

VALUE OF CONTINUAL GROWTH

"When I think about how much I've learned, and how much remains to be learned, it makes me very happy to be alive."

"Whatever happens, even if it's painful, I feel that if you can learn something for your future, you're way ahead."

KNACK OF FINDING INTEREST AND MEANING

"When the lecturer started droning on and on, I was dismayed, but then I concentrated on making a list of all the ways he had of being boring, so that I could learn never to be that way myself."

"At work, when I have to do routine tasks, I try to determine how to reorganize the job so that it can be done faster and with more value."

TOLERATING ANXIETY IN ORDER TO CHOOSE THE FUTURE

"My relationship with Al was at least comfortable, if unfulfilling, and that made it very hard to leave—but finally I was stagnating so much that it seemed as if my life was over, so I had to gulp twice and leave."

"My heart was in my mouth as I began to sign the contract that brought the new company to me. Suppose I failed and lost everything? But I had researched it too well to turn back. It could be the turning point of my life."

DECISIVE ACTIONS

"By the time I got home after the argument with my boss, I had thought the problem through enough to want to talk with her about it, so I just called her apartment."

"Whenever I have a problem, I'm the kind of person who wants to deal with it sooner rather than later."

The following are examples of expressions of psychopathological states:

ADVENTUROUSNESS

"I'm like an ambulance chaser, only with me it's causes. As soon as I finish working for one cause, I feel uncomfortable, bored, and empty until another comes along. I'm a creature of crisis, I suppose."

"I don't know why I keep breaking the law. All I know is that when I'm breaking into that house at night, or when I'm trying to get away from the cops chasing me, that's when I feel really alive."

"You know, being a commodities broker is really asinine. You can make a lot of money, but you can lose even more. And the tension is not to be believed. It's enough to make you a junkie. But it's the only thing that cancels out humdrum, everyday routines. Being a broker, you don't even need friends or lovers."

NIHILISM

"We can say whatever we want to about why things happen or don't happen—theories, religions, romance. But when you come right down to it, we don't understand anything because there's nothing to understand. There's no scientific or religious order. There's only chaos, if you can make that into a religion."

"We think of humans as the triumph of evolution, as so much more advanced than the animals. That's baloney. We are just like so many apes, or sharks, or cockroaches, nothing better."

"Amy took me to church, and it disgusted me so much to sit through that sermon. I should have walked out. What drivel about rising above pressures, and being tested by God. I'm amazed that Amy and the others could be so naive."

VEGETATIVENESS

"I don't have any reason to get out of bed in the morning. If anything in my day had the least bit of meaning, I'd bolt up, but it's the same emptiness day after day."

"I don't even feel anything any more. There are no reds or yellows, just grey. Nothing matters, nothing is now. I wish I could even get angry at it all."

"I sit there at my desk at the office and try to be pleasant and get something done. But I just don't care about the work, or the others, or myself, I guess. I'd commit suicide, but even that seems dumb."

As with any diagnostic approach, it is difficult to determine whether one is confronted with the premorbidity of conformism or with some outright psychopathological state. Patients often express aspects of conformism, adventurousness, nihilism, and vegetativeness within the same session. As with other approaches, the therapist must decide on a diagnosis based on the weight of evidence, and be prepared to revise conclusions as additional information becomes available.

A further complication is that patients do not always express themselves elaborately. In such cases, it behooves the therapist to ask questions designed to elicit relevant material. Interviewing techniques designed to provoke particular responses are sometimes useful. Binswanger (1963), for example, would insistently ask "Why?" or "Why not?" when patients appeared unable to communicate or experience richly. No sooner was one insistent "Why" answered then another would confront the respondent. Frankl's (1965) primary therapeutic technique of *paradoxical intention* can also be used for assessment interviewing. This technique involves listening discerningly to the patient and then suggesting some behavior that is a logical extension of the behavioral theme but seems paradoxical nonetheless. Thus, someone who complains about the emptiness and worthlessness of life can be asked "Why haven't you committed suicide?" The answer to such a question is often quite revealing of underlying assumptions about the self and the world.

I have employed a technique called *situational reconstruction* in a diagnostic (as well as therapeutic) manner (Maddi 1986). In this technique, patients are asked to describe a current stressful event in their own words. Then they must imagine three versions of the event that would have been even worse, from their viewpoint, and three versions that would have been better. They are then invited to investigate the plausibility of the three better and worse versions of the event by imagining others who might be involved, the roles they all play, and the relevant tasks and social forces that would have been necessary for these alternative versions to occur. If they have not covered this already, they are then asked to imagine what they themselves could do to increase the likelihood of the better versions of the event and to decrease the likelihood of the worse versions. It is helpful to record this entire exercise or to take notes, because in answering the questions, patients usually reveal much about their beliefs concerning themselves and their world that is relevant to existential diagnosis.

Take, for example, the case of Arthur, whose stressful event was the denial of an expected job promotion based on a negative evaluation from his supervisor. Arthur was so angry and hurt that he resisted my efforts to have him imagine better and worse versions of what had happened. This difficulty suggested that he did not make vigorous use of imagination in daily life (possible evidence for conformism or psychopathology). However much he tried, he could come up with only two worse versions of the event, suggesting just how bad what had happened was in his view (this suggests conformism, as the event provoked strong negative emotions and involved being rejected by an authority figure). Arthur's two worse versions of the event were combining the negative job evaluation with being fired, or with no salary increase. Both more negative versions suggest materialism (being without a job or money seemed as bad as he could imagine things getting). It was somewhat easier for Arthur to imagine three better versions of the event. They were (1) if the negative evaluation had been presented as tentative rather than definite, (2) if it had not been believed by the officers of the company, and (3) if it had occurred at a time when he had another attractive job offer. Versions 1 and 3 suggest some mature initiative on Arthur's part (he could perhaps influence a tentative negative evaluation or take another job entirely), but 2 suggests the powerlessness of conformism (he is subject to the whims of officers' beliefs). As the emphasis shifted to considering the plausibility of the better- and worse-event versions, the simple, almost stereotypical nature of his views of self and world became more apparent. He emerged as an ordinary, passive, fearful person buffeted about by the forces in the world, such as power-hungry peers, indifferent supervisors, incompetent officers, and crass, "bottom-line" thinking. There was little in all this to suggest psychopathological tendencies of adventurousness, nihilism, or vegetativeness. On balance, the diagnosis reached was conformism.

Existential Psychology: Questionnaires

There are also some questionnaires that are useful in assessment from an existential viewpoint. There are, for example, several measures of powerlessness, often called Internal-versus-External-Locus-of-Control Scales (Bialer 1961, Crandall et al. 1965, Rotter et al. 1962). Also, Crumbaugh and Maholik (1964) and Crumbaugh (1968) have offered a questionnaire, called the *Purpose-in-Life Test*, aimed at assessing Frankl's concept of the existential vacuum (meaninglessness). Another related test, the *Existential Study*, is under development by Thorne (Thorne 1973, Pishkin and Thorne 1973, Thorne and Pishkin 1973).

Although the Purpose-in-Life Test and the Existential Study are short and have face validity, more research must be done with them before they are accepted as reliable and valid enough for clinical use. Also, although much research has been reported using the various versions of the Internal versus External Locus of Control Scale, complications abound concerning reliability, homogeneity, and validity. It too must be used with caution.

Kobasa, Maddi, and their associates have developed a promising measure of hardiness, called the *Personal Views Survey* (Hardiness Institute 1985). Hardiness (Kobasa 1979) is a composite of three sets of beliefs about self and world concerning commitment (versus alienation), control (versus powerlessness), and challenge (versus threat). Considered a version of existential courage (Maddi 1986, 1988b) especially useful in coping with stressful events, hardiness has evidenced a buffering, or health-preserving, effect on subjects experiencing much stress (Kobasa 1979, Kobasa et al. 1982, Maddi and Kobasa 1984). Although earlier versions of the Personal Views Survey had homogeneity problems when used with adolescents and (sometimes) with females, the most current version, which consists of 50 rating-scale items balanced for positive and negative content, shows adequate reliability and validity (Hardiness Institute 1985). Persons high in hardiness can be expected to reflect the authentic life-style, whereas those achieving low scores will probably do so either out of existential premorbidity (conformism) or actual existential psychopathology.

Humanistic Psychology: Overview

There are both similarities and differences between existential and humanistic approaches to assessment. Among the similarities are the encouragement to patients to relate their current (rather than past) experiences, a deemphasis on dreams, and a generally supportive stance on the part of the therapist. As to differences, the humanistic interviewer will reflect rather than confront, and in asking questions, will take special care not to appear confrontational.

For some humanistic psychologists, there is no point to diagnostic assessment; the decision as to whether therapy is desirable is the patient's alone, and the nature of the therapy is the same regardless of the presenting symptoms. Other humanistic psychologists will find it a matter of interest to determine whether the patient is fully functioning (self-actualized) or maladjusted. For the latter practitioners, some diagnostic procedures can be specified.

Humanistic Psychology: Diagnostic Interviewing

The major task is to determine from patients' material whether they are maladjusted or fully functioning (self-actualized). The following are examples of maladjustment:

CONDITIONS OF WORTH

"I hate myself when I fritter away the whole day and get nothing of value done."

"I don't care what other people do, but I have to stay calm and collected no matter what."

INCONGRUENCE BETWEEN SELF AND POTENTIAL

"I work so hard, and for what? Just money. At the end of the day, I'm so tired, but also so dissatisfied. I don't even know what I want any more, but I know I'm not happy."

"Sometimes I have this vague sense that I could have done all sorts of things instead of having the orderly, mundane life I'm stuck with."

DEFENSIVENESS

"I don't understand myself. I try and try to figure things out, but the more I try, the less clear it all becomes."

"I'm just like other people; I do all the things you're supposed to do. So why am I having all these problems? Why am I the one who gets left behind all the time?"

RIGID PRECONCEIVED PLANS

"Ever since graduating from college, I've had this schedule for myself: Start as a junior exec, maybe making $40,000 a year, move up the ladder and make assistant VP by age 30, and be a major force in the company by 40, with a salary of $120,000."

"I always wanted a normal American life. You know, two children, a house in the suburbs, a Mercedes in the driveway, good standing in the community. What's so wrong with that?"

ORGANISMIC DISREGARD

"When I get that tightness in the chest, I just shrug it off. I've always been a little cowardly, and I'm not about to give in to it."

"When I'm with Amy, we have pleasant times, but I can't always think of things to say. On the other hand, Laura and I always have a ball, without ever making any plans, without ever feeling bored. But I'm going to see if Amy will marry me, because I respect her education and career too much, and I see myself as needing that."

FEELINGS OF MANIPULATION

"Life is a rat race. You just keep running to try to reach your goals before the guy behind you beats you out."

"I'm a loser. I've never won anything or been in the least bit lucky."

CONFORMITY

"I love shopping in Harold's because it has all the latest, trendy styles that you need in order to look acceptable."

"At staff meetings, it's important to know who the power brokers are so that you can say the right things and get on their side."

The following are examples of the fully functioning life-style (Rogers 1961):

OPENNESS TO EXPERIENCE

"When I meet a person, it's as if it's the first person I've ever met. I'm so excited about getting to know him."

"When Joe hurt me so much, I thought I'd never want anything to do with him again. But then, whenever we'd get together, I realized that despite my hurt pride, I enjoyed and appreciated what we could have together. I began to realize that life and relationships are complicated, and you have to let them go wherever they go."

EXISTENTIAL LIVING

"When people ask me where I'm going on vacation next year, I never know what to say. I don't feel like making big, unchangeable future plans. Who knows what I'll want to do next year?"

"I know I change my mind a lot, but it's not just arbitrary. There's always a lot of input that I mull over before I decide what to do and think."

ORGANISMIC TRUSTING

"I know everyone was counting on me to marry Jim. All the plans were made, and we seemed to be such a nice couple. But, when push came to shove, I just didn't feel right enough or excited enough down deep."

"You know, all the odds were against making a success of that business. But something in me kept saying I should give it a shot, so I did."

EXPERIENTIAL FREEDOM

"You know, if you try to influence what's going on around you, you often can. Not always, but many times."

"Sometimes I have this great sense of power, like I can do anything I want to if I believe in it and am willing to work at it."

CREATIVITY

"When I am assigned a task at work, I always start by asking myself what's the best solution to the problem. I have to discard the usual ways the problem has been approached. Sometimes it's best to think of some way that seems outlandish because it may turn out to be the best."

"I don't like to do things the same way twice. Better to explore new solutions."

The implications of Maslow's (1962) version of maturity, the self-actualized person, are sufficiently different from those just explicated to warrant separate treatment.

REALISTIC ORIENTATION

"Relationships are two-way streets. When I try to understand some problem I have with another person, I try to listen to his point of view as carefully as I listen to my own."

"Every piece of information on some topic has truth to it. You have to consider it all."

ACCEPTANCE OF SELF, OTHERS, AND WORLD

"The older I get, the more I realize that my limitations are as important in making me who I am as are my strengths. Finally, it's all me, and that's okay."

"It doesn't make sense to blame everything on the politicians and bosses. Everyone more or less tries their best sometimes and goofs around sometimes. People aren't perfect, but they're all we have."

SPONTANEITY

Same as Rogers's Existential Living.

TASK ORIENTATION

"When there's a job to be done, that pulls me out of myself. It doesn't much matter how I and the others are or are not feeling that day, and who likes whom. There's work to be done."

"Even at times when I've been really down, I can get into working with the tasks at hand."

SENSE OF PRIVACY

"I really get a kick out of people. But sometimes I just need to be alone, to hear my inner voice."

"Just because I can open up to my intimate friends doesn't mean that I wear my heart on my sleeve wherever I go."

INDEPENDENCE

"Although it's more fun to travel with someone you like a lot, I also enjoy going places by myself."

"More and more, I find that I have my own point of view on various matters."

APPRECIATIVENESS

"Last night, the sunset was unbelievably beautiful. I just felt the whole power of the universe and it made me happy to be part of it."

"When I think of my past, I realize how wonderful people have been to me."

SPIRITUALITY

"Sometimes I'm overwhelmed at the ability of people—artists, writers, even ordinary people—to take giant steps forward."

"We all have such power in us, for good or evil."

INTIMACY

Same as in existential psychology.

DEMOCRATIC VALUES

"We are all brothers under the skin, as the saying goes."

"I like having all sorts of friends—rich, poor, educated, uneducated—it makes for a more meaningful life."

DIFFERENCE BETWEEN MEANS AND ENDS

"It's fine to want to rise to the top of the heap, but it's not fine to do so by lying and cheating."

"I care too much about my family's well-being to cast them aside and pursue my own freedom."

PHILOSOPHICAL HUMOR

"It's funny to see how we all try to cover up those wrinkles as we get older. We primp and preen, and spend all that money on oils and massages. I guess we just don't want to part with life."

"Here we are telling each other lies about ourselves, for fear that we aren't acceptable to each other. We humans are so frightened, and yet so wonderful."

CREATIVITY

Same as in Rogers.

NONCONFORMISM

Same as in existential psychology.

In the humanistic approach, there is little reliance on aids to interviewing such as Binswanger's "Why?" technique and Kobasa and Maddi's Situational Reconstruction. Such techniques would appear too manipulative of the patient to be acceptable to humanistic psychologists. But these psychologists have found the Experiencing Scale (Gendlin and Tomlinson 1967) useful. Experiencing is described as "the quality of an individual's experiencing of himself, the extent to which his ongoing, bodily, felt flow of experiencing is the basic datum of his awareness and communications about himself, and the extent to which this inner datum is integral to action and thought" (Klein et al. 1969, p. 1). Although the name may imply it, the Experiencing Scale is not a questionnaire to be filled out by the patient. Rather, the patient verbalizes in the interview, and then these verbalizations are rated by the therapist on a scale of degree of experiencing. There are seven stages of experiencing, ranging from the lowest, in which the patient seems distant or remote from feelings, through the middle range, in which feelings are brought into clearer perspective as the patient's own, to the highest, in which feelings have been scrutinized and explored such that they become a trusted and reliable source of self-awareness. Clearly, low experiencing is akin to maladjustment, whereas high experiencing suggests a fully functioning life-style. Klein and colleagues (1969) provide a scoring manual for the Experiencing Scale and report adequate interscorer reliability after practice.

Humanistic Psychology: Questionnaires

There is a questionnaire aimed at measuring the components of self-actualization included in Maslow's theories. Called the *Personal Orienta-*

tion Inventory (Shostrom 1965, 1966), this test consists of 150 paired, opposing statements. Responses yield scores on two major scales (inner-directedness and time competence) and ten complementary scales (self-actualizing values, existentiality, feeling reactivity, spontaneity, self-regard, self-acceptance, nature of man, synergy, acceptance of aggression, and capacity for intimacy). Adequate reliability is reported for the scales, and there is also evidence for construct validity.

Not all existential and humanistic psychologists will agree with the position I have taken in this chapter—namely, that there is an assessment technology inherent in these approaches. Admittedly, there is little acceptance in these approaches of DSM-III-R as a guide to psychopathology; nor is there even general acceptance of the concept that psychopathology is of value. Nonetheless, it seems to me that there is a surprising amount of conceptual and technical material relevant to existential and humanistic practice. I have tried to highlight this material.

REFERENCES

Bialer, I. (1961). Conceptualization of success and failure in mentally retarded and normal children. *Journal of Personality* 29:303–320.

Binswanger, L. (1963). *Being-in-the-World: Selected Papers of Ludwig Binswanger*, trans. J. Needleman. New York: Basic Books.

Boss, M. (1963). *Psychoanalysis and Daseinanalysis*, trans. L. B. Lefebre. New York: Basic Books.

Crandall, V. C., Katkovsky, W., and Crandall, V. J. (1965). Childrens' beliefs in their own control of reinforcement in intellectual-academic achievement situations. *Child Development* 36:91–109.

Crumbaugh, J. C. (1968). Cross-validation of the Purpose-in-Life Test based on Frankl's concepts. *Journal of Individual Psychology* 24:74–81.

Crumbaugh, J. C., and Maholik, L. T. (1964). An experimental study in existentialism: the psychometric approach to Frankl's concept of noogenic neurosis. *Journal of Clinical Psychology* 20:200–207.

Frankl, V. (1965). *The Doctor and the Soul*, 2nd ed., trans. R. Winston and C. Winston. New York: Knopf.

Gendlin, E. T., and Tomlinson, T. M. (1967). The process conception and its measurement. In *The Therapeutic Relationship and Its Impact: A Study of Psychotherapy with Schizophrenics*, ed. C. R. Rogers et al., pp. 109–131. Madison, WI: University of Wisconsin Press.

Hardiness Institute (1985). *The Personal Views Survey: A Measure of Hardiness.* Chicago: Hardiness Institute.

Kierkegaard, S. (1954). *Fear and Trembling and the Sickness unto Death*, trans. W. Lowrie. Garden City, NY: Doubleday Anchor.

Klein, M. H., et al. (1969). *The Experiencing Scale: A Research and Training Manual*, vol. 1. Madison, WI: Wisconsin Psychiatric Institute.

Kobasa, S. C. (1979). Stressful life events, personality, and health: an inquiry into hardiness. *Journal of Personality and Social Psychology* 37:1–11.

Kobasa, S. C., and Maddi, S. R. (1977). Existential personality theory. In *Current Personality Theory*, ed. R. Corsini, pp. 243–276. Itasca, IL: Peacock.

Kobasa, S. C., Maddi, S. R., and Kahn, S. (1982). Hardiness and health: a prospective study. *Journal of Personality and Social Psychology* 42:168–177.

Laing, R. D. (1967). *The Politics of Experience*. New York: Ballantine.

Maddi, S. R. (1967). The existential neurosis. *Journal of Abnormal Psychology* 72:311–325.

——— (1970). The search for meaning. In *Nebraska Symposium on Motivation*, ed. M. Page, pp. 137–186. Lincoln, NB: University of Nebraska Press.

——— (1986). Existential psychotherapy. In *Contemporary Psychotherapies: Models and Methods*, ed. S. Lynn and J. Garske, pp. 191–215. New York: Merrill.

——— (1988a). *Personality Theories: A Comparative Analysis*, 5th ed. Chicago: Dorsey Press.

——— (1988b). On the problem of accepting facticity and pursuing possibility. In *Hermeneutics and Psychological Theory: Interpretive Perspectives on Personality, Psychotherapy, and Psychopathology*, ed. S. B. Messer, L. A. Sass, and R. L. Woolfolk, pp. 182–209. New Brunswick, NJ: Rutgers University Press.

Maddi, S. R., and Kobasa, S. C. (1984). *The Hardy Executive: Health Under Stress*. Chicago: Dorsey Press.

Maslow, A. H. (1955). Deficiency motivation and growth motivation. In *Nebraska Symposium on Motivation*, ed. M. R. Jones, pp. 1–30. Lincoln, NB: University of Nebraska Press.

——— (1962). Some basic propositions of a growth and self-actualization psychology. In *Perceiving, Behaving, Becoming: A New Focus for Education*. Washington, DC: Yearbook of the Association for Supervision and Curriculum Development.

May, R., Angel, E., and Ellenberger, H. F., eds. (1959). *Existence: A New Dimension in Psychiatry and Psychology*. New York: Basic Books.

Pishkin, V., and Thorne, F. C. (1973). A factorial study of existential state reactions. *Journal of Clinical Psychology* 29:392–402.

Rogers, C. R. (1959). A theory of therapy, personality, and interpersonal relationships, as developed in the client-centered framework. In *Psychology: A Study of a Science*, vol. 3, ed. S. Koch, pp. 184–256. New York: McGraw-Hill.

——— (1961). *On Becoming a Person*. Boston: Houghton Mifflin.

Rotter, J. B., Seeman, M., and Liverant, S. (1962). Internal versus external control of reinforcements: a major variable in behavior theory. In *Decisions, Values, and Groups*, vol. 2, ed. N. F. Washburne, pp. 473–516. London: Pergamon Press.

Shostrom, E. (1965). An inventory for the measurement of self-actualization. *Educational and Psychological Measurement* 24:207–218.

——— (1966). *Manual for the Personal Orientation Inventory (POI): An Inventory for the Measurement of Self-Actualization*. San Diego: Educational and Industrial Testing Service.

Thorne, F. C. (1973). The existential study: a measure of existential status. *Journal of Clinical Psychology* 29:387–392.

Thorne, F. C., and Pishkin, V. (1973). The existential study. *Journal of Clinical Psychology* 29:389–410.

5
The Behavioral Interview

DANIEL A. BEACH, Ph.D.

BEHAVIORAL PRINCIPLES

Behavioral psychology, or behaviorism, has gained in popularity and respect as an approach to clinical treatment over the past several decades. However, many clinicians fail to understand its basic principles or the way in which these principles can be applied in a clinical setting.

Many treatment approaches are included under the rubric of behaviorism. They differ in many ways, but they all operate from the same set of fundamental assumptions. One assumption is that behavior is lawful; that is, behavior is influenced by identifiable laws whether or not the individual is aware of their influence. Behaviorists do not create the laws, they discover them. The behavioral therapist attempts to provide patients with the opportunity to take control of the contingencies that affect their lives.

A second assumption is that in humans, behavior is primarily learned. Adaptive behavior as well as maladaptive behavior can be learned, unlearned, and modified. Certain kinds of learning can be more resistant to change than others, and may require various forms of intervention to modify the resultant behavior. Maladaptive behavior is not qualitatively different from adaptive behavior, and it can be understood by applying our general understanding of the acquisition of any behavior pattern.

A third assumption is that both public behavior (that which can be viewed by others) and private behavior (thought) are influenced by the same basic laws. An individual's cognitions are controlled by contingencies in much the same way that public behavior is controlled. Anxieties, fears, and other thoughts can be learned, unlearned, and modified just as public behaviors, such as table manners, driving skills, and social skills, can be altered.

There are three primary modes by which we acquire behavior: classical conditioning, operant conditioning, and modeling.

Classical Conditioning

Ivan Pavlov, an early twentieth-century Russian physiologist, was interested in studying the process of digestion. His research methods included feeding dogs and measuring the amount of saliva they produced while eating. He noted that they not only salivated when they were being fed, but they also salivated when the laboratory assistant who regularly fed them entered the room. They even salivated to the sound of the laboratory door opening. The study of this phenomenon so intrigued Pavlov that he abandoned his research in digestion and spent the rest of his life studying this process.

He found that many behaviors involving the smooth muscles of the body (nonskeletal muscles) could be conditioned to occur in the presence of an apparently unrelated stimulus. This learning process begins with an *unlearned stimulus* (US) being associated with the elicitation of an *unlearned response* (UR). For example, salivating is an unlearned response to the presence of food in the mouth. This is a behavior that is natural to the organism; it is not learned, but rather is present in the organism at birth. A new stimulus is then presented by the researcher in the presence of the unlearned stimulus. The organism experiences both of them at the same time. This new learned stimulus is referred to as the *conditioned stimulus* (CS). When these two stimuli (US and CS) are experienced together often enough, the organism will respond to the new stimulus (the CS) in much the same way it responded to the US. When the behavior is produced in the presence of the CS alone, we call it a learned, or *conditioned, response* (CR).

To use Pavlov's research as an example, we can say that the US (the food), which produces the UR (salivation), was frequently presented at the same time that the CS (the laboratory assistant) happened to be nearby. Thus, later, when the dog saw the CS it salivated, producing a CR that was similar to the one it produced in the presence of the food. Pavlov showed that bells, tones, lights, and many other stimuli, when paired with the unlearned stimulus of food, could be made to elicit this same response.

Behaviors learned through classical conditioning can be unlearned. This learning reversal is known as *extinction*. A behavior is extinguished when the CS is presented often enough without being paired with the US. The association between the two stimuli is thus weakened, and the CR will fail to occur in the presence of the CS. Extinction can be produced more quickly by classically conditioning a new response (CR) to the CS. The new CR must be incompatible with the old CR. That is, it should not be possible for the subject to produce the new response and the old response at the same time. This process of rapid extinction through new learning is called *counterconditioning*.

Many different kinds of behavior have been shown to be learned according to the principles of classical conditioning as discovered by Pavlov. Not only simple reflex behavior, but also more complex forms of human behavior are subject to these laws. Such behaviors can include the flushed or weak feeling one has when an examination is being returned by a teacher, or the sinking feeling in the pit of the stomach when one hears a noise in a dark, empty house.

Operant Conditioning

Several psychologists in the United States contributed to the discovery and understanding of another form of learning called *operant conditioning*. The foremost researcher in this area is Skinner, whose discoveries came from laboratory research, primarily with rats and pigeons. This type of learning affects what we refer to as voluntary behavior.

In order to understand operant conditioning we must have a fundamental understanding of another concept: namely, reinforcement. *Reinforcement* is the consequence of a behavior that always *increases* the probability that a behavior will occur again. There are two types of reinforcement: positive and negative. *Positive reinforcement* is equivalent to reward. A reward can be something tangible, such as money, food, or awards, or it can be intangible, such as attention from others, a smile, or a pleasurable feeling.

Negative reinforcement involves the termination or avoidance of a negative stimulus. It is not the negative stimulus itself. Remember that reinforcement always increases the probability of the occurrence of a behavior. A negative stimulus (punishment, pain, or the like) does not typically result in one's desiring to repeat the behavior that resulted in that experience. Rather, when one is about to experience the negative situation or is currently experiencing it, one will usually attempt to terminate it or avoid it. Whatever behavior works to avoid or terminate that experience will be reinforced, and we call that type of reinforcement negative reinforcement.

For example, if you were to step into a darkened room off a hallway in order to avoid seeing someone with whom you had had an argument earlier in the day, your avoidance of that individual and the awkward or aversive experience that would accompany that encounter would have been negatively reinforced. The next time you saw that person, you would be even more likely to take steps to avoid contact.

When we are dealing with simple organisms, it is not difficult to determine in advance what will be reinforcing. In dog training, we often use food or praise and a scratch behind the ear. Few people would be willing to accept that as sufficient reward for a week's labor. A paycheck is the usually expected reinforcement. Because humans are so complex, we can never be sure what will be reinforcing and what will not. Reinforcement is always in the eye of the receiver.

In any given circumstance there are various behaviors in which we might engage, ranging from those that are most likely to occur to those that might occur rarely. We could rank order these behaviors, with those that are most probable at the top of a column to those that are least probable at the bottom. If we chose a low-probability behavior and reinforced it when it occurred, we could raise its probability of occurrence by a slight amount each time reinforcement was received. If we continue this process, the probability of occurrence would be raised sufficiently to make the behavior much more likely to occur, and therefore we would see the behavior being performed more frequently. When this behavior becomes the most probable behavior to occur in the set of circumstances, we say that the behavior is conditioned, or learned. Nonreinforced behavior tends to drop in terms of its probability of occurrence. By identifying a target behavior and selectively reinforcing or not reinforcing it, we can affect its probability of occurrence and the frequency with which it is performed.

Reversal of an operantly conditioned behavior is also called *extinction*. Extinction is produced by withdrawal of reinforcement. When a behavior occurs in the absence of reinforcement, its probability of recurrence drops. When it has been nonreinforced often enough, it drops very low in the individual's repertoire of behavior. At this point we refer to the behavior as having been extinguished.

In a classroom, we might wish to have a particular child sit in his seat more frequently. If this were a low-frequency behavior, we could provide reinforcement each time we noticed the child in his seat. The reinforcement could be a positive verbal statement, eye contact and a smile, a tangible reward, or another method that the child perceives as reinforcing. After sufficient reinforcement, the probability of occurrence will increase and we will see more in-seat behavior. As a by-product, we will also see less disruption of others, a more organized classroom, a less frustrated teacher, and a child who views the teacher as a source of reward rather than punishment.

Modeling

A third mode of behavior acquisition that is stressed by behaviorally oriented psychologists is *modeling*, which is a process of learning through imitation. It is a method that we all use in everyday life to acquire skills. When we see another person performing a behavior that appears to be effective or that is reinforcing for that person, we are likely to attempt that behavior ourselves. The learning does not come from merely observing the behavior, but from practicing our imitation of that behavior until we have mastered it. The mere observation of a model being reinforced for a particular behavior increases the probability that one will imitate the behavior. Whether it is learned, and hence repeated, will depend upon the consequences.

Such a process places great emphasis upon the individual's thoughts and perceptions rather than upon external factors, as is the case in classical and operant conditioning. In addition, through modeling, as compared to conditioning techniques, rather complex behaviors can be acquired in a relatively short period.

LEARNED EMOTIONAL RESPONSES

Although our emotional responses feel natural to us and appear to most of us to be innate responses to various experiences, they are learned in much the same way that other behaviors are learned.

The first demonstration of this was conducted by Watson, who classically conditioned a fear response in the now famous "little Albert." In this study, Watson placed Albert in a chair and put a cage containing a white rat on a table top immediately in front of the young child. The child had previously exhibited no fear of the animal; in fact, he exhibited curiosity and some enjoyment of its presence. The cage was then covered with a cloth. Watson's assistant stood behind Albert and struck an iron bar with a hammer each time the cloth was raised from the cage. Not surprisingly, Albert was startled and began to cry at the sound of the hammer striking the iron. After a number of such trials, the cloth was raised without the loud noise being produced in its presence. Albert became fearful and cried. This demonstration was a success for Watson, if not for Albert, in showing that fears can be learned through the process of classical conditioning.

Albert not only learned a fear response to this previously neutral stimulus, but he also exhibited this same fear in response to a whole class of stimuli, including white mice, white rabbits, and a white ball of cotton. He generalized his learned fear to an entire class of stimuli that he perceived as being similar to the original CS (the white rat). We refer to this process as *stimulus generalization.* What is most important here is that the person perceives the stimuli to be similar whether or not most other people might agree that a similarity exists. Once again, as in reinforcement, the judgment is made by the one affected.

How does such learning affect individuals who enter the therapeutic situation? Many behavioral disorders, particularly those that fall into neurotic categories, are associated with learned fear or anxiety responses.

> Sara, for example, came to see her psychologist with a complaint that many of her relationships had fallen apart and that she was unable to maintain relationships, especially those with men, for very long. She desired to be close to others, but it never worked out for her. After several sessions, she revealed that she had been physically and emotionally abused by her alcoholic father, to whom she had been very close during her early childhood years.
>
> A behavioral analysis of this situation would first describe the learned fear response. Sara learned to fear her father, who had inflicted pain upon her. The physical violence and emotional rejection are the US. Under these conditions, the associated pain is the UR. The presence of the father who inflicts this pain is the CS, and the subsequent fear of closeness with the father becomes the CR. In Sara's case we find that she has learned to fear not only her father's closeness, but the closeness of any other individual. Through stimulus generalization she has learned that emotional closeness, or even the possibility of it, is a cue for her to begin to experience anxiety. This cuts her off from the possibility of engaging others and developing intimacy.
>
> If that was all there was to it, then Sara could simply live her life without being close to others, finding enjoyment in solitary activities. However, Sara has a serious flaw. She is human. Sara possesses the same needs that we all have for closeness, love, affection, caring, and understanding, and these needs can be satisfied only through interpersonal relationships. Because of these human

needs, Sara approaches others with the desire to establish relationships despite her fear.

The anxiety-producing stimulus (closeness) now requires her to find some way of reducing the anxiety. She is in an operant-conditioning situation in which, through trial and error, she attempts to discover ways to reduce anxiety. Those behaviors that are effective will be negatively reinforced, since she is attempting to terminate or avoid the negative stimulus (anxiety or fear). Such behaviors might include keeping people at a distance through polite, nonrevealing conversation, continued use of humor to prevent serious discussion, engaging only others who have similar fears of closeness, or thousands of other possibilities that keep her insulated from the dangers of emotional vulnerability. Not all, or even most, close relationships result in pain. By continuing to avoid the anxiety-provoking situation, Sara prevents herself from experiencing interpersonal closeness in the absence of pain. Thus she is not allowing extinction of the fear response to take place.

Sara may eventually feel that she has exposed too much of herself or has reached a point at which she is being pressured by another to develop a closer relationship. This is a cue for strong feelings of anxiety that might only be reduced by ending the relationship. If either person ends the relationship, Sara is likely to feel pain, which serves to strengthen the original classical-conditioning experience and to justify her feelings that closeness inevitably leads to pain and must be guarded against.

The fear of intimacy described in this example could develop from a classical-conditioning experience that does not necessarily include physical pain or abuse. Rejection, nonacceptance, disapproval, and other responses could have similar effects and result in fear of closeness. In addition, Sara might not generalize her response to the entire population; rather, she might be somewhat selective and experience such responses only to men, older men, men who look like her father, men who act like her father, people who act in an authoritative manner, or any other individuals or groups that she might perceive as being similar to her father.

Psychoanalytic theory recognizes that such responses may occur in the therapeutic situation, and its literature has documented such occurrences and has named them *transference*. That is, the patient feels the same way toward the therapist that he feels toward some other significant individual. *Countertransference* is a similar process, whereby the therapist begins to experience feelings toward the patient that are similar to his feelings toward someone else in his life. A behaviorist would say that both the patient and the therapist are experiencing stimulus generalization. Such generalization appears to have survival value for our species. If every situation in which we found ourselves were unique, so that previous adaptive behaviors could not be used, we would find life exceedingly stressful. Just as adaptive behaviors can be generalized, so maladaptive behaviors (including emotional responses) can be generalized to new situations, causing problems and nonadaptive responses.

Humans are able to symbolize the events of their lives. We can think about our experiences and can relive them in a very powerful way through imagery. In a sense, we can replay our experiences so that they have virtually the same emotional impact that the real-life experience had. By re-experiencing life events through imagery, one can repeat trials, much like the repeated trials that we use in classically conditioning a laboratory subject. As a consequence, the learned emotional response becomes well fixed and very resistant to extinction.

The process just described is referred to as the *two-factor theory* of avoidance learning. It involves the classical conditioning of a fear (anxiety) response to a previously neutral stimulus, the generalization of that stimulus to a variety of situations, and then an operantly conditioned response to reduce that anxiety. These two factors, when working together in this manner, can describe a wide range of maladaptive behaviors that are frequently seen by therapists in the therapeutic situation.

VERBAL CONDITIONING: A PROCESS ISSUE

When we speak to others, we selectively reinforce statements that we may agree with or may be interested in hearing more about. Reinforcement in this setting usually involves such actions as statements of agreement, attention, smiles, nods of the head, maintenance of eye contact, and nonverbal vocalizations.

In Greenspan's (1955) well-known study on this topic, subjects were asked to say as many words as they could think of in an allotted period. In one group, the experimenter said "mmm-hmm" every time the subject mentioned a plural noun and said nothing when other words were mentioned. A second group of subjects heard "huh-uh" (a statement of disapproval) after each plural noun. A control group received no verbal responses at all from the experimenter.

The results showed that the subjects reinforced with "mmm-hmm" produced the largest number of plural nouns. In second place came the control group, and the least number of plural nouns were produced by the group receiving disapproval. The results of this study and others (Isaacs et al. 1960, Konecni and Slamecka 1972, Verplanck 1955) have provided clear evidence for the process of conditioning of verbal responses.

In therapy, especially the more traditional forms, verbal exchanges between the therapist and the patient are critical. The therapist may express concern about the patient's feelings of depression and rejection, suicidal ideation, and low self-esteem. At the same time, the patient may receive little or no response when speaking of more positive issues. To the extent that the therapist's remarks are reinforcing to the patient, the therapist may be reinforcing the patient's negative self-statements, while positive self-statements may be extinguished.

Attention from another person, particularly one who is in a powerful position, can be highly reinforcing. In therapy, as in institutional mental health settings, problem behaviors tend to receive more attention than positive behaviors. This is referred to as the "squeaky-wheel" principle:

The part that makes the most noise (negative behavior) gets the most grease (attention and reinforcement). By attending to problems, which, of course, is what therapists are trained to do, we risk more firmly solidifying these negative self-statements and making the process damaging rather than therapeutic. Such occurrences may not be rare. After all, we do speak of casualties in psychotherapy.

Careful attention must be paid by the therapist in the clinical interview to those statements that are in need of reinforcement and those that are not. Of course, the therapist's theoretical orientation will influence the decision of which statements are reinforced. In the initial portions of the interview when the patient is presenting his formulation of the problem, the therapist must not take control prematurely and risk losing valuable information by directing the patient away from his own issues. By ignoring the effects of verbal conditioning, the therapist may restrict conversation to topics with which he feels comfortable or to those that are related to his own biases.

Verbal reinforcement affects all forms of therapy, not only the form used by behaviorists. The analytically oriented therapist who chooses to positively interpret a statement made by the patient reinforces that statement and can expect to hear others similar to it. When Rogers smiled at his client and nodded his head, he was manipulating the direction of conversation in his own nondirective way. When the family therapist fails to respond positively to an observation made by a family member, that person is less likely to speak out in the future. Verbal reinforcement occurs whether or not the therapist decides to take control of the contingencies of reinforcement.

Verbal reinforcement is an important issue in therapy, and it deserves the therapist's continuous attention. Maintenance or extinction of problem behavior can be closely related to the contingencies of reinforcement involved in the verbal exchange between therapist and patient.

CAUSATION

All therapists, regardless of theoretical orientation, look for the cause of the behavior that the patient defines as problematic. What is meant by *cause* and how it affects the behavior in question is what separates the various therapeutic schools.

When the general public looks at behavioral causation, the approach, for the most part, tends to be rather simplistic. A recent television news program reported that a man had been found unconscious on the street and was taken to the local hospital. The cause of this incident was reported to be an overdose of heroin. Was this indeed the case? In part, yes. But this is neither the whole picture nor an accurate description of the actual cause of this incident.

Behavior is multicausal. No single event can be isolated as *the* cause. In order to understand the causal aspects of a behavior and to develop an intervention strategy, we must understand the importance of the causal chain leading to the behavior in question. In the example just noted, the drug overdose was clearly related to the fact that the man was found unconscious, but it was one of many causes that put him in that position. It was *a* cause, not *the* cause.

One effective means of understanding the causal chain of events is to organize it in chronological order. There are three types of causes: predisposing, precipitating, and perpetuating. These three P's of causation are a way of conceptualizing the important variables necessary for the production of any behavior. All three must occur before the behavior is manifested. No one of these events is solely responsible for the behavior we see. In other words, each is a necessary cause, but none is sufficient by itself to cause the behavior.

Predisposing causes are the historical antecedents of the behavior. They set the stage, as it were, for the other causes. They establish the general conditions that permit the individual to engage in the behavior. Predisposing causes can include such factors as genetic endowment, physical illness, reinforcement history, various life experiences, environmental variables, and the person's history of learned emotional responses.

The *precipitating* cause is the triggering mechanism of the behavior. It is the immediate, observable event that sets the behavior in motion. This is the occurrence that people usually point to as *the* cause of a behavior.

The *perpetuating* cause is the set of contingencies that sustains the behavior. Unless the behavior is maintained in some fashion, it will not continue to be produced. Perpetuating causes are responsible for the fact that the problem continues to adversely affect the patient's quality of life.

At what point should the therapeutic intervention take place? Since all three forms of causation are necessary to produce the behavior, an intervention strategy aimed at any one of the three causes would result in the termination of the behavior. The clinical interview seeks to identify these factors so that treatment can be directed to intervene at any one of these three points.

How can we intervene with a predisposing cause? Most traditional forms of therapy have this as their goal. Their emphasis upon underlying causes of behavior presumes that the predisposing cause is the primary and determining cause of the behavior. Behaviorists recognize the importance of early experiences and other predisposing factors but do not view them as the only or primary point of intervention.

Genetic predispositions, physical disease processes, and environmental variables indigenous to a patient's community setting may not be fruitful points of intervention. More effective strategies might involve the elimination of learned emotional responses to various types of interpersonal situations.

Wolpe's (1973) use of systematic desensitization is a form of intervention directed at predisposing causes. It seeks to extinguish a classically conditioned fear or anxiety response that in the past has placed the patient in the position of avoiding or terminating that anxiety through a behavior that has proven to be maladaptive or unsatisfying. In such an approach, the behavioral therapist uses a counterconditioning technique to have the CS evoke a relaxation response rather than an anxiety response. The reversal of early learning through conditioning or modeling techniques can reduce or eliminate the effectiveness of the predisposing cause.

As mentioned earlier, we can replay painful life events through imagery and thus strengthen a classically conditioned emotional response. Positive visualization, thought-stoppage techniques, relaxation techniques, biofeedback, quieting-reflex techniques, and others can be employed to extinguish this response and thus intervene at the level of the predisposing cause.

The precipitating cause is often obvious or can be clarified through the interview. Sometimes the precipitating event can be controlled or managed in a very direct manner. The patient who feels most depressed when alone on a Sunday night can plan community, church, or family activities at such times. The parent who feels most frustrated after six consecutive hours with the children can arrange a short period of child care in the middle of the day with a neighbor. The student who experiences tremendous stress at exam time can practice more effective study habits through the semester, and thus feel more confident when the exam date arrives. The precipitating cause may not always be identifiable or may have occurred only once at some time in the distant past. In such cases, an intervention at this point may not be profitable or practical.

In examining the perpetuating cause, the behavioral therapist is evaluating the system of reinforcement that maintains the behavior at a sufficiently high level to be identifiable and problematic. Based upon the principles of reinforcement, we know that when the behavior is reinforced by reward or by avoidance or termination of an aversive experience, it tends to be repeated. Reinforcement maintains behavior, since behavior is under the control of its consequences. The withdrawal of reinforcement reduces the occurrence of a behavior. In the clinical interview, the behaviorist seeks to identify those sources of reinforcement that are sustaining the problem behavior. Such sources can include attention from others, satisfaction of physical needs, avoidance of learned anxiety responses, or a myriad of other forms of reinforcement. Therapeutic strategy is then aimed at eliminating the reinforcement from the problem behavior. Such withdrawal of reinforcement leads to the extinction of the behavior in question. Verbal reinforcement in the therapeutic setting can maintain negative self-statements, or their extinction can be produced by the elimination of reinforcement. At the same time, positive self-statements can be strengthened by their selective reinforcement.

In a social system, the identification of cause-and-effect relationships is made more difficult by the fact that an individual's action may be both a cause of another's behavior and an effect of some behavior of that other individual. This circularity of causation is certainly present in family systems. In order to understand interactive patterns, the therapist must be aware that every behavior is both a cause and an effect.

INTERVIEW AND ASSESSMENT

The therapist's approach to assessment defines the nature of the interview. As previously mentioned, the major point of departure between behavioral and traditional assessment approaches appears to be in the understanding of the nature of the causes of the patient's behavior. Traditional assessment views these causes as essentially intrapsychic. Consequently, the traditionalist would view the behaviors as symptoms of an underlying cause and only of trivial significance in their own right. These causes produce a generalized response and therefore can produce behaviors across a variety of situations.

Behavioral assessment emphasizes *response specificity*. Behaviorists believe that a behavior is produced in relation to the environmental and personal variables that are present in specific circumstances (Cone and Hawkins 1977). The behaviors themselves may be problematic, but they are not symptomatic. The behavior itself is the problem; it is not a symptom of a hypothetical personality construct. The orientation of the behavioral interview is derived from this position. A behaviorist addresses problem behavior in detail rather than attempting to paint the patient with a broad brush that seeks to describe his entire personality functioning.

The primary goal of the clinical assessment is to find out what the patient's problem is and develop a working hypothesis about what actions can relieve the problem. This involves gathering relevant data and deciding which variables can be effectively addressed in therapy. The use of the interview has been advocated by many behaviorally oriented therapists as one of various methods of acquiring such information (Bijou and Peterson 1971, Goldfried and Pomeranz 1968, Kanfer and Saslow 1969, Lewinsohn et al. 1976). Although other purposes have been associated with the use of this technique, most behaviorists agree that its primary use is to assess specific behavioral targets (Lichtenstein 1971). Traditional approaches have oriented the interview to the individual patient, whereas behavioral interviewing may include many significant others in the patient's environment in order to gather additional data and to clarify hypotheses about variables that may be contributing to the patient's behavior.

The clinical interview is seen as one part of the behavioral assessment. Aside from interviews with significant others, the assessment may include observations in vivo, observations in structured situations, self-monitoring, role playing, review of records, or any other method of assembling information about the possible variables contributing to the patient's behavior.

According to Linehan (1977), the behavioral interview should include at least these five basic elements: (1) identification of the behaviors that are perceived to be problematic, (2) determination of the variables related to the causal chain of events, (3) identification of those characteristics of the patient that may facilitate or interfere with a method of treatment, (4) assessment of environmental variables that may facilitate or interfere with treatment, and (5) choice of a treatment intervention technique. Such an approach may not differ dramatically from the elements of other theoretical approaches. The types of variables that are attended to as salient factors will differ depending upon orientation.

With respect to elements 3 and 4, the interview is used to evaluate the effectiveness of the variables used to treat the target behavior. For example, if we plan to use a certain form of reinforcement to increase the frequency of a behavior that is incompatible with the problem behavior, we must be certain that the patient perceives the reinforcement to be reinforcing or it will not have the desired effect. Similarly, we must assess whether the system in which the patient lives can provide this source of reinforcement. Through the interview we can gather information that can lead to a conclusion on these issues.

The clinical interview is often used to determine the likelihood of being able to establish a productive relationship with the patient. The quality of interaction may be predictive of future behavior patterns. The quality of the relationship is directly related to the effectiveness of information gathering (Cozby 1973).

The clinical interview is not only effective in aiding the patient to conceptualize the problem he is experiencing; it may be therapeutic in and of itself (Linehan 1977). For a patient who is experiencing feelings of desperation, lack of control, or guilt, a behavioral explanation of the variables contributing to this behavior can bring immediate relief and assurance. Such information can raise expectations and feelings of self-efficacy, which are closely tied to treatment effectiveness. The knowledge that he has a clear definition of the situation and can potentially gain control of the contingencies that affect these problem behaviors and feelings can go a long way toward alleviating the patient's immediate distress. In this way the initial interview can serve not only as a method for making an assessment for future intervention, but also as an intervention itself.

CONTENT OF THE BEHAVIORAL INTERVIEW

Many formats for the structure of the behavioral interview have been proposed. Among the most influential of these approaches has been that of Kanfer and Saslow (1969). They suggest an evaluation of past and present patterns of behavior and environmental influences. Their model consists of assembling information in seven primary areas: (1) an analysis of the presenting problem, (2) a clarification of the problem and the causes of the behavior, (3) a motivational analysis, (4) a developmental analysis, (5) an analysis of self-control, (6) an analysis of social relationships, and (7) an analysis of the social-cultural-physical environment (Linehan 1977). This model is certainly a most thorough and comprehensive approach.

Wolpe (1973) also recommends securing a large amount of data about past and present functioning in five areas, including (1) early family history, (2) education, (3) employment history, (4) sexual history, and (5) current relationships with others. Lazarus (1973, 1976) suggests a comprehensive assessment of the important facets of the patient. He uses the helpful acronym BASIC ID to organize the information that needs to be assessed in the behavioral interview. In this scheme the letters represent the following: *B*, identification of behavioral deficiencies and excesses; *A*, affective responses that require modification; *S*, sensory deficits, oversensitivities, or pain; *I*, imagery in which the patient habitually engages; *C*, cognitions that are illogical or mistaken and lead to "emotional disturbance"; *I*, patterns of interpersonal relationships; *D*, drugs, which also includes fitness and general well-being.

The contents of the aforementioned models should be viewed as salient areas to search for important information rather than as a critical outline of information that must be filled in for every patient.

STRUCTURE OF THE INTERVIEW

Based upon the preceding discussion, a general structure emerges for the behavioral interview. The first step involves defining the patient's presenting problem. The patient is not likely to offer a list of various stimulus–response situations or to divide his problems between those that were conditioned and those that were modeled. Nor is it necessary at this point to translate the patient's complaints into behavioral terms. It is important that the therapist attend carefully to specific behavioral situations that have generated the patient's concerns, and refrain from overdirecting the conversation by verbally reinforcing those points that may be of interest to him but may have no relevance to the patient's presenting problem.

The second step involves collecting broad-based information that might relate to the problem. Models, such as those by Kanfer and Saslow, Wolpe, or Lazarus, are helpful in identifying major areas in which information collection should be concentrated.

The third step requires the gathering of more precise data from those areas that appear most salient based on the foregoing process. Close inspection of the problem behavior from this perspective will help to establish preliminary hypotheses that can be supported or disconfirmed through the acquisition of additional information.

In the fourth step, we establish a working hypothesis regarding the variables affecting the patient's behavior, with emphasis on the three P's of causation. By examining the causal chain and identifying the elements that operate at these three critical junctures, we can begin to think about potential points of intervention. Such hypotheses involve the understanding of the origins and maintenance of the behavior through the processes of conditioning and modeling.

The fifth step requires that we conduct an initial test of this hypothesis. This test can begin with a detailed questioning of the patient's perceptions of the contingencies that are controlling the behavior.

Beyond this the therapist can use role playing to assess skills and imagined-exposure techniques to evaluate beliefs and emotional reactivity to particular events. Interviews with significant others can also be used to evaluate environmental contingencies. This step requires flexibility on the part of the therapist, since the original hypothesis may be disconfirmed or require some modification.

The sixth and final step in the interview involves the design of a treatment approach that permits the patient to gain control of those variables affecting the problem behavior. An understanding of the behavioral approaches to treatment is necessary in order to design the most effective strategy possible.

The behavioral interview is based upon the understanding of the acquisition of behavior through the processes of conditioning and modeling. Behaviorally oriented therapists attempt to determine the causes of the problem behavior with respect to the predisposing, precipitating, and perpetuating events that are necessary for the production of such behavior. The goal of the interview is to define the contingencies that control the behavior and to establish a treatment plan that permits the patient to gain more control over those contingencies.

As research increasingly supports the efficacy of behavioral interventions, behavioral approaches to treatment are gaining in popularity. The roots of the behavioral approach are in the psychology laboratory, and its value is established both by convincing research evidence and by clinical observations of its effectiveness in treating human problems.

REFERENCES

Bijou, S., and Peterson, R. (1971). Functional analysis in the assessment of children. In *Advances in Psychological Measurement*, ed. P. McReynolds, pp. 63–78. Palo Alto: Science and Behavior Books.

Cone, J., and Hawkins, R. (1977). *Behavioral Assessment: New Directions in Clinical Psychology*. New York: Brunner/Mazel.

Cozby, P. (1973). Self-disclosure. *Psychological Bulletin* 79:73–91.

Goldfried, M., and Pomeranz, D. (1968). Role of assessment in behavior modification. *Psychological Reports* 23:75–87.

Greenspoon, J. (1955). The reinforcing effect of two spoken sounds on the frequency of two responses. *American Journal of Psychology* 68:409–416.

Isaacs, J., Thomas, M., and Goldiamond, I. (1960). Application of operant conditioning to reinstate verbal conditioning. *Journal of Speech and Hearing Disorders* 25:8–12.

Kanfer, F., and Saslow, G. (1969). Behavioral diagnosis. In *Behavior Therapy: Appraisal and Status*, ed. C. M. Franks, pp. 417–444. New York: McGraw-Hill.

Konecni, J., and Slamecka, N. (1972). Awareness in verbal nonoperant conditioning: an approach through dichotic listening. *Journal of Experimental Psychology* 94:248–254.

Lazarus, A. (1973). Multimodal behavior therapy: Treating the "BASIC-ID." *Journal of Nervous and Mental Disease* 156:404–411.

—— (1976). *Multimodal Behavior Therapy*. New York: Springer.

Lewinsohn, P., Biglan, A., and Zeiss, A. (1976). Behavioral treatment of depression. In *The Behavioral Management of Anxiety, Depression, and Pain*, ed. P. O. Davidson, pp. 91–146. New York: Brunner/Mazel.

Lichtenstein, E. (1971). Techniques for assessing outcomes of psychotherapy. In *Advances in Psychological Assessment*, ed. P. McReynolds, pp. 178–197. Palo Alto: Science and Behavior Books.

Linehan, M. (1977). Issues in behavioral interviewing. In *Behavioral Assessment: New Directions in Clinical Psychology*, ed. J. Cone and R. Hawkins, pp. 30–51. New York: Brunner/Mazel.

Verplanck, W. S. (1955). The control of the content of conversation: reinforcement of statements of opinion. *Journal of Abnormal and Social Psychology* 51:668–676.

Wolpe, J. (1973). *The Practice of Behavior Therapy*. New York: Pergamon.

6 The Family Therapy Interview

DAVID GOODMAN, Ph.D.

Family therapy is a treatment approach that works with the family as the identified patient rather than with any one family member. Of course, it is usually true that it is one individual rather than the family that first seeks treatment.

Consider the following case:

> Mrs. J. contacted a psychologist on the recommendation of her family physician because of her concern that her 16-year-old son's grades were slipping. Martin's attitude at home was also disturbing; when he was upset, he would often slam doors, kick walls, and sometimes even break his own possessions.
>
> At the initial interview with Martin, his parents, and two older siblings, the boy was sullen, withdrawn and uncommunicative.

All therapists would agree that how the problem is defined determines how the problem is resolved. The therapist working from an individual treatment philosophy would look at the case just described as one in which Martin would need help in identifying his anger, exploring more effective ways of his communicating feelings, and becoming more assertive. The family therapist would want Martin's family to be present in the treatment room along with the adolescent. The therapeutic focus would be on the processes of communication, power, influence, and conflict resolution. Successful family treatment would see a change in the structure of family relationships, while successful individual treatment would look for improvement in intrapsychic processes.

Systematic family therapy is built on answering the following questions:

1. What are the advantages of Martin's current behavior to other family members? For example, does Mrs. J. find herself more needed as a mother because of Martin's temper tantrums, or is Mrs. J. more involved because her husband is aloof and dominant with his son?

2. Is Martin's current behavior a successful adaptation to an even more dysfunctional family problem? For instance, should his father's depression be the actual focus in the treatment? Or, does it matter that the

death of Martin's grandfather, with whom he was extraordinarily close, has never been talked about in the family because this older man died by suicide?

3. What is the developmental history and current stage of the family system? Should the father's recent job change, which requires more time away from home, be considered as a condition influencing the emergence of the present symptoms?

4. What other problems do family members see in Martin's behavior or in the family as a whole? Does the lack of conversation at the dinner table cause family members to avoid one another or to turn to television as a way of distracting themselves from their discomfort?

The family therapy approach then looks beyond how the therapist can help Martin individually deal with his problem. Individual symptoms are viewed as serving family needs.

THE ROOTS OF FAMILY THERAPY

Psychoanalytic

The family therapy treatment approach is a descendant of psychoanalysis (Ackerman 1958) on both a theoretical and practical level. Freud's contribution to medicine and to the treatment of mental illness was in his bold and brilliant explanation that mental illness could be caused by dysfunction in parent–child relationships in the patient's early years of development (Freud 1964, Kerr 1981). Freud's treatment method was to correct this past negative experience through a therapeutic relationship between doctor and patient. Family therapy today uses this same principle of dysfunction in human relationships as an explanation for aberrant behavior, but the context of treatment has vastly changed. The relationship between therapist and patient is sacrificed in the interest of improving the relationship between family members.

As analytic thinking was accepted as the most comprehensive explanation of behavior during the 1930s and 1940s, this approach was applied, with modifications, to the most treatment-resistant of mental illnesses—schizophrenia. However, therapists felt increasingly frustrated in helping this disabled population when it was found that the way in which the schizophrenic's family related to him was, at times, as dysfunctional as the patient's individual symptoms.

Communications Theory

In the early 1950s, a research group including Bateson, Weakland, Haley, and Jackson described a form of communication that they discovered occurring in many families with a schizophrenic member. The *double bind* (Bateson et al. 1956, Wynne et al. 1968) is the exquisite damned if you do–damned if you don't type of communication that leaves the patient unable to choose an alternative because neither choice is acceptable and yet the choice cannot be escaped. Double-bind communication is occurring when, for example, the assertion to a disobedient child that "all is forgiven" is confounded by a hostile facial expression and a sarcastic verbal tone. The recipient of such a message is confused as to what he should believe; even more damaging to the child's mental health is his lack of awareness that this communication contradiction exists. The double-bind principle is one of the earliest contributions to family therapy thinking.

On a practical level, working with the severely mentally ill increasingly required involvement with the patient's immediate family. Aside from the application of analytic principles to schizophrenic patients and the resulting impetus to involve the family in treatment, the necessity of working with children at risk and with delinquent adolescents again forced therapists to consider the family as a logical focus of treatment.

Freud's (1964) celebrated treatment of a phobic child demonstrated an awareness of the symptom's relationship to the interaction between the boy and his father. Freud handled the treatment of Little Hans by directing the boy's father in understanding his son's behavior. In fact, the entire treatment program was carried out by correspondence between Freud and Hans's father.

As Freud directed attention to the relationship between Little Hans and his father, many professionals working in child-guidance clinics in the 1940s and 1950s began to look at the patient's family, at first as a source of information regarding the child, and then slowly as the source of the dysfunctional behavior.

Social Conceptions

Before we conclude this brief historical perspective, two other theorists deserve mention. Adler (1918) saw the individual as influenced more by social roles than by instinctual drives. The need for power, status, and belonging influenced the development of self-esteem. Adler saw the family as a place where social and purposeful goals could first be met. He also theorized on the importance of sibling position. Finally, Adler's focus on the conscious provided an anchor upon which family therapy still relies, since fantasies, dreams, and the like are rarely the material of family therapy treatment encounters.

Interpersonal

Sullivan (1974) was the first to begin building the bridge from intrapsychic theory to interpersonal interaction. Family therapy today has continued to build that bridge by going from an interpersonal view of dysfunction to a systemic one (Foley 1979, Framo 1972, Kaslow 1987).

FAMILY THERAPY RESEARCH IN THE 1950s

The Bateson study group also produced the principle of *family homeostasis*. This concept suggested that an improvement in one family member's symptoms might lead to an increase in disruptive behavior by another family member. Consequently, the family therapist learned to look as much at the forces resisting change as at those encouraging it. In fact, a specific tactic in some family therapy situations is for the therapist to push in the direction of the resistance as opposed to against it. For example, prescribing greater effort on the part of an already over-involved parent in the life of his child may do more in the short run to hasten the collapse of this destructive behavior than would constantly opposing it. This paradoxical tactic has become a principal tool for the family therapist.

Bowen trained at the Menninger Clinic and worked there from 1946 through 1954. Early in his career, he began to work with families in order to improve the outcome of individual therapy. He described a characteristic of families with a schizophrenic member, that of emotional stuck-togetherness, that continues to be quite useful in defining the importance of family boundaries between individuals as well as between generations.

At Yale University, Lidz and colleagues (1957) published an article on marital relationships in families with a schizophrenic member. They noted the frequent absence of a primary bond between husband and wife in such families. In its place was noted an allegiance between a spouse and his or her parent(s).

The term *pseudomutuality* was used to describe the inauthentic interaction between members of families with a schizophrenic member. This concept, devised by Wynne and colleagues in 1958, emphasizes the unity of the family at the expense of the separateness of individuals. Individual overdependency on the family is the hallmark of this dysfunction.

Finally, in England, Laing (1965) observed the miscommunication and manipulation occurring between hospitalized adolescent female schizophrenics and their families. He published his observations in 1965. Laing was tempted at times to conclude that the healthiest members of these families were the identified patients themselves.

It is important for the reader to appreciate that these researchers were unaware of their colleagues' efforts throughout most of the 1950s. The explosive enthusiasm that has characterized the family therapy field these last 25 years got its start because so many practitioners and researchers concluded that they were not the only ones viewing the family as a most powerful force. The excitement was contagious and led, for example, to the founding of the journal *Family Process* in 1961.

FROM FAMILY THEORY TO FAMILY THERAPY: THE 30 YEARS' WAR

New ideas in the field of psychotherapy have a history of rejecting the old ways for the sake of modern approaches. This experience has been true as much for family therapy as it sought recognition in the world of traditional individual treatment approaches as it has been, in more recent times, in the field of family treatment itself, which has been caught up in skirmishes and conflicts among practitioners within the school. The 1950s were a time in which researchers looked at family phenomena and conceptualized various ways of understanding family data. As theory moved into practice, specific techniques and approaches became identified, formalized, and, sometimes, canonized.

The movement in family treatment today is toward integration and accommodation. This point of view is the result of pushing various schools of family treatment to their limits. This perspective on trends in family work is, of course, not meant to suggest that this area is one big, happy family.

It is appropriate to begin the examination of various family treatment approaches by looking at the one that is closest to the traditional analytic view of pathology and its remediation. Ackerman (1958), Framo (1972), Zuk (1975), and Paul (1975) are the individuals most closely associated with the psychodynamic family therapy school. This position holds that unresolved issues, conflicts, and losses in the family of origin cause problems in present-day family functioning. Consequently, treatment efforts looked as much at the individual family member's psychological history and identity as it did at the functioning of the family itself. The importance of flexibility in times of crisis in regard to family roles and behavior was emphasized. In addition, matters of both individual and family identity were attended to by the family therapist. In contrast to the analytic model of a passive, receptive analyst, Ackerman, in particular, advocated a highly energetic chairman-of-the-meeting role for the family therapist. For example, the family therapist who practices this approach might ask a parent to describe his own experience as a child responding to the demands of his parents, in an effort to illuminate the silent expectations of this adult in the parenting role. The essential quality that characterizes this treatment approach is the continued allegiance to intrapsychic processes in the midst of expanding attention to family relationships.

In contrast to this psychodynamic orientation is a systemic view of family functioning identified with Bowen, Jackson, Haley, and Minuchin. For the sake of accuracy, it is important to see these individuals as gathered around the family systems view, with varying styles of treatment and particular theoretical emphases.

Bowen is most often described as defining the family systems model. The goal of Bowen's therapy approach is to enable the identified patient to achieve a separate self within the family system. This *differentiated self*

(Kerr 1981) is capable of responding to family needs as an intellectual choice, as opposed to reacting from an unclear emotional position. Bowen asserted that those family members in whom intellect and emotion were indistinct were frequently ruled by feelings. This *more primitive position* (Okun and Rappaport 1980) made the achievement of independence in the family more difficult. When crisis and stress begin to influence a family, the way in which the individual and the family respond depends on the level of self-differentiation and healthy integration of the members with one another. Although Bowen himself did not use a vertical and horizontal matrix, self-differentiation can be seen as the *x* axis and family integration as the *y*. Bowen developed a scale of differentiation ranging from the emotionally and intellectually fused to those who function according to intellect, emotions, and needs of those in their family.

The extent of an individual's success in achieving self-differentiation, Bowen theorized, was determined by childhood experiences with a particular element of the family structure that he defined as *triangles* (Kerr 1981). When a crisis overwhelms the resources of two family members, a third is often drawn in to reduce tension. It is usually the less self-differentiated who are made the third point of the relationship. Instances of marital conflict, parental dysfunction, or problems with children account for many occasions of the triangling process (Okun and Rappaport 1980). Further, as an individual grows to adulthood, he must resolve for himself the emotional separation from the family of origin. If this separation is generally incomplete, then subsequent significant interpersonal relationships are affected. Consequently, how the nuclear family comes to manage stress and whether an increasingly dysfunctional triangled relationship is set in motion become focal points of family therapy investigation. Bowen enlarged his perspective to include a generational view of schizophrenia; that is, he saw increasing dysfunction over succeeding generations as leading to decreasing self-differentiation.

Jackson was a psychiatrist member of the Bateson study group. He continued to develop communication theories related to family functioning during the 1960s. He drew upon the principle of family homeostasis to focus on the importance of dysfunctional family stability. Jackson theorized that a number of unexpressed rules governed family communication. He saw successful family intervention as helping family members both to identify the rules by which they operate and to redefine the meaning of their behaviors. Jackson focused on these communication and relationship rules and avoided interpretation of individual behavior. He believed that changing the way in which family members communicate is a here-and-now process that requires little historical information. Jackson's style was active and directive. He examined communication between husband and wife, parent and child, sibling and sibling. Jackson used a *prescribing-the-symptom* (Watzlawick et al. 1967) tactic to upset dysfunctional family equilibrium; he directed the members to continue a dysfunctional behavior but offered an entirely new meaning as to its use in the family. For example, a husband and wife would be urged to continue their chronic bickering because such behavior really fosters the intimate, loving relationship they both want. The couple receiving this instruction is forced to choose either to continue this behavior with the new meaning attached or to abandon the behavior in order to prove the therapist wrong and thus indirectly achieve a reduction in bickering and an improvement in family functioning.

Another tactic associated with Jackson's communication approach is the *relabeling* technique. Relabeling is a process of redefining pathological behavior in a most benign way. In the example just cited, relabeling occurs as the therapist offers a new definition of the advantages of bickering.

In summary, Jackson's emphasis on the cognitive aspects of family communication led family therapists to pay close attention to the meaning of behavior for a dyad or family. Jackson's conceptualizing shift allowed troubled family members to change present behavior by design or to continue old ways with new understanding.

Haley brings into the family treatment model a perspective on the importance of *power struggles* in the family. A corollary to power issues is control concerns. Consequently, while Jackson emphasized conceptualization in family communication, Haley saw power as the more predominant quality. Symptoms in a family allow an individual to control a relationship. Haley views it as the therapist's responsibility to identify the effect of the dysfunction on family members and to engage in altering the symptom itself. His style is directive and present oriented, and he advocates short-term therapeutic engagement. He uses paradoxical instruction, relabeling, and other assignments to effect family renegotiation of power exchanges.

Jackson and Haley have both been identified in the development of family treatment as focusing on strategic intervention. Both view the presenting symptom as the true problem. Their interventions are aimed at altering the behaviors of family members. Their style is less distant and objective than that of a true behaviorist, however. They place themselves in the family and may offer personal opinions, share their ignorance when puzzled, or prescribe a behavior for the sake of encouraging direct resistance and the achievement of a greater goal.

Minuchin drew on his early professional experience as a psychiatrist working with delinquent boys to elaborate a family therapy approach that has come to be known as a *structural treatment orientation*. His work with children and adolescents from economically disadvantaged families continues a tradition of seeing disruptive individual behavior as more than just the result of intrapsychic conflict. Minuchin stated that the work of the therapist was first to challenge the view that there is one certain identified patient. He wanted the therapist to confront the linear notion of causality—that is, the idea that the identified patient or some other family member is entirely accountable for all the difficulties in the family. In place of this linear notion, Minuchin advocated a view that each family member provides, and is provided with, a context for responding by the action of others in the family. This principal of complementarity emphasizes the increasing reciprocal and multilevel nature of causality within the family unit. For example, the therapist, on observing the behavior of an immature, selfish adolescent, might tell the teenager that he is acting like a 2-year-old and then ask the parents how they had succeeded in keeping him that way (Minuchin and Fishman 1981).

Minuchin elaborated on the concept of alignment that Wynne first conceived. He emphasized the importance of boundaries within the family between the subsystems of husband and wife and parent and child. Minuchin saw family growth as the result of modifying family structure as different developmental tasks and crises affected the family. *Family boundaries* are essentially the communication and participation rules that define the subsystem. Problems occur when the boundaries are unclear, being either too rigid (disengaged) or too diffuse (enmeshed). Symptoms occur when boundary rules become inflexible, and what may occur temporarily as a result of a family transition (for example, an enmeshed mother–child relationship following the birth of the child) then settles into an unhealthy family adaptation. Consequently, Minuchin's approach looks closely at environmental stress and developmental transition points as diagnostic material for assessing effective family interaction. The consideration of these factors forms a pattern of structural questions that the family therapist uses to analyze family functioning.

Minuchin's efforts in family treatment have continued a tradition of testing a treatment model by applying it to difficult cases. Minuchin and his advocates have worked with families with eating disorders and severe substance abuse problems. It is understandable, then, that his field experience has enriched family therapy techniques with a number of specific strategies and tactics.

The structural family therapist begins his work by decreasing the gap between himself and the troubled family. Minuchin encourages the development of a nonconfrontive treatment alliance at the start of therapy. Rapport allows the therapist to assess the sturdiness of boundaries and the areas of dysfunction. Once the diagnosis has been made, the therapist can propose a contract to work on the identified problem.

Minuchin's second phase of treatment permits the therapist to withdraw to a more neutral position in the service of encouraging communication between family members rather than between family and therapist. Specific direction may be used to reduce or strengthen subsystem boundaries as the case requires; for example, the therapist might recommend to the parents that they preserve more time for each other as a way of clarifying parent–child boundaries that have become enmeshed. Another strategy (and one best used in the hands of a skilled therapist) is for the therapist to become critical of a child for the sake of drawing in a more distanced parent in a disengaged family. As with other family treatment approaches, Minuchin uses homework assignments as well as specific tasks during the treatment session to increase the effectiveness of family interaction.

Recent trends in family therapy have sought to integrate the treatment models and strategies proposed over the last 30 years. It is clear even in the review of the treatment approaches presented in this chapter that rigid differences stand out only rarely. Therefore, the blending of complementary theories (and sometimes even conflicting ones) is occurring with increasing regularity in professional literature. Stanton published an article on an integrated approach to family therapy involving structural–strategic models (Stanton 1981). His article provides decision-making rules on when to use components of either system. Pinsof and Feldman (1982) developed an integrative model for understanding problem maintenance in families. Pinsof (1983) continued this line of theorizing with an attempt at synthesizing family and individual psychotherapies.

There have been other attempts at integration both within the family treatment approach as well as across modalities. Psychologists, as one professional group active in both family research and treatment, voted to establish the Division of Family Psychology in 1984. The inaugural issue of the *Journal of Family Psychology* was published in September 1987. This professional effort symbolically culminates the integration that has occurred within family treatment theory and practice and across treatment modalities.

It is appropriate to end this introduction to the field of family therapy by identifying the current movement of integration as a natural and positive outcome of working with difficult families and discovering what is most effective.

TREATMENT SESSION STRATEGY AND TACTICS

Indications for family treatment often involve disruptive behavior with children, parent–child distress, and marital dissatisfaction. The way in which the presenting problem is given to the family therapist, whether by telephone contact or third-party referral, influences the strategies employed in setting up the initial interview. Usually the parent will call because of personally identified concerns related to a child. It is crucial for the therapist to listen closely to the description of the problem in order to be sure that the difficulty is accurately a parent–child problem. Sometimes the marital relationship is clearly the major trouble spot, in which case a first session with children present is inappropriate. Unless the children are at risk of significant physical or emotional harm, marital therapy has priority over family treatment. In addition, while many family therapists view drug and alcohol problems as a symptom of marital and family dysfunction, I believe that if either of the spouses is the substance-abusing individual, practical intervention again requires that only adults be present at the initial interview. In the latter case, psychological intervention may point to the need for inpatient chemical dependency treatment. (There are those in the drug treatment field who rely on a family-confrontation strategy to motivate the substance-abusing individual to seek professional help.) With these exceptions noted, the first interview with the therapist includes everyone living in the family residence. Ordinarily, the therapist can successfully encourage all family members to attend by telephoning those described as reluctant by the caller requesting the appointment. The therapist can build on the natural concern and desire to be helpful that most people share for those they care about. If necessary, the recalcitrant individual can be reassured that he will have to talk only when he wishes.

The way in which the family members arrange themselves in the treatment room is a valuable nonverbal diagnostic indicator. Those members who select large distances between themselves and other family members may be pointing to emotional distance as well as to a preference for individual space. The therapist begins the session with an introduction and greeting to each of the members. For example, discussing preferences for the use of titles or first names is a logical starting point. Depending on the problem at hand, it may be advantageous to judiciously emphasize one or the other. A child-custody evaluation perhaps best exemplifies a situation in which professional titles are best used. My preference is ordinarily to use first names for both myself and family members as a quicker and more effective way of establishing trust and candor.

Inquiring as to what problems or concerns bring the family to the therapist lets the family define the problem and the cause. Moving beyond the identified-patient perspective and introducing multilevel causality permits an effective shift from an individual to a family treatment orientation. In the case of a substance-abusing adolescent, for example, identifying family treatment needs will help to establish particular strategies necessary to help the adolescent in his recovery.

Less than 15 years ago, the field of family therapy was uniformly skeptical of psychological testing because of its connection with individual diagnosis. The value of formal assessment has not been lost, however, and a number of structured rating scales are now available. The clinical rating scale for the circumplex model (Olson and Killorin 1985) permits the therapist to rate the family on the dimensions of cohesion, adaptability, and communication. Other assessment strategies involve the use of projective instruments like the Rorschach that the family works on together to provide data on family interactional patterns (Wahlstrom 1986).

In private-practice work, the therapist frequently finds that the family or some of its members have previously been involved in counseling. The importance of previous treatment cannot be overstated. What the individual or family learned, liked, and disliked about that experience is fundamental to plotting a current treatment direction. For example, if the therapist discovers that the previous therapist saw only the adolescent in individual treatment and that the parents were not reassured about the adolescent's progress, since they were not consulted, then the therapist has an excellent opportunity to underline the importance of specific behavioral goals and mutual assessment of progress by all family members in the present treatment experience.

While everyone at the initial treatment session has an opportunity to identify the problem and their solution to it, the therapist must reserve time before the session ends to offer preliminary estimates of the problem and a general direction for future sessions. An orientation to the therapist's expectations as well as the family's is advised. I usually counsel that the family will know within two or three sessions whether treatment is proceeding in a helpful direction and that they can trust their intuitions as well as their informed judgment. Such direction does not convey that treatment will be finished after two or three hours (although it will not take two or three years). Those therapists who favor structural and strategic approaches ordinarily will complete treatment in a shorter time than family system therapists and psychodynamic family therapists because of the differences in problem identification and the perceived magnitude of the treatment task.

Many system therapists use a genogram to identify members of the family across three generations. Such information is useful as a diagram of boundaries and of emphasized and unemphasized family relationships. In addition, family therapists place much importance on measurable change as evidence of progress in treatment. An increase in positive feelings toward family members is considered secondary to the elimination of an adolescent's eating disorder, for example.

Evaluation of the success of family therapy is confounded by some of the same problems that beset any therapeutic evaluation. In addition, the presence of a family, as opposed to an individual, complicates and multiplies the process-observation task. Research findings published by the University of Minnesota (Aldous and Hill 1967) provide reviews of family investigations.

Bowen was among the first in this field to advocate the importance of the therapist's evaluation of his role in his own family of origin. This counsel is advantageous to all who would attempt to help other families, since what occurs within our own families often contains principles that can be generalized to others. The greater our grasp of family interaction, the more we can help families achieve productive change.

REFERENCES

Ackerman, N. (1958). *The Psychodynamics of Family Life.* New York: Basic Books.

Adler, A. (1918). *Understanding Human Nature.* New York: Permabooks, 1949.

Aldous, J., and Hill, R. (1967). *International Bibliography of Research in Marriage and the Family*, vol. 1, *1900–1964.* Minneapolis: University of Minnesota Press.

Bateson, G., et al. (1956). Towards a theory of schizophrenia. *Behavioral Science* 1:251–264.

Foley, V. D. (1979). Family therapy. In *Current Psychotherapies*, ed. R. J. Corsini, 2nd ed., pp. 460–499. Itasca, IL: Peacock.

Framo, J. (1972). *Family Interaction: A Dialogue Between Family Researchers and Family Therapists.* New York: Springer.

Freud, S. (1964). Analysis of phobia in a 5-year-old boy. In *The Complete Works of Sigmund Freud*, ed. J. Strachey, pp. 3–149. London: Hogarth Press.

Kaslow, F. (1987). Trends in family psychology. *Journal of Family Psychology* 1:77–90.

Kerr, M. (1981). Family systems theory and therapy. In *Handbook of Family Therapy*, ed. A. Gurman and D. Kniskern, pp. 226–264. New York: Brunner/Mazel.

Laing, R. (1965). Mystification, confusion, and conflict. In *Intensive Family Therapy*, ed. I. Boszormenyi-Nagy and J. Framo, pp. 343–363. New York: Harper & Row.

Lidz, T., et al. (1957). The intrafamilial environment of schizophrenic patients: marital schism and marital skew. *American Journal of Psychiatry* 114:241–248.

Minuchin, S., and Fishman, H. (1981). *Family Therapy Techniques*. Cambridge, MA: Harvard University Press.

Okun, B., and Rappaport, L. (1980). *Working with Families: An Introduction to Family Therapy*. Belmont, CA: Brooks/Cole.

Olson, D. H., and Killoran, E. (1985). *Clinical Rating Scale for the Circumplex Model of Marital and Family Systems*. St. Paul, MN: University of Minnesota, Department of Family Social Science.

Paul, N., and Paul, B. (1975). *A Marital Puzzle*. New York: W. W. Norton.

Pinsof, W. (1983). Integrative problem-centered therapy: toward the synthesis of family and individual psychotherapies. *Journal of Marital and Family Therapy* 1:19–35.

Pinsof, W., and Feldman, L. (1982). Problem maintenance in family systems: an integrative model. *Journal of Marital and Family Therapy* 7:295–308.

Stanton, M. (1981). An integrated structural/strategic approach to family therapy. *Journal of Marital and Family Therapy* 10:427–439.

Sullivan, H. S. (1973). *The Interpersonal Theory of Psychiatry*. New York: W. W. Norton.

Wahlstrom, J. (1986). *Consensus Rorschach interaction patterns of families with an asthmatic child*. Paper presented at the Fifth International Congress of Family Therapy, Jerusalem, June.

Watzlawick, P., Beavin, J., and Jackson, D. (1967). *Pragmatics of Human Communication*. New York: W. W. Norton.

Wynne, L., Ryckoff, I., Day, J., and Hirsch, S. (1958). Pseudomutuality in the family relations of schizophrenics. *Psychiatry* 21:205–220.

Zuk, G. (1975). *Process and Practice in Family Therapy*. Haverford, PA: Psychiatry and Behavioral Science Books.

PART III

Interviewing Patients with Specific Psycho-pathologies

7
Affective Disorders

JOSEPH A. FLAHERTY, M.D.
and F. MOISES GAVIRIA, M.D.

Depression, in the broadest sense, is one of the most common psychological disturbances. It is a rare individual who has not had a dysphoric period lasting hours, days, or even weeks. In fact, psychoanalytic theorists have postulated that the capacity to bear depression is a positive indicator of psychological development. Nonetheless, there is a world of difference between the ubiquitous "blues" and a suicidal state of psychotic depression. This difference compels clinicians to search for diagnostic distinctions that can have predictive validity and treatment implications.

DIAGNOSTIC DISTINCTIONS

Diagnostic efforts since the beginning of this century have related depressive disorders (and all psychiatric disorders) to a variety of etiologic factors, in some cases favoring psychological predilection (as in cases of dependent and obsessive compliance personality), and in other situations favoring social factors (intercurrent life events) or biological origins (genetic or neurochemical pathophysiology). In each case the etiologic link was tenuous and too parsimonious to explain the entire phenomenon, leading to competing criteria and rendering diagnostic comparisons between treatment centers meaningless. The authors of DSM-III-R have recognized this dilemma and have made diagnoses dependent on the clinical phenomena, while understanding that multiple etiologic factors are relevant for each diagnosis and each patient.

It is important to note here old diagnostic dichotomies in the literature on affective disorders and to show their limited utility. The first is the endogenous reactive division. As originally proposed, *endogenous depression* referred to a depression presumably biologically based and without evident precipitant events, while *reactive depression* described those individuals whose depression seemed to arrive as a result of a serious life event such as the death of a spouse. However, current research on life events and depression fails to show that antecedent life events differentiate these two entities; in other words, individuals with "endogenous" depression are as likely as individuals with "reactive" depression to have experienced a serious life event prior to the onset of their depression. The remnant of utility of this division is the fact that individuals with severe sleep and appetite disturbance (more common in the "endogenous" type) are more likely to respond to an antidepressant pharmacotherapy or electroshock therapy than those without such neurovegetative symptoms.

A second historical distinction is the primary–secondary one. *Primary depression* was reserved for individuals without another major psychiatric disorder (particularly schizophrenia or alcoholism), while *secondary depression* referred to depressed individuals who had already been diagnosed as schizophrenic or alcoholic. This distinction creates a hierarchy of psychiatric diagnoses that is, at best, arbitrary. It is more important to recognize that depressive disorders can, and frequently do, occur in the course of schizophrenia, and that many alcoholic or substance-abusing patients suffer from concurrent affective conditions. The *neurotic–psychotic* distinction is a carry-over from early etiologic thinking favoring psychic conflict as the causative factor in neurosis. Confusion arose when "neurotic" conflict occurred concurrently with the obvious psychotic states. The DSM-III found it useful to employ the term *with psychosis* to recognize those patients with affective disorders who have an obvious impairment of reality orientation, determined by the presence of hallucinations, delusions, or other thought disorder.

Finally, the distinction of *melancholia* has also undergone revision. The term *involutional melancholia* (DSM-II) referred to a depression in individuals over the age of 50 with a particular constellation of symptoms including excessive guilt, psychomotor retardation, and early-morning insomnia. The DSM-III-R recognizes this distinction but does not reserve a separate category for it.

PRESENTATION OF DEPRESSIVE SYMPTOMS

Due to differences in personality and coping style, patients vary in the extent to which they manifest specific symptoms. Some patients may present with predominantly neurovegetative symptoms while denying feeling sad or "down." Others may initially complain of existential anguish and later will admit to other aspects of the disorders. It is not uncommon for patients to minimize their symptomatology or attribute it to a specific life event. In some cases, family members may notice the symptoms first, while the patient denies them.

Social-occupational dysfunction and depressive symptoms do not always co-vary directly. Some patients have a marked symptom picture but remain productive at work and do not have a marked deterioration in family functioning. Others may present with a diminished capacity to work before a clear symptom picture emerges. These individual variations require the clinician to make a comprehensive assessment of each patient with a potential affective disorder. The high prevalence of depression, the risk of suicide, and the potential benefits of treatment all underscore this need.

The following are common signs and symptoms of depressive illness:

1. *Dysphoric mood.* Most patients describe feeling sad, "blue," or "down in the dumps." Some patients are merely anxious and irritable.

2. *Feelings of hopelessness or helplessness.* Depressed patients commonly feel there is nothing that will get them out of a depressed slump.

3. *Loss of pleasure*, capacity to work, and interest in hobbies and personal relationships, including sexual activity.

4. *Changes in appetite and/or weight.* Most depressed people lose appetite and may lose weight; less commonly there is an increase in food intake and a consequent weight gain, although often little pleasure is reported while eating.

5. *Self-attribution.* Many depressed patients have a cognitive style that focuses the blame for the illness on themselves.

6. Decrease in total sleep time associated with initial, mid-sleep cycle, and early-morning *insomnia.* Many depressed patients try unsuccessfully to sleep during the day. A minority of depressed patients have *hypersomnia* and sleep 12 hours or more each day.

7. *Psychomotor retardation.* This common symptom is manifested by extremely slow movements and speech or by decreased attention and a delayed response to questioning. Alternatively, some depressed patients have *psychomotor agitation*, manifested by pacing, handwringing, fidgeting, increased smoking, anxiety, and agitations.

8. *Cognitive difficulties.* Many patients manifest a decreased attention span and an inability to complete tasks or make decisions. This problem may result in apparent deficits in mental status, or *pseudodementia.* Such deficits may improve with increased efforts to make the patient attend to questions.

9. *Excessive guilt.* Some patients experience guilt even to the point of delusion. Depressed patients often remember minor transgressions or slights rendered to others and blame themselves excessively.

10. *Obsessive rumination.* Depressed patients may obsessively focus on events in the past or on specific problems.

11. *Decreased energy.* There is also sometimes a decreased variation in energy levels. Patients who suffer from major depression often feel worse in the morning and feel more energy by afternoon or evening (*diurnal variation*).

12. *Suicidal ideation.* Thoughts of suicide are very common in depression. Some depressed patients become preoccupied with death, with thoughts of reuniting with loved ones after death, or the response of family to their death.

13. *Narcissistic preoccupation with bodily functions* and concerns about somatic dysfunction.

DSM-III-R CATEGORIES OF AFFECTIVE DISORDERS

The following are DSM-III-R categories of affective disorders, along with brief descriptions of their clinical course and epidemiology.

Major Depression

DIAGNOSTIC CRITERIA

The presence of a dysphoric mood is a major criterion for the diagnosis of depression. The mood may be one of sadness or overriding anhedonia. Other affective symptoms include anger, anxiety, and irritability. The DSM-III-R requires the presence of at least four of the following symptoms for a period of at least two weeks:

1. Appetite disturbance
2. Sleep disturbance
3. Psychomotor retardation or agitation
4. Anhedonia
5. Loss of energy
6. Feelings of worthlessness or guilt
7. Decreased cognitive functioning
8. Suicidal thoughts

These symptoms may develop insidiously or rapidly. Major depression may be diagnosed in the presence of other personality disorders, anxiety states, and cyclothymic or dysthymic disorders. If major depression occurs with a history of manic or hypomanic episodes, the condition is referred to as a *bipolar disorder*. The term *unipolar disorder* is reserved for those individuals who have recurrent episodes of depression but not mania. The condition cannot be diagnosed if

1. There is a preoccupation with mood-incongruent delusions or hallucinations.
2. The symptoms are superimposed on schizophrenia or on schizophreniform or paranoid disorder.
3. The symptoms are due to an organic mental disorder or to bereavement.

SUBTYPES OF MAJOR DEPRESSION

Major depression with melancholia is a variant of major depression characterized by a marked loss of the capacity for pleasure and by the presence of three of the following:

1. Distinct quality of depressed mood
2. Feeling worse in the morning
3. Early morning awakening
4. Marked psychomotor retardation or agitation

5. Inappropriate or excessive guilt
6. Anorexia or weight loss

Major depression with psychosis occurs in 15 to 20 percent of cases; these manifestations include the following:

1. *Mood-congruent delusion.* These are delusions typical of the depressed state and are usually related to extremely low self-esteem, poverty of thought and affect, guilt, death, nihilism, or punishment.
2. *Hallucinations* of any senses may occur, although single-word or single-phrase auditory hallucinations, such as a voice saying "help" or calling the patient's name, are most common.
3. *Depressive stupor* exists when the patient is mute and unresponsive.

It should be recognized that much of the error in diagnosing major depression as schizophrenia is due to the failure to recognize that individuals with major depression may be very psychotic. Mood-congruent delusions are related to the dysphoric mood and may include fear of punishment for minor wrongdoing in the distant past, delusions of poverty, and somatic delusions ("My body is rotting"; "I have a brain cancer that they can't find"). Auditory hallucinations may also be present and are commonly a single word or phrase ("Help," "Bad," "Go to hell") or a voice calling the patient's name.

EPIDEMIOLOGY

The overall prevalence of major depression in the United States is between 3 and 5 percent. The lifetime risk for developing a major depressive episode is 3 to 12 percent for men and 20 to 26 percent for women (Weissman and Boyd 1985). This risk is higher for individuals with a first-degree relative who has a diagnosis of major depression, bipolar disorder, or alcoholism. The mean age of onset is in the mid-20s, although the incidence of depression appears to be increasing in children and adolescents.

In women, the first episode of depression often occurs within six months of postpartum period. Women with a postpartum depression are more vulnerable to a recurrence in each subsequent postpartum period. There does not appear to be an increased incidence of major depression in the menopausal period.

Possible risk factors for depression include the absence of a close, confiding relationship; occurrence of a loss (for example, the death of a family member); and high levels of introversion, neuroticism, and dependency.

CLINICAL COURSE

An untreated major depression lasts an average of six months, although some episodes have a much shorter duration, while others go on to a chronic course. This six-month period in a treated patient may be viewed as a period of increased vulnerability to relapse. Relapse is always a possibility, but 50 percent of patients with major depression have only one episode. Factors associated with relapse include (1) several recent episodes; (2) continued social dysfunction despite symptom improvement; and (3) lack of compliance with treatment. A relapse within six months of the initial episode places the patient at high risk for chronicity.

Pharmacologic treatment changes the severity and length of major depression episodes but does not reduce the frequency of episodes. Treatment clearly decreases the risk of suicide, which occurs in about 15 percent of these patients.

Manic Episode

DIAGNOSTIC CRITERIA

The occurrence of periods of elevated, elated emotion or irritable mood, sometimes interrupted by a depressive mood, is a major diagnostic criterion for the diagnosis of manic episode. Another criterion is hospitalization, or the presence of at least three of the following symptoms (four if mood is only irritable) for a duration of at least one week:

1. Increased activity
2. Pressured speech or increased talkativeness
3. Flight of ideas
4. Inflated self-esteem (grandiosity)
5. Reduced sleep
6. Distractibility
7. Severe risk taking and poor judgment

No mood-incongruent delusions or hallucinations and no bizarre behavior is manifested if the affective syndrome (mania) is absent. Manic episode cannot be diagnosed if the symptoms are associated with schizophrenia or with schizophreniform or paranoid disorder. The clinician must also rule out organic or toxic mental disorder as the etiology of these symptoms.

While the happy, elated, and gregarious interactive style has become the stereotype of the manic patient, a lability of mood, with rapid shift to anger or sadness, is common. Manic patients will frequently begin an interaction with humor that quickly becomes sarcastic and tactless. They become annoyed when people react negatively to them, and they may eventually become tearful after such a rebuff.

Mood-congruent delusions are those that are consistent with the manic patient's elated mood and grandiosity. Common themes are superhuman physical and intellectual capacity, unrealistic plans and schemes for fame and fortune, and unreal feelings of personal connectedness to favorite people. The delusions do not have the bizarre or idiosyncratic flavor of those described by the schizophrenic patient. Also absent are the delusions most commonly seen in schizophrenia, such as the belief that one is being controlled by unknown forces (or by machines, radar, electricity, or computers) or that one's thoughts are being transmitted (thought broadcasting), placed in one's head (thought insertion), or controlling one's activities (thought control). Hallucinations are rare in the course of mania, although visual hallucinations and illusions, such as flashing lights, may be present at the peak of the manic episode.

EPIDEMIOLOGY

The lifetime risk for developing an affective disorder is approximately 1 percent (0.6 to 1.3 percent) in industralized nations (Weissman and Boyd 1985). The prevalence rate for manic episodes ranges from 0.4 to 0.9 percent for men and for women.

Most studies suggest that the age of onset of bipolar illness occurs from adolescence to about age 35 and then declines. Compared to major depression (unipolar), for which the peak age of onset is the late 30s, the peak onset for bipolar illness is in the late 20s. However, episodes recur every three to nine years, and the length of time between episodes declines with age. This results in a predominance of older patients in treatment.

While bipolar illness is more prevalent in the upper social classes, it is unclear whether this is a cause or a consequence of the illness and/or of the somewhat typical premorbid personality of the bipolar patient, which is characterized by ambition and overachievement (Flaherty 1983).

There does not appear to be a racial or ethnic distribution in bipolar illness, although small, inbred ethnic groups may have a higher incidence. Having a close genetic relative with bipolar illness may be a predisposing factor. Twin studies show concordance rates of 0.68 for monozygotes and 0.23 for dizygotes (Price 1968).

CLINICAL COURSE

The untreated manic episode is usually shorter than the depressive episode; manic episodes usually last from three to seven months. However, brief episodes of only 1 to 2 weeks in duration are known to occur and may be missed in the history.

While most (untreated) bipolar patients will experience four to twelve episodes of mania in a lifetime, some bipolar patients will have up to four episodes a year. These patients are referred to as "rapid cyclers" and are less responsive to treatment with lithium carbonate (Annitto and Shopsin 1979).

Some bipolar patients enjoy their initial manic episodes and therefore avoid treatment. Continued occupational, marital, and legal difficulties as a result of their imprudent activities frequently reduce this pleasure and force these patients to see the benefits of treatment. Patient and family psychoeducation after a manic episode may greatly increase treatment compliance.

Dysthymic Disorder

DIAGNOSTIC CRITERIA

The diagnosis of dysthymic disorder describes the patient who has been bothered most or all of the time for the two years preceding presentation by symptoms that are characteristic of the depressive syndrome but that are not of sufficient severity and duration to meet the criteria for a major depressive episode. The manifestations of the depressive syndrome may be relatively persistent, or they may be separated by periods of normal mood lasting a few days to a few weeks but no more than a few months at a time.

During the depressive periods, the patient experiences either prominent depressed mood (reports feeling sad, blue, down in the dumps, or low) or marked loss of interest or pleasure in all or almost all usual activities or pastimes. At least three of the following symptoms are present during the depressive periods:

1. Insomnia or hypersomnia
2. Low energy
3. Feelings of inadequacy
4. Decreased effectiveness at work or study
5. Reduced concentration
6. Loss of interest or enjoyment
7. Irritability
8. Inability to be pleased by praise
9. Reduced activity or talkativeness
10. Brooding and pessimism or feeling sorry for self
11. Tearfulness
12. Thoughts of death or suicide

The absence of psychotic symptoms is a criterion for this diagnosis. The disorder is difficult to establish in the presence of a major depression. However both dysthymic disorder and major depression may appear in the same individual ("double depression").

EPIDEMIOLOGY

The prevalence of the dysthymic disorder is estimated at between 4.5 and 10.5 percent, with more women affected than men. There may be a higher prevalence among individuals who report early parental loss.

CLINICAL COURSE

This disorder has, by definition, a chronic course. Symptoms usually begin in late adolescence or early adulthood. Treatment may be effective in reducing the severity of symptoms or the associated impairment in social and occupational functioning.

Cyclothymic Disorder

DIAGNOSTIC CRITERIA

Like dysthymic disorder, cyclothymic disorder is generally a chronic illness of mood that does not reach the severity of a major depression or mania and that is unaccompanied by psychotic symptoms. The mood state alternates between depressive and hypomanic periods. Unlike the dysthymic patient, the patient with cyclothymic disorder may experience a normal mood between periods of disordered mood. The depressive periods have the diagnostic criteria described for dysthymic disorder. The *hypomanic periods* are characterized by an elevated, expansive, or irritable mood accompanied by three of the following:

1. Reduced need for sleep
2. Increased energy
3. Increased self-esteem
4. Increased productivity and long work hours
5. Creative thinking
6. Uninhibited gregariousness and sexuality
7. Irresponsibility and poor judgment
8. Restlessness
9. Increased talkativeness
10. Excessive optimism
11. Inappropriate laughing and joking

EPIDEMIOLOGY

The prevalence of this disorder is estimated at approximately 10 percent. It is more common in patients with a family history of bipolar disorder or major depression.

CLINICAL COURSE

Like dysthymia, cyclothymia usually has a chronic course. Although affective periods often seem related to specific stresses, they occur without apparent precipitating stress as well. Patients often self-medicate periods of exacerbation with alcohol and other substances of abuse, complicating the clinical picture. There is often associated social dysfunction, particularly marital and familial, as the disorder progresses.

Depression and Physical Illness

There are a variety of ways in which depressive symptomatology is related to physical illness: (1) depression can be a first sign of physical illness; (2) depression can be secondary to physical illness; (3) depression can be caused by pharmacotherapy; and (4) depression can be masked by complaints of physical illness. Table 7–1 provides a partial list of signs and symptoms of depression.

DEPRESSION AS A FIRST SIGN OF PHYSICAL ILLNESS

Depression is often present in the following disorders: hypothyroidism, Cushing's syndrome, primary aldosteronism, Addison's disease, early stages of Parkinson's disease, chronic infectious diseases, carcinoma of the pancreas, early diabetes, lupus erythematosus, and vitamin deficiencies such as pellagra, thiamine deficiency, and pernicious anemia. Dementia may also initially present with depressive symptoms.

TABLE 7-1. Signs and Symptoms of Depressive Disorders

Emotional
Sadness ("blue," "down in the dumps")
Anxiety
Irritability
Anhedonia
Psychological
Guilt
Hopelessness
Helplessness or worthlessness
Loss of capacity for pleasure
Cognitive
Obsessive thoughts and rumination
Decreased memory
Poor concentration
Suicidal ideation
Social
Social withdrawal
Social-occupational dysfunction
Neurovegetative
Decreased energy
Psychomotor agitation or retardation
Insomnia or hypersomnia
Decreased libido
Appetite disburbances
Diurnal variation in mood
Constipation
Psychotic manifestations (Present in a subgroup only)
Delusions
Hallucinations

DEPRESSION SECONDARY TO PHYSICAL ILLNESS

Depression is one of the most common ways in which a patient reacts to the development of a physical illness. Some of the factors that play a role in this reaction are (1) age of onset, (2) degree of disability, (3) nature of the disease, (4) the patient's premorbid body image and the changes in his perception of his body imposed by a specific illness or treatment (such as heart surgery). Depression is commonly associated with cardiac disease; over 60 percent of hospitalized cardiac patients are depressed. Following a myocardial infarction, individuals remain at high risk for depression for over 18 months. Depression is a common accompaniment of many other chronic diseases, such as rheumatoid arthritis and other collagen diseases.

DEPRESSION AND PHARMACOTHERAPY

Although approximately 200 specific drugs have been implicated as possible causes of depression, only a few agents have been associated with any frequency. These are as follows: (1) oral contraceptives, (2) antihypertensive drugs (particularly reserpine, alpha-methyldopa, propranolol, hydralazine, and clonidine), and (3) psychotropic drugs (such as the phenothiazines, barbiturates, and benzodiazepines).

DEPRESSION MASKED BY COMPLAINTS OF PHYSICAL ILLNESS

A masked depression is one in which the patient has symptoms of a somatic disturbance but denies a depressed mood. These patients often visit a nonpsychiatric physician with somatic complaints that most often affect the central nervous system or the gastrointestinal, cardiovascular, and musculoskeletal systems. The chief complaints include lethargy, palpitations, abdominal pains or spasms, headaches, backaches, chest pains, and many vague and poorly defined somatic disturbances. The diagnosis is made by establishing (1) the lack of an organic disorder to explain the physical complaint and (2) the presence of the usual vegetative signs of depression.

Grief and Bereavement

Grief is the normal reaction to loss, whether of a person, object, state of health, prestige, or self-esteem; *mourning* refers to the process by which grief is resolved (grief work), and *bereavement* refers to the state accompanying the mourning process. The normal grief reaction is an adaptational process that, when successfully completed, results in a reorganization phase in which the bereaved individual regains the capacity to develop new attachment.

The normal process of grief and mourning may be disturbed in various ways. Grief can present as a general, nonspecific stress and, as such, can affect the individual as any other stressor would. Clinical evidence supports the hypothesis that bereavement may be a factor in the development of a wide range of physical and emotional disorders, including fatal illness (Clayton 1974). Alternatively, any of the stages of a grief reaction may be altered, intensified, or prolonged, qualifying for a diagnosis of pathologic grief.

Seasonal Affective Disorders (SAD)

Individuals with seasonal depression are less severely ill than many depressives but share features in common with those in the depressed phase of bipolar illness (Rosenthal et al. 1985). Approximately 75 percent of those who suffer from SAD are women. In the typical case the symptoms begin in the fall and increase until the beginning of spring, following which a slow remission develops. The individuals report feeling much better during the summer months and during bright, sunny days in general. In addition to irritability, sadness, and some thought and motor retardation, they have a carbohydrate craving and frequently gain weight during the winter. They are also hypersomnic and tend to withdraw from elective social activities, but most individuals maintain their work and family responsibilities. This diagnostic distinction is useful because of the availability of a low-risk treatment for the disorder: The use of high-intensity ultraviolet lights for one to two hours a day in the winter frequently has prophylactic and treatment value.

Depression and Demoralization

Demoralization is a condition (not a disorder) in which the individual feels hopeless, despondent, and unable to effect a change that will improve his status (Dohrenwend et al. 1974, Frank 1973). It appears to be more related to stressful events and transitions than does clinical depression. However, there is a strong overlap in symptoms, and many depressed patients become demoralized and stay so in the initial stages of treatment. Patients who are both demoralized and depressed may require both pharmacotherapy and psychotherapy, so the clinician should be alert to this condition.

Personality Disorders and Affective Disorders

Theoretically, personality disorders and affective disorders may be related in various ways: (1) A certain personality type or style may predispose to an affective disorder. (2) A personality style may be a sequela of an affective state. (3) Both personality styles and affective disorders may result from a basic genetic or psychosocial predisposition, or both. (4) A personality disorder may exist only when the affective state is present. It is wise to reassess personality after the affective episode is over. Certain personality traits, such as interpersonal dependency, may only be a manifestation of depression (Hirshfield and Klerman 1979). Personality conditions may also influence the symptomatology of the affective disorder. Bipolar patients with a borderline personality disorder usually experience more delusions and hallucinations when manic and have poorer functioning between episodes (Gaviria et al. 1982).

DIFFERENTIAL DIAGNOSIS OF DEPRESSION

ADJUSTMENT DISORDER

Adjustment disorder with depressed mood may be considered if the symptoms seem to be related to a recent (within three months) psychosocial stressor. Expect these symptoms to remit when the stress is over. Since many major depressions are anteceded by life events, this diagnostic differential is confusing and somewhat academic. If the patient has symptoms of a major depression, he should be treated as such.

ORGANIC AFFECTIVE DISORDER

Organic affective disorder can be diagnosed if there is clinical evidence for an organic factor causing the symptom picture. Withdrawal from amphetamines, cocaine, and other sympathomimetic drugs are often associated with transient depressive symptoms.

SCHIZOPHRENIA OR SCHIZOAFFECTIVE DISORDER

Schizophrenia or schizoaffective disorder should be considered if the individual has psychotic symptoms such as delusions and hallucinations. The differential diagnosis stresses the presence of Schneiderian first-rank symptoms in schizophrenia and mood-congruent delusions in affective disorders. During an acute episode, however, it can be extremely difficult to differentiate an affective from a schizophrenic state. It is often necessary to confirm the diagnosis by clinical course and response to treatment.

POSTTRAUMATIC STRESS DISORDER

Posttraumatic stress disorder may often mimic a depression. The major criterion for this disorder is the antecedent catastrophic stress; commonly associated symptoms include night terrors, flashbacks, and intrusive thoughts.

PERSONALITY DISORDERS

Personality disorders, particularly narcissistic and borderline, are often accompanied by periods of dysphoric mood, intense feelings of loneliness, and emptiness. Therefore, personality disorders must be considered in the differential.

DIFFERENTIAL DIAGNOSIS OF MANIA

SCHIZOPHRENIA

Schizophrenia is the most common entity in the differential of mania. The lack of delusions of control and continued, complex auditory hallucinations characterize mania. Manic speech is usually rapid and often replete with clang associations, as opposed to the loose and idiosyncratic associations in mania.

ORGANIC MENTAL DISORDERS

Organic mental disorders associated with toxic and medical conditions may mimic the manic state. The most common medical conditions with manic symptoms are hyperthyroidism and hypercortisolism (Cushing's syndrome). Thyroid function studies and plasma cortisol levels, along with other clinical signs and symptoms, can usually rule these out. Partial complex seizures (psychomotor seizures) and interictal behavior may resemble mania at times; an electroencephalogram (EEG) would be helpful in questionable cases. Intoxication with psychotomimetics, cocaine, opiates, and amphetaine can usually be differentiated by a urine toxicology screen. Dementia occasionally presents with manic symptoms (affective lability and poor judgment); the frequency of dementia in patients with acquired immune deficiency syndrome (AIDS) makes it an important differential.

BRIEF REACTIVE PSYCHOSIS

A *brief reactive psychosis* may also present with the symptoms of mania. As both may initially respond to antipsychotic drugs, the long-term course of the illness may be the essential factor in making this differential diagnosis.

BORDERLINE AND NARCISSISTIC PERSONALITY DISORDERS

Borderline and narcissistic personality disorders may be characterized by the psychotic symptoms, hypersexual and erratic behavior, and poor judgment that are common in mania. The favorable response to treatment with lithium carbonate in the manic, along with the long-term course, are critical in making the distinction.

INTERVIEW FORMAT FOR AFFECTIVE DISORDERS

Presenting Symptoms

The therapist should assess when, how, and if the patient began to recognize his symptoms as abnormal and sought treatment. First episodes of affective illness may come to treatment only as a result of family intervention or, in the case of mania, police referral. Public nudity is not infrequently a presentation of mania. Patients with major depression may have previously sought help from internists for a variety of somatic complaints.

History of the Present Episode

The therapist should query all symptoms common to mania and depression and should establish a chronology of the present episode. Particularly important are the following symptoms: insomnia (early, middle, or late), hypersomnia, weight loss or gain, or diurnal variation in mood (depressives typically feel more depressed in the morning), a loss of pleasure in activities including sex, and suicidal ideation. The efficacy of efforts to ameliorate the condition, including the use of prescribed or street drugs, should be elicited. Amphetamines may result in a temporary improvement in depressive symptoms. The occurrence of a severe loss (the anniversary of a loss or the presence of ongoing stresses, such as mental, occupational, or financial difficulties) should be examined. The absence of a close, confiding relationship and an ongoing social support system may both increase the vulnerability to an affective episode and worsen the clinical course (Flaherty et al. 1983).

Past History

The chronology of affective episodes, starting with the first, should be elicited along with past treatments and responses to treatment. The therapist should look for symptoms of other psychiatric disorders, including substance abuse, schizophrenia, and borderline personality disorder. The patient should be asked about prescribed and illicit drug use. A postmedical history should be performed.

FAMILY HISTORY

The therapist should ask the patient whether there is a history in his family of any of the entities in the "depressive spectrum"—depression, mania, and alcoholism—or of any other psychiatric disorder. Response to treatment should also be assessed; if a family member has responded to a specific antidepressant drug, this is a good prediction of the patient's response.

DEVELOPMENTAL HISTORY

A developmental assessment is important in considering an Axis II (personality) disorder. Here the patient's adaptive style and relationships from childhood through early adulthood and early functioning in occupation, marriage, and family are critical.

SOCIAL HISTORY

A history emphasizing the patient's current social network, including a description of individuals who are helpful or detrimental to the patient, should be elicited. The patient's relative social adjustment and performance in his various roles should also be assessed.

FAMILY OR MARITAL INTERVIEW

A session with the patient's spouse and family is useful in checking the history as well as in evaluating the family's potential to offer support and willingness to engage in family therapy.

MENTAL STATUS EXAMINATION

An assessment of mental status should be made on each patient. This examination should be more extensive and formal if there is the possibility of an organic mental disorder; depressed patients may have evidence of a pseudodementia. Basic assessments of orientation, judgment, memory (past, recent, and recall), abstract thinking, and ability to calculate are essential.

SUICIDALITY

Every depressed patient and every patient suspected of being depressed should be carefully evaluated for suicide potential. Some 40 to 60 percent of all suicides occur in patients with affective disorders; as many as one out of ten patients in a major depressive episode will make a serious suicide attempt. Suicide occurs more frequently in men (although women make more attempts), in older people, and in those whose occupations provide access to the means of suicide (such as hospital employees, pharmacists, and police officers). In addition to the diagnosis, the following parameters must be assessed in the suicide evaluation:

1. The presence of psychiatric symptoms. Psychiatric states increase the risk, particularly the presence of auditory hallucinations (often a suicide "command") or delusions of reunion with a deceased loved one.
2. Use of alcohol or other drugs. This both increases impulsivity and may potentiate any drug used in an overdose.
3. The loss (particularly sudden and recent) of a close relationship.
4. The presence of a severely debilitating or fatal illness.
5. The presence of severe and unrelenting physical pain.
6. A profound feeling of hopelessness about improvement, coupled with the idea that suicide will provide an end to the current state.
7. A suicide plan, particularly one that is possible for the patient (that is, for which the patient has the necessary means) is potentially lethal. Females usually attempt (and complete) suicide by drug overdose; males more commonly employ a gun or use hanging or jumping.

MEDICAL ASSESSMENTS

Because of the possibility that depression may be caused by a medical condition and because of the need to ensure that concurrent somatic complaints are not serious, a thorough physical examination and medical history is usually necessary in a suspected affective disorder. The patient can be referred to an internist, and these assessments can be performed in the hospital setting or in the ambulatory setting.

LABORATORY DIAGNOSTIC ASSESSMENT

Dexamethazone Suppression Test (DST)

The DST is based on the abnormally excessive secretion of cortisol in many patients with major depression and, in particular, on their failure to reduce (suppress) this secretion when given an exogenous form of cortisol (dexamethazone). An abnormal plasma cortisol level (greater than 10 mg at 4:00 P.M.) and, in particular, nonsuppression of cortisol 24 hours after dexamethazone ingestion (1 mg) is found in approximately 50 percent of patients with major depression. False-positive results occur in other disorders, such as schizophrenia and alcoholism, limiting the utility of this test. The conversion of nonsuppression to suppression could be useful in monitoring treatment outcome of depressed patients.

Thyroid-releasing Hormone Response

The response of drug-free, fasting patients to 500 mg of thyroid-releasing hormone, with subsequent collection of serum thyroid-stimulating hormone at 15-, 30-, 45-, and 90-minute intervals, is sometimes blunted in patients with unipolar disorder and elevated in bipolar depression.

Sleep Electroencephalogram Recordings

An EEG taken during sleep may also aid the diagnostic process. Depressed patients characteristically have both a reduced total sleep time before the first rapid eye movement (REM) phase and alterations in the REM architecture.

RATING SCALES AND OTHER DIAGNOSTIC INSTRUMENTS

Several reliable instruments have become available for the systematic assessment of symptoms of depression. Although initially used for research purposes, some of the instruments have become useful to clinicians who wish to systematically document the course of depressive illness. The following are some commonly used instruments:

THE HAMILTON RATING SCALE FOR DEPRESSION

The Hamilton Rating Scale for Depression (HRSD) is a 24-item rating of depressive symptoms; it must be administered by a clinician during the course of the interview. It is very easy to complete and requires virtually no additional time other than that spent in gathering data on the progress of the illness.

THE CARROL SELF-RATING SCALE

The Carrol Self-Rating Scale (CSRS) is a 52-item self-report that measures the same symptom picture as the HRSD does; the two instruments have a high correlation (Carroll et al. 1981).

THE BECK DEPRESSION INVENTORY

The Beck Depression Inventory is a 21-item survey of common symptoms of depression. It is useful in picking up milder forms of depression in general populations.

THE MODIFIED MANIC RATING SCALE

The Modified Manic Rating Scale (MMRS) is the counterpart to the HRSD and can be rated by any experienced clinician.

THE SCHEDULE OF AFFECTIVE DISORDERS AND SCHIZOPHRENIA

The Schedule of Affective Disorders and Schizophrenia (SADS) is a detailed, structured interview that establishes the presence of affective disorders. It is a useful corollary to the criteria presented in DSM-III-R, upon which most clinicians rely in diagnosing affective symptoms. The SADS interview can be conducted in 45 to 90 minutes. While it has produced few false positives, false negatives have been known to occur.

PROJECTIVE TESTS

Projective tests, such as the Rorschach and the Thematic Apperception Test (TAT), while arguably helpful in diagnosis, may suggest important underlying psychosis, impulsivity, or suicidality.

PERSONALITY INVENTORIES

Personality inventories, such as the Minnesota Multiple Personality Inventory (MMPI) or the Millon Clinical Multiaxial Inventory (MCMI), may provide a broader picture of the patient's basic personality. They all have scales that assess depression.

PRACTICAL CONSIDERATIONS IN THE ASSESSMENT OF AFFECTIVE DISORDERS

Countertransference is common in the assessment of affective disorder and varies with the interviewer's personality. Strong reactions of frustration in response to hopeless and depressed patients and anger toward manic patients are common and, if unrecognized, lead to diagnostic and assessment errors. Due to the high prevalence of depressive symptoms, the inexperienced clinician may be co-opted by the depressed patient into minimizing the severity of the depression and may assume that the patient is having a normal reaction to a disappointment.

Manic patients are notorious for splitting staff members into rival camps and playing one staff member against another. They also tend to have great observation skills and can attack the interviewer's vulnerable points and ask embarrassing questions; alternatively, the manic patient may attempt to engage the therapist in humor. It is essential that the therapist maintain a professional, firm posture and that he not be "sidetracked" by the patient's verbal out-pouring. This may require a considerate but firm redirecting of the interview. The manic patient who is severely agitated may well be violent. In such a case, the interview should be conducted in the presence of other staff.

The depressed patient's current state may cloud his view of the past, such that he conveys a false impression of his past achievements, functioning, and symptom picture. Many patients with major depression provide a history of long-standing dysthymic disorder; this "history" may change when the patient's mood improves. While it is tempting to confront or interpret the depressed patient's obvious defenses or negative cognitive sets, the therapist should refrain from doing so until a careful treatment plan has been established. Such a plan may or may not include psychodynamic or cognitive therapy.

Patients with clear intrapsychic, familial, or social conflicts may initially be willing to address these issues but may later relegate their problems to "chemistry" if their symptoms improve with antidepressant pharmacotherapy. Treatment planning should carefully address the cost–benefit ratio in further exploration of the conflicts.

DEPRESSION AND THE LIFE CYCLE

While our discussion has been limited to depression in adults, the high prevalence of depression in children has come to recent attention. The increased incidence of suicide among adolescents and even younger children make this issue even more important to the clinician. Parallel to this interest have been new inroads into our diagnostic assessment of depression in children. Twenty years ago, depression was considered rare in childhood; when it existed, it was characterized primarily by "depressive equivalents," such as eating difficulties, school problems, and risk-taking behavior. It is now recognized that in addition to these behaviors, children also manifest many symptoms similar to those that characterize adult depressions. (The reader is referred to overviews on this topic [Puig-Antich 1980].)

Depression in the elderly, even in the very old (those over 85), has also been better appreciated in recent years. Issues that complicate this diagnosis include the need to separate real somatic difficulties from those secondary to depression, the tendency of the elderly to experience a "pseudodementia" when depressed, and the relative lack of social and occupational roles for the elderly that would bring symptoms to attention earlier in the younger patient.

CASE HISTORY

A 54-year-old white female complained that "my sins are coming back to haunt me," and reported the fear that she was "slipping back to another nervous breakdown," and that she felt like it was "1962 all over again." Despite the patient's insistence that she was "having a nervous breakdown" and her constant return to a description of how her brain felt "like it's melting," she was able to provide a detailed history over the course of two interviews. She reported taking badly the news of her daughter's remarriage and move to California two months ago. Since that time, she had been worrying about her daughter's mental stability and about the problems she had caused her daughter because of her own hospitalization when the daughter was only a year old. These concerns made it difficult for her to sleep; she reported waking up after only two or three hours' sleep during recent weeks. She also reported anorexia, coupled with a fear that she might be developing a bowel cancer like her mother had before her death. Additional somatic concerns included constipation, urinary frequency, and headaches, accompanied by a fear that her brain was "rotting." She denied auditory hallucinations or feelings of being controlled by outside forces, thought broadcasting, grandiosity, or thought insertion. She reported active suicidal ideation, including a plan. A mental status examination showed marked psychomotor retardation and sadness. Orientation, judgment, and memory were intact. The patient's cognition was sluggish but appeared intact with effort. Her response to proverbs confirmed the ability to abstract.

The patient's psychiatric history revealed episodes similar to the current one, with only fair between-episode functioning. In addition to these depressive episodes, she had had at least two periods (lasting two to four weeks each) of increased anxiety, hypersexual ideation (but not actual sexual activity), lack of sleep and increased activity manifested in poetry writing and excessive walking (12 to 15 miles at a time). She had been hospitalized in 1967 (at age 35), 1972, and 1980; each time she was diagnosed as schizophrenic and treated with an antipsychotic agent.

The patient's family history was positive for alcoholism (father) and for probable sociopathy (father and brother); she also had a maternal grandmother who "was depressed a lot." The patient was the first of five siblings. She reported that her parents had fought continually (both verbally and physically) throughout their lives together. Her father had died 15 years ago; her mother, 9 years ago. Her only happy childhood memories were the positive feedback she had received from teachers and her friendships with female friends up until the time of her marriage. She reported always feeling "down" about herself—about both her personality and her body. She also stated that she had always felt powerless to change her life. These features had continued to make it difficult for her to seek employment or to begin new social relationships. The patient tended to blame herself for all her difficulties.

The patient had completed high school and college and had worked as an editorial assistant for a popular magazine. She reported having many friends and was reasonably happy until she began to become depressed over minor disappointments. Her marriage, and her husband's subsequent development of an alcohol problem, added to her distress. She had been recently divorced at the time of her first psychiatric admission.

The patient denied using alcohol but smoked two packs of cigarettes a day. She had also had a continued problem with weight control. She had not abused street or prescription drugs.

Psychological testing showed the following:

MCMI–Higher than the norm in depressive, narcissistic, and dependency scales
Weichler Adult Intelligence Scale–115 (verbal, 121; performance, 108)
Hamilton Depression Scale–25

Diagnosis

Axis I–Major depression with psychosis; past history of manic episodes
Axis II–Mixed personality disorder, dependent and narcissistic
Axis III–Developing emphysema
Axis IV–Daughter leaving home
Axis V–5 (poor)

Initial Treatment Plan

1. Admit to a psychiatric unit.
2. Begin tricyclic antidepressants. Start on imipramine 50 mg per day and increase to 150 mg by day 10.
3. Institute suicide precautions.
4. Consult with pulmonary medicine for further evaluation of emphysema.
5. Schedule for group therapy to renew skills, confidence, and satisfaction in social relationships and to decrease social isolation.
6. Provide opportunity to develop a therapeutic relationship with one therapist to evaluate capacity/need for individual psychotherapy.

Later Considerations

1. Consider another antidepressant if imipramine (at adequate blood level) does not improve mood in three weeks.
2. Begin patient education on bipolar illness, with stress on possible use of lithium in the future.
3. Consider the advisability of cognitive therapy, particularly if cognitive style of helplessness and self-attribution continues after mood improves.
4. Evaluate social support resources in patient's life and her resistance to seeking them.
5. Refer to a smoking-cessation program.
6. Include maintenance antidepressants and individual psychotherapy in discharge plans.

This case highlights several features in the presentation and history of the patient with an affective disorder.

1. Life events, particularly losses, frequently antecede an affective episode.
2. Patients previously diagnosed and treated for schizophrenia may well have been misdiagnosed and may actually have had a recurrent affective illness (Akiskal and Puzantian 1979).
3. Unsuccessful treatment of affective states frequently results in marked social deterioration, further confusing the diagnostic picture.
4. Manic episodes may occur late in the clinical course of bipolar illness.

Affective disorders generally respond favorably to treatment. The efficacy of lithium in bipolar states, of tricyclics or electroshock therapy in major depression, and of cognitive or interpersonal psychotherapy (alone or in combination with antidepressants) in major depression without psychosis are well established (Weissman and Prusoff 1979). Individual and family therapy, psychoeducation, group psychotherapy, and support groups are also beneficial in preventing relapse and in early symptom recognition. The potential for successful treatment, coupled with the awareness of the consequences of misdiagnosis (in terms of, for example, suicide, loss of social-occupational functioning, and loss of self-esteem) makes the evaluation of affective disorders critical. In the absence of any definitive psychological or biological test, the clinical interview is the essential tool of the diagnostic process.

REFERENCES

Akiskal, H. S., and Puzantian, V. R. (1979). Psychiatric forum of depression and mania. *Psychiatric Clinics of North America* 2:419.

Annitto, W., and Shopsin, B. (1979). Neuropharmacology of mania. In *Manic Illness*, ed. B. Shopsin. New York: Raven Press.

Carroll, B. J., Feinberg, M., Smouse, P. E., Rawson, S. G., and Greden, J. F. (1981). The Carroll rating scale for depression. *British Journal of Psychiatry* 138:194-201.

Clayton, P. (1974). Mortality and morbidity in the first year of widowhood. *Archives of General Psychiatry* 30:747.

Dohrenwend, B. P., Shrout, P. E., and Egri, G. (1980). Nonspecific psychological distress and other dimensions of psychopathology. *Archives of General Psychiatry* 37:1229–1230.

Flaherty, J., et al. (1983). The role of social support in the functioning of patients with unipolar depression. *American Journal of Psychiatry* 140:473–476.

Frank, J. (1973). *Persuasion and Healing*. Baltimore: Johns Hopkins Press, pp. 113–315.

Gaviria, F. M., and Flaherty, J. A. (1988). Diagnostic assessment of depression. In *Psychiatry: Diagnosis and Therapy*. Norwalk, CT: Appleton & Lange.

Gaviria, M., Flaherty, J., and Val, E. (1982). A comparison of bipolar patients with and without borderline personality organization. *Psychiatric Journal of the University of Ottawa* 7:190–198.

Hirschfield, R., and Klerman, G. (1979). Personality attributes in affective disorders. *American Journal of Psychiatry* 137:67.

Paykel, E., et al. (1969). Life events and depression: a controlled study. *Archives of General Psychiatry* 21:753.

Poznansky, E. O. (1982). Depression in children and adolescents. In *Affective Disorders: Psychopathology and Treatment*, ed. Val, E., Gaviria, F. M., and Flaherty, J. A. Chicago: Yearbook Medical Publishers.

Price, J. (1960). The genetics of depressive behavior. *British Journal of Psychiatry* 2:37.

Puig-Antich, J. (1980). Affective disorders in childhood. *Psychiatric Clinics of North America* 3:403–424.

Rosenthal, N. E., Sach, D. A., Carpenter, C. J., et al. (1985). Antidepressant effects of light in seasonal affective disorder. *American Journal of Psychiatry* 172:163–170.

Weissman, M., and Prusoff, B. A. (1979). The efficacy of drugs and psychotherapy in the treatment of acute depressive episodes. *American Journal of Psychiatry* 136:555.

Weissman, M. M., and Boyd, M. (1985). Epidemiology of affective disorders. In *Comprehensive Textbook of Psychiatry*, vol. 4, ed. Kaplan, H. I., Freedman, A. M., and Sadock, B. J. Baltimore: Williams & Wilkins.

8

Substance Abuse

ROBERT J. CRAIG, Ph.D.

Mental health clinicians are increasingly faced with the need to assess substance abuse. However, graduate school curricula often do not provide sufficient training in this area (Lubin et al. 1986), and only a few articles in isolated contexts have appeared on the subject (Senay 1983, Milby and Rice 1985). Therefore, the purpose of this chapter is to provide a broad overview of clinical interviewing with substance abusers, emphasizing drug (not alcohol) abuse in adult male patients.

DSM-III-R CLASSIFICATION OF SUBSTANCE DISORDERS

The DSM-III-R contains two major classification headings on Axis I for substance-induced conditions: substance-induced organic mental disorder and psychoactive substance use disorder. For substance-induced organic mental disorders, the criteria are mostly substance-specific intoxication or withdrawal states. The diagnoses in the category psychoactive substance use disorders are to be used when the patient meets the substance-specific criteria and when he is currently not in a state of intoxication or withdrawal. As an aside, any individual with a substance use disorder most certainly has had, at some point, substance-induced organic mental disorder.

The substance use disorders are divided into the categories of (1) substance-specific abuse (indicated by a pattern of pathological use, social or occupational impairment, and duration of at least one month) and (2) dependence (indicated by demonstration of tolerance or symptoms of withdrawal). These diagnoses also allow further specification of the course of the disorder (continuous, episodic, in remission, or unspecified).

Because drug addicts tend to be polydrug abusers, it is technically correct to give them multiple diagnoses on Axis I for the many drugs that they use; often the use of each drug takes a different course. By convention, however, we generally place on Axis I only those drugs that require treatment or are the focus of concern for the therapist.

In DSM-III-R, the distinction between abuse and dependence is removed; the definition of dependence is broadened to include clinically significant behaviors that indicate the degree of involvement with drugs;

an identical set of symptoms and behaviors is used to determine dependence on all classes of drugs; and a system for rating the severity of dependence is provided (Rounsaville et al. 1986).

DSM-III-R is likely to be most useful regarding treatment concerns when the patient meets the criteria for substance-specific dependence or withdrawal. In such circumstances, referral for medical management is indicated.

ABUSE LIABILITY

The Controlled Substances Act was passed to enable the federal government to minimize the quantity of drugs of abuse that are available to persons prone to abuse drugs. The Food and Drug Administration and the Drug Enforcement Administration share the responsibility for enforcing the act. This law set up a five-tier system to classify psychoactive drugs in terms of their abuse potential and accepted use in medicine. Each class of drugs may also differ in terms of registration requirements, record keeping, manufacturing quantity, distribution restrictions, dispensing limits, security precautions, reporting mechanisms, and criminal penalties for trafficking. Table 8–1 contains the Schedule of Drugs set up by this classification system.

RELIABILITY OF ADDICT SELF-REPORTS

Because most information about drug-abusing patients is based on clinical interview and self-report data, a major question is whether the information provided by addicts can be trusted. Surprisingly, most of the research has indicated a high degree of correspondence between self-reported history information and data obtained from family, criminal records, and other significant sources (Bale 1979, Bale et al. 1981, Ben-Yehuda 1980, Bonito et al. 1976, Maddux and Desmond 1975, Maisto et al. 1982–1983, Pompi and Shreiner 1979, Rounsaville et al. 1981). Discrepancies have been attributable to normal memory decay and the possible masking of specific crimes.

These conclusions are based on a patient–therapist relationship in which trust and rapport have been established and in which the patient believes that the therapist is on his side (Senay 1983). When evasiveness and suspiciousness have been eliminated and when addicts believe that therapists will keep the information confidential, they give reliable and valid life-history information.

DIAGNOSTIC INTERVIEW SCHEDULES FOR ADDICTIVE DISORDERS

Diagnostic interviews can be unstructured or structured. Before we cover the unstructured interview, which is most prevalent, we will

Table 8-1. The Controlled Substances Act Schedule of Drugs

Schedule	Basic requirements	Examples
I	Substances with a high potential for abuse and no currently accepted medical use. They are available for research only.	heroin marijuana LSD
II	Substances with high potential for abuse, but with a currently accepted medical use. These drugs may lead to severe physical and psychological dependence. They are available only by written prescription with no refills.	morphine methadone Demerol amphetamines cocaine PCP
III	Substances with potential for abuse, but less so than for drugs in Class II. They have an accepted medical use. Abuse may result in low to moderate physical dependence or high psychological dependence. They are available only by written or oral prescription, with 5 refills permitted in 6 months with medical authorization.	Dilantin Doriden Preludin butabarbital
IV	Substances with less potential for abuse and with accepted medical use. Abuse may lead to low physical or psychological dependence. Refills are permitted as in Class III drugs.	Dalmane chloral hydrate phenobarbital pentazocine phenfluramine
V	Substances with low potential for abuse and accepted medical use. Abuse may lead to limited physical or psychological dependence. Some may be available without a prescription depending on state laws.	Cheracol cough syrup with codeine Robitussin A-C cough syrup

review the published interview schedules available for use with the addictive disorders.

Addiction Severity Index (ASI)

The ASI is a structured clinical interview designed to assess dysfunctional areas affected by substance abuse. Its administration time is 20 to 30 minutes, and it provides a 9-point problem severity rating in each of six areas (substance abuse, employment, and medical, legal, family/social, and psychiatric functioning). It has excellent reliability and validity with substance-abusing patients (McLellan et al. 1980, 1985, Kosten et al. 1983).

Substance Abuse Problem Checklist (SAPC)

Carroll (1984) developed the SAPC as a paper-and-pencil, self-report inventory. It consists of 377 problem statements grouped into eight categories (motivation for treatment, health, personality, social relationships, job, misuse of leisure time, and religious/spiritual and legal problems). It is designed as a cost-effective, rapid screening instrument for use in initial assessment and for treatment planning.

The ASI appears to be more psychometrically established than the SAPC, has a more solid research base, and is becoming well received among substance abuse researchers. The SAPC is a new clinical instrument that has potential practicality in clinical settings but requires further validation.

DIAGNOSTIC INSTRUMENTS

Laboratory Tests

In settings in which medical tests are available, the most useful test is the urinalysis, in this case as a toxicology screen for the presence of illicit drugs. There are many analytic drug-screening methods, but the most frequently used are the enzyme multiplied immunoassay technique (EMIT), the radioimmunoassay (RIA), and the thin-layer chromotography (TLC). Each method has advantages and disadvantages. Most urine samples are tested with one procedure and confirmed with an alternate procedure to reduce error rates.

Before accepting laboratory test results on urine, the clinician must ensure that the test has been confirmed with another procedure. Even with confirmation, there are many problems with mass urine-screening programs, such as sensitivity levels, lack of specificity, cross-reactivity, and human error, that can produce false positive or false negative results (DeAngelis 1973, Morgan 1984). Furthermore, patients will attempt to influence urine results by diluting their urine with water or vinegar or by using a drug immediately before the test to ensure positive results if it meets their interests. All urine samples with this population should be taken under direct observation. However, the half-lives of psychoactive drugs vary, and hence the detectability of drugs in urine also varies. Some drugs (including barbiturates, marijuana, and opiates) are stored longer in tissue than are others (such as cocaine). A positive urine test result may indicate past use (seven to ten days ago) but not current use. A negative result could mean that the patient has used no drug, or it could indicate a low dose and low purity levels that go undetected. Also, a patient may believe that he or she is buying one drug but is actually getting another.

The urine test itself may be invalid for other reasons. Hansen and colleagues (1985) evaluated the performance of 13 laboratories servicing 262 methadone clinics. These labs were sent preanalyzed urine as if it were from routine patient samples. The error rate ranged from 0 to 100 percent, which suggests that these labs are often unable to detect drugs at clinically useful concentration levels.

There are also ethical and sociopsychological aspects of drug tests (Lewis et al. 1972) that must be understood. Urine tests must be clinically interpreted with the same degree of scrutiny that one would apply to psychological tests.

Psychological Tests

The Minnesota Multiphasic Personality Inventory (MMPI) is the most frequently used psychological test for assessing substance abuse (Craig 1982). Drug addicts tend to have T scores above 70 on the clinical scales of Pd (psychopathic deviance), Sc (schizophrenia), and Ma (hypomania). They also have moderate elevations on the F (validity) and D (depression) scales. Craig (1984a) compared 442 profiles of narcotic addicts in treatment based on multiple methods of classification. He found that the 49′/94′, 42′/24′, and 48′/84′ two-point configurations accounted for 44 percent of the MMPI configurations. However, 33 different MMPI profiles were obtained so that clinicians would expect to find heterogeneity within this population (Craig 1984a).

The MacAndrew Alcoholism scale (MAC) of the MMPI was developed to detect alcoholism among psychiatric outpatients. Subsequent research has indicated that the MAC should be construed as a generic substance abuse scale because drug addicts also attain significant elevations on this scale (Craig 1984b, Preng and Clopton 1986). Patients with elevated MAC scores should be interviewed specifically for substance abuse.

A few other psychological tests may be useful with drug addicts. The Millon Clinical Multiaxial Inventory (MCMI) drug abuse scale shows excellent concurrent validity (Flynn and McMahon 1984) and reveals distinct personality patterns and styles among substance abusers (Craig et al. 1985). The Inwald Personality Inventory also has a drug abuse scale, although it is based more on self-reported patterns of drug use and relies on honesty.

Concurrent Psychiatric Diagnosis

Drug abuse may be a primary disorder, may be a disorder secondary to other psychiatric conditions, or may coexist independently with current psychiatric disorders. It is therefore required that the presence of other Axis I conditions be routinely assessed in substance abusers. Research has shown that depression, alcoholism, and antisocial personality disorders are frequently associated with drug abuse (Gawin and Kleber 1986, Khantzian and Treece 1985, O'Brien et al. 1984, Rounsaville et al. 1982), although the full range of DSM-III-R personality disorders can be expected (Craig 1988). Consideration of concurrent psychiatric conditions has important treatment implications because drug abusers rated high in psychiatric severity tend not to improve despite various kinds of treatment (McLellan et al. 1983).

ALCOHOLISM AND DRUG ABUSE

Alcohol plays a significant role for many drug addicts. Some were alcoholic before developing a drug habit; others used alcohol (1) to maintain or intensify a high, (2) to ease withdrawal, or (3) as a substitute when their preferred drug was not available. Prevalence estimates of alcoholism among drug addicts range from 10 percent to 50 percent, with modal prevalence at around 20 percent (Green and Jaffe 1977, Belenko 1979). However, there is widespread variation depending on local base rates. I examined 100 drug addicts in treatment and found that 70 percent met DSM-III criteria for alcohol abuse and 30 percent of this group met the criteria for alcohol dependence one month before admission. Thus drug addicts must be thoroughly assessed for alcohol use.

CONFIDENTIALITY

It is extremely important that psychologists dealing with drug addicts become familiar with the federal regulations governing patient records for alcohol and drug abusers (US Department of Health and Human Services 1987). These laws are considered the most restrictive and the most protective and are a model for other medical and mental health records (Lanman 1980). As a general rule, all patient records related to the treatment of drug or alcohol abuse are considered confidential, although this status may be waived with the patient's written informed consent. Recipients of the information may not redisclose the information without obtaining another signed consent. Medical emergencies, audits, and court orders are situations in which these regulations allow for disclosure of confidential information without consent. The regulations also prohibit undercover agents or informants from being enrolled in drug and alcohol programs unless they are granted permission by a court order. If a law enforcement agency wants to know whether a certain patient is attending a program, the program is prohibited by these regulations from acknowledging or denying the patient's participation. The regulations provide a very specific format and content for "consent to release information" documents, and the reader is urged to review these regulations.

COUNTERTRANSFERENCE

Drug addicts have the capacity to engender powerful countertransferential reactions, even in a brief diagnostic interview. These patients are often aggressive, demanding, confrontive, or defensive, and they enjoy exposing the therapist's vulnerabilities (Levine and Stephens 1971). This "oral insatiability" is further complicated by the behaviors and life-style that accompany drug abuse, especially criminal activity. It strains the most objective clinician not to experience emotional reactions to these processes.

Imhof and colleagues (1983) detailed common countertransferential attitudes evoked by the drug-abusing population. They included the following reactions: (1) acting in the role of a good parent rescuing a bad, impulsive child, (2) reacting with anger when the patient challenges the therapist's knowledge or authority, (3) aligning with the patient by identifying with antiauthority stories or by vicariously romanticizing the drug addict life-style, and (4) emotionally withdrawing, becoming indifferent, or feeling bored, angry, or burnt out.

It is recommended that clinicians constantly monitor their emotional reactions when interviewing drug addicts and seek consultation or supervision for catharsis and growth. Some of the therapist's reactions may have important therapeutic implications and may form the basis of treatment recommendations for the future management of the patient.

RECOMMENDED INTERVIEW FORMAT

Table 8–2 suggests an interview format to be used with drug addicts. This format should not be followed in a rote, sequential manner; it merely depicts the content areas that should be covered by the time the interview process has been completed.

General Assessment

Because drugs affect cognitive processes, it is necessary to evaluate the patient's mental status and concurrent psychiatric condition. The mental status exam need not be a formal one. One can obtain most of the necessary information from the patient by asking content questions in other areas.

Presenting Complaint

Drug addicts rarely seek treatment out of a desire to change themselves. Their motivation for treatment is almost always external and precipitated by pressures or a crisis. Loss of a residence, a spouse's or boyfriend's or girlfriend's threats to leave unless the patient stops using drugs, running out of drugs, unexpected physical symptoms, untoward reactions to drugs, and pending legal difficulties are typical reasons that drug addicts seek treatment. Many have hidden agendas, and it is important to identify them early in the treatment relationships.

Drug Use

The therapist must determine whether the patient needs medical referral for detoxification, withdrawal, or possible delirium tremens (DTs). The list of items presented in Table 8–2 provides for this type of assessment.

TABLE 8-2. Recommended Format for Diagnostic Interviews with Substance Abusers

General assessment
- Do a mental status exam
- Evaluate the patient for presence of concurrent psychiatric disorders

Presenting complaint
- Assess the patient's motivation for treatment
- Determine what brought the patient in
- Determine the patient's goals (look for hidden agendas)

Drug use
- Identify drugs used
- Determine the amount and the frequency of use (currently and over time)
- Determine the route of administration
- Identify amount and time of last use
- Determine the pattern or context of use
- Assess tolerance, dependence, and withdrawal states
- Include an assessment for alcohol abuse and alcoholism

Effects of drug abuse
- Assess the patient's work history
- Inquire about legal problems
- Explore the nature and the quality of interpersonal relationships and family interaction
- Assess the patient's psychological state for subjective distress
- Explore leisure time and the recreational use of drugs
- Determine presence of physical problems
- Look for enabling situations or relationships

Special considerations
- Evaluate sexual dysfunction
- Review for suicide history
- Review for child abuse history

Treatment considerations
- Identify previous treatment for both drugs and alcohol
- Determine whether there were any previous psychiatric treatment episodes and the reasons for them
- Check for overdose history
- Determine whether the patient participated in any major drug treatment modality (detoxification, methadone maintenance, antagonist treatment, therapeutic communities, outpatient counseling) and evaluate the effects
- Explore the patient's history of abstinence (length and circumstances)
- Determine the patient's previous attempts at self-treatment

DSM-III-R diagnoses
- Expect multiple diagnostic categories to be present on Axis I
- Expect at least one personality disorder on Axis II

Treatment recommendations
- Review with the patient your suggested treatment plan
- Attempt to reach mutually agreeable goals

For treatment purposes, information about the pattern and context of drug use is particularly useful and can lead to meaningful intervention strategies.

Effects of Drugs

Drugs affect cognitive, social, and familial relationships, affect ability to function at work and play, and result in legal difficulties or illegal activities. They also lead to an array of physical problems, most commonly abscesses, cellulitis, chest pains, seizures, hepatitis, toxic psychotic states, panic reactions, flashbacks, and belligerent and aggressive behavior.

Male drug addicts tend to structure their relationships in certain kinds of ways. Some get women to take care of them, satisfying their unresolved dependency needs, but all the while they manifest a pseudoassertive manner (Ganger and Shugart 1966, Wellish et al. 1970). They tend to be enmeshed with their parents or parent surrogates in alliances that cross generational lines and are in reversal of the hierarchical organization of their families, which may perpetuate addictive behavior (Kaufman 1981, Kosten et al. 1982, Madanes et al. 1980).

Addicts create "enabling" relationships with others that are characterized by family behaviors that perpetuate drug abuse. Awareness of these relational patterns can form the basis of a treatment plan that may involve significant others.

Special Considerations

Drugs interfere with sexual performance in both sexes and produce a variety of sexual dysfunctions (Abel 1984, Buffum 1982). Addicts frequently present with suicidal histories of recent overdoses (Murphy et al. 1983) and may have been abused as children. Although suicide history is frequently assessed, many clinicians ignore a review of sexual functioning and child abuse history in routine assessment. A complete assessment should include these important treatment variables.

Treatment Considerations

The areas listed in Table 8–2 provide many key variables to explore when assessing treatment history. A history of previous abstinence gives some good clues to ego strength and alerts the therapist to possible recalcitrant or refractory behaviors.

Diagnosis and Treatment

After a diagnosis has been reached and a tentative treatment plan has been developed, the plan should be explored with the patient. The therapist should check for resistance and attempt to reach mutually agreeable goals. The most common treatment modalities for drug abusers include detoxification, maintenance or antagonist treatment, therapeutic communities, outpatient drug-free counseling, and group and family therapy, although a multimodal approach is the most popular (Craig 1985).

CASE HISTORY

The patient was a 32-year-old, married, unemployed, white man in stable condition who was seen on consultation in a medical intensive care unit after an overdose of Valium. He had a history of one previous outpatient psychiatric treatment and two previous inpatient treatment episodes for drug abuse. He had also been on methadone maintenance as an outpatient for several years.

An immediate precipitant for his request for another treatment attempt was the fact that his methadone maintenance clinic was being closed, and the patient, having no other legal source of methadone, had begun to buy street methadone to avoid withdrawal. He called me to arrange admission to my program. Before coming to the hospital he had been in a car accident that caused a seizure disorder. He was placed on methadone to avoid withdrawal, barbiturates to control seizures, and Percodan for pain and was then released from the hospital.

The patient telephoned again to arrange admission, requesting detoxification from methadone. His speech was slurred and he sounded confused and lethargic, but his reasoning was intact. Arrangements were made for him to come for admission the following morning.

He reported to the hospital not on the prearranged day, but on the following day. He arrived too late to be processed and was told by the physician to return the next day. Instead, he went to a local public hospital, where he was placed on an alcoholic ward, despite the fact that he did not drink. He left the next day and claimed that he had walked 30 miles (he probably had hitched rides also) back to my hospital and applied for admission to the drug abuse program. Upon arriving, he experienced significant delays in processing. His medical records could not be located quickly, and he was sent to several locations in the hospital. He was among the last patients scheduled to be seen that day and reported feeling "depressed and anxious; I wasn't being taken care of." He began to feel that he was "getting sick" (he was experiencing symptoms of withdrawal), so he "went into the bathroom and took 25 Valium tablets." The patient took another 25 Valium tablets shortly thereafter. He was taken to the emergency room and treated for a drug overdose. He denied that this was a suicide attempt, claiming that he had taken the Valium "to calm down."

His history included a father who "was a heavy drinker" but provided for his family and was not abusive. The patient had been involved in race riots while in high school, and his parents had sent him to live out of state. He had several brothers who were career military men, so he enlisted in the army after graduation; he was sent to Vietnam and was made a medic in a triage hospital. He said, "I couldn't handle it." A physician had given him drugs to keep him awake and later offered him "whatever I wanted" from "pills laying all around." He began using opium, hashish, and heroin from the illegal market as well. He said that men "kept coming in with missing limbs and open guts and I couldn't take it." He reported abusing drugs almost continually since leaving the service.

The patient reported a history of nightmares (twice a year), mildly intrusive memories of Vietnam, and occasional, infrequent flashbacks. He refused to talk to anyone about his war experiences. He denied having an exaggerated startle response, and he had no survivor guilt.

He had not worked since leaving the service, but he had a financial interest in a family business that provided for the support of his wife and children. He said that there was a communication problem between him and his wife, and he admitted to delayed ejaculation, which his wife did not consider normal. He said that his wife was talking about leaving him, but he denied that there was a "conflict" because, he said, he was "the problem." He blamed doctors for causing his problems, saying that a doctor had called his wife and told her that he had overdosed and was in intensive care and that the doctors had not successfully treated his drug abuse problem. He said that he had recently taken a temporary job as a mailman and feared losing it as a result of recent hospitalization. He denied any history of legal problems.

His urine test results were positive for methadone and barbiturates and negative for all other drugs. His psychological test files were searched for previous results, and his MMPI profile during psychiatric admission was 8617′. Two years later, upon first treatment for drug abuse, the MMPI profile was 7934′. One year later, the MMPI profile was 4′29.

DSM-III-R Diagnoses

1. Psychoactive substance use disorder; opioid (methadone) dependence, continuous (304.01); rule out (r/o) posttraumatic stress disorder (PTSD), chronic, delayed (309.89). Sexual disorder was not classified elsewhere (delayed ejaculation secondary to drug use, 302.90).
2. Provisional diagnosis was mixed personality disorder, dependent and passive-aggressive traits (301.90); r/o dependent personality (301.60); r/o passive-aggressive personality disorder (301.84).
3. Status posttrauma seizure disorder.
4. a. 4–closing of methadone clinic;
   b. 2–lack of immediate attention during hospital processing.
5. Global assessment functioning (GAF) 1: 60; GAF 2: 55

Treatment Plan

1. Detoxify patient from opiates.
2. Observe for signs of PTSD after patient has been detoxified.
3. Observe for suicidal ideation.
4. Schedule for individual and group therapy to improve patient's ability to deal with stress and frustrations, to reduce his tendency to internalize anger and hostility, and to reduce his externalization of blame.

5. Contact patient's wife for further history; evaluate for possible marital therapy after discharge.
6. Encourage patient to complete maximum length of stay in order to begin to learn how it feels to be off drugs.
7. Develop posthospitalization plan geared toward relapse prevention.
8. Maintain patient on barbiturates for seizure disorder; provide education if necessary.

SOME PRACTICAL SUGGESTIONS FOR THE THERAPIST

1. Do not be judgmental. You are a therapist, not a judge.
2. Remind the patient that the relationship is confidential. If necessary, remind the patient of this again when you discuss legal problems and illegal activities.
3. Do not present yourself as an expert in drug abuse if you are not an expert. Be an expert on human behavior. Allow the patient to educate you. When patients use unfamiliar drug slang, ask for clarification. Do not pretend to understand if you do not; patients will immediately sense such insincerity.
4. Make sure that you determine the patient's motivation for treatment and the effects of drug use, in addition to identifying the type and the pattern of drug use.
5. Do not assume that drug abuse is the patient's only problem. Explicitly evaluate him for concurrent psychiatric disorders, especially depression, personality disorders, and alcoholism.
6. When there is a discrepancy between the addict's self-report and the urinalysis results, do not assume that the laboratory data are correct.
7. Look for the "con" (the patient's lies). Confront the patient when you see it. Ask for the truth.
8. Get collateral information, if possible. If you plan to contact a significant other, remember that you must have a signed consent form before initiating such contact.
9. All other principles of good diagnostic interviewing apply to drug addicts as well. Set aside enough time to do a thorough job of interviewing the patient. Avoid interruptions. Be empathic, genuine, understanding, and congruent. Above all, be professional. Drug addicts like to relate to therapists as if they are peers. Keep your professional distance and boundaries.
10. After completing the interview, give the patient feedback on your observations. If a hospital staff will be treating the patient, tell him that "we'll put our heads together and figure out the best approach to your situation." Keep promises. Later, try to get the patient to agree to the treatment plan.

SUBSTANCE ABUSE REFERRALS

When should a therapist refer a patient to a substance abuse program or to a therapist who specializes in substance abuse? Until research establishes reliable guidelines, the following clinical indicators are offered:

Therapists should refer patients to a substance abuse program when (1) the therapist does not possess the expertise to treat either the primary substance abuse problem or any coexisting psychiatric condition; (2) the patient's drug abuse is out of control; (3) the patient's drug abuse becomes a serious danger to himself, to friends or family, or to the general public; (4) the patient has medical problems associated with drug abuse; or (5) the patient cannot be managed on an ambulatory basis.

Therapists should refer patients to a substance abuse specialist (1) when the therapist does not possess the expertise to treat the primary substance abuse problem or any coexisting psychiatric condition; (2) as part of a plan to follow the patient after release from inpatient care for relapse prevention; and (3) when the patient's substance abuse is reactive to other primary problems that can be resolved by psychotherapy.

SPECIAL POPULATIONS

This chapter was geared toward the treatment of adult male drug abusers. Treatment of special populations of drug abusers (such as female addicts, adolescent drug abusers, Mexican-American and black addicts, iatrogenic medical addicts, and impaired professionals) requires further knowledge in key content areas and somewhat different approaches modified to their particular circumstances. The reader is urged to consult the many references dealing with these special populations.

REFERENCES

Abel, E. L. (1984). Opiates and sex. *Journal of Psychoactive Drugs* 16:205–216.

American Psychiatric Association (1987). *Diagnostic and Statistical Manual of Mental Disorders*, 3rd ed., rev. Washington, DC: APA.

Bale, R. N. (1979). The validity and reliability of self-reported data from heroin addicts: mailed questionnaires compared with face-to-face interviews. *International Journal of the Addictions* 14:993–1000.

Bale, R. N., Van Stone, W. W., Engelsing, T. M., and Zarcone, V. P. (1981). The validity of self-reported heroin use. *International Journal of the Addictions* 16:1387–1398.

Belenko, S. (1979). Alcohol abuse by heroin addicts: review of research findings and issues. *International Journal of the Addictions* 14:965–975.

Ben-Yehuda, N. (1980). Are addict self-reports to be trusted? *International Journal of the Addictions* 15:1265–1270.

Bonito, A. J., Nurco, D. N., and Shaffer, J. W. (1976). The veridicality of addict self-reports in social research. *International Journal of the Addictions* 11:719–724.

Buffum, J. (1982). Pharmacosexology: the effects of drugs on sexual function: a review. *Journal of Psychoactive Drugs* 14:5–44.

Carroll, J. F. (1984). The Substance Abuse Problem Checklist: a new clinical aid for drug and alcohol treatment dependency. *Journal of Substance Abuse Treatment* 1:31–36.

Craig, R. J. (1982). Personality characteristics of heroin addicts: review of empirical research 1976–1979. *International Journal of the Addictions* 17:227–248.

——— (1984a). A comparison of MMPI profiles of heroin addicts based on multiple methods of classification. *Journal of Personality Assessment* 48:115–120.

——— (1984b). MMPI substance abuse scales on drug addicts with or without concurrent alcoholism. *Journal of Personality Assessment* 48:495–499.

——— (1985). Multimodal treatment package for substance abuse treatment programs. *Professional Psychology: Research and Practice* 16:271–285.

——— (1988). A psychometric study of the prevalence of DSM-III personality disorders among treated opiate addicts. *International Journal of the Addictions* 23:115–124.

Craig, R. J., Verinis, S. J., and Wexler, S. (1985). Personality characteristics of drug addicts and alcoholics on the Millon Clinical Multiaxial Inventory. *Journal of Personality Assessment* 49:156–160.

DeAngelis, G. G. (1973). Testing for drugs: techniques and issues. *International Journal of the Addictions* 8:997–1014.

Flynn, P. M., and McMahon, R. C. (1984). An examination of the drug abuse scale of the Millon Clinical Multiaxial Inventory. *International Journal of the Addictions* 19:459–468.

Ganger, R., and Shugart, G. (1966). The heroin addict's pseudoassertive behavior and family dynamics. *Social Casework*, December, pp. 643–649.

Gawin, F. H., and Kleber, H. D. (1986). Abstinence symptomatology and psychiatric diagnosis in cocaine abusers: clinical observations. *Archives of General Psychiatry* 43:107–113.

Green, J., and Jaffe, J. H. (1977). Alcohol and opiate dependence: a review. *Journal of Studies on Alcohol* 38:1274–1293.

Hansen, H. J., Caudill, S. P., and Boone, J. (1985). Crisis in drug testing: results of CDC blind studies. *Journal of the American Medical Association* 253:2382–2387.

Imhof, J., Hirsh, R., and Terenzi, R. E. (1983). Countertransferential and attitudinal considerations in the treatment of drug abuse and addiction. *International Journal of the Addictions* 18:491–510.

Kaufman, E. (1981). Family structure of narcotic addicts. *International Journal of the Addictions* 16:273–282.

Khantzian, E. J., and Treece, C. (1985). DSM-III psychiatric diagnosis of narcotic addicts. *Archives of General Psychiatry* 42:1067–1071.

Kosten, T. R., Jalali, B., and Kleber, H. D. (1982). Complementary marital roles of male heroin addicts: evaluation and intervention tactics. *American Journal of Drug and Alcohol Abuse* 9:155–169.

Kosten, T. R., Rounsaville, B. J., and Kleber, H. D. (1983). Concurrent validity of the Addiction Severity Index. *Journal of Nervous and Mental Disease* 171:606–610.

Lanman, R. B. (1980). The federal confidentiality protections for alcohol and drug abuse patient records: a model for mental health and other medical records? *American Journal of Orthopsychiatry* 50:666–677.

Levine, S., and Stephens, R. (1971). Games addicts play. *Psychiatric Quarterly* 45:584–592.

Lewis, V. S., Petersen, D. M., Geis, G., and Pollack, S. C. (1972). Ethical and socio-psychological aspects of urinalysis to detect heroin use. *British Journal of Addictions* 67:303–307.

Lubin, B., Brady, K., Woodward, L., and Thomas, E. A. (1986). Graduate professional psychology training in alcoholism and substance abuse: 1984. *Professional Psychology: Research and Practice* 17:151–154.

Madanes, C., Lic, J. D., and Harbin, H. (1980). Family ties of heroin addicts. *Archives of General Psychiatry* 37:889–894.

Maddux, J. F., and Desmond, D. P. (1975). Reliability and validity of information from chronic heroin users. *Journal of Psychiatric Research* 12:87–95.

Maisto, S. A., Sobell, L. C., and Sobell, M. D. (1982–1983). Corroboration of drug abusers' self-reports through the use of multiple data sources. *American Journal of Drug and Alcohol Abuse* 9:301–308.

McLellan, A. T., Luborsky, L., Cacciola, L., et al. (1985). *Guide to the Addiction Severity Index: background, administration, and field testing results* (National Institute on Drug Abuse Treatment Research Report, DHHS Publication No. AD 85-1419). Rockville, MD: US Department of Health and Human Services.

McLellan, A. T., Luborsky, L., Woody, G. E., and O'Brien, C. P. (1980). An improved diagnostic evaluation instrument for substance abuse patients: the Addiction Severity Index. *Journal of Nervous and Mental Disease* 168:26–33.

McLellan, A. T., Luborsky, L., Woody, G. E., et al. (1983). Predicting response to alcohol and drug abuse treatments: role of psychiatric severity. *Archives of General Psychiatry* 40:620–625.

Milby, J., and Rice, J. A. (1985). Drug abuse. In *Diagnostic Interviewing*, ed. M. Hersen and S. Turner, pp. 183–204. New York: Plenum.

Morgan, J. P. (1984). Problems of mass urine screening for misused drugs. *Journal of Psychoactive Drugs* 16:305–317.

Murphy, S. L., Rounsaville, B. J., Eyre, S., and Kleber, H. D. (1983). Suicide attempts in treated opiate addicts. *Comprehensive Psychiatry* 24:79–89.

O'Brien, C. P., Woody, G. E., and McLellan, A. T. (1984). Psychiatric disorders in opioid-dependent patients. *Journal of Clinical Psychiatry* 45:9–13.

Pompi, K. F., and Shreiner, S. C. (1979). The reliability of biographical information obtained from court-stipulated clients newly admitted to treatment. *American Journal of Drug and Alcohol Abuse* 6:79–95.

Preng, K. W., and Clopton, J. R. (1986). The MacAndrew scale: clinical application and theoretical issues. *Journal of Studies on Alcohol* 47:228–236.

Rounsaville, B. J., Kleber, H. D., Wilber, C., et al. (1981). Comparison of opiate addicts' reports of psychiatric history with reports of significant other informants. *American Journal of Drug and Alcohol Abuse* 8:51–69.

Rounsaville, B. J., Spitzer, R. L., and Williams, J. B. (1986). Proposed changes in

DSM-III substance use disorders: description and rationale. *American Journal of Psychiatry* 143:463–468.

Rounsaville, B. J., Weissman, M. M., Kleber, H. D., and Wilber, C. (1982). Heterogeneity of psychiatric diagnosis in treated opiate addicts. *Archives of General Psychiatry* 38:161–166.

Senay, E. C. (1983). *Substance Abuse Disorders in Clinical Practice*. Littleton, MA: PSG Publishing.

US Department of Health, Education, and Welfare (1987). Confidentiality of alcohol and drug abuse patient records. *Federal Register* 52:21796–21814.

Wellish, D. K., Gay, G. R., and McEntee, R. (1970). The easy rider syndrome: a pattern of hetero- and homosexual relationships in a heroin addict population. *Family Process* 9:425–430.

9
Alcoholism

J. SCOTT VERINIS, Ph.D.

It is now almost universally accepted that alcoholism and alcohol abuse is a major health problem in the United States. One in ten Americans is believed to be an abuser of alcohol, and it is believed that one in three Americans has been affected in some adverse way by either their own alcohol problem or someone else's. The economic, social, and human cost to our society is incalculable. The suffering is unimaginable.

One of the ways we as mental health professionals can help with this crisis is to make an accurate diagnosis of alcohol-related problems as early in the treatment process as possible. And yet that is not as easy as it sounds. Alcoholism is an elusive, wily phenomenon that more often than not goes undiagnosed. It is the purpose of this chapter to help the therapist reverse this trend.

DIAGNOSTIC CONCEPTUALIZATIONS

When the word *alcoholism* is used in the media or in everyday conversation, there are assumptions that everyone is talking about the same phenomenon. Alcoholism can take many forms, however, and the diagnostic process can be a frustrating search. Experts themselves aren't in total agreement, although there is some common ground. A brief review of some of the major attempts to conceptualize alcoholism will illuminate this point. (Clinicians interested in further details can consult the excellent review by Paredes [1986], from which much of this material was taken.)

Jellinek

Jellinek is generally regarded as the pioneer who first attempted to diagnostically conceptualize alcoholism. In a series of articles from the 1940s through to the 1960 publication of his *The Disease Concept of Alcoholism* and beyond, he wrestled with the notions of alcohol addiction, chronic alcoholism, and related diagnoses (Jellinek 1952, 1960). What came out of this work is simply the notion of alcoholism as a progressive disease that follows a steady, predictable course once the person is addicted. He listed 43 symptoms and a series of stages that he felt characterized the development of this disease (Table 9–1). These

TABLE 9-1. Progression of the Disease of Alcoholism

Prealcoholic phase
Occasional relief drinking
Constant relief drinking commences
Increase in alcohol tolerance
Prodromal phase
Onset of memory blackouts
Surreptitious drinking
Increasing dependence on alcohol
Urgency of first drinks
Feelings of guilt
Inability to discuss problem
Memory blackouts increase
Crucial phase
Decrease in ability to stop
Drinking when others do so
Drinking bolstered with excuses
Grandiose and aggressive behavior
Persistent remorse
Efforts to control fail repeatedly
Promises and resolutions fail
Tries geographical escapes
Loss of other interests
Family and friends avoided
Work and money troubles
Unreasonable resentments
Neglect of food
Tremors and early-morning shakes
Decrease in alcohol tolerance
Physical deterioration
Chronic phase
Onset of lengthy intoxications
Moral deterioration
Impaired thinking
Drinking with inferiors
Indefinable fears
Unable to initiate action
Obsession with drinking
Vague spiritual desires
All alibis exhausted
Complete defeat admitted
Obsessive drinking continues in vicious circles

Adapted from Jellinek (1952).

phases are described in many texts (for example, Blum and Blum 1967, Taylor and Helzer 1983) but Forrest's (1975) description is especially detailed.

1. PREALCOHOLIC PHASE

The prealcoholic phase is characterized by experimentation and frequent social drinking and is highlighted by the use of alcohol to obtain relief or to escape from unpleasant feelings. Alcohol consumption increases and the person starts to develop a capacity to drink more and more alcohol without becoming intoxicated (*tolerance*).

2. PRODROMAL (OR EXCESSIVE DRINKING) PHASE

The prodromal (or excessive drinking) phase encompasses an increasing preoccupation with alcohol. Drinking is more frequent and excessive. Drinks are gulped; social activities and friendships are alcohol-centered. Memory blackouts also start to occur, and the person starts to hide bottles and avoids talking about drinking. Problems in social, marital, or job functioning also start to occur.

3. CRUCIAL (OR ADDICTION) PHASE

The crucial (or addiction) phase is characterized by the loss of control over drinking. Once the person starts drinking, nothing stops him short of sickness, unconsciousness, or lack of funds. His behavior starts to change: Loss of sexual desire, grandiose promises, paranoid ideation, self-pity, remorse, and aggressive outbursts all start to appear. He becomes increasingly ineffective on the job. Tardiness, absenteeism, and episodes of showing up at work intoxicated start to occur, with the inevitable termination soon following. Memory blackouts increase. His family life becomes severely disrupted, and marital separation or divorce is likely. Physical illnesses related to alcohol abuse start to occur. The morning-after shakes appear. His drinking pattern is characterized by daily, day-long consumption and hoarding of alcohol supply. There are attempts to go on the wagon and even seek treatment during this phase.

4. CHRONIC PHASE

The chronic phase is characterized by serious physical health problems as a result of both alcohol consumption and lack of nutrition. Such problems include alcoholic cirrhosis, pancreatitis, alcoholic neuropathy (at first, numbness in feet and hands; later, loss of control and eventual paralysis), ulcers, alcoholic cardiomyopathy, and severe neurological impairment (confusion, memory impairment, inability to problem solve or perform the simplest life-maintenance tasks). Delirium tremens (the DTs) and tremors are common. Loss of moral values, association with social inferiors, and even a drift downward to skid-row living occur. The drinking pattern is characterized by week-long, and even month-long, periods of constant intoxication and occasionally by the drinking of alcohol-containing products such as shaving lotion because of the unavailability of alcohol.

Jellinek identified five types or species of alcoholism. In *alpha alcoholism*, there is psychological dependence and constant use, but not a progression to the chronic phase. In *beta alcoholism*, there is a serious physical problem as a result of alcohol use, but there are no signs of physical withdrawal or progression to chronic alcoholism. In *gamma alcoholism*, the progression just described occurs. *Delta alcoholism* is characterized by many of the symptoms of gamma alcoholism except that the person can still occasionally control the amount drunk. *Epsilon alcoholism*, or binge drinking, is characterized by long periods of abstinence, and there is not necessarily a progression to chronic alcoholism.

Much of Jellinek's description of types of alcoholism was quickly overlooked, and the gamma type of progressive alcoholism was assumed to be the prototype of the disease. It was apparent to other workers that many alcoholics did not conform to Jellinek's model. Many alcoholics showed only some of the gamma symptomatology, and the orderly progression to chronic status occurred in only a minority. The fact that many alcoholics, after developing problems characteristic of the addictive phase, could then return to less problematic drinking, sometimes without help, was a phenomenon also unexpected from Jellinek's model. Taylor and Helzer (1983) reviewed the evidence and found that (1) symptoms often occurred out of sequence, (2) loss of control is not a universal phenomenon, and (3) drinking tended to moderate rather than worsen over the years for many alcoholics.

World Health Organization

The World Health Organization (1977) conceptualized alcoholism as the "alcohol dependence syndrome." This description focuses primarily on the pattern of drinking, its regularity, its reconstruction of the person's world around drinking, the loss of control, and the development of tolerance and withdrawal symptomatology. Also critical is the ease which one can be readdicted after a period of abstinence. The health, social, and cognitive results of excessive alcohol abuse are considered separately, and a person can have varying degrees of both.

National Council on Alcoholism

The National Council on Alcoholism, or NCA (1972), has approached the problem of classification in a more empirical way. They have developed a list of symptoms that they believe are indicative of an alcoholism disorder to varying degrees (Table 9–2).

The symptoms are divided into major and minor criteria and into three levels depending on how strongly (in the eyes of the NCA com-

TABLE 9-2. NCA Level 1 Major Criteria for the Definite Diagnosis of Alcoholism

1. Physiological dependence as demonstrated by a withdrawal syndrome (gross tremors, hallucinations, seizures, DTs—all coming from the withdrawal from alcohol, all other etiology ruled out)
2. Physiological evidence of tolerance (blood alcohol level of 0.15% with no signs of intoxication, consumption of the equivalent of a fifth of whiskey a day for more than one day for a 180-pound individual)
3. Alcoholic hepatitis
4. Alcoholic cerebellar degeneration
5. Continued drinking despite strong medical contraindications
6. Continued drinking despite strongly identified social contraindications (such as joblessness, marital disruption, drinking-related arrests).

mittee) they indicate the presence of alcoholism. Thus the presence of a "major" symptom from level 1 (such as alcohol withdrawal syndrome, DTs, alcoholic hepatitis, consumption of a fifth of whiskey or its equivalent by a 180-pound individual for more than one day, blood alcohol of more than 0.15 percent with no signs of intoxication, or continued drinking despite strong medical or social contraindications) means an automatic alcoholism diagnosis (Table 9–2). The presence of major symptoms from level 2 (such as alcohol-induced amnesic states, Lannec's cirrhosis, pancreatitis, or reported loss of control) are strongly indicative of an alcoholism diagnosis, but more evidence should be obtained. Major symptoms from level 3 (such as chronic gastritis, anemia, or beriberi) indicate possible alcoholism and necessitate a detailed search for other evidence.

Several of the minor criteria must be present before a diagnosis of alcoholism can be made. Level 1 minor criteria include blood alcohol level of 0.300 mg at any time, and blatant, indiscriminate use of alcohol. Some level 2 minor criteria are surreptitious drinking, morning drinking, abstinence attempts, loss of interest in nonalcohol-related activities and nondrinking companions, suicide attempts or outbursts of rage while drinking, peripheral neuropathy, and odor of alcohol on breath. Level 3 minor criteria are such symptoms as frequent traffic accidents, sudden unexplained changes in family and occupational status, flushed face, tachycardia, cigarette burns on clothing, decreased tolerance, and a variety of laboratory test abnormalities (such as hematology, electroencephalogram, and liver enzymes). There are also two tracts—(1) a physiological, clinical laboratory test and disease tract and (2) a behavioral, psychological, and attitudinal tract—that transect all levels.

In an intriguing study conducted in West Germany, Ringer and his associates (1977) examined control subjects and alcoholics for the existence of these symptoms. They found that some symptoms occurred in a large number of alcoholics and rarely or never in controls (gross tremors, drinking more than 0.757 liters of whiskey a day, blackouts, fatty degeneration of the liver, chronic gastritis, drinking despite medical or social contraindications, loss of control, odor of alcohol on breath, surreptitious drinking, and morning drinking). Other symptoms occurred in only a small percentage of alcoholics and never in controls (hallucinosis, withdrawal seizures, DTs, Wernicke-Korsakoff syndrome, alcohol facies, vascular engorgement, living on skid row, and using alcohol to relieve anxiety). However, there were many NCA criteria that failed to discriminate between alcoholics and nonalcoholics, either because they were so rare (cerebellar degeneration is one example) or because they occurred with enough frequency in the nonalcoholic sample to make a diagnosis based on that symptom alone fairly unreliable (hepatitis, attempts at abstinence, loss of interest in nondrinking activities, frequent automobile accidents, spouse complaints about drinking, and job loss are such criteria). Again it should be emphasized that the whole pattern of symptomatology should be taken into account; the existence of one symptom is not sufficient for diagnosis.

Feighner

Feighner and his associates (1972) group the symptoms of alcoholism into four categories:

CATEGORY 1

Category 1 is characterized by symptoms of alcohol withdrawal, diagnosis of an alcohol-related disease, blackouts, or two days or more of continued drinking.

CATEGORY 2

Category 2 is characterized by loss of control, failed attempts to abstain, morning drinking, drinking of alcohol-containing products because of the unavailability of liquor.

CATEGORY 3

Category 3 includes such symptoms as legal problems because of alcohol use (including citations for DUI), work-related alcohol problems, alcohol-related fights.

CATEGORY 4

Category 4 is characterized by complaints from family and friends about the patient's drinking, and loss of either as a result, and by the patient feeling that his drinking is inappropriate and experiencing guilt over his drinking behavior.

At least one symptom from three of these four groups must be present in order to justify a diagnosis of alcoholism.

Pattison

Pattison (1985) contends that there are a variety of types of alcohol problems, some of which involve physical dependence and others of which involve psychological dependence. Continued abuse of alcohol will result in a variety of alcohol-related life problems. The developmental course of alcohol abuse is not necessarily progressive, and there is a great deal of movement in both directions between the various stages. Pattison proposes an individual profile or pattern that allows the alcoholic to be placed somewhere on a continuum for ten factors:

1. *Alcohol consumption*—quantity, frequency, and volume.
2. *Drinking behavior*—preoccupation with alcohol, craving, attempts to control, inability to control, and pursuit of drinking despite high social and physical costs.
3. *Psychic dependence*—change in a patient's state of mind or behavior once he begins drinking.
4. *Physical dependence*—the existence of tolerance and withdrawal symptoms.
5. *Physical consequences*—health-related consequences of alcohol abuse.
6. *Emotional consequences*—the guilt, shame, grandiosity, paranoia, anxiety, depression, and regressive ego defenses connected with alcoholism.
7. *Interpersonal consequences*—alcohol-related problems with family and friends.
8. *Vocational consequences*—alcohol-related problems in the work area.
9. *Informal social consequences*—alcohol-related embarrassing and offensive social behavior.
10. *Legal consequences*—alcohol-related legal problems.

DSM-III

The final diagnostic conceptualization is the by-product of much of the previous work and is liable to be the most widely accepted because of its endorsement by the American Psychiatric Association and its inclusion in DSM-III-R (1987). It includes three categories of symptoms:

1. PATTERN OF PATHOLOGICAL ALCOHOL USE

Includes need for daily use of alcohol for adequate functioning; inability to cut down or stop drinking; repeated efforts to control or reduce excess drinking by "going on the wagon" (periods of temporary abstinence) or restricting drinking to certain times of the day; binges (remaining intoxicated throughout the day for at least two days); occasional consumption of a fifth of spirits (or its equivalent in wine or beer); amnesic periods for events occurring while intoxicated (blackouts); continuation of drinking despite a serious physical disorder that the individual knows is exacerbated by alcohol use; drinking of nonbeverage alcohol.

2. *IMPAIRMENT IN SOCIAL OR OCCUPATIONAL FUNCTIONING DUE TO ALCOHOL USE*

Includes violence while intoxicated; absence from work; loss of job; legal difficulties (such as arrest for intoxicated behavior and traffic accidents while intoxicated); arguments or difficulties with family or friends because of excessive alcohol use.

3. *EITHER TOLERANCE OR WITHDRAWAL*

Tolerance includes the need for markedly increased amounts of alcohol to achieve the desired effect, or markedly diminished effect with regular use of the same amount. *Withdrawal* includes the development of alcohol withdrawal symptoms (such as morning "shakes" and malaise relieved by drinking) after cessation of or reduction in drinking.

Three patterns of use are acknowledged: (1) regular, or daily, (2) weekend, or (3) periodic binge. Alcohol dependence is distinguished from alcohol abuse by the fact that the former is characterized by physical dependence, with evidence of withdrawal symptomatology or tolerance or both. A diagnosis of alcohol abuse can be made (versus no diagnosis) if the pathological pattern or impairment in social or occupational functioning is of more than a month's duration. The DSM-III-R also describes other alcohol-related disorders under the section on organic mental disorders:

ALCOHOL INTOXICATION

The criteria for this diagnosis include recent ingestion of alcohol, maladaptive behavioral effects (such as impaired judgment and inability to function on the job), physiological signs (such as slurred speech or unsteady gait), psychological signs (including loquacity, impaired attention, and mood changes) and evidence that these symptoms are not attributable to any other physical or mental disorder.

ALCOHOL IDIOSYNCRATIC INTOXICATION (PATHOLOGICAL INTOXICATION)

The criteria for this diagnosis include recent ingestion of alcohol but not in an amount that would cause intoxication in most people, marked behavior change (such as aggressive-assaultive behavior) that is atypical of the person when he is sober, and evidence that these symptoms are not attributable to any other disorder.

ALCOHOL WITHDRAWAL

This disorder is diagnosed when the following symptoms appear: evidence of cessation or reduction of heavy, prolonged drinking (several days' duration or longer) followed by coarse tremors in hands, tongue, or eyelids and any of the following: nausea and vomiting, malaise or weakness, autonomic hyperactivity such as sweating and elevated heart rate and blood pressure, anxiety, depression, irritability, or orthostatic hypotension. These symptoms also must not be attributable to any other disorder.

ALCOHOL WITHDRAWAL DELIRIUM (DTS)

The diagnostic criteria are delirium (rapidly developing clouding of consciousness, hallucinations, delusions, incoherent speech, disturbance of the normal sleep and wakefulness cycle, increased or decreased psychomotor activity, and memory disorientation) and autonomic hyperactivity that follow the cessation or rapid reduction of alcohol consumption following a period of heavy alcohol use. These symptoms must not be attributable to any other disorder.

ALCOHOLIC HALLUCINOSIS

The criteria for this diagnosis are vivid auditory hallucinations, not attributable to any other disorder, that follow the cessation or reduction of alcohol consumption after a period of heavy alcohol use. There is no clouding of consciousness or other signs of delirium.

ALCOHOL AMNESTIC DISORDER (KORSAKOFF'S SYNDROME)

This is a pronounced impairment in both recent and long-term memory that is not accompanied by a state of alcohol ingestion. There is no other etiology to explain this impairment.

DEMENTIA ASSOCIATED WITH ALCOHOLISM

This is a state of dementia (impaired social or occupational functioning, impaired intellectual ability, impaired memory, impaired abstract thinking and/or judgment, the existence of a variety of aphasias and agnosias, and personality change) following a period of heavy alcohol use. The symptoms are not attributable to a state of intoxication or delirium, although these may be present. The dementia persists for at least three weeks after alcohol use has stopped.

SYNTHESIS

It is difficult to find a core of symptomatology that can be found in all people with alcohol problems, but there are some symptoms that are *frequently* found in this population. There is usually some abnormality in the pattern of alcohol use, and if this abnormal pattern continues, there are usually some problems in the significant areas of the person's life (including health, social, and vocational functioning, and family relationships). Signs of physical and psychological dependence are often present, and they become more likely the more a person continues to use alcohol in an aberrant fashion. Thus there is much for the interviewer to investigate, and the presence of any one symptom neither confirms nor disconfirms the diagnosis of alcoholism.

A variety of syndromes are encompassed under the label *alcoholism.* Jellinek's and the other models that assume a common pattern and disease process for all alcoholics are really describing just one of the many patterns of alcoholism. To add to one's sense of caution, the research literature continues to show that alcohol use for some individuals is fluid in that it can flow from problematic and abusive to nonproblematic and controlled, and back again (Pattison et al. 1977). Thus it is possible for an individual to have earned a diagnosis of alcohol dependence in the past and not be drinking in an alcoholic manner at present. The Alcoholics Anonymous (AA) axiom of "once an alcoholic, always an alcoholic" does not always apply. For others, the course of drinking can remain static for long periods of time, not necessarily progressing into the chronic stages but remaining mildly abusive for a lifetime. One needs to know at what point in this process the interview is taking place.

CASE HISTORY

The patient is a 42-year-old black male seeking treatment for his alcoholism because of pressure from the courts. He had had a series of alcohol-related accidents and he was required to obtain treatment in order to reobtain his license. He had had his first drink at age 8; it was given to him by his father, also an alcoholic. The patient's father had died of hepatic cirrhosis at age 56. More regular drinking began at age 13. The patient started to miss class and to perform poorly in school because of his alcohol use. He reported getting drunk frequently and was eventually held back a grade and then expelled for coming to school drunk. His first blackout occurred at this time. He also started smoking marijuana regularly.

He entered the armed services and reported no adjustment problems despite regular, heavy drinking bouts. At age 22 he was honorably discharged. One week later, he urinated in his mother's bedroom during a blackout. He was asked to move out of the house, and he subsequently began to have more alcohol-related problems. He began to miss work due to his drinking. He raped his girlfriend while drunk, and he married her when he found that she was pregnant. He started drinking at work, and at age 28 he lost his first job for this reason. His marriage began to deteriorate, and he started experimenting with other drugs, such as cocaine, but alcohol remained his drug of choice. He was drinking every day. He explained this away by citing his unhappiness at home and at work. He found himself increasingly preoccupied with alcohol. He would not go anywhere where alcohol was not available, and he felt that drinking enhanced everything he did. At the same time, he recognized that he was drinking too much. He would try to control it, but he never tried to stop. His wife left him after six months of marriage.

At age 30 he entered his first alcohol treatment program. It was not successful, the patient claimed, because he had sought treatment only because the woman with whom he was living had put him out. At age 32 he obtained a job as a security guard and made a serious attempt to reduce his drinking. This, too, was unsuccessful. He lost this job a year later and began driving a cab, but he demolished the cab in an accident while drinking.

At age 36 he remarried, but this relationship too began to sour because of his drinking. He was irresponsible, verbally abusive, and couldn't hold a job. He secured a job working for the General Service Administration. He began to drink more heavily. If he wasn't working, he would reach for a drink as soon as he awoke and would drink throughout the day until he passed out. If he was working, he would drink a half pint in the morning and then use mouthwash and cologne so that the alcohol odor would not be noticed. He would not drink while under his supervisor's scrutiny and would resume drinking after work. In the field, he would stop for half pints throughout the day. After wrecking a government car while intoxicated, he was again propelled into treatment. This also was unsuccessful.

His wife divorced him when he was 38, and he lost his job the following year. His blackouts were becoming more frequent. He continued to eke out a living as a cab driver until he was 42, when he was involved in yet another accident and his license was revoked. This incident forced him once again to seek treatment. Throughout he reported neither withdrawal symptoms (no tremors, no DTs, no nausea or hangover) nor impaired physical health because of his drinking. A medical examination confirmed the absence of health problems. He continued to manifest a high tolerance level up to the time of seeking treatment.

The patient earns a diagnosis of alcoholism according to the DSM-III criteria: He manifests a pathological alcohol use pattern, impairment in social and occupational functioning, and evidence of tolerance. It is notable that the patient lacks many significant symptoms (such as health impairment and withdrawal symptoms) despite over 25 years of alcohol abuse. Using the NCA major criteria, only "continued drinking despite strongly identified social contraindications" from level 1 applies, in addition to a good sampling of items from other levels (morning drinking, memory blackouts, futile attempts to cut down, work absenteeism, marital discord). The patient could be assigned a diagnosis of alcoholism based on these standards also. A brief review of Feighner's and Pattison's criteria would lead to the same conclusion.

DSM-III Diagnosis

Axis I: Alcohol dependence (303.91)
Axis II: No diagnosis given, but elements of an antisocial personality disorder (301.70) are present
Axis III: No diagnosis
Axis IV: No major stressors apparent in year prior to the diagnostic interview. Minimal or mild.
Axis V: Level of functioning: poor

SPECIAL POPULATIONS AND PATTERNS

The following section distills the essence of several excellent reviews. Further readings are encouraged.

Women

Studies comparing the pattern of alcoholic symptomatology across the sexes reveal several differences (Gomberg 1986, Lex 1985, Wilsnack 1982). For one, female alcoholics tend to be characterized by a later onset of their problem drinking and a more rapid course. They seem especially vulnerable to certain alcohol-related problems, such as family disruption, development of cirrhosis and other liver disorders, depression, and suicide attempts. They are less vulnerable than men to work-related problems, arrests and other legal problems, DTs, blackouts, and extended binges. There was also less morning and daily drinking noted in some female samples and more solitary drinking, usually in the home. The notion of women as pantry drinkers apparently still has some validity. There is also a link between certain types of cancer (breast, oral) and alcohol abuse.

Men are still more likely than women to have an alcoholism diagnosis, but several studies report that the gap is narrowing. Homosexuals of both sexes are at greater risk than their heterosexual counterparts (Brandsma and Pattison 1982).

Aged

Two general patterns of alcohol abuse appear in the aged population (Hoffman and Heinemann 1986, Lex 1985, Maletta 1982). The majority of older people with alcohol problems were young alcoholics who managed to survive. They generally drink as frequently as they did when they were younger but their volume is less. The effect of alcohol on their health is more pronounced, especially in the central nervous system. The usual deficits attributed to aging (such as poor memory and diminished concentration) are magnified by the alcohol abuse. Many of them appear to be demented, bland, apathetic, passive, irritable, confused, and impulsive. They may also have other serious central nervous system impairments (such as aphasia). Falling, and related injuries, is also more common. A portion of this group lives permanently on skid row, having destroyed any existing social network through their alcohol abuse.

The other pattern is that of a recently developed tendency to abuse alcohol in response to the stress of old age (such as retirement, loss of spouse, loss of health, and loneliness). This pattern accounts for approximately one third of the alcohol problems affecting the elderly and is indistinguishable from the first pattern except in terms of onset.

Alcohol problems in the elderly often go undetected because of several factors. They often live in isolated situations, so there is little in terms of family or social life to be disrupted. Since the majority of the elderly no longer work, there is no occupational life to be disrupted, and if they do not drive or leave their living quarters very often, they are less likely to be arrested. Their alcohol problems are often well camouflaged behind serious health problems, and if they are demented, they cannot relate an accurate history to the interviewer.

Adolescents

For adolescents, the social consequences of alcohol abuse are primary, and the physical dependence symptoms and health consequences are relatively rare (Bennett 1986, Filstead 1982, Lex 1985). Thus, the adolescent with a drinking problem will show disruptions in the areas of school performance (poor grades, truancy, and disciplinary problems) and family and peer relationships. Legal problems will come about through drunken driving, fighting, and petty crimes. Experimentation and abuse of other drugs are also very common.

Without the existence of the signs of physical dependence (they hardly have the chance to develop given the relatively short drinking life of the average adolescent), one wonders whether these adolescents truly deserve the diagnosis of alcoholism. Follow-up and natural-history studies support this notion, as many adolescents with drinking problems turn out to be normal, nonabusive drinkers as adults. At this stage in our knowledge, it is not possible to reliably distinguish the eventual alcoholic from his moderate-drinking counterpart by his adolescent drinking pattern.

Ethnic and Cultural Factors

Different ethnic groups have different views of problem drinking, different patterns of drinking, and different susceptibilities to the development of alcoholic drinking styles (Abel et al. 1987, Heath 1983, MacCready et al. 1983). The Irish, Scandinavians, British Canadians, and French have long been targeted as more likely to develop alcoholism as compared to the Italians, Greeks, and Jews. Much of the theorizing has focused on child-rearing practices and culturally reinforced drinking styles as a partial explanation. No convincing evidence points to a genetic predisposition in these alcoholism-prone ethnic groups. The degree of assimilation to American culture also has surprisingly little impact on alcoholism rates. An awareness of these factors is helpful to the diagnostician.

When it comes to exploring ethnic difference in drinking patterns, it becomes difficult to separate the ethnic factor from the effects of low socioeconomic status—a direct result of racial discrimination.

BLACKS

Blacks are less likely to see abusive drinking as a problem requiring treatment. They are more likely than white alcoholics to have DTs, hallucinosis, alcoholic psychosis, and hypertension. Legal problems are especially prevalent among black alcoholics, with disorderly conduct, public intoxication, and other similar arrests occurring much more frequently than in white alcoholics. Family problems are also prevalent in black alcoholics (Harper 1976, Lex 1985).

HISPANICS

It is impossible to make a statement that will cover the wide variety of Hispanic groups in the United States. The only general statement that can be made is that, like blacks, they are less likely to see alcoholism as a problem needing treatment. Drinking is encouraged, but losing control over it seems to be more stigmatized than it is in other groups (Johnson and Matre 1978, Lex 1985).

AMERICAN INDIANS AND ESKIMOS

It is well established that these groups are especially prone to alcoholism and alcohol abuse. Heavy alcohol use and drunkenness is prevalent in young Indians, and this behavior quickly leads to more serious problems. This finding is so firmly established that many theorists propose a biological sensitivity to alcohol for these racial groups (Lex 1985, Mello 1983, Westermeyer and Baker 1986).

ASIAN AMERICANS

These groups have very few problems with alcohol, although there is a slight tendency for these problems to increase in more assimilated individuals or in the very poor where the family unit is fractured.

DIAGNOSTIC OVERLAP WITH OTHER PSYCHIATRIC DISORDERS

Alcohol abuse may coexist with, cause, suppress, or be a result of a variety of psychiatric disorders. This complicates the diagnostician's job as he tries to sort out the exact relationship of the alcoholism to the other disorders.

Affective Disorders

The relationship between the affective disorders and alcoholism is extremely complex. It is very common for an alcoholic to be depressed while actively drinking and even after stopping (Schuckit 1983, 1986, Solomon 1983). This appears to be a result of the naturally depressant effect of alcohol as a drug when used extensively and of the fact that alcoholism is a disease of losses. However, most depression experienced by alcoholics is notoriously short lived (Schuckit 1986, Verinis 1985, 1986b) and will dissipate with a short period of abstinence. Studies with our own alcoholic population revealed a different rate of depression resolution for hospitalized alcoholics as compared with those maintained on an outpatient basis, with the inpatients showing a much faster rate of improvement. It was hypothesized that removal of the patient from the stressful environment contributed to this finding. Most depression seen in alcoholic patients appears to be of this kind. The alcoholism would be diagnosed as the primary disorder and the depression, if diagnosed at all, would be secondary.

In some patients with a primary diagnosis of affective disorder (the primary–secondary issue is usually resolved by a careful history that determines which problem became a problem first), alcohol is often used in an attempt to self-medicate. In a depressed patient, alcohol appears to have a short-term mood-elevating effect (Solomon 1983), and frequent reliance on this coping mechanism can result in the development of alcohol dependence. The depressive symptoms should worsen when the alcohol is removed from the patient's system.

In many of our patients, alcoholism became a problem only after a significant loss (such as the death of a parent or spouse, loss of a job, retirement, or divorce) had occurred. They began drinking heavily to facilitate their coping with the pain of their loss, and an adjustment reaction with depression or uncomplicated bereavement (DSM-III-R 1987) became alcohol abuse or dependence.

Alcohol can serve several purposes for manic patients. Drinking sprees can be one of the channels for manic excitement. Alcohol can also be used as a self-medicating attempt to modulate the excitement.

Schuckit (1986) speaks of depression and alcoholism coexisting as secondary diagnoses, with another diagnosis (such as drug abuse or schizophrenia) being primary. A patient can also suffer from both alcoholism and depression that are relatively independent of each other. Such a patient would be depressed regardless of whether he were drinking or not.

Suicide

As might be expected, suicidal ideation, suicide attempts, and successful suicide are also closely linked to alcoholism. Various studies show that a significant percentage of alcoholics contemplate and attempt suicide and that alcohol use is a factor in a large percentage of suicide attempts (Fowler et al. 1986, Rich et al. 1986, Solomon 1983). Menninger (1938) even contended that alcoholism was a form of suicide.

Schizophrenia

Alcohol abuse can cause many psychotic symptoms, including hallucinations, paranoid delusions, confusion and disorientation, and unpredictable aggressive outbursts. These alcohol-originated disorders can be present during intoxication and especially during the withdrawal stages. On the whole they are relatively transient disorders and will disappear with an extended period of abstinence.

Alcohol abuse is relatively common in individuals with a primary diagnosis of schizophrenia. Freed's (1975) review indicates that anywhere from 3 to 63 percent of schizophrenics abuse alcohol. One of the reasons appears to be an attempt at self-medication. Many of the patients coming through our clinic are resistant to taking psychotropic medication because of the stigma or the side effects, or both, and they turn to alcohol as a substitute. Occasionally the alcohol abuse can effectively mask the symptoms of schizophrenia, and only after a period of abstinence do the psychotic symptoms start to reappear.

Sociopathy

There is a close relationship between alcoholism and sociopathy. Many alcoholics engage in a wide variety of antisocial acts, ranging from drunk driving to rape and child molestation to theft and murder. Alcohol abuse becomes one of the many ways an antisocial personality acts out his impulses and seeks pleasure. In order to distinguish which disorder is primary, the diagnostician should determine whether the patient engages in the act only when he has been drinking and whether the patient experiences remorse (Guze et al. 1969, Schuckit 1983).

Drug Abuse

Increasing evidence confirms the tendency among alcoholics to abuse other substances and the tendency of other substance abusers to abuse alcohol (Carroll 1977, Cohen 1982, Craig 1989, Kanig and Kofoed 1984), especially among younger Americans. This further complicates diagnostic attempts because of the ways in which alcohol interacts with various drugs (Cohen 1982). Marijuana and alcohol appear to be the most frequent combination, with the result that the cognitive deficits noted in alcohol abuse alone are magnified. Sedatives and tranquilizing drugs also magnify the effects of alcohol. Stimulants and alcohol will be used as the individual attempts to alleviate the lethargy induced by the alcohol or blunt the effects of the stimulants. The latter group is more likely to be talkative, euphoric, and restless. Abuse of other substances, such as nicotine (Dreher and Fraser 1967, 1968) and caffeine (Verinis 1986a), is also common in alcoholic populations.

Anxiety

Symptoms of excessive anxiety (heart palpitations, insomnia, hand tremors, accelerated thoughts) are also quite common in patients with alcohol problems. Withdrawal from alcohol seems to highlight these symptoms. The symptoms usually improve dramatically with a short period of abstinence (Verinis et al. 1986), although some writers (Miller et al. 1980) note that anxiety and excessive tension remain a problem for one to two years after the last drink.

Because of its depressive nature, alcohol abuse can develop as a self-medicating attempt on the part of a patient with an anxiety disorder. The removal of the alcohol in these cases will result in an exacerbation of these symptoms. Our clinic has noted a few cases of agoraphobia masked by alcoholism as the patient attempted to cope with his feelings of panic through the use of alcohol. Several cases of post-traumatic stress disorder also emerged once the alcoholism was brought under control.

Organic Brain Syndromes

The existence of cognitive and neurological impairment in alcoholics is well documented (Becker and Kaplan 1986). Symptoms of confusion, disorientation, poor attention span, memory deficit, inability to reason effectively or to comprehend simple instructions, and poor judgment have all been noted. Much of this impairment is a result of acute intoxication, and it is aggravated by the nutritional deficits that often accompany this condition. These symptoms persist and may even peak during withdrawal but are then thought to largely dissipate as the period of abstinence lengthens. Increasingly, however, researchers are finding that there is some lingering impairment even in relatively healthy alcoholics that may take months to clear up. The impairment is more pronounced in older alcoholics.

Some damage to the brain is permanent or much more obstinate in its response to treatment. In such cases, the impairment in intellectual functioning is severe enough that the patient cannot function or can function only marginally. His work and family roles are affected. The patient's personality is often altered, and he may behave in a manner atypical for him; shallow, flattened affect, poor impulse control, apathy, and blandness are frequently noted. Specific aphasias (that is, the inability, not attributable to impaired sensory apparatus, to recognize familiar objects or persons) are not uncommon. Wernicke's syndrome is often, although not always, associated with chronic alcohol abuse. The primary presenting symptoms are confusion, excitement, occasional delirium, ataxia, abnormal eye movements, impairment of memory, and dysarthria. Stupor and death may follow (Thompson 1959). The patient who recovers runs a risk of developing Korsakoff's syndrome, or alcoholic amnestic syndrome, as it is now called. Profound permanent impairment of memory, both recent and long-term, is the primary feature of this syndrome. The patient will confabulate outlandish stories to fill in these memory gaps and often cannot remember the events of a few minutes ago. The alcohol-related nature of these disorders is usually established by history obtained from someone who has been familiar with the patient over an extended period of time.

CASE HISTORY

The patient is a 43-year-old divorced, unemployed white male who presented himself to the clinic asking for alcohol treatment. He gives a drinking history of almost 30 years' duration. He took his first drink at age 15 and had been drinking regularly since. He would frequently drink to intoxication during his teenage years and described himself as a "hell raiser." Minor delinquent behavior was reported.

He enrolled in the armed services at age 20 and was sent to Vietnam. It was there that he began to drink daily and in increasing volume. He reported falling asleep on guard duty, experiencing memory blackouts, and drinking to the point of unconsciousness. He experimented with marijuana at this time but felt that it made him "too paranoid." He reacted strongly to his combat experiences and reported depression, insomnia, nightmares, and agitation. He was seen by a psychiatrist at this time.

Upon discharge he continued the heavy, daily drinking habit established in Vietnam. It wasn't long before he developed withdrawal tremors. His blackouts increased in frequency. He was anxious and frequently depressed. He was bothered by nightmares and flashbacks of Vietnam. He had trouble sleeping and used alcohol as a soporific. A girlfriend left him when he was 30 years old because she could not tolerate his excessive drinking. He was not abusive, but he spent long hours away from her in the bar and wasted his money. He married at age 33, and his wife left him two years later for the same reason. His work record was unstable; and although he was never fired, he resigned or walked off three jobs. At age 35 he developed a pancreatic cyst, which was surgically removed. He continued to drink steadily. At age 36 he was diagnosed as diabetic.

At this point he began to come to grips with the fact that he was drinking too much, and he made conscious attempts to abstain. Although he was unable to do so, he did begin to drink periodically rather than daily. He would go for weeks to occasional months between drinking periods. When he did drink, he would binge. He reported some alleviation of his depression and anxiety during his sober periods. At age 38 he was admitted to a psychiatric unit with insomnia, depression, suicidal thoughts, nightmares, and flashbacks of Vietnam. He was diagnosed as having depression and a post-traumatic stress disorder.

Three weeks before coming for treatment, the patient lost his job for reasons he felt were unfair. This precipitated a drinking binge, which ended in a diabetic coma. During the first interview he was depressed and anxious; he reported trouble sleeping and recent, although not current, suicidal ideation. He was still troubled by Vietnam-related flashbacks. He was admitted into an alcohol clinic and encouraged to go to AA. Within three weeks his depression had lifted, and he reported feeling more relaxed and sleeping better. This improvement continued after three months of treatment.

The multiplicity of problems in this case complicates the diagnosis. Which is primary? Certainly the seeds of an abusive alcohol-use pattern were present, and the trauma of the patient's wartime experiences seemed to propel his alcohol use into serious abuse. Yet his depressive symptoms appear so chronic and pervasive that they also seemed to require special attention. However, they followed the transient pattern of depression secondary to alcoholism and disappeared with an extended period of abstinence.

DSM-III Diagnosis

Axis I: Post-traumatic stress disorder, Chronic (309.81)
Axis: II: Alcohol dependence (303.91)
Axis III: Diabetes
Axis IV: Current stress considered moderate, but original wartime stress rated severe
Axis V: Level of functioning: poor

THE ALCOHOLIC PERSONALITY

Much effort has been directed toward the establishment of a unique combination of character traits that distinguish the alcoholic from the nonalcoholic (Barnes 1979, Blum and Blum 1967, Donovan 1986, Forrest 1975). This constellation includes weak ego, hypersensitivity to physical and emotional distress, low frustration tolerance, immaturity, passivity, dependency, insecurity, impulsivity, poor self-concept, sociopathy, hostility, anxiety, and depression. Still debated is the question of whether this constellation is present before the alcoholism and is therefore instrumental in its development, or whether it is instead the result of many years of alcohol abuse. For the diagnostician, however, the debate over which came first is relatively unimportant compared to the fact that if there is some validity to this research, then the existence of this constellation of traits can confirm or disconfirm a diagnosis of alcoholism.

Like most issues in the treatment of alcoholism and related disorders, diagnosis is not that simple. These traits do appear in some form or another in many alcoholics. They do not appear in every alcoholic nor do they invariably appear in a constellation. Nor are they the sole property of alcoholics: It is possible to have a number of these characteristics and not develop alcoholism.

Supporting some of these statements is the research, usually involving some form of factor analysis or cluster analysis, that establishes several types of alcoholic pesonalities (Bartsch and Hoffman 1985, Craig et al. 1985, Nerviano and Gross 1983). Unfortunately the nature and number of personality subtypes seem to depend on the instrument used and the nature of the subject population. Nevertheless, a rough consensus appears to be emerging (Miller and Hester 1986a); many of the subtypes appear to have primarily sociopathic features, with a relative absence of neurotic symptoms (such as depression and anxiety). Still other subtypes have more psychotic or borderline features—some with a strong paranoid trend, and others with more of a schizoid quality. There also appears to be a number of patterns with primarily neurotic symptoms and little sociopathy. A fourth pattern—that of abusive alcohol use with no other symptomatology—is also found.

INTERVIEWING AN ALCOHOLIC

As the therapist approaches the interview, there are many factors of which to be aware in order to make as accurate an assessment as possible. This section will focus on these factors and will give some helpful hints on symptoms to listen for, ask about, or test for.

Validity of the Patient's Self-Report

The self-report of alcoholics is not always valid, although the rate of concordance with the report of collaterals or with previous records is generally high (Sobell and Sobell 1980, Verinis 1983). In our study involving the use of collaterals, it was found that the validity of the patient's self-report shifted depending on the area being assessed. The reports on drinking status and family relationships were less valid than those on occupational and health status.

One of the factors involved here is the denial, minimization, or outright lying so common in alcoholic patients. Another is the continuing stigma connected with being an alcoholic, and a third is the alcoholic's impaired recall, due either to the occurrence of blackouts or to an alcohol-related organic condition (whether temporary or permanent).

The *use of collateral information*, whether an interview with a relative or an examination of the patient's records, *is recommended*. The only point of caution is that family members can also be in denial.

An awareness of the purpose of the interview is also helpful. In our experience, the most defensive and least reliable interviews are those conducted with individuals who are being coerced into the interview (by the courts, or a job supervisor, or family members). An open admission of alcohol-related problems is usually a good sign. Alcoholism remains a stigmatized, low-status disease, so there is very little to be gained by admitting to alcohol problems. The only exceptions, in our experience, have been patients with a primary drug abuse or schizophrenic diagnosis who will endorse whatever symptoms necessary to obtain hospital admission. In addition, for some schizophrenic patients, being an alcoholic is preferable and less stigmatizing than being "crazy."

State of Intoxication

As has been made clear throughout this chapter, the alcoholic's complicated diagnostic picture can change depending on his state of intoxication or phase of withdrawal. Much of the emotional and organic-cognitive pathology often associated with alcoholism clears up with two weeks of abstinence. Disorders that are well masked by drinking begin to emerge. Even the reliability of the alcoholic's responses is influenced by his state of intoxication (Verinis 1986b). For this reason, a follow-up interview should be scheduled whenever possible, and the therapist should attempt to determine intoxication status at both times. A period of detoxification certainly increases the validity of the diagnostic conclusions. Caddy

(1986) recommends the use of a breathalizer to determine blood alcohol level.

Family History

It is becoming a well-established fact (Bohman 1978, Goodwin et al. 1973) that alcoholism tends to run in families. Alcoholism in a mother or father dramatically increases the chances that an offspring will develop alcoholism. This holds true whether the child is raised with the biological parent or apart, thus establishing a strong genetic link in many cases of alcoholism. Those who have other alcoholic blood relatives are also at increased risk.

Research has specified other family-history signs that increase the risk of an individual's developing alcoholism. A family history of alcohol abstinence in a sociocultural group that would normally drink is sometimes found. A history of clinical depression among female relatives is also being found to occur more regularly in the family background of alcoholics, as is a history of family disruption. Divorce, separation, absent and/or unknown parents (often the father), and marital conflict are the forms that this disruption takes. Childhood hyperactivity, school adjustment problems, and learning disabilities are also worth noting.

It should be emphasized that while the existence of any of the foregoing patterns does not conclusively indicate an alcohol problem, the patterns can serve as markers or warning signs to the alert interviewer that the possibility of an alcohol problem should be investigated. The information already cited on ethnic differences should also be taken into account.

Physical Complaints

Alcoholism has a profound effect on physical health. Certain diseases, including hepatic cirrhosis, pancreatitis, peripheral neuropathy, and alcoholic dementia (NCA 1972), almost invariably indicate alcoholism in the advanced stages. It is much more difficult to recognize the disease in the early or middle stages because it can be masked behind seeming unrelated physical disorders. The NCA level 2 and 3 signs (such as minor cardiac problems, flushed face, vitamin deficiencies) are of some help here. Estes and Heinemann (1986) and Chafetz (1983) cite other disorders that often mask alcoholism. Fatigue, insomnia, and sexual dysfunction, as well as clinical depression and anxiety disorders, are often associated with alcohol abuse. Fractures, falls, scars, unexplained seizures, and burns also qualify, as does heartburn, nausea, edema, and hypertension. An illness that is not responding to conventional treatment may also be a sign, as may a request for tranquilizers. The individual himself is often not aware of the connection between his alcohol abuse and the foregoing problems and will focus on the masking symptoms in the interview.

Whenever possible, a thorough physical examination should accompany the diagnostic interview. Laboratory tests (especially liver enzymes) and a blood alcohol level may be particularly helpful in diagnosing a patient who is currently manifesting high tolerance and showing no other physical signs of alcohol abuse. Alcohol on the individual's breath or the odor of stale alcohol, indicating abuse the night before the interview, should also be noted. Heavy use of colognes and breath mints may point to an attempt to mask the signs of alcohol abuse. An individual who appears much older than his chronological age may also be an alcohol abuser. Heavy smoking during the interview is another indicator.

Behavioral Indicators

Alcoholism may also be hidden behind certain behavioral problems. Family problems can be one indicator. Frequent quarreling, violence and discord, unexplained divorces and separations, and spouse complaints about the patient's drinking, even though brushed off by the patient, are all symptoms worth investigating.

Vocational problems may also indicate alcohol abuse. Frequent absenteeism, especially on Mondays, tardiness, unexplained demotions or failure to progress, frequent job changes, vague "personality conflicts" and other problems with employers, and maximum use of sick leave can all be alcohol related. The tendency to choose jobs that are clearly beneath the patient's capabilities or that have a maximum of unsupervised time (for drinking) may also be indicative. Certain jobs appear to be associated with a high risk for the development of alcohol-related problems (Whitehead and Simpkins 1983). Physicians, enlisted armed services personnel, bartenders, workers in the beverage industry, bar owners, entertainers, executives, salespersons, seamen, restaurant workers, construction and other types of blue-collar, unskilled or semiskilled workers (such as painters, printers, and oil rig workers), journalists, firefighters and police officers have all been found to have a greater-than-average chance of developing alcohol-related problems. In some cases it is the stress of the jobs themselves that make them high risk. In others, certain features of the jobs (such as the availability of alcohol or the predominance of unsupervised blocks of time) can encourage an alcohol problem or can attract individuals with already-existing alcohol problems.

Legal problems also mask alcohol problems. Most frequently they take the form of driving while intoxicated, disturbing the peace, or disorderly conduct charges. Alcohol use is also tied to more serious crimes, from homicide to incest, rape, and check forgery. Frequent victimization can also be related.

Other behavioral patterns connected with drinking itself can also be indicative, and many of these have already been noted in the section on diagnostic conceptualization. To briefly recapitulate, the tendencies to center one's social and recreational activities around drinking-related activities and to choose friends of a lower social stratum are frequent markers of ongoing alcohol problems, as is a history of unexplained or unsuccessful attempts to "go on the wagon." The patient may admit that he drinks too much on occasion but will insist that he could cut down if he had to. The drinking is well rationalized and overjustified. The patient will point to others or problems as the reason for this alcohol abuse. The lack of control is made to sound like the individual's choice to overdrink.

Diagnostic Aids

There are many questionnaires that, if answered honestly, could provide confirmation of a diagnosis of alcoholism (Miller 1976). Certainly the most thoroughly researched is the Michigan Alcoholism Screening Test, or MAST (Selzer 1971), which consists of 24 straightforward questions that call for yes or no answers. Examples include the following: Have you ever gone to anyone for help because of your drinking? Can you stop drinking without a struggle after one or two drinks? Has your drinking ever created problems between you and your wife, husband, a parent, or other relative?

Mayfield and his associates (1974) developed the four-question CAGE questionnaire:

1. Have you ever felt you should *cut* down on your drinking?
2. Have people *annoyed* you by criticizing your drinking?
3. Have you ever felt bad or *guilty* about your drinking?
4. Have you ever had a drink first thing in the morning to steady your nerves or get rid of a hangover (*eye-opener*)?

For the therapist who prefers an alcoholism questionnaire imbedded in the context of a more comprehensive personality inventory, the Millon Multiaxial Clinical Interview (Craig et al. 1985) appears to be as good a choice as any.

These tests discriminate alcoholics from nonalcoholics and are often used as an initial screening device when a large number of people must be assessed. They help to distinguish those for whom a future interview may be necessary. They seem to work well when the patient openly admits or is totally unaware of the existence of an alcohol problem; they are less effective with defensive individuals who are trying to minimize and sanitize their alcohol use.

A structured clinical interview can be equally effective. Several, such as the one developed by Estes and Heinemann (1986) for nurses, and the 31-item Drinking Behavior Interview (Shelton et al. 1969), are available. They are thorough and have the advantage of the rapport between interviewer and patient to increase their validity.

A detailed assessment of the patient's alcohol consumption pattern can also be helpful (Armor and Polich 1982). Miller and Marlatt (1984) have developed an assessment mode that divides the individual's week down into days and days into morning, afternoon, and evening. The number of drinks consumed during each period is broken down into number of ounces (alcohol content of beverage, size of drink) of alcohol consumed, and the blood alcohol content can be determined for each drinking episode. These results are then projected over a three-month period. When this information is given to the patient in the form of objective feedback, the effect can help to break through some of the denial as the patient becomes aware of how much he is actually drinking (Miller and Hester 1986a).

Nathan (1982) describes a technique in which individuals are asked to discriminate their own blood alcohol level. Research shows that alcoholics are impaired in this self-monitoring, which may help explain their consistent tendency to drink to intoxicating levels. Nathan believes that this technique could be used as a diagnostic aid. Research is beginning to detail different physiological reactions when alcoholics or those at high risk for alcoholism (such as children of alcoholics) and control subjects are given a specified dose of alcohol. Differences in brain activity (Propping et al. 1981) and enzyme release (Schuckit 1984) have been noted. These findings are at the very preliminary stages and are of no practical value to the interviewer at present. However, future interviewers may have available dependable physiological assessment instruments that will help confirm their diagnostic impression of alcoholism.

The Interview Itself

Little can be added to the well-established principles of being friendly, establishing rapport, being nonjudgmental and matter-of-fact, and talking about "safe" topics first to put the patient at ease (Caddy 1986, Miller and Hester 1986a). Estes and Heinemann (1986) emphasize the "blind spots" that many interviewers have that often result in alcoholism's being overlooked or minimized. Naivete and lack of knowledge can often result in the interviewer's focusing on the masking symptom and neglecting to look for the underlying alcoholism. In addition, many beginning interviewers fear upsetting their patients or evoking their anger by invading their privacy. The result is that the issue of alcoholism is carefully skirted rather than objectively confronted.

The interviewer's own drinking patterns may prevent him from thoroughly examining a patient's pattern. Not to be ignored is the anger that interviewers may feel toward the alcoholic—because of their own family experiences with an alcoholic, because of past frustrations of trying to work with other alcoholics who have been noncompliant and manipulative, because of reactions to some of the alcoholic's behavior and his lack of guilt, and because of the general defensive and antagonistic posture that some alcoholics will adopt in the interview. This anger can distort an interviewer's assessment. Therapists must carefully monitor their own attitudes, beliefs, and experiences before trying to deal with alcoholic patients. An objective focus on patients and their problems is essential.

TREATMENT DECISIONS

After the diagnostic work is completed and the alcohol-related diagnosis is certain, the therapist should begin to devise an effective treatment plan. Treatment referrals may be necessary.

Detoxification

It is foolhardy to try to treat an alcoholic who is still actively drinking. If the patient is currently consuming alcohol, the therapist must choose among a variety of detoxification alternatives.

MEDICALLY SUPERVISED DETOXIFICATION

The patient spends from five to ten days in a hospital. This form of detoxification is usually recommended for patients with accompanying serious medical problems or with a history of withdrawal seizures or delirium. It should also be considered for patients with concomitant psychiatric disorders, especially when a masked psychotic disorder is suspected or suicidal ideation is present.

SOCIAL DETOXIFICATION

This form of detoxification also takes place in an inpatient setting but usually not one connected with a hospital. The treatment staff is usually composed of alcoholism counselors, although some backup medical personnel are often available. The stay at a social detoxification facility is usually five to seven days. This resource is recommended for individuals who have a relatively uncomplicated history of withdrawal and who report an inability to stop drinking on their own. It is helpful, too, for individuals whose social support structure is exhausted and who might benefit from a brief period of removal from these stressful circumstances.

OUTPATIENT DETOXIFICATION

Many patients are able to stop drinking on their own without a dramatic inpatient intervention. This capacity is usually revealed in the patient's history. Outpatient detoxification usually requires a commitment to stop and a short follow-up interview to monitor the success of this effort. The individual often reports spending a few days in bed at home. Support can be provided through AA meetings and outpatient clinics as well as medication. At our clinic, we recommend daily attendance with constant monitoring and medical intervention if necessary.

Treatment Alternatives

Once detoxification is complete, a variety of other treatment decisions must be made.

INPATIENT REHABILITATION

These are hospital-based programs of 21 to 28 days' duration. Along with a thorough medical evaluation, the patient is educated about the disease of alcoholism and participates in a variety of other psychotherapeutic treatments, depending upon the orientation of the treatment staff. Individual, group, and family counseling are usually offered, although many units also provide aversive conditioning and social skills training. Inpatient rehabilitation used to be a preferred treatment modality for any alcoholic, but treatment evaluation studies have consistently shown it to be no more effective than much less expensive outpatient care (Miller 1986). There is still a place for inpatient rehabilitation (Miller and Hester 1986b), but only for physically deteriorated patients whose social support structure has been destroyed by their drinking and who are in need of an extended time-out period for stabilization.

OUTPATIENT CLINICS

There is a wide diversity in the therapeutic services provided by these clinics, but the main therapeutic modality is usually inclusion in a sobriety-enhancing, supportive milieu of other alcoholic patients who are also trying to avoid returning to drinking. Group therapy is a common feature. Patients with a relatively intact social support system can benefit from once-a-week contact, but those with little remaining support need more regular contact. These clinics are generally connected with medical centers.

AA MEETINGS

These self-help meetings of recovering alcoholics are held in virtually every area of the United States. They are usually listed in the telephone book and are free of charge. They are especially ubiquitous in urban areas, where they can be found at such a variety of times as to fit any schedule. In many areas, AA provides clublike settings where members can go to socialize or just to spend time in an alcohol-free environment. The meetings themselves can take a variety of forms: Some involve passively listening to the testimony of a recovering alcoholic; others involve a discussion of the AA principles; and still others are similar to group therapy, where an open discussion of current problems is encouraged.

Some patients are disconcerted by the structure and heavy spiritual overtones of many AA meetings. In fact, studies report that those who are able to effectively use AA are more likely to be middle-class, compulsive, guilt-ridden, socially dependent individuals who can be comfortable in groups of people.

INDIVIDUAL COUNSELING

The decision to refer a patient to this treatment modality should be made with a great deal of caution; its effectiveness with alcoholics is not impressive (Miller 1986). It is generally recommended that the patient also be expected to attend AA or outpatient clinic groups, or both, as well. Patients with a secondary diagnosis of depression or anxiety seem to benefit from these individual sessions. The transient nature of much of the alcoholic's emotional distress appears to be part of the reason that other alcoholics tend to derive little benefit. The inclusion of regular breathalizer tests and collateral contacts to verify continued abstinence is also suggested.

MEDICAL CONSULTATION

As has been emphasized throughout this chapter, a thorough physical examination is helpful in establishing the diagnosis of alcoholism. The alcoholism-related diseases must be medically monitored and treated.

Medication is sometimes appropriate, and nonphysician counselors must seek the expertise of their medical colleagues in these situations. The long-term use of antianxiety agents is generally discouraged because of the potential for readdiction, although they can be useful in easing outpatient detoxification or in helping the patient weather an immediate crisis. Antipsychotic medication to reduce mania is needed if the secondary diagnosis is psychosis or bipolar disorder. Antidepressant medication is also helpful with secondary or primary depressions.

Disulfiram (Antabuse) is a drug that interacts adversely with alcohol; in sufficient quantity, it can induce severe illness if taken with alcohol-containing products. It serves as an immediate deterrent to alcohol consumption. Antabuse is effective only as long as the patient takes it. It can be helpful in patients with a history of impulsive drinking, as it does initially deter the drinking episode. Some treatment programs insist that patients take Antabuse, but this is effective only if there are some means to enforce compliance (such as if it is possible to have the patient swallow the pill as a staff member observes). Antabuse is contraindicated in severely physically deteriorated alcoholics whose health might not be able to withstand an Antabuse reaction or in the demented alcoholics who might not remember that they have taken Antabuse. It should be prescribed with caution to patients with a history of suicidal acting out, as the ingestion of Antabuse and alcohol in sufficient quantity can be fatal.

This chapter has focused on the signs, symptoms, and subterfuges of the alcoholisms. Although there have been problems with every major attempt to classify alcoholism, there is enough substance in these attempts to assist the diagnostic interviewer. The therapist should look intensively at the patient's drinking pattern, at the effects of the alcohol use on the patient's physical and mental health and on his ability to function socially and occupationally, and at the symptoms that result when the patient stops drinking. There is a complex interplay between alcoholism and other psychiatric disorders, with alcoholism having the potential to cause, mask, or aggravate these problems.

REFERENCES

Abel, T., Metraux, R., and Roll, S. (1987). *Psychotherapy and Culture.* University of New Mexico Press

American Psychiatric Association (1987). *Diagnostic and Statistical Manual of Mental Disorders*, 3rd ed., rev. Washington, DC: APA.

Armor, D. J., and Polich, J. M. (1982). Measurement of alcohol consumption. In *Encyclopedic Handbook of Alcoholism*, ed. E. M. Pattison and E. Kaufman, pp. 72–82. New York: Gardner Press.

Barnes, G. E. (1979). The alcoholic personality: a reanalysis of the literature. *Journal of Studies on Alcohol* 40:571–634.

Bartsch, T., and Hoffman, J. (1985). A cluster analysis of MCMI profiles: more about a taxonomy of alcoholic subtypes. *Journal of Clinical Psychology* 41:707–713.

Becker, J., and Kaplan, R. (1986). Neurophysiological concomitants of brain dysfunction in alcoholics. In *Psychopathology and Addictive Disorders*, ed. R. E. Myer, pp. 263–292. New York: Guilford.

Bennett, G. (1986). Alcohol problems among the young. In *Alcoholism: Development, Consequences, and Interventions*, ed. N. J. Estes and E. Heinemann, pp. 221–240. St. Louis: C. V. Mosby.

Blum, E. M., and Blum, R. H. (1967). *Alcoholism: Modern Psychological Approaches to Treatment.* San Francisco: Jossey-Bass.

Bohman, M. (1978). Some genetic aspects of alcoholism and criminality. *Archives of General Psychiatry* 35:269–276.

Bohman, M., Sigvardsson, S., and Cloning, C. R. (1981). Maternal inheritance of alcohol abuse. *Archives of General Psychiatry* 38:965–969.

Brandsma, J., and Pattison, E. M. (1982). Homosexuality in alcoholism. In *Encyclopedic Handbook of Alcoholism*, ed. E. Pattison and S. Kaufman, pp. 736–741. New York: Gardner Press.

Caddy, G. R. (1986). Alcoholism. In *Diagnostic Interviewing*, ed. M. Herson and S. M. Turner, pp. 161–182. New York: Plenum.

Carroll, J. F. (1977a). Drug abuse by alcoholics and problem drinkers: a literature review and evaluation. *American Journal of Drug Abuse* 4:317–341.

——— ed. (1977b). National Drug/Alcohol Collaborative Project (NDACP), final report. Eagleville, PA: Eagleville Hospital and Rehabilitation Center.

Chafetz, M. (1983). *The Alcoholic Patient: Diagnosis and Management.* Oradell, NJ: Medical Economics Books.

Cohen, S. (1982). Combined alcohol–drug abuse and human behavior. In *Perspectives in Alcohol and Drug Abuse*, ed. J. Solomon and K. Keeley, pp. 89–116. Boston: John Wright.

Craig, R. J., Verinis, J., and Wexler, S. (1985). Personality characteristics of drug addicts and alcoholics. *Journal of Personality Assessment* 49:156–160.

Donovan, J. M. (1986). An etiologic model of alcoholism. *American Journal of Psychiatry* 143:1–11.

Dreher, K., and Fraser, J. (1967). Smoking habits of alcoholic outpatients I. *International Journal of Addictions* 2:259–270.

——— (1968). Smoking habits of alcoholic outpatients II. *International Journal of Addictions* 3:65–80.

Estes, N. J., and Heinemann, E. (1986). Issues in identification of alcoholism. In *Alcoholism: Development, Consequences, and Interventions*, ed. N. J. Estes and E. Heinemann, pp. 317–333. St. Louis: C. V. Mosby.

Feighner, J. P., Robins, E., Guze, S., et al. (1972). Diagnostic criteria for use in psychiatric research. *Archives of General Psychiatry* 26:57–68.

Filstead, W. (1982). Adolescence and alcohol. In *Encyclopedic Handbook of Alcoholism*, ed. E. M. Pattison and E. Kaufman, pp. 769–778. New York: Gardner.

Forrest, G. (1975). *The Diagnosis and Treatment of Alcoholism.* Springfield, IL: Charles C Thomas.

Fowler, R. C., Rich, C. L., and Young, D. (1986). San Diego suicide study II: substance abuse in young cases. *Archives of General Psychiatry* 43:962–965.

Freed, E. X. (1975). Alcoholism and schizophrenia: the search for perspectives. *Journal of Studies on Alcohol* 36:853–881.

Gomberg, E. S. L. (1986). Women with alcohol problems. In *Alcoholism: Development, Consequences, and Interventions*, ed. N. J. Estes and E. Heinemann, pp. 221–240. St. Louis: C. V. Mosby.

Goodwin, D. W. (1979). Alcoholism and heredity. *Archives of General Psychiatry* 36:57–61.

Goodwin, D. W., Schulsinger, F., and Hermansen, L. (1973). Alcohol problems in adoptees raised apart from alcoholic biological parents. *Archives of General Psychiatry* 28:238–243.

Guze, G. B., Goodwin, D. W., and Crane, J. B. (1969). Criminality and psychiatric disorders. *Archives of General Psychiatry* 20:583–591.

Harper, F., ed. (1976). *Alcohol Abuse and Black America.* Alexandria, VA: Douglass.

Heath, D. B. (1983). Alcohol use among North American Indians: a cross-cultural survey. In *Research Advances in Alcohol and Drug Problems*, vol. 7, pp. 343–396. New York: Plenum.

Hoffman, A., and Heinemann, E. (1986). Alcohol problems in elderly persons. In *Alcoholism: Development, Consequences, and Interventions*, ed. N. J. Estes and E. Heinemann, pp. 257–272. St. Louis: C. V. Mosby.

Jellinek, E. M. (1952). Phases of alcohol addiction. *Quarterly Journal of Studies on Alcohol* 13:673–684.

——— (1960). *The Disease Concept of Alcoholism.* Highland Park, NJ: Hillhouse.

Johnson, L. V., and Matre, M. (1978). Anomie and alcohol use: drinking problems in Mexican American and Anglo neighborhoods. *Journal of Studies on Alcohol* 39:894–902.

Kania, J., and Kofoed, L. (1984). Drug use by alcoholics in outpatient treatment. *American Journal of Drug Abuse* 10:529–534.

Lex, B. (1985). Alcohol problems in special populations. In *The Diagnosis and Treatment of Alcoholism*, ed. J. Mendelson and N. Mello, 2nd ed., pp. 89–188. New York: McGraw-Hill.

MacGready, N., Greely, A., and Thieson, G. (1983). Ethnicity and nationality in alcoholism. In *The Biology of Alcoholism. The Pathogenesis of Alcoholism: Psychosocial Factors*, vol. 6, ed. B. Kissin and H. Beleiter, pp. 309–340. New York: Plenum.

Maletta, J. (1982). Alcoholism and the aged. In *Encyclopedic Handbook of Alcoholism*, ed. E. M. Pattison and E. Kaufman, pp. 779–794. New York: Gardner.

Mayfield, D., McCleod, G., and Hall, P. (1974). The CAGE questionnaire: validation of a new alcoholism screening instrument. *American Journal of Psychiatry* 131:1121–1123.

Mello, N. (1983). Etiological theories of alcoholism. In *Advances in Substance Abuse*, ed. N. Mello, pp. 271–312. Greenwich, CT: JAI.

Menninger, K. (1938). *Man Against Himself.* New York: Harcourt Brace.

Miller, M., Gorski, T., and Miller, D. (1980). *Learning to Live Again.* Hazel Crest, IL: Human Ecology Systems.

Miller, W. R. (1976). Alcoholism scales and objective assessment methods: a review. *Psychological Bulletin* 83:649–674.

——— (1986). The effectiveness of alcoholism treatment: what research reveals. In *Treating Addicting Behaviors: Process of Change*, ed. W. E. Miller and N. Heather, pp. 121–174. New York: Plenum.

Miller, W. R., and Hester, R. (1986a). *Problem drinking: assessment, motivation, and intervention.* Paper presented at the annual meeting of the American Association of Behavioral Therapy, Chicago, November.

——— (1986b). Inpatient alcoholism treatment: who benefits? *American Psychologist* 41:794–805.

Miller, W. R., and Marlatt, A. (1984). *Manual for the Comprehensive Drinker Profile.* Odessa, FL: Psychological Assessment Resources.

Nathan, P. (1982). Blood alcohol level discrimination and diagnosis. In *Encyclopedic Handbook of Alcoholism*, ed. E. M. Pattison and E. Kaufman, pp. 64–71. New York: Gardner Press.

National Council on Alcoholism (1972). Criteria for the diagnosis of alcoholism. *American Journal of Psychiatry* 129:2–14.

Nerviano, V., and Gross, W. (1983). Personality types of alcoholics in objective inventories. *Journal of Studies on Alcohol* 44:837–851.

Paredes, A. (1986). Models and definitions of alcoholism. In *Alcoholism: Development, Consequences, and Interventions*, ed. N. J. Estes and E. Heinemann, pp. 53–66. St. Louis: C. V. Mosby.

Pattison, E. M. (1985). The selection of treatment modalities for the alcohol patient. In *The Diagnosis and Treatment of Alcoholism*, ed. J. Mendleson and N. Mello, 2nd ed., pp. 189–294. New York: McGraw-Hill.

Pattison, E. M., Sobell, M., and Sobell, L., eds. (1977). *Emerging Concepts of Alcohol Dependence.* New York: Springer.

Propping, P., Kruger, J., and Mark, N. (1981). Genetic disposition to alcoholism: an EEG study in alcoholics and their relatives. *Human Genetics* 59:51–59.

Rich, C. L., Young, D., and Fowler, D. C. (1986). San Diego suicide study I: young vs. old subjects. *Archives of General Psychiatry* 43:577–582.

Ringer, C., Kufner, H., Antons, K., and Feuerlein, W. (1977). The NCA criteria for the diagnosis of alcoholism. *Journal of Studies on Alcohol* 38: 1259.

Schuckit, M. (1983). Alcoholism and other psychiatric disorders. *Hospital and Community Psychiatry* 39:1022–1027.

——— (1984). Subjective responses to alcohol in sons of alcoholics and controls. *Archives of General Psychiatry* 41:879–884.

——— (1986). Genetic and clinical implications of alcoholism and affective disorders. *American Journal of Psychiatry* 143:140–147.

Selzer, M. L. (1971). The Michigan Alcoholism Screening Test: the quest for a new diagnostic instrument. *American Journal of Psychiatry* 3:176–181.

Shelton, J., Hollister, L., and Gocka, E. (1969). The Drinking Behavior Interview: an attempt to quantify alcoholic impairment. *Diseases of the Nervous System* 30:464–467.

Solomon, J. (1983). Psychiatric characteristics of alcoholics. In *The Biology of Alcoholism. The Pathogenesis of Alcoholism: Psychosocial Factors*, vol. 6, ed. B. Kissin and H. Begleiter, pp. 67–112. New York: Plenum.

Sobell, L. C., and Sobell, M. B. (1980). Covergent validity: an approach to increasing confidence in treatment outcome conclusions with alcohol and drug abusers. In *Evaluating Alcohol/Drug Abuse Treatment Effectiveness*, ed. L. C. Sobell, M. B. Sobell, and E. Ward, pp. 177–183. New York: Pergamon.

Taylor, J., and Helzer, J. (1983). The natural history of alcoholism. In *The Biology of Alcoholism. The Pathogenesis of Alcoholism: Psychosocial Factors*, vol. 6, ed. B. Kissin and H. Begleiter, pp. 17–66. New York: Plenum.

Thompson, G. N. (1959). Acute and chronic alcoholic conditions. In *American Handbook of Psychiatry*, vol. 2, ed. S. Arieti, pp. 1203–1221. New York: Basic Books.

Verinis, J. S. (1983). Agreement between alcoholics and relatives when reporting follow-up status. *International Journal of Addictions* 18:891–894.

——— (1985). *Patient improvement upon entering alcohol treatment: a week-by-week comparison*. Paper presented at the 25th annual meeting of the New England Psychological Association, New Haven, CT, October.

——— (1986a). Caffeine use in recovering alcoholics. *Alcohol Health and Research World* 11:64.

——— (1986b). Characteristics of patients who continue with alcohol outpatient treatment. *International Journal of Addictions* 21:25–31.

Verinis, J. S., Wetzel, L., Vanderporten, A., and Lewis, D. (1986). Improvement in men inpatients in an alcoholism rehabilitation unit: a week-by-week comparison. *Journal of Studies on Alcohol* 47:85–88.

Westermeyer, J., and Baker, J. (1986). Alcoholism and the American Indian. In *Alcoholism: Development, Consequences, and Interventions*, ed. N. J. Estes and E. Heinemann, pp. 273–282. St. Louis: C. V. Mosby.

Whitehead, D., and Simpkins, J. (1983). Occupational factors in alcoholism. In *The Biology of Alcoholism. The Pathogenesis of Alcoholism: Psychosocial Factors*, vol. 6, ed. B. Kissin and H. Begleiter, pp. 17–66. New York: Plenum.

Wilsnack, S. (1982). Alcohol abuse and alcoholism in women. In *Encyclopedic Handbook of Alcoholism*, ed. E. M. Pattison and E. Kaufman, pp. 718–735. New York: Gardner.

World Health Organizaton (1977). *Manual of the International Statistical Classification of Diseases, Injuries, and Causes of Death*. Geneva: WHO.

10

Anorexia and Bulimia

CHERYL MARSHALL, Psy.D.

The eating disorders—anorexia nervosa and bulimia nervosa—have become much more prevalent in the past 20 years, perhaps owing to changing cultural life-styles and values. These disorders are particularly evident in industrialized societies, and in the United States they represent a major health problem (Mitchell and Eckert 1987). Along with the increased prevalence has appeared a growing body of literature on anorexia nervosa and bulimia nervosa. Specialized treatment centers continue to become available (Garner and Garfinkel 1985). One apparent gap in the literature is found in compendia on diagnostic interviewing, in which assessment of the eating disorders is either omitted or granted cursory review. It is likely that eating disorders will be encountered in a variety of settings, making it incumbent upon healthcare professionals to be familiar with these life-threatening ailments so that effective assessment and treatment recommendations can be made.

Anorexia nervosa and bulimia nervosa are believed to be multidetermined disorders, with each having significant medical, nutritional, and psychological implications and consequences. This chapter provides an introduction to diagnostic procedures for assessment of eating disorders. It is organized into three sections. First, diagnostic categories will be reviewed. Next, various medical, nutritional, and psychological complications and consequences of these disorders will be presented, with an eye toward holistic understanding. Finally, an interview format will be put forth, along with suggestions for treatment planning.

DSM-III-R CLASSIFICATION OF EATING DISORDERS

The eating disorders are a subclass of disorders characterized by a significant disturbance in eating behavior (American Psychiatric Association 1987). The focus here will be on anorexia nervosa and bulimia nervosa, disorders which typically begin in adolescence and early adulthood and which predominantly affect females (approximately 95 percent of these patients are female). It is possible that more males are affected than clinical and community samples would suggest, and that categorizing these disorders as feminine afflictions has deterred men from admitting problematic eating behaviors (Johnson and Connors 1987) and from seeking treatment.

Anorexia Nervosa

The essential features of anorexia nervosa include low body weight, morbid fear of becoming overweight, distorted body image, and amenorrhea. Patients with anorexia nervosa are profoundly underweight, and weight loss (or failure to gain weight as expected) is achieved via restrictive dieting or fasting, sometimes with the additional weight-reduction methods of self-induced vomiting, laxative or diuretic abuse, and vigorous exercise. Although amenorrhea typically follows weight loss, it can also occur prior to noticeable reduction in weight (Ohlrich and Stephenson 1986). The diagnostic criteria for this disorder are listed in Table 10–1.

Clinically, anorexic patients often deny having any problems. Upon inquiry, they are likely to say that they are "fine" and that other aspects of their lives are "fine" too; not surprisingly, they are unlikely to be self-referred. Frequently observed, however, is an emaciated-looking person whose excessive thinness belies disavowal of a problem. The pervasive denial encountered in these patients can make the assessment interview quite challenging for the therapist interested in understanding the patient.

The onset of anorexia nervosa typically follows a stressor that was accompanied by loss of appetite and related weight loss, or a "successful" restrictive diet in which desired weight loss was found to be particularly reinforcing. In some cases, the disorders may also appear consequent to exposure to media coverage (Chiodo and Latimer 1983) or educational presentations in the school setting, where, along with heightened aware-

Table 10-1. DSM-III-R Criteria for Anorexia Nervosa

1. Refusal to maintain body weight over a minimal normal weight for age and height; weight loss leading to maintenance of body weight 15 percent below that expected; or failure to make expected weight gain during period of growth, leading to body weight 15 percent below that expected.
2. Intense fear of gaining weight or becoming fat, even though underweight.
3. Disturbance in the way in which the patient's body weight, size, or shape is experienced; for example, the patient claims to "feel fat" even when emaciated, or believes that one area of the body is "too fat" even when obviously underweight.
4. In females, absence of at least three consecutive menstrual cycles when other etiology has been ruled out (primary or secondary amenorrhea). (A woman is considered to have amenorrhea if her menses occur only following hormone administration.)

ness of the problem, an attraction emerges to the idea of developing the disorder. Bruch (1986) has noted that the later phenomenon is seen in "me-too" anorexia, in which the imitative basis of the problem may represent a syndrome clinically distinct from the primary anorexia nervosa seen prior to the 1970s. She has also speculated that the traditional psychodynamic conceptualization of the disorder as an original, passionate, and fierce expression of independent strivings may come to lose its meaning as the "me-too" anorexic begins to predominate. Genuine primary anorexia nervosa may in fact disappear until cultural conditions are once again right for its reemergence.

Bulimia Nervosa

The essential feature of bulimia nervosa (previously called "bulimia") is binge eating, coupled with overconcern about body weight and shape. There is a feeling of lack of control over eating behavior during the binges, and compensatory activities are used in an attempt to prevent weight gain as a result of the binges. These methods typically include self-induced vomiting, use of laxatives or diuretics, strict fasting or restrictive dieting, and excessive exercise. The diagnostic criteria for bulimia nervosa are listed in Table 10–2.

Studies have shown that, like the anorexic patient, the patient with bulimia nervosa often follows a restrictive diet (Fairburn and Cooper 1984, Pyle et al. 1981). Other factors associated with the onset of bulimic behavior include heightened awareness of bodily appearance and increased interest in the opposite sex (Abraham and Beumont 1982), loss or separation (Johnson and Connors 1987, Johnson et al. 1982, Pyle et al. 1981), and important life transitions (Johnson and Connors 1987).

In contrast to anorexics, bulimics tend to view their symptoms as pathological; also unlike anorexics, who take pride in their behavior, bulimics often feel ashamed of their symptoms. In addition, the bulimic is more likely to be self-referred, troubled by eating-disordered behavior, unhappy, and longing for more effective solutions to personal problems.

TABLE 10-2. DSM-III-R Criteria for Bulimia Nervosa

1. Recurrent episodes of binge eating (rapid consumption of a large amount of food in a discrete period of time).
2. A feeling of lack of control over eating behavior during the eating binges.
3. Regular engagement in self-induced vomiting, use of laxatives or diuretics, strict dieting or fasting, or vigorous exercise in order to prevent weight gain.
4. A minimum average of two binge-eating episodes a week for at least three months.
5. Persistent overconcern with body shape and weight.

Eating Disorder Not Otherwise Specified

Sometimes it happens that a patient shows prominent disturbances in eating behavior but does not meet the criteria for a specific eating disorder. In atypical cases such as this, the residual category of eating disorder not otherwise specified (NOS) is used. DSM-III-R examples are listed in Table 10–3.

Differential Diagnosis

The process of identifying the correct diagnosis from among conditions with similar features is known as *differential diagnosis* (Maxmen 1986). For any apparent psychiatric problem with physiological involvement, etiological distinction must be made between organic and functional conditions. When there is no known physiological cause for a disorder, it is said to be *functional*. Thus, even though biological factors are involved in the eating disorders, they are considered to be functional because no known biological cause is necessary to produce the disorder. Instead, the etiology is believed to be primarily psychosocial. The eating disorders are a unique type of psychopathology in that the culture, as an environmental variable, appears to be a major etiological factor in their development (Mitchell and Eckert 1987). Nevertheless, a thorough physical evaluation is always mandatory, due to the medical consequences of the disorders and because certain medical illnesses can mimic anorexia nervosa and bulimia nervosa (Mitchell 1986).

Experimental research on starvation in normal subjects (Keys et al. 1950) has revealed that its cognitive and behavioral effects (such as irritability, poor concentration, anxiety, emotional lability, and obsessive thinking) are also observed in semistarvation associated with anorexia nervosa and bulimia nervosa (Garner et al. 1985). This research has clarified the contribution of the effects of starvation to the eating disorders, while highlighting the importance of weight gain as fundamental to the treatment process (Andersen 1983, Garfinkel and Garner 1982).

Once an organic basis for the illness has been ruled out, eating-disordered patients must be distinguished from weight-preoccupied dieters. Noting that dieting and concern about weight have become "normative," Polivy and Herman (1987) pointed out that these two groups

Table 10-3. DSM-III-R Criteria for Eating Disorder (NOS)

Disorders of eating that do not meet the criteria for a specific eating disorder. Examples:

1. Average weight and no binge-eating episodes, but frequent engagement in self-induced vomiting for fear of gaining weight
2. All of the features of anorexia nervosa in a female except absence of menses
3. All of the features of bulimia nervosa except the frequency of binge-eating episodes

share some pathological attitudes and behaviors, such as binge eating, purging, body image dissatisfaction, and a drive for thinness. Fortunately, the weight-loss criterion for anorexia nervosa and the frequency and duration criteria for bulimia nervosa will help clarify this issue.

Regarding differential diagnosis among psychiatric disorders, there may be weight loss and anorexia (loss of appetite) in depressive disorders, but there is rarely a genuine loss of appetite in anorexia nervosa except in the late stages. Also assisting with the distinction is the fact that depressed patients without anorexia nervosa will not manifest a disturbance in body image or a morbid fear of obesity.

In bulimia nervosa (without associated anorexia nervosa) there may be a fear of obesity, and weight loss may be significant, but the patient will not meet the 15 percent weight-loss criterion. However, anorexia nervosa can occur in patients with bulimia nervosa, in which case both diagnoses are given.

Although the DSM-III-R states that anorexia nervosa and bulimia nervosa are related disorders, Garner and Garfinkel (1985) have noted that the theoretical relationship between the disorders is not clear; nor is the extent to which they benefit from common or unique therapeutic approaches. However, these authors and others (Garner et al. 1983, Norman and Herzog 1983) have offered the suggestion that the symptom of bulimia among normal-weight and anorexic patients may be of diagnostic significance. Research has differentiated bulimic anorexics from restricting anorexics based on evidence that the former subgroup resembles bulimics more than they do anorexics. Although the distinctions—bulimic anorexic and restricting anorexic—are not used for formal diagnosis, some awareness of these subgroups may be helpful.

The presence of bulimic symptoms has important clinical implications, whether they appear among normal-weight bulimics or anorexia nervosa patients with bulimic symptoms (Johnson and Connors 1987). The symptom of bulimia has been associated with impulse-dominated behavior, indirect expression of aggression, stereotypical views of feminity (Norman and Herzog 1983), and affective instability (Johnson and Connors 1987). Overall, however, bulimic anorexics are believed to have the greatest degree of psychopathology and the poorest prognosis (Hsu et al. 1979). This group is characterized by more severe affective instability with suicidal ideation (Casper et al. 1980, Garfinkel et al. 1980), as well as self-mutilation, sexual acting out, shoplifting, and substance abuse (Bruch 1973, Casper et al. 1980, Garfinkel et al. 1980).

Concurrent Psychiatric Diagnosis

Although there appear to be broad similarities among patients diagnosed as manifesting anorexia nervosa and bulimia nervosa, and several writers have associated these disorders with specific psychopathologies, it is probably more accurate at this stage in our understanding to construe the disorders as syndromes representing "a final common symptomatic pathway for a large number of psychopathologies" (Swift 1985, p. 385). Heterogeneity is being stressed here in the interest of the patients whom the therapist will be assessing. Knowledge of research suggesting apparent uniformity of personality correlates is important, but only in conjunction with efforts to understand the individual with whom one is working. The eating disorders are best understood from a biopsychosocial framework, and, as with any patient, a thorough diagnostic assessment is indispensible to effective treatment planning.

Recent research has revealed a link between the eating disorders and the primary affective disorders, particularly for bulimic patients (Johnson 1985). Both affective disorders and substance abuse disorders have been found to be prevalent among first- and second-degree relatives of eating-disordered patients (Strober et al. 1982, Winokur et al. 1980), and there is some evidence to suggest that bulimia may be a symptom of a biologically mediated affective disorder that might respond to pharmacotherapy (Pope and Hudson 1982). When a mood disorder is observed, it should be diagnosed on Axis I.

BEYOND THE DSM-III-R

Diagnostic labels by themselves do not begin to capture the wide spectrum of behaviors, implications, and consequences found in the eating disorders. The classification of anorexia nervosa and bulimia nervosa as "mental disorders" immediately suggests psychological and social impairment, but omits biological facets of the problem. Since careful assessment based on holistic understanding of the eating disorders is essential to responsible and ethical treatment, the therapist must be familiar with medical, nutritional, and psychological perspectives on the problem.

Medical Aspects of Assessment

The medical consequences of eating disorders differ significantly depending on the particular symptom. Minimally, a comprehensive assessment should include a medical evaluation, both to rule out an organic basis for the disturbed eating and to evaluate for the presence of physical effects of an eating disorder. The potential physical consequences of various eating-disordered behaviors are quite numerous (Table 10–4), with the most medically dangerous combination of behaviors being restriction of calorie intake and vomiting (Ohlrich and Stephenson 1986).

Among the more common physical side effects of the eating disorders are menstrual difficulties or absence of menses, electrolyte imbalance, dehydration, edema, dental decay, parotid gland enlargement, and gastrointestinal difficulties. The physical consequences can range from minor, reversible problems to death. Involvement of a physician who is knowledgeable in the assessment and treatment of eating disorders is an absolute necessity in the overall care of these patients. A thorough

TABLE 10-4. Major Medical Consequences of Behaviors Associated with Eating Disorders

Restrictive eating—low weight	Vomiting
Amenorrhea	Electrolyte problems
Lanugo	Dehydration: dizziness, syncope
Bradycardia	Muscle weakness
Acrocyanosis	Dental enamel erosion, caries
Dehydration: dizziness, syncope	Cardiac arrhythmias
Hypothyroidism: coldness, constipation, dry skin, coarse hair	Sore throat; sores in mouth, gums
Osteoporosis	Nasal congestion
Retardation of growth in height	Enlarged salivary glands
Edema of feet, legs, hands, body	Hematemesis
Congestive heart failure	Calluses
Depression, suicide	Laxative abuse
Kidney stones	Dehydration: dizziness, syncope
Decreased kidney function	Electrolyte problems
Binge eating	Cardiac arrhythmias
Obesity	Muscle weakness
Edema of feet, legs, hands	Rectal bleeding
Acute stomach dilation; rupture possible	Feel constipated upon discontinuing laxatives
Depression, suicide	Edema of feet, legs, hands upon discontinuing laxatives
Diet pill abuse	Depression, suicide
Elevation of blood pressure	Diuretic abuse
Stroke	Electrolyte problems
Myocardial infarction	Dehydration
Seizures	Cardiac arrhythmias
Restlessness, anxiety	Muscle weakness

From Ohlrich, S. E., and Stephenson, J. N. (1986). Pitfalls in the care of patients with anorexia nervosa and bulimia, in *Seminars in Adolescent Medicine*, Volume 2, Number 1, New York, 1986, Thieme Medical Publishers, Inc. Reprinted by permission.

physical examination should be conducted, along with standard laboratory tests such as a complete blood count, urinalysis, and a multiple-channel chemistry analysis (Johnson and Pure 1987).

Nutritional Aspects of Assessment

Assessment of nutritional status is an integral part of the comprehensive evaluation of an eating-disordered patient. If your clinical setting does not afford opportunity for collaboration with a multidisciplinary team, an outside registered dietician should be consulted. A dietary assessment will reveal in-depth information about the patient's past and present eating patterns, activity level, food dislikes and preferences, and knowledge about nutrition. In order to understand the patient's degree of nutritional compromise, the dietician will conduct an anthropometric assessment, which involves the accurate measurement of height and weight, and the evaluation of body composition (Kilbourne 1986). Once an ideal body weight is determined (usually from charts), current weight is used in calculating the patient's current percentage of ideal body weight. For adults, the percentage of ideal body weight is calculated as follows:

$$\frac{\text{current weight}}{\text{ideal body weight}} \times 100$$

For adolescents, the calculation is more complex, since predicted weights must be obtained by evaluating past growth records (Kilbourne 1986).

Psychological Aspects of Assessment

The eating disorders have profound psychosocial implications, and it is the therapist's task to assess the patient's overall occupational intrapsychic, and interpersonal functioning. The therapist should inquire in depth about eating patterns, weight history, and related life events. Also evaluated are the type and degree of psychopathology, assets and strengths, and motivation for treatment. In the care of eating-disordered patients, the therapist generally determines the diagnosis, develops a working conceptual understanding of the patient and his or her behavior, and makes treatment recommendations. Hypotheses should be developed regarding the adaptive, functional role of the patient's symptoms as a solution or resolution to underlying conflict.

THE INITIAL ASSESSMENT

The therapist's approach will differ depending on the setting and availability of professional resources. In a formal program dedicated to the assessment and treatment of eating disorders there is typically found a multidisciplinary professional team, usually comprising a physician, a nurse, a dietician, and a psychologist. The solitary practitioner should not attempt diagnosis or treatment in the absence of collaborative relationships with other professionals. When outside professionals are consulted, an alliance must be formed so that the therapeutic aspects of a "team" might be simulated. The team approach provides a "holding environment" for the patient, in which clinical management is based on developmental object relations theory (Stern 1986). Most major programs for eating adhere to some guiding team philosophy in their assessment, treatment, and management of the eating disorders.

Assuming that eating and weight difficulties are known and are part of the presenting complaint, it is essential that the therapist understand the circumstances of the referral. The initial few minutes of the interview are important in understanding attitudes that might affect data collection, as well as motivation for subsequent treatment (Johnson 1985). Generally speaking, patients with anorexia nervosa appear for evaluation at the behest of others in their lives; thus, they may be resistant or, at best, reluctant to engage in the assessment process. Patients with bulimia nervosa tend more often to be self-referred, and to have some self-awareness as to the pathological nature of their behavior. Consequently, despite their shame and embarrassment, bulimics may be more motivated to provide reliable information. In assessing anorexics, particularly adolescents, it's a good idea to interview parents about the youngster's eating patterns.

Significant countertransference reactions may be evoked in working with eating-disordered patients, even in the initial consultation (Johnson 1985). The term *countertransference* refers to the emotional reactions that arise in the therapist as a result of the patient's influence on the therapist's unconscious feelings (Freud 1910). Interviewers, in keeping with traditional technique, are advised to monitor their own reactions so as to avoid any deleterious effects of countertransference on the patient. Johnson (1985) has suggested that the interviewer can "maintain perspective" in the face of provocative or resistant behavior by understanding the "adaptive context" of the eating disorder—that is, by conceptualizing the eating disorder as an attempt to adapt to desperate circumstances.

Eating and Weight History

Once a medical examination has ruled out an organic basis for abnormal eating behavior, the therapist is free to investigate the psychosocial contributions to the problem. Inquiry will be made into the patient's weight history, including weight fluctuations and methods of weight control, and body image. Onset of weight and food preoccupation should be explored, and the patient should be encouraged to reconstruct the life circumstances that coincided with the development of overconcern with food and weight. Patterns of problematic eating following onset can be explored in a similar vein. Weight-control methods tried by the patient must be investigated in detail, since this information may bear significantly on the patient's physical health and on degree of medical risk involved. Methods of weight control may include any single one of the following activities, or some combination thereof: (1) restrictive dieting; (2) self-induced vomiting (possibly with use of syrup of ipecac); (3) laxatives, diuretics, and diet pills; and (4) physical exercise. Vomiting and use of laxatives and diuretics are considered to be purging behaviors. All have serious side effects, and the exact extent of the behaviors should be ascertained. Patients who use syrup of ipecac, in particular, are at risk for cardiac arrest and sudden death (Adler et al. 1980).

The patient's phenomenological experience of all food and weight-related behaviors can be explored, including dieting behavior, binge eating, and purging. Similarly, the perception of body image can be explored. Body-image difficulties among these patients can range from mild dissatisfaction to severe distortion, and the extent to which such difficulties interfere with life adjustment should be assessed (Johnson 1985).

Social History

The nature of patients' interpersonal functioning is assessed by inquiring about their relationships with family and friends. An interview with the family of the patient provides an opportunity to observe the family in action and to note styles of relating, ways in which members manage the stress of the interview, and the patient's apparent role in the family.

In the context of an interpersonal assessment, sexual adjustment can be assessed via inquiry into significant romantic relationships in the individual's life. In this context, sexual attitudes can come to be understood as part of the patient's overall life adjustment.

Mental Status Examination

It is a sound practice to conduct a mental status examination on all patients seen for an eating-disorders assessment. Much of the mental status examination for this population can be informal, ascertained by observations of the patient when covering background history. However, because of the established relationship between affective disorders and eating disorders, a more direct assessment of mood and affect should be made. Any history of suicidal ideation or self-harm should be noted, along with any current suicidal thinking or inclinations.

Potential for insight is best determined by offering patients a few interpretations during the assessment. Patients' reactions can provide some data from which to conjecture about openness to the therapeutic process. See Table 10–5 for recommended interview format.

Assessment Instruments

As part of the assessment process, patients can be asked to complete some questionnaires. The Eating Disorders Inventory (EDI) (Garner et al. 1983) is a psychometric instrument designed to assess for a broad range of eating-related pathology associated with anorexia nervosa and bulimia. The EDI is a paper-and-pencil inventory that has eight subscales that may help to distinguish eating-disordered individuals from "normal" dieters.

Another instrument that can be used either as a self-report survey or as a semistructured interview is the Diagnostic Survey for Eating Disorders-Revised (DSED-R; Johnson and Connors 1987). The questionnaire covers demographic information, body image, dieting behavior, binge-eating behavior, purging behavior, exercise behavior, sexual history, medical and psychiatric history, life adjustment, and family history.

TABLE 10-5. Suggested Format for the Assessment of Eating Disorders

1. Background information
   Inform patient of what to expect from comprehensive assessment.
   Establish rapport.
   Determine circumstances of the referral and patient's attitudes about coming for an evaluation.
2. Eating and weight history
   Explore history of the problem.
   Determine onset of weight preoccupation.
   Assess for unusual eating patterns, including binge eating and restrictive dieting. (Determine frequency and duration.)
   Note any significant weight fluctuations.
   Inquire about life events that have coincided with any of the foregoing items.
3. Weight-control methods
   Account for nature of restrictive dieting.
   Identify purging methods used by the patient. (Determine frequency and duration for each method.)
   —Vomiting (Self-induced? Reflexive? How induced? Ipecac used?)
   —Laxatives (Type used)
   —Diuretics (Over-the-counter or prescription)
   Look for history of use of diet pills or appetite suppressants.
   Evaluate activity level and use of exercise to control weight.
   Assess patient's recent pattern with foregoing information.
4. Self-image
   Explore perceptions of body-image, including self-perceptions and patient's beliefs about others' perceptions.
   Assess feelings of self-efficacy.
   Explore concerns and complaints not related to food or weight.
5. Social history
   Gather family history, assessing quality of patient's relationships with parents and siblings.
   Inquire about family environment.
   Explore relationships with peers.
   Explore sexual history, which may range from total retreat from sexual maturation to self-destructive acting out.
   Inquire about history of sexual abuse.
6. Mental status examination
   Evaluate patient formally when sufficient data have not been obtained informally during the interview.
   Determine history of substance abuse.
   Identify disturbances in mood and affect.
   Conduct a suicide assessment, including any history of self-mutilation or self-harm.
   Explore long-term goals and goals for treatment.
7. Treatment recommendations
   Discuss patient's diagnosis.
   Provide feedback on medical, nutritional, and psychological needs.
   Make treatment recommendations.

Treatment Recommendations

When a diagnosis has been determined, feedback is given to the patient, and if they have been involved, to the family as well. Any concerns raised by the diagnosis can then be discussed. Specific medical, nutritional, and psychological needs are highlighted, followed by discussion of a treatment plan. The most obvious treatment decision to be made is between inpatient and outpatient care, since some eating-disordered patients require hospitalization. The recommendation to hospitalize is based on the following criteria: serious medical compromise resulting from the eating disorder, suicide risk, and failure of previous outpatient treatment to assist patient with refeeding or with interruption of the binge–purge cycle.

Treatment recommendations should be based on the individual patient's needs, which may require a variety of treatment approaches, such as individual, group, or family psychotherapy; nutritional counseling; medical care; and psychiatric consultation for pharmacotherapy. Because of the nature of these disorders, psychotherapy alone is not enough; the symptoms must be treated too. Symptom management must be a component of every patient's treatment. Typically, this is a medically monitored program conducted by a registered nurse who regularly checks patients' weight and vital signs while also providing psychoeducational material to assist patients in their management of symptoms. Symptom management is conducted in conjunction with ongoing psychotherapies, with attention given to coordinating psychological and medical treatment.

REFERENCES

Abraham, S., and Beumont, P. J. V. (1982). Varieties of psychosexual experience in patients with anorexia nervosa. *International Journal of Eating Disorders* 1:10–19.

Adler, A. G., Walinsky, P., Kroll, R. A., and Cho, S. Y. (1980). Ipecac syrup poisoning. *Journal of the American Medical Association* 243:1927–1928.

American Psychiatric Association (1987). *Diagnostic and Statistical Manual of Mental Disorders*, 3rd ed., rev. Washington, DC: APA.

Andersen, A. E. (1983). Anorexia nervosa and bulimia: a spectrum of eating disorders. *Journal of Adolescent Health Care* 4:15–21.

Bruch, H. (1973). *Eating Disorders: Obesity, Anorexia Nervosa, and the Person Within.* New York: Basic Books.

——— (1986). Four decades of eating disorders. In *Handbook of Psychotherapy for Anorexia Nervosa and Bulimia*, ed. D. M. Garner and P. E. Garfinkel, pp. 7–18. New York: Basic Books.

Casper, R. C., Eckert, E. D., Halmi, K. A., et al. (1980). Bulimia: its incidence and significance in patients with anorexia nervosa. *Archives of General Psychiatry* 37:1030–1035.

Chiodo, J., and Latimer, P. R. (1983). Vomiting as a learned weight-control technique in bulimia. *Journal of Behavior Therapy and Experimental Psychiatry* 14:131–135.

Fairburn, C. G., and Cooper, P. J. (1984). The clinical features of bulimia nervosa. *British Journal of Psychiatry* 144:238–246.

Freud, S. (1910). The future prospects of psychoanalytic therapy. *Standard Edition* 3:43–68.

Garfinkel, P. E., and Garner, D. M. (1982). *Anorexia Nervosa: A Multidimensional Perspective*. New York: Brunner/Mazel.

Garfinkel, P. E., Moldofsky, H., and Garner, D. M. (1980). The heterogeneity of anorexia nervosa. *Archives of General Psychiatry* 37:1036–1040.

Garner, D. M., and Garfinkel, P. E. (1985). Introduction. In *Handbook of Psychotherapy for Anorexia Nervosa and Bulimia*, ed. D. M. Garner and P. E. Garfinkel, pp. 3–6. New York: Basic Books.

Garner, D. M., Garfinkel, P., and O'Shaughnessy, M. (1985). The validity of the distinction between bulimics with and without anorexia nervosa. *American Journal of Psychiatry* 142:581–587.

Garner, D. M., Olmsted, M. P., and Polivy, J. (1983). Development and validation of a multidimensional eating disorder inventory for anorexia nervosa and bulimia. *International Journal of Eating Disorders* 2:15–34.

Garner, D. M., Rockert, W., Olmsted, M. P., et al. (1985). Psychoeducational principles in the treatment of bulimia and anorexia nervosa. In *Handbook of Psychotherapy for Anorexia Nervosa and Bulimia*, ed. D. M. Garner and P. E. Garfinkel, pp. 513–572. New York: Basic Books.

Hsu, L. K. G., Crisp, A. H., and Harding, B. (1979). Outcome of anorexia nervosa. *Lancet* 1:61–65.

Johnson, C. (1985). Initial consultation for patients with bulimia and anorexia nervosa. In *Handbook of Psychotherapy for Anorexia Nervosa and Bulimia*, ed. D. M. Garner and P. E. Garfinkel, pp. 19–51. New York: Basic Books.

Johnson, C., and Connors, M. E. (1987). *The Etiology and Treatment of Bulimia Nervosa*. New York: Basic Books.

Johnson, C., and Pure, D. L. (1986). Assessment of bulimia: a multidimensional model. In *Handbook of Eating Disorders*, ed. K. D. Brownell and J. P. Foreyt, pp. 405–449. New York: Basic Books.

Johnson, C., Stuckey, M., Lewis, L., and Schwartz, D. (1982). Bulimia: a descriptive survey of 316 cases. *International Journal of Eating Disorders* 11:1–16.

Keys, A., Brozek, J., Henschel, A., et al. (1950). *The Biology of Human Starvation*. Minneapolis: University of Minnesota Press.

Kilbourne, K. A. (1986). Nutritional evaluation and management of anorexic and bulimic patients. *Seminars in Adolescent Medicine* 2:47–55.

Maxmen, J. S. (1986). *Essential Psychopathology*. New York: W. W. Norton.

Mitchell, J. E. (1986). Anorexia nervosa: medical and physiological aspects. In *Handbook of Eating Disorders*, ed. K. D. Brownell and J. P. Foreyt, pp. 247–265. New York: Basic Books.

Mitchell, J. E., and Eckert, E. D. (1987). Scope and significance of eating disorders. *Journal of Consulting and Clinical Psychology* 55:628–634.

Norman, D. K., and Herzog, D. B. (1983). Bulimia, anorexia nervosa, and anorexia nervosa with bulimia: a comparative analysis of MMPI profiles. *International Journal of Eating Disorders* 2:43–52.

Ohlrich, S. E., and Stephenson, J. N. (1986). Pitfalls in the care of patients with anorexia nervosa and bulimia. *Seminars in Adolescent Medicine* 2:81–88.

Polivy, J., and Herman, C. P. (1987). Diagnosis and treatment of normal eating. *Journal of Consulting and Clinical Psychology* 55:635–644.

Pope, H. G., and Hudson, J. I. (1982). Treatment of bulimia with antidepressants. *Psychopharmacology* 78:176–179.

Pyle, R. L., Mitchell, J. E., and Eckert, E. D. (1981). Bulimia: a report of 34 cases. *Journal of Clinical Psychiatry* 42:60–64.

Stern, S. (1986). The dynamics of clinical management in the treatment of anorexia nervosa and bulimia: an organizing theory. *International Journal of Eating Disorders* 5:233–254.

Strober, M., Salkin, B., Burroughs, J., and Morrell, W. (1982). Validity of the bulimia-restrictor distinction in anorexia nervosa: parental personality characteristics and family psychiatric morbidity. *Journal of Nervous and Mental Diseases* 170:345–351.

Swift, W. J. (1985). Assessment of the bulimic patient. *American Journal of Orthopsychiatry* 55:384–396.

Winokur, A., March, V., and Mendels, J. (1980). Primary affective disorder in relatives of patients with anorexia nervosa. *American Journal of Psychiatry* 137:695–698.

11 Obesity

PIERRE-EMMANUEL LACOCQUE, Ph.D.

Eating-disordered patients are often quite complex and difficult to treat. This chapter will present a basic guideline as to what to look for when working with adult obese eating-disordered patients. First, a few notes of caution: Therapists working with overweight patients must be sensitive to the fact that obesity, in and of itself, is not synonymous with psychopathology. Moreover, if present at all, a psychological disturbance may be more the result of years of discrimination for being overweight and less the result of a pathogenic childhood environment. Anyone living in a deprecating environment can indeed experience mild to severe psychological distress. Some obese individuals develop psychiatric symptoms such as depression or low self-esteem in response to the rejections or criticisms they have had to endure. Many clinicians argue that the most devastating consequences of obesity are the social and psychological hazards rather than the associated health risks (Brownell 1981, 1982, Leon 1982, National Institutes of Health 1985, Wadden and Stunkard 1985, 1987, Striegel-Moore and Rodin 1986). Obese individuals are as prone to psychopathology as anyone else. Our aim will be to highlight symptoms and psychodynamics common among adult obese eating-disordered patients and to propose techniques to detect and evaluate them.

This chapter is divided into two interrelated parts. The first reviews the varieties of obesities and their multifarious etiologies. We then turn to obesity—specific DSM-III-R differential and concurrent psychiatric diagnoses. Eating-disorders inventories tailored for obese patients are provided, and commonly used psychological assessment tools are highlighted. The second part focuses on the psychological interview. We will consider motivation for treatment, psychosocial functioning and life-style analysis, insight level, the capacity to mourn, self-efficacy beliefs, perfectionistic strivings, body-image disparagement, hunger awareness, psychological pay-offs for remaining obese, and the night eating syndrome.

Throughout, the need for an interdisciplinary approach to the treatment of eating disorders will be emphasized. The help of a nutritionist, and often a physician and an exercise physiologist, is essential to treating the obese eating-disordered patient. Moreover, therapists working with obese patients must be sensitive to the possible medical or physiological processes contributing to the obesity. The therapist who intends to help an obese patient lose a significant amount of weight will need to refer to objective physiological data gathered through such means as indirect calorimetry or bioelectrical impedence machines, which assess the specific number of calories per day needed to maintain the present weight and body fat percentage, respectively.

TYPES OF OBESITY

There are many known etiological factors leading to obesity. Some are independent variables, while others are linked and interrelated. In some types of obesity, we can detect a precise, specific etiology. For example, obesity may be the result of endocrine or genetically based dysfunctions. The Prader-Willi syndrome, the Lawrence Moon-Biedl syndrome, and the Summitt syndrome are examples of such disorders. It can also result directly from diseases of the central nervous system, from epilepsy, or from neuromuscular diseases.

Endocrine and genetically based disorders are rare compared with other types of obesities, however. Among the more typical determinants leading to obesity are the following: physical inactivity, low metabolic rate, high fat-cell count and size, genetics, childhood environment, brain damage, chronic overeating, poor nutrition, a defect in dietary thermogenesis (heat production via calorie metabolism), or emotional-psychological disturbances (Table 11–1).

The obese person is not immune from psychological conflicts. Clinicians tend to agree that the longer the period of obesity, the more likely it is that psychopathology will be present. Research shows that dieting childhood-onset obese adults experience more pronounced emotional

Table 11-1. Etiologic Factors Leading to Obesity

1. Environment (including family environment, culture, ethnicity, and socioeconomic level)
2. Genetic factors (obesity resulting from a chromosomal abnormality as is found in Prader-Willi syndrome or in Cushing's syndrome)
3. Neurological damage (for example, injury to the ventromedial hypothalamus)
4. Medication use (such as phenothiazines and cyproheptadine)
5. Endocrine pathology (abnormal basal metabolic rate, hypothyroidism, defects in dietary thermogenesis, hyperinsulinism, hypercorticism, and so forth)
6. High-fat diet
7. Hyperphagia
8. Inadequate knowledge of nutrition
9. Physical inactivity
10. Psychosocial functioning

turmoil than dieting adult-onset obese patients (Glucksman and Hirsch 1969, Grinker et al. 1973, Leon 1982). Symptoms such as body-image distortion, obsession over food, perfectionistic strivings, a low tolerance for conflict (impulsivity), and an inordinate susceptibility to food cues often apply to the juvenile-onset severely obese person. The obesity in this case may be but a camouflage for other long-standing problems.

A striking feature of many developmentally obese individuals is their inability to correctly identify physiological hunger and other visceral sensations (Bruch 1973a, Stunkard 1976, 1985). The obese person afflicted by this deficit will be prompted to eat for a wide variety of reasons, ranging from internal arousal or tension to external cues such as seeing other people eat. Nonobese people will eat for similar reasons, but their hunger awareness and sense of satiation are usually better defined and more reliable. The obese person afflicted by the inability to correctly register internal sensations, including affects, will tend to eat indiscriminately in response to any arousal, be it pleasantly or unpleasantly experienced (Leon 1975, Leon and Chamberlain 1973, McKenna 1972, Robbins and Fray 1980, Rodin 1977a, 1977b, 1981, Slochower 1976).

DSM-III-R DIAGNOSES

There are dangers in giving any individual a diagnosis. For example, labeling a patient "borderline" or "narcissistic" may be more a reflection of therapists' inability to contain their anxieties than an accurate clinical picture (Lacocque and Loeb 1988). It is therefore suggested that the patient be evaluated for a few weeks before a definitive diagnosis is assigned. Medical and nutritional assessments are often necessary when treating overweight patients, especially when working with the severely obese. An Axis V diagnosis may therefore be best at first until a comprehensive assessment is conducted.

No predictable personality profile has been found for the obese. Indeed, what they have in common is more their physical appearance than their psychological characteristics. There are, however, specific diagnoses that can be assigned to *disturbed* obese patients. The main diagnosis proposed by DSM-III-R for obesity is that of psychological factors affecting physical condition (316.00). However, a number of other diagnoses, including the following, may apply: bulimia nervosa (307.51), eating disorder not otherwise specified (307.50), dysthymia (depressive neurosis, 300.40), depressive disorder not otherwise specified (311.00), and impulsive personality disorder (301.90).

Psychological Factors Affecting Physical Condition

This diagnosis recognizes that emotional factors play an important role in the etiology or course of obesity. It is placed on Axis I, with "obesity" placed on Axis III to describe the physical condition being treated.

Bulimia Nervosa

The term *bulimia* comes from the Greek word *boulimia* (*bous*, meaning "ox," and *limos*, meaning "hunger"). The diagnosis of bulimia implies an impulsive and unpredictable eating pattern in which a large food intake takes place rapidly and in a short period of time. The DSM-III-R notes self-loathing and remorse among the diagnostic criteria for bulimia nervosa. However, we have not invariably found these emotional reactions in obese bulimics. The defense mechanisms of denial, repression, and suppression, among others, are often so deeply rooted that long-term, intensive psychotherapy is required before some patients allow guilt feelings, self-deprecation, anxiety, or depression to come to their awareness. In our estimation, hyperphagia without guilt in the obese patient also falls under the category of bulimia. Should this be the case, eating disorder not otherwise specified (NOS) would be an appropriate diagnostic choice.

Bulimia nervosa is seldom an accurate diagnosis for obese binge-eating patients. Indeed, while hyperphagia is a common characteristic among obese and nonobese bulimics, one rarely finds self-induced vomiting, vigorous exercising, or laxative and diuretic abuse in the former group. This does not mean that obese patients do not express the wish to induce vomiting after binge-eating episodes. In fact, many do report such a desire. However, it seems that the mere idea of vomiting is repulsive enough to them to deter them from acting on the wish. (Bulimia is found in about 5 percent of the obese population. See Stunkard [1983].)

There are, nevertheless, at least two common characteristics between obese and nonobese bulimics: (1) the engagement in strict dieting or fasting to lose excess weight, and (2) a persistent concern with body image (two of the five diagnostic criteria for bulimia nervosa). When obese patients display symptoms close but not identical to bulimia nervosa, the diagnosis of eating disorder NOS can be considered.

Dysthymia

Obese patients often complain of depression. For some it is severe, and they "medicate" it through food abuse; for others, the depression is mild to moderately incapacitating. Overeating is one of the DSM-III-R criteria for this diagnosis. Dysthymia has two distinctive types under the DSM-III-R: primary and secondary. When the depression is attributable to an eating disorder, the diagnosis should be of a secondary type. Primary dysthymia should be considered if the depression is not associated with a pre-existing or more severe disorder, such as affective disorder, for instance.

The DSM-III-R also distinguishes between early- and late-onset depressive neurosis. If the dysthymia has its onset prior to age 21, then it is referred to as dysthymia, early onset. If the symptoms first appear after that age, then it is called dysthymia, late onset. Any of the depressive conditions just described may fit the obese patient, depending upon his specific life circumstances and psychological functioning. Also, if the clinical picture is that of a nonpsychotic depression not matching dysthymia in symptoms or diagnostic criteria, then a depressive disorder NOS should be considered.

Impulsive Personality Disorder

While the so-called oral personality has been overplayed in the clinical literature to describe obese patients, there is some truth to this view, especially with adult patients suffering from a juvenile-onset obesity. These patients often display impulsivity and identity diffusion. Therefore, the diagnoses of borderline personality disorder, narcissistic personality disorder, personality disorder NOS (for example, impulsive personality disorder), and impulsive control disorder NOS may be accurate diagnoses for some of these patients. The diagnosis of impulsive control disorder, for example, is pertinent for compulsive overeaters who are addiction prone. Alcohol or drug abuse, heavy cigarette smoking, and suicidal gestures can also be part of this diagnostic picture.

TOOLS FOR ASSESSING OBESITY

Many inventories have been devised to assess the wide spectrum of eating disorders. We will focus on those geared toward obesity. It should be noted, however, that measures developed for the diagnostic evaluation of anorexia nervosa and bulimia nervosa are also useful for the assessment of obesity. Scales designed for evaluating body-image disparagement, preoccupation with food, and hunger and satiety awareness in anorexics can be equally useful assessment tools with obese patients. Tests such as the Eating Attitudes Test (Garner and Garfinkel 1979) or the Bulimia Test (Smith and Thelen 1984) can therefore be revised and adapted for use with obese compulsive overeaters.

Our discussion of assessment instruments will be divided into two parts. First we will highlight eating-disorders questionnaires geared toward the obese; then we will review psychological tests commonly used in obesity research and assessment. For a more detailed review and analysis of eating-disorders inventories, the reader is referred to Brownell (1981), Mahoney et al. (1982), Drewnoski (1983), Leon and Rosenthal (1984), Miller et al. (1984), and Grommet (1988).

Some of the most comprehensive interdisciplinary screening and interviewing devices have been developed by Agras and colleagues (1976), Bray (1976), Bray and co-workers (1976), Brownell (1981), Johnson (1985) and Mahoney et al. (1982). The Stanford Eating Disorders Questionnaire by Agras and his colleagues (1976) is an impressive tool assessing such areas as diet, weight and medical histories, psychosocial functioning, and precipitants to excessive eating. The questionnaire can be used either as a self-report measure or in structured therapeutic interviews.

One of the most reliable and valid questionnaires is the Eating Behavior Inventory (EBI), by O'Neil and co-workers (1979), which assesses a wide variety of situations and psychosocial events leading to overeating or binge eating. Night eating, emotional eating, shopping behaviors and habits, the extent of the ability to refuse food offered, rate of eating, snacking behavior, and many other pertinent areas are explored. This inventory emphasizes behaviors associated with successful weight loss and can serve as a diagnostic tool to predict prognosis for success in maintaining it.

The Restraint in Eating Questionnaire (Stunkard and Messick 1979, Stunkard 1981) is a reliable and valid predictive measure of the degree to which a person can restrain eating. Three factors are measured: cognitive restraint, tendency toward disinhibition (emotional lability), and perceived hunger.

Specific yet less interdisciplinary scales also exist. The Eating Patterns Questionnaire (Hagen 1974, Wollersheim 1970), is a 60-item tool assessing six areas concerned with eating: emotional and uncontrolled eating, eating in response to interpersonal or social situations, eating between meals, extent of eating used as self-reward, and eating when alone. (Gormally and colleagues [1980] have devised an abridged questionnaire.) The Hunger-Satiety Questionnaire by Monello and Mayer (1967) and Garfinkel's modified scale (1974) for anorexics, based on the latter inventory, are useful diagnostic tools for the assessment of hunger awareness and sense of fullness after eating. The Eating Analysis and Treatment Schedule (Coates 1977), also known as EATS, has received much attention despite its untested validity. The inventory is designed to be used at home by nonparticipant observers—that is, by relatives of the obese patient. The schedule takes into consideration the types of meals prepared, how they are served, how many bites and chews are involved in the eating process, where specific foods are located in the home, and so forth. This type of recording is often inaccurate due to the commonly occurring "closet eating" behaviors by the obese.

Other scales, the validity of which is also untested, are the Eating Habits Booklet by Mahoney (1974) and the Mahoney Master Questionnaire (Wollersheim 1970), which assess habit changes and the extent of influence of external cues on eating behaviors, respectively.

Psychological Assessment Tools

Many attempts have also been made to assess the psychological status of the obese person. These efforts have not been useful in detecting a specific or predictable obese personality profile. Among the most widely used psychological measures are the Minnesota Multiphasic Personality Inventory (MMPI), the Beck Depression Inventory (BDI; Beck 1967), the Symptom Checklist (Derogatis 1977, Gough and Heilbrun 1965, Lipman et al. 1979), and the Spielberger Trait Inventory (Spielberger et al. 1971, Taylor 1953).

There are numerous scales based on the MMPI that can be adapted to the wide spectrum of eating disorders, including obesity. The MacAndrew Scale is one such device. It is a reliable measure of addiction proneness, including food abuse (Graham 1978, Leon et al. 1979, Leon et al. 1979, MacAndrew 1965). *The Addiction Severity Index* (McLellan et al. 1980) also assesses addiction proneness and is applicable to obese patients.

The Beck Depression Inventory (BDI) is one of the scales most often used in the diagnostic assessment of dysthymia in the obese (Craighead et al. 1981). Designed by Beck (1967), it measures the severity of depression and its psychomotor, affective, cognitive, and vegetative components. This tool is highly reliable and valid. In conjunction with Beck's depression scale, clinicians can also use the Mood Adjective Checklist (Nowlis 1965), the Profile of Mood States (McNair et al. 1981) or the Symptom Checklist (Derogatis 1977).

The Clinical Analysis Questionnaire (CAQ), developed by Cattell and associates, is also a helpful diagnostic device (Krug and Cattell 1980). It provides information on such areas as psychological inadequacy, boredom, tension, insecurity, emotional stability, impulsivity, and self-sufficiency. The CAQ correlates well with the MMPI, especially with its anxiety and depression scales. Finally, the Tennessee Self-Concept Scale (TSCS), by Fitts (1964), is sometimes used as an assessment tool with obese patients (Eppinger and Lambert 1983). In fact, the TSCS is one of the best scales available for measuring self-perception (Crandall 1973).

Although these scales provide useful information, I tend to reserve them for research or for use with patients who are diagnostically puzzling. Much of the data supplied by these screening devices can as easily be obtained through clinical interviews and consultation with an interdisciplinary team.

THE DIAGNOSTIC INTERVIEW

Mental Status

Although mental status assessment of the obese patient follows the same lines as that for any other patient, there are some areas that are crucial to explore with obese patients (Table 11-2). One is the family history of psychiatric illness. A high percentage of patients, especially those who are moderately to severely obese, come from families whose members have clearcut affective or alcoholic illnesses, or both. For some of these patients, severe depression is allayed through compulsive overeating (Crisp and Stonehill 1970, Johnson 1985, Johnson et al. 1982, Pyle et al. 1981, Strober et al. 1982). Medication assessment should therefore be considered if the data lean toward a hereditary predisposition toward psychiatric illness.

TABLE 11-2. A Guide for the Diagnostic Interview of the Obese Eating-Disordered Patient

1. Mental status
   Inquire into events that led the patient to seek therapy.
   Ask about living arrangements, marital status, support system.
   Assess psychosocial functioning, job history, hobbies, and contentment with life in general.
   Inquire into psychiatric history, somatic symptoms, and medication history.
   Conduct a life-style analysis.
   Assess the patient's stress level, degree of addiction proneness and impulsivity (cigarette use, alcohol and drug abuse, suicide attempts or ideation, shopping sprees, and so forth).
   Evaluate the extent of body-image distortion, the ability to interpret mood states, and the capacity to detect physiological hunger.
   Obtain a chronological weight history.
   Identify the age of onset of the obesity.
   Inquire about first diet and weight loss attempt. Whose idea was it?
   Explore the first binge episode.
   Ask about the highest weight and lowest weight ever reached.
   Determine the extent of teasing and discrimination experienced for being overweight as a child and as an adult.
   Check for severe weight fluctuation.
   Determine whether the patient knows his set-point weight range.
   Ask the patient to describe a typical eating day: Are meals skipped? Does the patient pay attention to hunger pangs? Are there indications of poor nutritional knowledge?
   Check for the night eating syndrome.
   Determine how much effort is required to maintain the present weight.
   Ask whether the patient loses quickly when determined to lose.
   Assess whether physiological problems contribute to the obesity.
2. Motivation for treatment
   Assess insight level, denial, perfectionistic strivings, self-efficacy, and locus of control, as well as the possible psychological pay-offs experienced for not changing.
   Begin formulating hypotheses of etiology, and assess whether motivation is endogenous or exogenous.
3. Types of obesities
   Start to identify the possible causes of the obesity. (There are typically a combination of factors, such as a sedentary life-style coupled with a slow metabolic rate and poor psychosocial functioning due to chronic ostracism.)
4. Diet and weight history
   Inquire about previous weight loss attempts.
   Identify preferred weight-loss methods.
   Ask about family history of obesity and parents' attitude toward food and obesity.
   Rule out a family history of substance abuse and impulsivity.
   Try to identify predictable precipitants to diet lapses.
   Ask patient about exercise routine, if any.
   Evaluate the capacity for self-control when confronted with food cues.

TABLE 11-2. *(continued)*

5. Special considerations
   Child abuse.
   Emotional neglect and/or abuse.
   Overprotective or perfectionistic parents.
   Conditional-love messages from primary caretakers.
   Ability to tolerate the present without reverting to food abuse.
   Ability to contain and manage the mourning process.
   Education, socioeconomic level, ethnicity, religious affiliation, culture.
   Menstrual cycle and its impact on moods and food cravings.
   Feelings of deprivation when dieting.
   Nonverbal behaviors.
   Identity disturbances.
6. Extent of food abuse
   Inquire into daily habits.
   Ask the patient to define a binge.
   Assess the times of the day when the patient is most liable to overeat, snack, or binge.
   Ask whether there are predictable circumstances or specific people that lead the patient to overeat.
   Look for ruminations over food and begin formulating hypotheses about their adaptive functions.
   Review the periods of time without serious lapses: When? How long? Under what circumstances?
   Inquire into moods experienced prior to overeating or binge eating.
7. DSM-III Diagnoses
   Rule out the presence of a clear-cut eating disorder, including bulimia nervosa (307.51), psychological factors affecting physical condition (316.00), and eating disorders NOS (307.50).
   Consider the affective and anxiety disorders, as well as the personality disorders.
8. Treatment recommendation
   Initiate a short-term contract with the patient to decrease the risk of a premature withdrawal from psychotherapy.
   Assess the need for an immediate referral to a physician or nutritionist.
   Refer the patient to an exercise physiologist if he wishes to engage in an exercise program.
   Arrange for the patient's body fat and metabolic rate to be assessed during weight-loss process.

Motivation for Treatment

As for any patient seeking therapy, the obese individual's motivation for treatment and change must be carefully assessed. This is especially true of the severely obese, who often claim that they wish to change their eating habits because of the associated physical discomforts and symptoms (such as joint pains, arthritis, high blood pressure, and sleep apnea). While the reasons presented for wanting to lose weight seem attributable to an ego-syntonic drive, motivation must be further explored. Physical discomfort is rarely a predictor for success in weight-loss maintenance or life-style changes.

Eagerness to lose weight is not a sufficient criterion for predicting successful dieting. The enthusiasm typically apparent at the diagnostic interview often quickly abates, because the obese patient must confront the consequences of having chosen a new way of life. Losing weight is ordeal enough; keeping the lost pounds from reappearing can be even more emotionally taxing. Will power is not enough to sustain the long-term maintenance of a new weight. The patient must be able to identify an ongoing personal reward or meaning in remaining thin. Few patients are able to remain motivated for long, and clinicians face the difficult task of helping to keep their patients' newfound incentive from collapsing. Weight-loss projects are abandoned for a number of reasons, some of which can be averted or worked through with professional help and support.

For patients who believe or act as if weight loss will magically resolve all their problems—and, unfortunately, many obese patients hold this belief—relapse and weight regain is inevitable. Such obese persons should be warned against dieting. They should be advised that looking thin is not *sine qua non* to a conflict-free life. Patients who employ magical thinking about weight loss transforming their lives, rarely succeed in remaining thin. They may eventually look thin, but they will probably still think and act "fat." Bruch (1973a, 1973b) aptly calls these individuals "thin fat people."

The interviewer should assess the obese patient's motivation. The therapist should inquire about whether there is anything in the patient's life that might prevent or sabotage the weight-loss project. A spouse, for instance, might not approve or be supportive; a child might soon require surgery; or the patient might be in the process of a stressful divorce. This type of inquiry can clarify whether the patient is ready to lose weight or whether psychotherapy should be recommended first.

During the diagnostic interview, the clinician should also assess the patient's cultural and socioeconomic background. A question about who best understands the patient will reveal the degree to which the patient experiences loneliness and social isolation. The extent of environmental support must be explored in depth to find specific etiological variables involved in past and possibly future dieting failures.

Environmental Support

There is mounting evidence that social support is one of the better predictors of successful weight-loss maintenance and life-style changes. It is known to influence an obese dieter's motivation to persist in losing and in maintaining the loss (Brownell 1984a, 1984b, 1986, Brownell et al. 1978, Coletti and Brownell 1982, Mahoney and Mahoney 1976, Miller and Sims 1981, Pearce et al. 1981, Rosenthal et al. 1980, Saccone and Israel 1978, Wilson 1985). Similar results are found in the treatment of substance abusers when marital and family support is experienced (Cummings et al. 1980, Marlatt and Gordon 1985, Mermelstein and Lichtenstein 1983, Moos and Finney 1983). Conversely, the odds against a successful weight-loss maintenance are quite high if emotional support is lacking. When a patient's dieting is interpreted as a threat by a significant other, such as a spouse, the likelihood of success in losing weight and maintaining it over long periods of time is strongly diminished (Stuart and Davis 1972).

Interpersonal conflict correlates poorly with successful weight loss. In fact, it is often a prognosis for relapse (Brownell et al. 1986, Cummins et al. 1980). In my experience, however, interpersonal conflicts do not necessarily predict how a patient will fare in a weight-loss program. It remains that moral support helps ease the weight-loss ordeal and is preferable to no support at all. Peer support is also positively correlated with long-term successful maintenance of weight loss (Foster et al. 1985). Of all the treatment methods offered to obese patients, group support is one of the most potent and therapeutic. The popularity of Weight Watchers International, Take Off The Pounds Sensibly (TOPS), Overeaters Anonymous (OA), and scores of other group-oriented programs attest to this view. Attrition may be high in these programs, but many overweight individuals find the motivation and energy to stick to their dieting plans thanks to peer support offered by the programs.

Insight Level

The capacity for insight is also of paramount importance to assess because it has a direct bearing on treatment planning. Obese patients can be placed on a psychological continuum, ranging from the "genuinely puzzled" to the "pseudoinsightful." The genuinely puzzled patients are baffled about what is going on within themselves. These patients are similar to Jung's (1938) "sensing individual." They know only that they experience real emotions, but they are unable to put them into words. An insight-oriented approach is doomed to fail with genuinely puzzled patients because it tends to confound them and may be a precipitant to the premature termination of psychotherapy. What works well with such patients are concrete, down-to-earth interventions, relying basically on what is obvious to them. That is, the therapist should focus on the level of the patient's experience as the basis for deeper intrapsychic work.

At the other end of the psychological continuum we find pseudoinsightful patients. Initially, they impress clinicians with their perceptiveness. It is not unusual for therapists, especially inexperienced ones, to become so mesmerized by these patients' insights that they question their need for therapy. Pseudoinsightful obese patients often appear more psychologically sophisticated then they actually are: They may well bring forth impressive insights, but they may have an extremely poor tolerance for conflicts. They impulsively brush aside their (often accurate) self-understanding in the service of self-protective devices such as binge eating. Impulsivity is a cardinal psychological feature of many compulsive overeaters. An insight-oriented approach is appropriate with pseudoinsightful patients.

Level of intuition can be assessed in a variety of ways. The therapist may want to inquire about the patient's past therapeutic experiences, and the reasons for terminating. This will indicate the extent of self-understanding and will reveal the patient's ability to tolerate the unavoidable stress inherent in self-exploration.

A good prognostic sign is the patient's recognition of having to give up old, maladaptive ways of being. Working through obesity requires a mourning process. The five stages of the dying process—denial, anger, bargaining, depression, and acceptance/resolution—described by Kubler-Ross (1969) can be applied to the weight-loss process as well. For obese eating-disordered patients, such ability to mourn involves much more than tolerating the self without food as the primary emotional soother. It also includes working through long-standing conflicts with one's parents, coming to terms with a new body image, and distancing oneself from old friends who may be threatened or envious by the changes.

During the diagnostic interview, therapists must also watch for their patients' nonverbal behaviors. The interviewer must pay attention to the congruence between speech content and the moods or affects conveyed. Some patients have trained themselves to repress deep rage and yet betray this very affect in disguised form (such as by clenching their teeth when smiling).

Life-style Analysis

The life-style assessment technique developed by Adler and his followers can be used during the diagnostic interview of obese patients (Adler 1956, Baruth and Eckstein 1978, 1981, Dreikurs 1967, Mosak 1977, Mosak et al. 1980). The life-style analysis consists of historical information, such as family constellation and parents' personalities; recollections prior to age 8 (Mosak 1958); favorite childhood books, movies, and pastimes; childhood fears; perceived assets, talents, and character traits compared with those of their siblings, and beliefs as to who among the children was most and least favored by either parent. These data are then used to interpret the patients' present psychosocial functioning.

Life-style analysis reveals useful data about the obese patient's family of origin and formative years. It is a particularly helpful interviewing tool with genuinely puzzled patients. It provides a concrete structure on which they can focus, and the specific questions often serve as prods for detailed and spontaneous self-disclosure. While inquiring about the patient's childhood recollections, the interviewer may find that little about the formative years is at first remembered. This in itself is diagnostically significant as it may reveal a wish to avoid reflecting upon disappointing past events. The therapist should therefore proceed with tact and care. Some patients will not welcome the life-style analysis and will feel more at ease discussing concerns pertaining to their day-to-day lives or dysfunctional eating patterns.

Themes and areas specific to the obese must be added to the general life-style analysis. Exploring the obese patient's job history, for instance, can provide clues as to the quality of his psychosocial adaptations.

Another area to be assessed is the patient's satisfaction with or sense of meaning in life. If individuals do not experience clear purpose in their lives, they will be prone to depression, a sense of emptiness, and even psychosomatic illnesses (Frankl 1967, Kotchen 1960). Boredom, a common complaint among the obese, is a symptom often linked to the experience of meaninglessness or purposelessness in life.

Hobbies must be explored as well. Food, especially for the moderately and severly obese, is often *the* primary pleasurable activity relied upon. Therefore, the answer to the question "What do you do for yourself that pleases you?" may indicate that there are no substitutes for the food abuse. On the other hand, the answer can reveal a list of potential reinforcers to which the therapist might refer later in treatment to counteract dysfunctional eating habits.

Adaptive Purposes and Compensatory Functions to Remaining Obese

Beginning with the first diagnostic interview, the therapist should formulate tentative hypotheses about the compensatory functions underlying the obesity. Therapists should be sensitive to the fact that obesity may not be attributable to emotional conflicts. Nevertheless, it remains that patients may abuse food for a plethora of psychological reasons. Indeed, for some patients overeating may be related to the wish to repress anxiety or anger; for others, stuffing themselves serves the purpose of fulfilling the desperate wish to be loved; for still others, it represents the wish to be noticed and taken seriously (Hamburger 1951).

> Bernice W., a 37-year-old mother of three young children, had successfully lost 80 pounds over a period of a year and a half. Physiology or sociocultural factors did not seem to play a role in her relapses. Bernice found herself binge eating more and more frequently after having successfully lost weight and she was rapidly regaining. She reported being out of control and worrying continuously about her lapses. Once we explored the precipitating events to her motivational collapse, she relayed that her father had recently been diagnosed as having terminal cancer. Bernice soon came to the realization that she had created an out-of-control situation (binge eating) in order to avoid coping with something she felt unable to confront: her father's terminal cancer and impending death. This self-induced disorientation device was more in her control than was her father's illness, which she was powerless to change.

Psychological pay-offs abound for regaining weight or remaining obese (Bruch 1944, 1973a, Chessick 1985, Johnson et al. 1984, Stuart and Jacobson 1987). For many obese people, especially those with a history of repeated failures at maintaining weight loss, thinness is often associated (whether consciously or not) with unpleasant side-effects: vague yet profound anxieties or insecurities, a "sickly" physical appearance, or a fear of sexual promiscuity. Table 11–3 highlights some psychological pay-offs for remaining obese or for not maintaining lost weight.

Probably one of the best gifts that therapists can give their patients is an appreciation of why it is so frightening or difficult to change. For some, the fear of success is unmistakably linked to losing sanity or psychological equilibrium (Chessick 1985, Kobut 1984, Lacocque 1984, 1986).

It is usually not advisable to interpret to patients the meaning of their resistances to change during a diagnostic interview. Therapeutic alliance takes time, especially with patients who have been chronically teased, rejected, and humiliated, as many juvenile-onset obese patients have. The interviewer must begin to formulate silent hypotheses as to the possible adaptive functions that *not* changing has served for the patient. The better these are understood by therapists, the more their patients can be helped to work through their eating disorders.

Self-Efficacy

The obese patient's self-defeating expectations are a prognostic indicator prior to, during, and after weight loss. The higher the expectation of failure, the more likely it is that the weight-loss attempts will be unsuccessful; and the more the patient feels in control during a diet—or the more he experiences *self-efficacy*, as Bandura (1977) calls this cognitive skill—the better able he will be to lose weight and to maintain the loss (Jeffery et al. 1984, Leon and Rosenthal 1984, Mitchell and Stuart 1984, Sternberg 1985).

Studies with obese children demonstrate that the higher the perceived self-control over food temptations, the more successful the weight-loss and maintenance program (Cohen et al. 1980, Epstein 1986, Loro et al. 1979, O'Leary and Dubey 1979). In a study of adult obese individuals who lost 40 pounds or more and maintained their weight loss, Holmes and colleagues (1984) found that regular weight self-monitoring kept them from regaining. Similar results were obtained in a study of Weight Watchers participants (Stuart 1980, Mitchell and Stuart 1984). Self-efficacy correlates highly with the working through of addictive behaviors (Foreyt et al. 1982, Graham et al. 1983, Jeffery et al. 1983) and is positively associated with the prevention of relapse in alcoholism, heavy smoking, and obesity as well (Coletti et al. 1985, Condiotti and Lichenstein 1981, Killen et al. 1984, Supnick and Coletti 1984). If patients voice a generalized sense of helplessness during the diagnostic interview, they should be advised to postpone weight loss until they attain some sense of being in control of their lives and eating habits.

Locus of Control

The locus of control experienced has also attracted eating-disorders researchers. Many scales have been devised based on Rotter's (1966, 1975) concepts. Among the many are scales by Duttweiler (1984),

TABLE 11-3. Psychological Pay-offs for Not Losing Weight

1. Obese patients, especially women, may fear sexual harassment by the opposite sex if thinner.
2. Patients may anticipate increased pressures to act more responsibly if at a lower weight (for example, increased involvement in household chores or in social activities).
3. Anxiety, boredom, emptiness, and/or futility may be too pronounced if the patient is no longer obese.
4. The patient may fear sexual promiscuity.
5. Thinness may be associated with unassertiveness or sickly appearance.
6. Lower weight brings with it the reassessment of long-term relationships, life-style, vocational goals, and so forth, which the person is not ready to face.
7. The state of "pleasure discontrol" (overeating) may be perceived as more rewarding than the alternatives foreseen if thinner.
8. Overeating may allow the patient to function in society.
9. Preoccupation with food or weight may serve as disorientation or screening device against more disturbing truths (such as an unhappy marriage or a suffocating parent).
10. Remaining obese may symbolize the refusal to work through resentments for having to look thinner to attract others' genuine interest.
11. Being at a lower weight may evoke fears of losing environmental support as thinness may threaten a spouse and/or significant others.
12. The perfectionistic fiction will be shattered if weight loss fails. Staying overweight preserves this fantasy.
13. Stopping the overeating cycle may be perceived as giving in to someone else's conditional affection. Remaining obese may represent a conscious or unconscious rebellion against conditional acceptance.
14. Without food abuse, the patient may be exposed to anxiety and interpersonal awkwardness.
15. For some obese people, losing weight in the past did not bring about the wished-for self-esteem or environmental support. A spouse may have remained as aloof and unaffectionate as before, or fewer people than expected responded to the new look with admiration.

Levenson (1973), Reid and Ware (1973), and Rosenbaum (1980). Corcoran and Fisher (1987) provide a list of other inventories as well. Research has indicated that anorexic and obese people tend to experience an external locus of control (Hood et al. 1982, Mitchell and Straw 1981, Thomason 1983). Individuals with this psychological and motivational orientation tend to rely heavily on others' opinions, to be less able to think autonomously, to have a poor capacity for impulse control, and to have a greater identity disturbance compared with those who experience an internal locus of reference (Bellack and Tillman 1974, Bellack et al. 1974, Reid and Ware 1973, Rotter 1966, 1975). Clinically, this implies that the less the patient is able to think or feel autonomously, the poorer the prognosis for therapy or for a weight-loss program.

Perfectionistic Strivings

The wish to be perfect reflects a desperate need to be in control. Obese eating-disordered patients often do not contain and manage psychological discomfort well. Their aspiration is to have as much control over circumstances and themselves as possible, but they seldom attain such perfection. For many obese patients, this will likely lead to binge eating or overeating to assuage their frustrations. The perfectionistic wish to be in absolute control is then broken, exposing the patient to feelings of inadequacy and self-hatred.

Body Image: Dissatisfaction or Disparagement?

The concept of body image includes the mental image of one's physical appearance as well as the feelings or attitude toward it. Self-esteem is directly linked with this concept, and many clinicians speak of the two concepts as inseparable (Fischer and Cleveland 1968, Kolb 1975, Shontz 1969). Cultural norms, social standards, socioeconomic class, ethnicity, and gender identity also play determining roles in shaping body image. People seem to adjust their food intake on the basis of their body image (Drewnoski 1983).

Johnson (1985) emphasizes that when assessing patients' attitudes toward their bodies, a distinction should be made between dissatisfaction and distortion. In other words, disliking how one looks does not necessarily imply psychopathology. On the other hand, the more the distorted the body image is, the more likely it is that the person will be emotionally disturbed. It is well known, for instance, that anorexics typically see themselves as fatter than they actually are, while the severely obese tend to downplay their body size (Glucksman et al. 1973, Glucksman and Hirsh 1969, Traub and Orback 1964). A common fallacy regarding obese people is that most of them hold body image disturbances. Stunkard (1985) and Powers (1980), for example, bring evidence to support that only a minority of obese individuals, even those who are neurotic, do in fact suffer from this body image distortion.

Body-image disparagement has wide psychological ramifications for the obese. Self-consciousness, viewing the body as grotesque, expecting derogatory or contemptuous reactions from others, and impaired psychosocial functioning are symptoms often associated with this disparagement. The greater the body-image disparagement, the poorer the prognosis for successful treatment (Garfinkel et al. 1977). Body-image distortion is most prevalent among obese patients who have been humiliated, jeered at, ostracized, and belittled for their physical appearance in the past. Women in particular, especially juvenile-onset young obese women of the middle and upper-middle classes, are often afflicted with this body-image disparagement (Foreyt 1987). Avoiding looking at oneself naked in the mirror from toe to head, declining to have pictures taken at parties or family gatherings, refusing to know one's body weight, and wearing loose clothes all reinforce this experience of body-image disparagement. Obese patients who recover from a distortion in body image are often appalled at how fat they looked in old photographs. Reduction in body-image distortion may actually be the best indication of having worked through an eating disorder (Bruch 1973a, Casper et al. 1979, Casper et al. 1981, Chessick 1985, Garner et al. 1976).

An assessment of the extent to which a patient experiences a body-image distortion must therefore be included in the diagnostic interview. There are many ways to assess body-image distortion. The therapist can inquire about the extent to which the patient's attitude toward his body has led him to shy away from social events, or from dating, or from going to the beach or swimming pool.

Perhaps one of the most important areas to assess during the diagnostic interview is the extent of the patient's dysfunctional eating patterns. The exploration of past and recent weight-loss attempts will reveal whether the patient has chronically failed at weight-loss or maintenance. It will also indicate how realistic the dieting attempts were, the length of time the weight loss was maintained, the frustrations encountered with the new weight, and the patient's set-point weight range.

Reliability of Self-Reports

While therapists working with obese eating-disordered patients should be familiar with basic nutrition, dieticians are better able to evaluate eating behaviors and should therefore be consulted. Dieticians rely heavily upon food records, which help patients reflect on the foods they have eaten in the course of a day. Food records also offer feedback as to what times of day patients eat, how much they consume, whether their eating takes place privately or in the presence of others, and the moods experienced during and after eating. It is a useful method for detecting vulnerable times of the day for food binges and the events that tend to precipitate overeating.

Unfortunately, food records are not reliable when used independently. Experienced clinicians have repeatedly warned against placing too much emphasis on their validity because much eating is not disclosed in patients' self-reports (Brownell 1981, Brownell et al. 1978, Dwyer and Mayer 1969). Indeed, for some overeaters, denial of food intake is very high. Even when relatives agree to report patients' eating habits, they cannot measure the overeaters' *private* eating behaviors (Coates 1977, Stalonas et al. 1978. See Brownell [1981] for an extensive review of this topic).

Nutritionists should be the ones to take on the task of restructuring patients' eating patterns for at least three reasons: First, they are best equipped to advise patients about changing maladaptive behaviors into nutritionally sound ones. Second, if a nutritionist is involved in the case, the therapist can focus on emotional issues rather than nutritional issues. Third, and perhaps most important, the involvement of a dietician minimizes the chances of countertransference reactions on the part of therapists if, for example, the patient fails to follow dietary advice.

(It should be noted that nutritionists are not immune from these negative reactions and should seek psychological consultation to learn how to contain and manage their disappointment with patients who do not follow their dietary recommendations.)

Diet and Weight History

The therapist should inquire about the dieting methods that the patient has used thus far to lose weight. As controversial as it may sound, it should not be assumed that resorting to a drastic method such as surgery to lose weight necessarily reflects underlying psychopathology. This extreme intervention may be warranted for some obese individuals. Nevertheless, a history of employing magical thinking and unrealistic methods to lose weight may indicate emotional instability. Such methods as starvation or diuretic abuse may reveal a poor sense of internal control and mistrust in one's capacity to work through the obesity. A history of erratic and unpredictable weight may indicate psychopathology. In such cases, weight-reduction attempts will likely continue to fail unless more fundamental issues are addressed.

Specific events leading to gaining or losing weight will provide an understanding of the patient's emotional world. The loss of a friendship or a lover, an unhappy marriage, the dreaded visit of in-laws, or rejection from a prospective date can precipitate weight gain. On the other hand, having a boyfriend or girlfriend may motivate the obese person to lose weight and stay thinner. However, the patient who loses weight for egodystonic reasons has a poor chance of maintaining the weight loss.

The clinician will also want to know about the family of origin's attitudes toward overweight. An exploration of this area often reveals unresolved conflicts that will have to be confronted before the patient can work through the eating disorder. The interviewer will want to inquire about the nature of family meals in childhood. Was the patient forced to finish food on his plate, and was punishment likely if he did not oblige? The answers to these questions may provide clues to the etiology of the obesity.

Binge Eating

Inquiry into the patient's daily eating routines can reveal whether or not the patient has an eating disorder. The clinician will want to know how many times a day the patient eats, where, with whom, and whether there are any concurrent activities going on. Vulnerable times of day for overeating, snacking, or binge eating must also be addressed. Is the patient a morning anorexic, typically skipping breakfasts and lunches? Is he so busy during the day that physiological hunger isn't noticed? Do evenings trigger ravenous appetites and uncontrolled lapses? Is the patient resorting to vomiting to keep his weight down?

The therapist should ask the patient to define a binge (if appropriate) and should assess the extent of obsessive thinking about food, the length of the binges and the types of food eaten, the feelings experienced after the binge, the age at onset and circumstances surrounding the first binge, the intensity of the uncontrolled urges, and the events typically leading to the binges.

In assessing binge-eating behaviors, the interviewer will want to know what has historically helped the patient to avoid resorting to binges. Some patients may never have reflected upon this important question. Another important area of inquiry is the patient's mood during a binge. Many compulsive overeaters may be at a loss as to how to answer this question, because they may have excluded a wide range of emotions from consciousness. Indeed, for some obese patients, any psychological disequilibrium is unbearable. Depression as well as joy may be experienced as overstimulating. Food abuse becomes the means by which the patient keeps this disequilibrium at bay. The prognosis is better if the patient has some understanding of what he is trying to avoid.

Hunger Awareness

Patients who are unable to accurately detect physiological hunger and satiety find it difficult to work through their dysfunctional eating habits. Initially at least, these patients must learn not to trust their subjective food "cravings"; instead, they must rely on objective criteria to guide them with portion control and food choices. Such objective criteria can include calorie counting, portion measurement, and regular weighing. Later, these patients may be able to trust their own judgment about what and how much to eat. Unfortunately, some patients will never be able to detect their hunger and satiety accurately. To prevent themselves from regaining weight they are condemned, perhaps forever, to rely on objective feedback devices.

There are many diagnostic questions that clinicians can ask to assess hunger and satiety awareness. Does the patient know how it feels to be physiologically hungry? Does he eat when hungry? Does he eat indiscriminately, without regard for physiological hunger? Does he know how it feels to be satiated? If so, does he continue to beyond satiety to the point of nausea?

The Night Eating Syndrome

The assessment of night eating behaviors deserves special consideration. While I agree with Stunkard's observations (Stunkard et al. 1955, Stunkard 1985) that some patients (especially women) are afflicted with a night eating syndrome (morning anorexia, evening hyperphagia and insomnia), I believe that his estimate that 10 percent of the obese population experience this syndrome is far too low, and that the disorder afflicts as many men as women. In my experience, patients tend to overeat or lapse at the end of the day. This is especially true for patients who thrive on a busy work schedule. Many obese individuals fit this "type A" personality pattern. Because of their hectic life-styles, these individuals do not (or choose not to) notice hunger during the day. By nighttime, they have put their bodies in a state of biological starvation. Having neglected to take care of their personal needs during the day, night becomes the cherished time to do so. Food becomes a powerful and reliable reward.

The underlying theme to be worked through in therapy is the anxiety of being alone. Night and darkness have always evoked dread and anxiety in humans. And yet, night is also the symbol of potential, when one can achieve ontological security (Campbell 1968, Eliade 1948, Jung 1956, Lacocque 1984). Being alone is indeed difficult. Evening forces us to look at ourselves, with the outside world shut out in the darkness. For the disturbed obese personality, compulsive eating becomes a salvific mechanism, albeit temporarily. Research on hyperphagia has shown, for instance, that overeating or binge eating is most likely to occur when patients are alone in unstructured situations (Johnson 1985, Pyle et al. 1981).

It would be a grave clinical error to assume that obesity always results from emotional disturbance. While obesity can be brought by psychopathology , it can as easily arise from physiological factors. Obesity is far too complex a phenomenon to be explained in a simple, unidimensional fashion. Only through interdisciplinary cooperation can we hope to unravel the mysteries surrounding obesity and the other eating disorders.

REFERENCES

Adler, A. (1956). *The Individual Psychology of Alfred Adler*. Ed. H. Ansbacher and R. Ansbacher. New York: Harper & Row.

Agras, W. S., Ferguson, J. M., Greaves, C., et al. (1976). A clinical and research questionnaire for obese patients. In *Obesity: Behavioral Approaches to Dietary Management*, ed. B. J. Williams, S. Martin, and J. P. Foreyt, pp. 41–53. New York: Brunner/Mazel.

American Psychiatric Association (1987). *Diagnostic and Statistical Manual for Mental Disorders*, 3rd ed., rev. Washington, DC: APA.

Bandura, A. (1977). Self-efficacy: toward a unifying theory of behavior change. *Psychological Review* 84:191–215.

Baruth, L. G., and Eckstein, D. (1978). *Lifestyle: What It Is and How to Do It*. Dubuque, IA: Kendall/Hunt.

——— eds. (1981). *Lifestyle: Theory, Practice, and Research*. Dubuque, IA: Kendall/Hunt.

Beck, A. T. (1967). *Depression: Clinical, Experimental, and Theoretical Aspects*. New York: Harper & Row.

Bellack, A. S., Schwartz, J., and Rozensky, R. H. (1974). The contribution of external control to self-control in a weight reduction program. *Journal of Behavior Therapy and Experimental Psychiatry* 5:245–250.

Bellack, A. S., and Tillman, W. (1974). The effects of task and experimenter feedback on the self-reinforcement behavior of internals and externals. *Journal of Consulting and Clinical Psychology* 42:330–336.

Blackburn, G. (1987). *The medical significance and management of obesity*. Paper presented at the Optifast postgraduate seminar, Scottsdale, AZ, April.

Bray, G. A. (1976). *The Obese Patient*. Philadelphia: W. B. Saunders.

Bray, G. A., Jordan, H. A., and Sims, E. A. H. (1976). Evaluation of the obese patient: an algorithm. *Journal of the American Medical Association* 235:2008–2010.

Brownell, K. D. (1981). Assessment of eating disorders. In *Behavioral Assessment of Adult Disorders*, ed. D. H. Barlow, pp. 329–404. New York: Guilford.

——— (1982). Obesity: understanding and treating a serious, prevalent, and refractory disorder. *Journal of Consulting and Clinical Psychology* 50:820–840.

——— (1984a). The psychology and physiology of obesity: implications for screening and treatment. *Journal of the American Dietetic Association* 84:406–414.

——— (1984b). Behavioral, psychological, and environmental predictors of obesity and success at weight reduction. *International Journal of Obesity* 8:543–550.

——— (1986). Public health approaches to obesity and its management. *Annual Review of Public Health* 7:521–533.

Brownell, K. D., Heckerman, C. L., Westlake, R. J., et al. (1978). The effect of couples training and partner cooperativeness in the behavioral treatment of obesity. *Behavior Research and Therapy* 16:323–333.

Brownell, K. D., Marlatt, G. A., Lichtenstein, E., and Wilson, G. T. (1986). Understanding and preventing relapse. *American Psychologist* 41:765–782.

Bruch, H. (1944). Food and emotional security. *The Nervous Child* 3:165–173.

——— (1973a). *Eating Disorders: Obesity, Anorexia Nervosa, and the Person Within*. New York: Basic Books.

——— (1973b). Thin fat people. *Journal of the American Medical Women's Association* 28:187–208.

Campbell, J. (1968). *The Hero with a Thousand Faces*. Princeton, NJ: Princeton University Press.

Casper, R., Halmi, K., Goldberg, S., Eckert, E., et al. (1979). Disturbances in body image estimation as related to other characteristics and outcome in anorexia nervosa. *British Journal of Psychiatry* 134:60–66.

Casper, R., Offer, D., and Ostrov, J. (1981). The self-image of adolescents with acute anorexia nervosa. *Journal of Pediatrics* 98:656–661.

Chessick, R. (1985). Clinical notes toward the understanding and intensive psychotherapy of adult eating disorders. *Annual of Psychoanalysis* 13:301–322.

Coates, T. J. (1977). *The efficacy of a multimodal self-control program in modifying the habits and weight of three obese adolescents*. Unpublished doctoral dissertation, Stanford University, Stanford, CA.

Cohen, E. A., Gelfand, D. M., Dodd, D. K., Jensen, J., et al. (1980). Self-control practices associated with weight loss maintenance in children and adolescents. *Behavior Therapy* 11:26–37.

Colletti, G., and Brownell, K. D. (1982). The physical and emotional benefits of social support: applications to obesity, smoking, and alcoholism. *Progress in Behavior Modification* 13:110–179.

Coletti, G., Supnick, J. A., and Payne, T. J. (1985). The Smoking Self-Efficacy Questionnaire: a preliminary validation. *Behavioral Assessment* 7:249–254.

Condiotti, M. M., and Lichenstein, E. (1981). Self-efficacy and relapse in smoking cessation programs. *Journal of Consulting and Clinical Psychology* 49:648–658.

Corcoran, K., and Fischer, J., eds. (1987). *Measures for Clinical Practice: A Sourcebook*. New York: Free Press.

Craighead, L. W., Stunkard, A. J., and O'Brien, S. (1981). Behavior therapy and pharmacotherapy of obesity. *Archives of General Psychiatry* 38:763–768.

Crandall, R. (1973). The measurement of self-esteem and related constructs. In *Measures of Social Psychological Attitudes*, ed. J. P. Robinson and P. R. Shaver, pp. 45–67. Ann Arbor, MI: Institute for Social Research, University of Michigan.

Crisp, A. H., and Stonehill, E. (1970). Treatment of obesity with special reference to seven severely obese patients. *Journal of Psychosomatic Research* 14:327–345.

Cummings, C., Gordon, J. R., and Marlatt, G. A. (1980). Relapse: prevention and prediction. In *The Addictive Disorders: Treatment of Alcoholism, Drug Abuse, Smoking, and Obesity*, ed. W. R. Miller, pp. 291–322. New York: Pergamon.

Derogatis, L. R. (1977). *SCL-90-R Manual*. Baltimore: Clinical Psychometrics Research Unit, Johns Hopkins University School of Medicine.

Dreikurs, R. (1967). The psychological interview in medicine. In *Psychodynamics, Psychotherapy, and Counseling*, pp. 75–102. Chicago: Alfred Adler Institute, 1954.

Drewnoski, A. (1983). Cognitive structure in obesity and dieting. In *Obesity*, ed. M. R. C. Greenwood, pp. 87–101. New York: Churchill/Livingstone.

Duttweiler, P. C. (1984). The Internal Control Index: a newly developed measure of locus of control. *Educational and Psychological Measurement* 44:209–221.

Dwyer, J. T., and Mayer, J. (1969). Biases in counting calories. *Journal of the American Dietetic Association* 54:305–307.

Eliade, M. (1948). *Patterns in Comparative Religion*. New York: Sheed & Ward.

Eppinger, M. G., and Lambert, M. J. (1983). Assessment of habit disorders: a tripartite perspective in measuring change. In *The Assessment of Psychotherapy Outcome*, ed. M. J. Lambert, E. R. Christensen, and S. S. DeJulio, pp. 387–389. New York: Wiley.

Epstein, L. H. (1986). Treatment of childhood obesity. In *Handbook of Eating Disorders*, ed. K. D. Brownell and J. P. Foreyt, pp. 159–179. New York: Basic Books.

Fisher, S., and Cleveland, S. E. (1968). *Body Image and Personality*. New York: Dover.

Fitts, W. (1964). *Manual: Tennessee Self-Concept Scale*. Nashville, TN: Counselor Recordings and Tests.

Foreyt, J. P. (1987). Issues in the assessment and treatment of obesity. *Journal of Consulting and Clinical Psychology* 5:677–684.

Foreyt, J. P., Mitchell, R. E., Garner, D. T., et al. (1982). Behavioral treatment of obesity: results and limitations. *Behavior Therapy* 13:153–163.

Foster, G. D., Wadden, T. A., and Brownell, K. D. (1985). Peer-led program for the treatment and prevention of obesity in schools. *Journal of Consulting and Clinical Psychology* 53:538–540.

Frankl, V. E. (1967). The significance of meaning for health. In *Religion and Medicine*, ed. D. Belgum, pp. 177–185. Ames, IA: Iowa State University Press.

Garfinkel, P. E. (1974). Perception of hunger and satiety in anorexia nervosa. *Psychological Medicine* 4:309–315.

Garfinkel, P. E., Moldofsky, H., and Garner, D. M. (1977). Prognosis in anorexia nervosa as influenced by clinical features, treatment, and self-perception. *Canadian Medical Journal* 177:1041–1045.

Garner, D. M., and Garfinkel, P. E. (1979). The Eating Attitudes Test: an index of the symptoms of anorexia nervosa. *Psychological Medicine* 9:273–279.

Garner, D. M., Garfinkel, P. E., Stancer, H. C., and Moldofsky, H. (1976). Body image disturbances in anorexia nervosa and obesity. *Psychosomatic Medicine* 38:327–336.

Glucksman, M. L., and Hirsch, J. (1969). The response of obese patients to weight reduction: the perception of body size. *Psychosomatic Medicine* 31:1–7.

Glucksman, M. L., Hirsch, J., and Levin, B. (1973). The affective response of obese patients to weight reduction: a differentiation based on age at onset of obesity. *Psychosomatic Medicine* 35:57–63.

Gough, H. G., and Heilbrun, A. B. (1965). *Manual for the Adjective Checklist.* Palo Alto, CA: Consulting Psychologists Press.

Graham, J. R. (1978). A review of some important MMPI special scales. In *Advances in Psychological Assessment*, vol. 4, ed. P. McReynolds, pp. 141–160. San Francisco: Jossey-Bass.

Graham, L. E., Jr., Taylor, C. B., Hovell, M. F., and Siegel, W. (1983). Five-year follow-up to a behavioral weight-loss program. *Journal of Consulting and Clinical Psychology* 51:322–323.

Grinker, J. A., Hirsch, J., and Levin, B. (1973). The affective response of obese patients to weight reduction: a differentiation based on age at onset of obesity. *Psychosomatic Medicine* 35:57–63.

Grommet, J. K. (1988). Assessment of the obese person. In *Obesity and Weight Control*, ed. R. T. Frankle and M. U. Yang, pp. 111–132. Rockville, MD: Aspen.

Hagen, R. L. (1974). Group therapy versus bibliotherapy in weight reduction. *Behavior Therapy* 5:222–234.

Hamburger, W. W. (1951). Emotional aspects of obesity. *Medical Clinics of North America* 35:483–499.

Holmes, N., Ardito, E. A., and Stevenson, D. (1984). Maintenance of weight loss in a heavily overweight population. In *Behavioral Management of Obesity*, ed. J. Storlie and H. A. Jordan, pp. 137–150. New York: Spectrum.

Hood, J., Moore, T. E., and Garner, D. (1982). Locus of control as a measure of ineffectiveness in anorexia nervosa. *Journal of Consulting and Clinical Psychology* 50:3–14.

Jeffery, R. W., Wing, R. R., and Stunkard, A. J. (1983). Behavioral treatment of obesity: the state of the art in 1976. *Behavior Therapy* 9:189–199.

Jeffery, R. W., Bjornson-Benson, W. M., Rosenthal, B. S., et al. (1984). Correlates of weight loss and its maintenance over two years of follow-up in middle-aged men. *Preventive Medicine* 13:155–168.

Johnson, C. (1985). Initial consultation for patients with bulimia and anorexia nervosa. In *Handbook of Psychotherapy for Anorexia Nervosa and Bulimia*, ed. D. M. Garner and P. E. Garfinkel, pp. 19–51. New York: Guilford.

Johnson, C., Lewis C., and Hagman, J. (1984). Bulimia: review and synthesis. *Psychiatric Clinics of North America* 7:247–273.

Johnson, C., Stuckey, M., Lewis, L. D., and Schwartz, D. (1982). Bulimia: a descriptive study of 316 patients. *International Journal of Eating Disorders* 2:1–15.

Jung, C. G. (1938). *Psychological Types*. London: Harcourt, Brace & Company.

——— (1956). *Symbols of Transformation*. Princeton, NJ: Princeton University Press.

Killen, J. D., MacCoby, N., and Taylor, C. B. (1984). Nicotine gum and self-regulation training in smoking relapse prevention. *Behavior Therapy* 15:234–248.

Kohut, H. (1984). *How Does Analysis Cure?* Chicago: University of Chicago Press.

Kolb, L. C. (1975). Disturbances of the body image. In *American Handbook of Psychiatry*, vol. 4, ed. S. Arieti, 2nd ed., pp. 810–837. New York: Basic Books.

Kotchen, T. A. (1960). Existential mental health: an empirical approach. *Journal of Individual Psychology* 16:174–181.

Krug, S. E., and Cattell, R. B. (1980). *Clinical Analysis Questionnaire Manual*. Champaign, IL: Institute for Personality and Ability Testing.

Kubler-Ross, E. (1969). *On Death and Dying*. New York: Macmillan.

Lacocque, P. E. (1984). Fear of engulfment and the problem of identity. *Journal of Religion and Heath* 2:218–228.

——— (1986). An existential interpretation of success neurosis. *Journal of Religion and Health* 25:96–106.

Lacocque, P. E., and Loeb, A. J. (1988). Death anxiety: a hidden factor in countertransference hate. *Journal of Religion and Health* 27:95–108.

Leon, G. R. (1975). Personality, body image, and eating pattern changes in overweight persons after weight loss. *Journal of Clinical Psychology* 31:618–623.

——— (1982). Personality and behavioral correlates of obesity. In *Psychological Aspects of Obesity*, ed. B. Wolman, pp. 15–29. New York: Van Nostrand Reinhold.

Leon, G. R., and Chamberlain, K. (1973). Comparison of daily eating habits and emotional states of overweight persons successful or unsuccessful in maintaining a weight loss. *Journal of Consulting and Clinical Psychology* 41:108–115.

Leon, G. R., Eckert, E., Teed, D., and Buchwald, H. (1979). Changes in body image and other psychological factors after intestinal bypass surgery for massive obesity. *Journal of Behavioral Medicine* 2:39–59.

Leon, G. R., Kolotkin, R., and Korgeski, G. (1979). MacAndrew scale and other MMPI characteristics associated with obesity, anorexia, and smoking behavior. *Addictive Behaviors* 4:401–407.

Leon, G. R., and Rosenthal, B. S. (1984). Prognostic indicators of success or relapse in weight reduction. *International Journal of Eating Disorders* 3:15–24.

Levenson, H. (1973). Multidimensional locus of control in psychiatric patients. *Journal of Consulting and Clinical Psychology* 41:397–404.

Lipman, R. S., Covi, L, and Shapiro, A. (1979). The Hopkins Symptom Checklist: factors derived from the HSCL-90. *Journal of Affective Disorders* 1:9–24.

Loro, A. D., Fisher, E. B., and Levenkron, T. C. (1979). Comparison of established and innovative weight-reduction treatment procedures. *Journal of Applied Behavior Analysis* 12:141–155.

MacAndrew, C. (1965). The differentiation of male alcoholic outpatients from nonalcoholic psychiatric patients by means of the MMPI. *Quarterly Journal of Studies on Alcohol* 26:238–246.

Mahoney, M. J. (1974). Self-reward and self-monitoring techniques for weight control. *Behavior Therapy* 5:48–57.

Mahoney, M. J., and Mahoney, K. (1976). *Permanent Weight Control: A Total Solution to the Dieter's Dilemma.* New York: W. W. Norton.

Mahoney, K., Rogers, T., Straw, M. K., and Mahoney, M. J., eds. (1982). *Human Obesity: Assessment and Treatment.* Englewood Cliffs, NJ: Prentice-Hall.

Marlatt, G. A., and Gordon, J. R. (1980). Determinants of relapse: implications for the maintenance of behavior change. In *Behavioral Medicine: Changing Health Lifestyles*, ed. S. O. Davidson and S. M. Davidson, pp. 410–452. New York: Pergamon.

McKenna, R. J. (1972). Some effects of anxiety level and food cues on the eating behavior of obese and normal subjects: a comparison of the schachterian and psychosomatic conceptions. *Journal of Personality and Social Psychology* 22:311–319.

McLellan, A. T., Luborsky, L., Woody, G. E., and O'Brien, C. P. (1980). An improved diagnostic evaluation instrument for substance abuse patients: the Addiction Severity Index. *Journal of Nervous and Mental Diseases* 168:26–33.

McNair, D. M., Lorr, M., and Droppleman, L. F. (1981). *Manual: Profile of Mood States (POMS).* San Diego: Educational and Industrial Testing Service.

Mermelstein, R. J., and Lichtenstein, E. (1983). *Slip versus relapses in smoking cessation: a situational analysis.* Paper presented at the meeting of the Western Psychological Association, San Francisco, CA, April.

Miller, P. M., O'Neil, P. M., Malcolm, R. J., and Currey, H. S. (1984). Eating disorders. In *Comprehensive Handbook of Psychopathology*, ed. H. E. Adams and P. B. Sutker, pp. 653–682. New York: Plenum.

Miller, P. M., and Sims, K. L. (1981). Evaluation and component analysis of a comprehensive weight control program. *International Journal of Obesity* 5:57–66.

Mitchell, C., and Stuart, R. B. (1984). Effect of self-efficacy on dropout from obesity treatment. *Journal of Consulting and Clinical Psychology* 52:1100–1101.

Mitchell, W., and Straw, M. K. (1981). *Psychological predictors of outcome in behavioral obesity treatment.* Paper presented at the meeting of the Association for the Advancement of Behavior Therapy, Toronto, March.

Monello, L. F., and Mayer, J. (1967). Hunger and satiety sensations in men, women, boys, and girls. *American Journal of Clinical Nutrition* 20:253–261.

Moos, R. H., and Finney, J. W. (1983). The expanding scope of alcoholism treatment evaluation. *American Psychologist* 38:1036–1044.

Mosak, H. H. (1958). Early recollections as a projective technique. *Journal of Projective Techniques* 22:302–311.

——— (1977). Life-style assessment: a demonstration. In *On Purpose: Collected Papers of Harold H. Mosak*, pp. 198–215. Chicago: Alfred Adler Institute, 1972.

Mosak, H. H., Schneider, S., and Mosak, L. E. (1980). *Lifestyle: A Workbook.* Chicago: Alfred Adler Institute.

National Institutes of Health Consensus Development Panel of the Health Implications of Obesity (1985). Health implications of obesity: National Institutes of Health consensus development conference statement. *Annals of Internal Medicine* 103:1073–1077.

Nowlis, V. (1965). Research with the Mood Adjective Checklist. In *Affect, Cognition, and Personality*, ed. S. S. Tomkins and C. E. Izard, pp. 352–389. New York: Springer.

O'Leary, S. G., and Dubey, D. R. (1979). Applications of self-control procedures by children: a review. *Journal of Applied Behavior Analysis* 12:449–466.

O'Neil, P. M., Currey, H. S., Hirsch, A., et al. (1979). Development and validation of the Eating Behavior Inventory. *Journal of Behavioral Assessment* 1:123–132.

Pearce, J. W., LeBow, M. D., and Orchard, J. (1981). Role of spouse involvement in the behavioral treatment of overweight women. *Journal of Consulting and Clinical Psychology* 49:236–244.

Powers, P. S. (1980). *Obesity: The Regulation of Weight.* Baltimore: Williams & Wilkins.

Pyle, R. L., Mitchell, J. E., and Eckert, E. (1981). Bulimia: a report of 34 cases. *Journal of Clinical Psychiatry* 42:60–64.

Reid, D. W., and Ware, E. E. (1973). Multidimensionality of internal-external control: implications for past and future research. *Canadian Journal of Behavioral Science* 5:264–271.

Robbins, T. W., and Fray, P. J. (1980). Stress-induced eating: fat, fiction, or misunderstanding? *Appetite* 1:103–133.

Rodin, J. (1977a). Obesity: why the losing battle? *McMaster Lecture Series.* Washington, DC: American Psychological Association.

——— (1977b). Research on eating behavior and obesity: where does it fit in personality and social psychology? *Personality and Social Psychology Bulletin* 3:333–355.

——— (1981). The current status of the internal-external obesity hypothesis: what went wrong? *American Psychologist* 36:361–372.

Rosenbaum, M. (1980). A schedule for assessing self-control behaviors: preliminary findings. *Behavior Therapy* 11:109–121.

Rosenthal, B., Allen, G. J., and Winter, S. (1980). Husband involvement in the behavioral treatment of overweight women: initial effects and long-term follow-up. *International Journal of Obesity* 4:165–173.

Rotter, J. B. (1966). Generalized expectancies for internal versus external control of reinforcement. *Psychological Monographs* 80:1–28.

——— (1975). Some problems and misperceptions related to the construct of internal versus external control of reinforcement. *Journal of Consulting and Clinical Psychology* 43:56–57.

Saccone, A. J., and Israel, A. C. (1978). Effects of experimenter-versus significant other–controlled reinforcement and choice of target behavior on weight loss. *Behavior Therapy* 9:271–278.

Shontz, F. C. (1969). *Perceptual and Cognitive Aspects of Body Experience.* New York: Academic Press.

Slochower, J. (1976). Emotional labeling and overeating in obese and normal weight individuals. *Psychosomatic Medicine* 38:131–139.

Smith, M. C., and Thelen, M. N. (1984). Development and validation of a test for bulimia. *Journal of Consulting and Clinical Psychology* 52:863–872.

Spielberger, C. D., Lushene, R. E., and McAdoo, W. G. (1971). Theory and measurement of anxiety states. In *Handbook of Modern Personality Theory*, ed. R. B. Cattell, pp. 34–52. Chicago: Aldine.

Stalonas, P. M., Johnson, W. G., and Christ, M. (1978). Behavior modification for obesity: the evaluation of exercise, contingency management, and program adherence. *Journal of Consulting and Clinical Psychology* 46:463–469.

Sternberg, B. (1985). Relapse in weight control: definitions, processes, and prevention strategies. In *Relapse Prevention*, ed. G. A. Marlatt and J. R. Gordon, pp. 521–544. New York: Guilford.

Striegel-Moore, R., and Rodin, J. (1986). The influence of psychological variables in obesity. In *Handbook of Eating Disorders*, ed. K. D. Brownell and J. P. Foreyt, pp. 99–121. New York: Basic Books.

Strober, M., Salkin, B., Burroughs, J., and Morrell, W. (1982). Validity of the bulimia-restricter distinction in anorexia nervosa: parental personality characteristics and family psychiatric morbidity. *Journal of Nervous and Mental Disease* 170:345–351.

Stuart, R. B. (1980). Weight loss and beyond: are they taking it off and keeping it off? In *Behavioral Medicine: Changing Health Lifestyles*, ed. P. D. Davidson and S. M. Davidson, pp. 210–222. New York: Brunner/Mazel.

Stuart, R., and Davis, B. (1972). *Slim Chance in a Fat World: Behavioral Control of Obesity* Champaign, IL: Research Press.

Stuart, R. B., and Jacobson, B. (1987). *Weight, Sex, and Marriage: A Delicate Balance*. New York: W. W. Norton.

Stunkard, A. J. (1957). The "dieting depression": incidence and clinical characteristics of untoward responses to weight reduction regimens. *American Journal of Medicine* 23:77–86.

——— (1976). *The Pain of Obesity*. Palo Alto, CA: Bull.

——— ed. (1980). *Obesity*. Philadelphia: W. B. Saunders.

——— (1981). Restrained eating: what it is and a new scale to measure it. In *The Body Weight Regulatory System: Normal and Disturbed Mechanisms*, ed. L. A. Cioffi, pp. 243–251. New York: Raven Press.

——— (1983). Biological and psychological factors in obesity. In *Eating and Weight Disorders*, ed. R. K. Goodstein, pp. 1–31. New York: Springer.

——— (1985). Obesity. In *Comprehensive Textbook of Psychiatry*, vol. 2, ed. H. I. Kaplan and B. J. Sadock, 4th ed., pp. 1133–1142. Baltimore: Williams & Wilkins.

Stunkard, A. J., Grace, W. J., and Wolff, H. G. (1955). The night eating syndrome: a pattern of food intake among certain obese patients. *American Journal of Medicine* 19:78–86.

Stunkard, A. J., and Messick, S. (1979). *A new scale to assess restrained eating*. Unpublished manuscript, University of Pennsylvania.

Supnick, J. A., and Coletti, G. (1984). Relapse coping and problem-solving training following treatment for smoking. *Addictive Behaviors* 9:401–404.

Taylor, J. A. (1953). A personality scale of manifest anxiety. *Journal of Abnormal and Social Psychology* 48:285–290.

Thomason, J. A. (1983). Multidimensional assessment of locus of control and obesity. *Psychological Reports* 53:1083–1086.

Traub, A. C., and Orback, J. (1964). Psychophysical studies of body image: the adjustable body-distorting mirror. *Archives of General Psychiatry* 11:53–66.

Wadden, T. A., and Stunkard, A. J. (1985). Social and psychological consequences of obesity. *Annals of Internal Medicine* 103:1062–1067.

——— (1987). Psychopathology and obesity. *Annals of the New York Academy of Sciences* 499:55–65.

Wilson, G. T. (1985). Evaluating behavior therapy for obesity. In *Therapeutic Practice in Behavioral Medicine*, ed. D. I. Mostofsky and R. L. Piedmont, pp. 84–87. San Francisco: Jossey-Bass.

Wollersheim, J. P. (1970). Effectiveness of group therapy based on learning principles in the treatment of overweight women. *Journal of Abnormal Psychology* 76:462–474.

12
Personality Disorders

THOMAS A. WIDIGER, Ph.D.,
ALLEN J. FRANCES, M.D., and
TIMOTHY J. TRULL, M.A.

Personality disorders are patterns of inflexible and maladaptive personality traits that result in significant impairment in social or occupational functioning or subjective distress, or both (American Psychiatric Association 1987, Millon 1981). They are chronic behavior patterns with an early and insidious onset; they are evident by late adolescence or early adulthood. Personality disordered patients are unable to respond flexibly or adaptively to the changes and demands of life. Instead, they create and exacerbate stress by provoking aversive reactions in others, by failing to make optimal social, occupational, or other life decisions, and by creating situations that are problematic and pathogenic.

The diagnosis and treatment of personality disorders has been receiving increasing attention (Frances and Widiger 1986, Liebowitz et al. 1986, Siever and Klar 1986). The inclusion of a separate axis and the development of relatively explicit criteria for the diagnosis of personality disorders in the third edition of the DSM (APA 1980) were instrumental in the development of this clinical and empirical interest. Prior to DSM-III, the diagnosis of personality disorders was often overlooked in the presence of a conspicuous or prominent clinical syndrome (Frances 1980, Spitzer et al. 1980). The DSM-III and DSM-III-R (APA 1987), require a multiaxial clinical evaluation that recognizes the contribution and interrelationship of various biopsychosocial factors to the development of the patient's condition (Williams 1985). The diagnosis of the personality disorders on Axis II is particularly important because they will alter the presentation, course, and treatment of, and be a primary contributing factor to, the development of Axis I clinical syndromes (Docherty et al. 1986, Hyler and Frances 1985, Millon and Kotik 1985, Widiger and Hyler 1987).

The assessment of personality disorders is problematic, however (Frances 1980, 1987, Widiger and Frances 1987c). Personality disorder diagnosis has tended to be relatively unreliable, even with the development of the DSM-III criteria (Mellsop et al. 1982). In this chapter we will review techniques and principles of personality disorder interviewing, and we will discuss some of the more controversial issues that impair reliable and valid personality disorder assessment. (The theoretical basis and criteria sets of personality disorders, along with empirical supports, have been reviewed elsewhere (APA 1987, Frances 1980, Frances and Widiger 1986, Millon 1981, Siever and Klar 1986, Widiger and Frances 1985a).

INTERVIEWING TECHNIQUES AND PRINCIPLES

We will begin with a discussion of interviewing techniques and principles in the assessment of personality disorders. We will discuss in particular the assessment of items rather than disorders, the assessment of traits rather than opinions, the assessment of functional impairment, the assessment of chronic and pervasive trends rather than states or situations, and the use of subtle and indirect inquiry.

Assess Items, Not Disorders

One of the reasons for the failure of DSM-III to result in a substantial improvement in the interrater reliability of personality disorder diagnosis is that therapists do not systematically follow the DSM-III criteria sets, and instead form a subjective impression on the basis of symptoms or behaviors that they have found to be useful in their own clinical experience. Morey and Ochoa (1987) asked clinicians to assign Axis II diagnoses to one of their patients and to rate the patient on each of the DSM-III personality disorder items (presented in a randomized order). They found substantial discrepancies between the personality disorder diagnoses assigned by the clinicians and the diagnoses that would be assigned on the basis of the DSM-III personality disorder items that they rated as present. In other words, it was often the case that the clinicians' personality disorder diagnoses were not based on their assessment of the personality disorder items.

The failure to assess criteria sets systematically is understandable; such assessment can be time-consuming. Nevertheless, the specific and explicit criteria sets offered in DSM-III will not improve reliability if they are not used. Unreliable diagnoses are unlikely to be valid, and a major contributor to unreliability is dependence on subjective impressions and personal criteria. Each clinician may believe that he is providing a valid diagnosis of borderline personality disorder, but if agreement is no better than a kappa of 0.29 (Mellsop et al. 1982), then many of them must be wrong. The only way to ensure that diagnoses are replicable and reliable is to follow systematically a standard set of criteria. Reliability has been obtained when semistructured interviews that adhere closely to the criteria have been used (Widiger and Frances 1987c).

The criteria sets are not infallible, however (Widiger et al. 1984, Widiger and Frances 1987b). A patient can meet the criteria for paranoid personality disorder and not have the disorder. The criteria are meant to be guidelines, not sacrosanct edicts. One may at times find that diagnosing with DSM-III-R criteria results in an "obvious" misdiagnosis. One should use one's own best clinical judgment. Nevertheless, one should also realize that it is "best clinical judgments" that often result in poor reliability and poor validity. (Further discussion of clinical judgment will be provided later.)

Some of the semistructured personality disorder interview schedules not only assess each item systematically, but do so in a fashion that minimizes diagnostic halo effects. The Structured Interview for DSM-III Personality Disorders, or SIDP (Stangl et al. 1985), the Personality Disorder Examination, or PDE (Loranger et al. 1987), and the Personality Interview Questions-II, or PIQ-II (Widiger 1987) reorganize the items based on similarities in content or issues. In contrast, the Structured Clinical Interview for DSM-III-R, or SCID (Spitzer et al. 1985), assesses each personality disorder in turn. The SCID-II is consistent with traditional clinical interviews, but it may encourage halo effects by allowing the diagnoses to become "apparent" as the interview proceeds (Widiger and Frances 1987c). For example, once a patient has met the criteria for identity disturbance, unstable-intense relationships, and affective instability, an assumption may develop that the patient has a borderline personality disorder, resulting in a lowered threshold for the subsequent borderline items and a higher threshold for items of personality disorders seemingly incompatible with a borderline personality disorder.

Diagnostic assumptions should not affect the assessment of individual items. For example, some patients who are not schizotypal will display aspects of magical thinking (such as a belief in telepathy and clairvoyance). One may be tempted to score the symptom as absent because one knows with confidence that the patient is not schizotypal. However, if the patient is not schizotypal, then he will not have at least four of the remaining eight schizotypal items. Patients can have magical ideation without being schizotypal, and the presence of magical ideation should be assessed independent of the judgment regarding whether the patient is schizotypal.

The reorganization of the criteria sets in the PDE, SIDP, and PIQ-II do not prevent these halo effects, but they do inhibit them, and they encourage the assessment of each item independently of any assumptions (biases) about the disorder. One can then be more confident that the diagnoses are in fact based on the presence of the items as specified in the DSM-III-R criteria sets.

Assess Traits, Not Opinions

It is somewhat ironic that the recognition of low reliability of clinical judgments has resulted to some extent in greater dependence on patients' judgments regarding maladaptive personality traits (Widiger and Frances 1987c). Because the individual personality disorder criteria are relatively explicit and specific (for example, the patient has no close friends or confidants), it is tempting to simply ask patients directly whether the trait applies to them. Reliability is apparently improved because patients will maintain their opinion across time, and clinicians can agree on whether the patient provided an affirmative or a negative opinion. However, this reliability is somewhat deceiving. If patients are relied upon to tell the clinician whether they have close friends (avoidant, schizotypal, and schizoid), are indecisive (obsessive-compulsive), or have difficulty initiating projects (dependent), then the reliability at issue is the extent to which patients are using the same criteria when they are describing themselves. Would patients agree on what is a close friend, or what constitutes difficulty initiating projects?

Patients will likely vary considerably in their understanding of what is meant by the various trait terms and the threshold for their attribution. An antisocial patient will likely have a much higher threshold for the attribution of recklessness than will an obsessive-compulsive patient. It is therefore not realistic to simply ask patients if they are reckless.

One can at times rectify this by providing examples of what is meant by the various trait terms. Examples are provided in DSM-III-R for many of the items (for example, recurrent speeding and driving while intoxicated are examples of recklessness). But an additional, more intractable problem is that the personality disorder items concern socially undesirable traits of which the patient may be unaware or may simply deny. It is questionable whether the average person is aware, informed, and open about his socially undesirable traits. It is particularly problematic for persons who have a characteristic tendency to distort self-description and self-presentation. Narcissistic persons tend to deny negative features, and it is not realistic to ask them whether they have a sense of entitlement, require constant attention and admiration, and lack empathy. Borderline and dependent persons tend to exaggerate their symptoms and may then overestimate the extent to which they are indecisive, have difficulty initiating projects, and are reticent in social situations.

It is therefore important to base one's assessments on behavioral examples or incidents, rather than opinions. It is always useful to ask patients to give examples of what they mean by a particular trait or symptom, and to then base the assessment on these incidents rather than on the opinions. For example, the schizoid, avoidant, and schizotypal personality disorders include the item of having none or only one close friend or confidant (other than first-degree relatives). Subjects will vary in what they mean by a "close friend," and they may say that they have two or three close friends but they never confide in them, never visit them at their homes, never invite them over to visit, and never telephone them to talk. Associates with whom one goes to bars, business meetings, or formal events do not qualify as close friends.

Assess for Functional Impairment

The DSM-III-R provides rules for determining when a patient has each of the personality disorders. A patient is not considered to have a borderline personality disorder unless he displays at least five of the eight criteria. This cutoff point is somewhat arbitrary and debatable (Finn 1982, Grove 1985, Widiger et al. 1984), but it is the accepted convention.

The threshold for each of the items is not at all clear, however. There is no absolute, qualitative distinction between a normal, adaptive personality trait and an abnormal, maladaptive one (Cloninger 1987, Frances 1982, Widiger and Frances 1985b). The point at which impulsivity, unstable and intense relationships, and feelings of emptiness and boredom are above the threshold for clinical significance is not clear and may be somewhat arbitrary.

One guiding principle is that an item or symptom is above clinical threshold if it results in significant impairment in social or occupational functioning (APA 1987). Has the passive-aggressive, indecisive, or impulsive behavior resulted in a loss of a job, promotion, or raise? Has it resulted in loss of or rejection by friends, inability to get along with others, failure to develop friendships, or misperceptions and misunderstandings in relationships?

Subjective distress is another potential indicator (APA 1987). Patients' complaints that they are troubled by their preoccupation with feelings of envy will suggest the presence of this narcissistic trait. But subjective distress is often a less useful indicator than functional impairment. Some patients will be overly distressed by and critical of minor flaws, peccadilloes, and mistakes, and their exaggerated self-deprecation can result in an overestimation of personality disorder. On the other hand, some patients will not be distressed at all, will be unaware that the traits are detrimental to functioning, and may even value their presence. Lack of empathy and lack of remorse may be considered by some narcissistic and antisocial patients (respectively) as a sign of a tough-minded resilience.

Magical thinking, from the schizotypal criteria set, is a good example. A belief in clairvoyance and telepathy is an example of magical thinking, but it is not considered to be above clinical threshold until it is inconsistent with subcultural norms and influences behavior in some personally relevant manner (APA 1987). Many persons will believe in such phenomena as part of an open-minded, scientific interest. It is clinically relevant if they have altered their lives or acted on the belief in some personally relevant manner. Did they cancel a trip due to a precognition, attempt to communicate with a dead relative, or join some occult group to further explore the phenomena?

Obsessive-compulsive indecisiveness is another example. It is within normal limits to at times avoid, postpone, or protract decisions. Clinically significant indecisiveness results in a repeated failure to complete assignments on time (due to continual revisions), to ask someone out on a date (worrying about where to go, when to go, how to ask, and whether to ask), or to make necessary purchases (ruminating over various possible complications, details, and uncertainties).

Assess Traits, Not States or Situations

The symptoms of personality disorder are readily confused with situational reactions and temporary state conditions (Frances 1980, 1987, Frances and Widiger 1986). The interviewer should therefore determine whether the behavior or incident being reported is a recent or isolated phenomenon or has occurred throughout most of the patient's adult life. Patients should be informed and reminded that the interviewer is interested in their usual behavior throughout their lives, "prior to coming to the hospital" and "prior to the beginning of the recent illness or problems." The patient's current problems may be part of a long-standing pattern, but this must be assessed explicitly by determining whether the pattern was evident prior to a recent divorce, hospitalization, or major depression.

For example, the borderline item of chronic feelings of emptiness and boredom will be a common complaint during inpatient hospitalization. Similarly, marrying an abusive husband is an insufficient basis for determining that a woman chooses people or situations that lead to disappointment, failure, or mistreatment (self-defeating). It is necessary to determine whether she has a history of becoming involved with such persons when others were available and in such situations (for example, whether she has a history of accepting demeaning or exploitative jobs).

In general, the interviewer should not rely on only one example of a particular item. One example of deliberately working slowly to do a bad job (passive-aggressive), questioning the loyalty of a spouse (paranoid), or engaging in excessive, unsolicited self-sacrifice (self-defeating) is not enough to score the item as present. One should ask for additional examples in other relationships, situations, and time periods. It should be a standard practice to ask the following kinds of questions: Can you give me any other examples? Did anything like this occur earlier in your life? Was that at all unusual, or was it typical? Has this been a recent change for you, or were there similar experiences before? How often did this happen? or Did anything like this happen with your first wife (other job, or when you lived alone)? The differentiation of the constructs of traits, states, and situations is, of course, controversial, and will be discussed further in a later section.

Use Indirect and Subtle Inquiries

Simple, direct questions are often more effective than subtle, indirect questions (Holden and Jackson 1985, Wrobel and Lachar 1982). If the patient is aware of his traits and is motivated to provide an honest and open self-description, then direct questions are preferable to indirect. However, this quality cannot be assumed when interviewing patients with personality disorders. It is not realistic to ask an antisocial person whether he has repeatedly lied, has no regard for the truth, or lacks remorse. If a person is characteristically dishonest, then it is unrealistic to expect him to be honest during the interview, especially in response to questions about social responsibility and trust.

It may be similarly unrealistic to ask a narcissistic person whether he requires constant attention or admiration, lacks empathy, is interpersonally exploitative, or has a grandiose sense of self-importance. Narcissistic persons have a fragile self-esteem (Kohut 1971) and are often preoccupied with how they are regarded by others (Kernberg 1984). It may be expecting too much to ask them to openly acknowledge their faults and shortcomings, particularly those that concern their conflicts with respect to self-esteem.

Many of the personality disorder items must then be assessed with less reliable direct observation and indirect questions. Direct observation is necessary for some of the DSM-III-R items (odd speech, for example), and it is helpful for others. For instance, there will be times when patients fish for compliments during an interview and wear their achievements (whether minor or major) on their sleeve for the interviewer to notice and acknowledge. There is then little need to inquire about their need for attention and admiration.

The full range of personality disorder pathology is rarely evident during one interview, however, and subtle, indirect inquiry is then helpful and even necessary. For example, a grandiose sense of self-importance can be assessed by asking patients whether they have any special talents or abilities, to describe their future ambitions or goals, and to indicate how they plan to reach these goals (Widiger 1987). An inflated self-evaluation, exaggeration of talents and achievements, and an expectation to be noticed as special without appropriate achievement will often be evident in response to these questions. Lack of remorse can be assessed by asking patients to indicate why they did some harmful, exploitative, or criminal act. Justifying the act through some form of rationalization without any expression of guilt would indicate lack of remorse. Expressions of guilt might not qualify as actual remorse if the patient never attempted any reparation, penance, or direct apology.

Identity disturbance is one of the most difficult items to assess. One approach is to ask patients to describe themselves but to provide no guidelines or cues as to how to do so. An identity disturbance is indicated by the inability to provide a vivid or clear description of what is unique about themselves (Kernberg 1984). Generalities or concrete statements, such as "patient," "friendly," or "nervous," are insufficient. Patients should be asked to explain what they mean by general-trait terms to determine whether they can provide more specific or unique information. If still unsuccessful, useful follow-up questions are "What is distinct or unique about you?" and "What are your goals or values in life?" (Widiger 1987). Inability to provide anything but concrete statements or generalities in responses to these questions (for example "to get out of the hospital," "to get well," or "to get my wife back") would indicate an identity disturbance.

Lack of empathy can be assessed in a similar fashion. The DSM-III-R provides two examples (being unable to understand why a friend whose father has just died does not want to go to a party, and annoyance or surprise when a friend who is seriously ill cancels a date [APA 1987]), and while these are good illustrations of a failure to understand how others feel, they are likely to be too infrequent to be of much help in assessment. Another approach is to ask patients to describe or explain the feelings of another person, particularly someone with whom they are in conflict. The therapist then observes whether the patient is able to "stand in the shoes" of another person and understand and appreciate this person's feelings and perspective. It is important, though, to distinguish here a personal and sincere appreciation from simply an intellectual, cognitive description of a contrary, opposing position.

CONTROVERSIES AND ISSUES IN ASSESSMENT

The foregoing discussion provided techniques and guidelines for interviewing for personality disorders. The interviewer should also be aware of the various issues and problems that hinder reliable and valid personality disorder assessment. There are many inherent difficulties in the assessment of personality disorders. We will discuss issues with respect to states, situations, roles, subjective judgments, and categorical distinctions.

Traits versus States

A personality disorder involves a long-standing tendency (trait) rather than a temporary condition (state). Personality disorders are often confused with a temporally circumscribed Axis I condition (Widiger and Frances 1987a). Patients who present with an atypical depression will appear borderline, and patients with a social phobia may appear avoidant. Perhaps the two most controversial distinctions are borderline personality versus affective disorder (Akiskal et al. 1985, Gunderson and Elliot 1985) and self-defeating personality versus depression (Akiskal 1983, Liebowitz 1987). There are others, including social phobia versus avoidant personality (Widiger et al. 1987), but we will confine our discussion to the borderline and self-defeating personality disorders.

Differentiating borderline personality from affective disorder is particularly difficult because many of the borderline items directly, or at least indirectly, tap affective symptoms (for example, affective instability and inappropriate or intense anger). Most borderline patients, by definition, display affective instability. Borderline personality may in fact represent a disposition to affective dyscontrol. The distinction between states and traits is somewhat arbitrary because traits may include the disposition to experience or display particular states (Allen and Potkay 1981). Depression, then, neither suggests nor necessarily excludes the diagnosis of a borderline personality disorder.

Gunderson and Elliot (1985) suggest that a "borderline depression" may be characterized by loneliness, emptiness, and boredom, whereas a purely "affective depression" may be characterized more by guilt, remorse, and low self-esteem. These clinical distinctions may be useful at times, but they may also be difficult to make reliably. Diagnosing borderline personality in a depressed patient requires the further identification of the presence of borderline features that are relatively independent of depression (for example, identity disturbance) and a history of a stable pattern of interpersonal and affective instability.

The differentiation of self-defeating personality disorder from dysthymia is similarly problematic. Many depressed persons will appear to be self-defeating, and most self-defeating persons are likely to be depressed. Self-defeating persons tend to choose people and situations that lead to disappointment, reject opportunities for pleasure, and even respond to positive events with depression (APA 1987). The DSM-III-R self-defeating personality disorder diagnosis is based in part on the psychoanalytic and psychiatric concept of a "depressive character" (Bemporad 1985, Simons 1987, Widiger and Frances, in press), which describes a person who is chronically self-deprecating, pessimistic, and self-blaming and is therefore likely to be depressed much of the time.

Akiskal (1983) suggests that a characterological depression can be distinguished from a subaffective dysthymia by the presence of dependent, histrionic, or sociopathic traits, a history of parental separation or divorce, a family history of parent assortative mating, normal rapid eye movement (REM) latency, and lack of response to thymoleptic drugs. However, these indicators may be more useful in identifying a drug-responsive and/or a biogenetic depression than in ruling out a characterological depression (Widiger and Frances 1987a). Self-defeating personality disorder might have a biogenetic substrate and be responsive to pharmacologic interventions (Gunderson and Pollack 1985).

The DSM-III-R suggests that self-defeating personality disorder be distinguished from depression by the presence of the self-defeating behaviors when the person is not depressed. This determination will at times require a retrospective assessment of the patient's personality prior to or independently of a current depression. Retrospective reporting is necessary in the assessment of all of the personality disorders, but it may be especially problematic when the patient is depressed. Depressed persons are likely to provide an overly pessimistic and critical description of their past, future, and self (Sacco and Beck 1985). Interviews may be less susceptible to such state factors than self-report inventories (Reich et al. 1987, Widiger and Frances 1987c), but they are certainly not immune to them.

Interviewers may therefore wish to supplement their patient interviews with interviews with a close relative, friend, or associate of the patient (Widiger and Frances 1987c, Zimmerman et al. 1986). These "informants" can be particularly helpful in personality disorder assessment because they will have observed the patient over a much broader span of time than is available to the therapist, and they will not be viewing this history through the distorting lens of a depression, anxiety, or psychosis. In addition, they will be particularly familiar with the interpersonal style of the patient, which can be of central importance in the assessment of personality disorders (Kiesler 1986, Widiger and Frances 1985b, Wiggins 1982). Informants are certainly not infallible or objective. They may not have observed some aspects of some personality disorders (for example, schizoid persons may not have any useful informants), and they may have their own axe to grind, but they can offer a useful and informative perspective.

Traits versus Situations

The differentiation of traits and situations has been controversial for some time (Epstein and O'Brien 1985). It is less of an issue in personality disorder assessment because personality disorders are by definition the tendency to be consistent in one's behavior across situations to the point that it is maladaptive (Millon 1981). Patients with personality disorders are unable to respond flexibly to the demands of varying situations. Nevertheless, personality disorders may often be confused with situational reactions. The two most controversial examples are the passive-aggressive and the self-defeating personality disorders.

The passive-aggressive personality disorder was almost excluded from DSM-III because some considered it a reaction to being in a powerless, subordinate position (Gunderson 1983, Malinow 1981). Passive-aggressive behavior may at times be a response to being an inpatient who has lost the control, authority, and freedom experienced prior to hospitalization and who must follow the dictates and rules of a hospital staff. Similarly, self-defeating behavior may be seen in female victims of abusive relationships (Rosewater 1987, Walker 1987). Self-defeating persons are more likely than others to place themselves within and fail to leave an abusive relationship, but the apparently self-defeating behavior of an abused woman may at times reflect the spouse's ability to keep her involved through promises to reform, guilt-inducing pleas not to be abandoned, and threats of violence.

Complicating the distinction is that traits are at times not evident outside of particular situations. A trait is the disposition to respond in a particular manner within certain situations (Levy 1983). If the relevant situations do not occur, then the trait will not be evident. Passive-aggressive behavior that is confined to the hospital or work setting, then, is not necessarily simply a situational reaction. The passive-aggressive trait may be the disposition to respond to hospitalization (and comparable situations) with negativistic resistance, and the self-defeating trait may be the tendency to respond to victimization (and comparable situations) with self-blame and helplessness. The behavior would be solely situational if all persons responded in the same manner to these situations.

One is more confident, though, that the behavior is a reflection of a trait if the behavior is observed across a variety of situations (Epstein and O'Brien 1985). Interviewers should determine, for example, whether patients also display passive-aggressive behavior outside of the hospital in such situations as work, leisure, or family. For example, do they sulk and complain when their friends do something they don't want to do and then spoil the evening for everyone, including themselves? Do they often complain that their friends, as well as their therapists and employers, make unreasonable demands? Similarly, one should assess whether the self-defeating behavior has occurred prior to and between abusive relationships.

Traits versus Roles

Traits may also be confused with roles (Frances 1980). Persons will choose roles, positions, and jobs because they complement and support their personality, but a person's behavior will also at times reflect the demands or pressures of a social role (aggressive behavior in a soldier is less indicative of a sadistic personality than aggressive behavior in a professor). A role maintained over an extended period of time may have a substantial effect on personality, but at what point this occurs is difficult to determine.

Sociocultural expectations and biases with respect to certain roles can further handicap the assessment of personality disorders. The most controversial examples concern possible sex-role biases with respect to the dependent, histrionic, and self-defeating personality disorders. These disorders involve to some extent exaggerated or extreme variants of stereotypically feminine behavior (Brown 1986, Caplan 1987, Kaplan 1983, Simons 1987, Williams and Spitzer 1983). Clinicians, whether male or female, may possess masculine biases regarding socially desirable behavior and may thereby pathologize feminine behavior. Emotionality in a woman may be too readily diagnosed as histrionic, devotion as dependency, and sacrifice as self-defeating. On the other hand, feminist political convictions can also hinder a clinician from recognizing such traits in female patients.

The extent to which the dependent, histrionic, and self-defeating personality disorders involve sex biases is unclear. It is then important for clinicians to be aware of the controversy and of their own assumptions, expectations, and/or biases with respect to their female (and male) patients. None of us is without biases, and it is likely that sex-role biases do impact on the clinical diagnosis of personality disorders.

Clinical Judgment

It was stated earlier that the assessment of personality disorder should be based on specific behaviors and incidents, not opinions or descriptive statements. Reliability is increased to the extent that clinical judgment is curtailed. But reliability does not necessarily imply validity, and with increasing behavioral specificity, one may lose the construct that is being assessed (Michels 1987).

The best example of this may be the antisocial personality disorder (Frances 1980). The DSM-III-R antisocial criteria are reliably assessed because they often refer to specific criminal and delinquent acts. But they do not necessarily indicate the absence of guilt, loyalty, empathy, and responsibility that are central to many theories of psychopathy (Millon 1981). Similarly, the DSM-III-R histrionic item of overconcern with physical appearance is more reliably assessed than the DSM-III item concerned with vanity, but there are many other ways of displaying vanity and many other reasons for being overconcerned with physical appearance.

Any single behavior can reflect a variety of traits, and any trait can be associated with a variety of behaviors (Widiger and Frances 1985b, Widiger and Trull 1987). Accusing a husband of having an affair after he came home late from work may reflect an unjustified concern with the spouse's fidelity (paranoid), suspicious or paranoid ideation (schizotypal), a demand for reassurance (histrionic), or a preoccupation with the fear of being abandoned (dependent). It is unlikely that personality disorder assessment can be done without some degree of clinical judgment.

The degree of subjective (expert) judgment that is necessary or tolerable is unclear. The explicit criteria provided in DSM-III-R are helpful in improving communication and agreement among clinicians (Spitzer and Williams 1985). Validity does assume reliability, and the latter requires adherence to the diagnostic criteria. Nevertheless, clinical judgments are still necessary with respect to particular traits and are then best made on the basis of assessments fully informed by the relevant literature (Frances 1980, 1987, Frances and Widiger 1986, Millon 1981, Siever and Klar 1986, Widiger and Frances 1985a, 1985b).

Categorical Distinctions

One of the factors contributing to low reliability is the necessity of making arbitrary categorical distinctions. There is no clear boundary between normal and abnormal personality traits (see earlier discussion on item threshold), nor between one particular personality disorder and another (Cloninger 1987, Frances 1982, Widiger and Frances 1985b).

The requirement to assess a personality disorder as present or absent forces the clinician to make an arbitrary categorical distinction for which there is then likely to be considerable disagreement. If there is no clear boundary and the distinction is to a large extent arbitrary, it is not surprising that clinicians disagree on when the item is present.

DSM-III and DSM-III-R allow clinicians to make more than one personality disorder diagnosis. There is then no requirement to distinguish among them. Nevertheless, clinicians do provide fewer personality disorder diagnoses than are obtained with semistructured interviews (Pfohl et al. 1986), reflecting in part perhaps a tendency to consider personality disorders to be discrete syndromes with distinct boundaries. It may not seem meaningful or appropriate to say that a patient suffers from four personality disorders, and clinicians may typically stop diagnosing when they have provided one or two diagnoses.

Categorical distinctions also tend to lose information by providing only two broad classes of presence versus absence of, for example, borderline personality disorder or identity disturbance. It is more likely the case that patients vary in the extent to which they have an identity disturbance or a borderline personality disorder. This information is lost in the DSM-III-R diagnostic system.

It may be more accurate and realistic to use a dimensional model to classify the personality disorders and their items (Frances 1982). Interviewers may find it useful to record not only the presence versus absence of each of the personality disorders, but also the number of items possessed by each patient. This will provide some information about the degree to which each patient displays each of the personality disorders. The number of items possessed is not the optimal dimensional system (Frances and Widiger 1986, Widiger and Frances 1985b). It is unlikely, for example, that presence of seven borderline items and seven dependent items suggests a comparable degree of dependent and borderline pathology, respectively. But until a dimensional system has been formally adopted, a record of the number of personality disorder items possessed by each patient will facilitate an increasing familiarity with the dimensional perspective that might eventually be used in a future DSM.

The diagnosis of personality disorders is essential in clinical assessment because most patients will display some degree of an inflexible and maladaptive behavior pattern that has characterized their functioning throughout most of their adult life. This behavior pattern may have contributed to the development of their anxiety disorder, sexual dysfunction, depression, or other Axis I syndrome, and it will often affect the presentation, course, and treatment of these disorders. It may even be the primary concern and the principal focus of treatment.

The assessment of personality disorders is complex and controversial, however. Personality disorders are often confused with states and situations, are affected by sex-role biases and subjective impressions, and are diagnosed with arbitrary categorical distinctions. The guidelines and suggestions provided in this chapter are intended to facilitate reliable and valid personality disorder assessment.

REFERENCES

Akiskal, H. (1983). Dysthymic disorder: psychopathology of proposed chronic depressive subtypes. *American Journal of Psychiatry* 140:11–20.

Akiskal, H., Yerevanian, B., Davis, G., et al. (1985). The nosologic status of borderline personality: clinical and polysomnographic study. *American Journal of Psychiatry* 142:192–198.

Allen, B. P., and Potkay, C. (1981). On the arbitrary distinction between states and traits. *Journal of Personality and Social Psychology* 41:916–928.

American Psychiatric Association (1987). *Diagnostic and Statistical Manual of Mental Disorders*, 3rd ed., rev. Washington, DC: APA.

Bemporad, J. (1985). Long-term analytic treatment of depression. In *Handbook of Depression*, ed. E. Beckham and W. Leber, pp. 82–99. Homewood, IL: Dorsey.

Brown, L. (1986). Gender-role analysis: a neglected component of psychological assessment. *Psychotherapy* 23:243–248.

Caplan, P. (1987). The Psychiatric Association's failure to meet its own standards: the dangers of self-defeating personality disorder as a category. *Journal of Personality Disorders* 1:178–182.

Cloninger, C. (1987). A systematic method for clinical description and classification of personality variants. *Archives of General Psychiatry* 44:573–588.

Docherty, J., Fiester, S., and Shea, T. (1986). Syndrome diagnosis and personality disorder. In *Psychiatry Update: American Psychiatric Association Annual Review*, vol. 5, ed. A. Frances and R. Hales, pp. 315–355. Washington, DC: American Psychiatric Press.

Epstein, S., and O'Brien, E. (1985). The person–situation debate in historical and current perspective. *Psychological Bulletin* 98:513–537.

Finn, S. (1982). Base rates, utilities, and DSM-III: shortcomings of fixed-rule systems of psychodiagnosis. *Journal of Abnormal Psychology* 91:294–302.

Frances, A. (1980). The DSM-III personality disorders: a commentary. *American Journal of Psychiatry* 137:1050–1054.

——— (1982). Categorical and dimensional systems of personality diagnosis: a comparison. *Comprehensive Psychiatry* 23:516–527.

——— (1987). *DSM-III Personality Disorders: Diagnosis and Treatment.* New York: BMA Audio Cassettes.

Frances, A., and Widiger, T. (1986). The classification of personality disorders: an overview of problems and solutions. In *Psychiatry Update: American Psychiatric Association Annual Review*, vol. 5, ed. A. Frances and R. Hales, pp. 240–257. Washington, DC: American Psychiatric Press.

Grove, W. (1985). Bootstrapping diagnoses using Bayes's theorem: it's not worth the trouble. *Journal of Consulting and Clinical Psychology* 53:261–263.

Gunderson, J. G. (1983). DSM-III diagnosis of personality disorders. In *Current Perspectives on Personality Disorders*, ed. J. Frosch, pp. 20–39. Washington, DC: American Psychiatric Press.

Gunderson, J. G., and Elliott, G. (1985). The interface between borderline personality disorder and affective disorder. *American Journal of Psychiatry* 142:277–288.

Gunderson, J. G., and Pollack, W. S. (1985). Conceptual risks of the Axis I-II division. In *Biologic Response Styles: Clinical Implications*, ed. H. Klar and L. Siever, pp. 81–95. Washington, DC: American Psychiatric Press.

Holden, R., and Jackson, D. (1985). Disguise and the structured self-report assessment of psychopathology: I. An analogue investigation. *Journal of Consulting and Clinical Psychology* 53:211–222.

Hyler, S., and Frances, A. (1985). Clinical implications of Axis I–Axis II interactions. *Comprehensive Psychiatry* 26:345–351.

Kaplan, M. (1983). A woman's view of DSM-III. *American Psychologist* 38:786–792.

Kernberg, O. (1984). *Severe Personality Disorders.* New Haven: Yale University Press.

Kiesler, D. (1986). The 1982 Interpersonal Circle: an analysis of DSM-III personality disorders. In *Contemporary Directions in Psychopathology*, ed. T. Millon and G. Klerman, pp. 571–597. New York: Guilford.

Kohut, H. (1971). *The Analysis of the Self.* New York: International Universities Press.

Levy, L. (1983). Trait approaches. In *The Clinical Psychology Handbook*, ed. M. Hersen, A. Kazdin, and A. Bellack, pp. 123–142. New York: Plenum.

Liebowitz, M. (1987). Commentary on the criteria for self-defeating personality disorder. *Journal of Personality Disorders* 1:197–199.

Liebowitz, M., Stone, M., and Turkat, I. (1986). Treatment of personality disorders. In *Psychiatry Update: American Psychiatric Association Annual Review*, vol. 5, ed. A. Frances and R. Hales, pp. 356–393. Washington, DC: American Psychiatric Press.

Loranger, A., Susman, V., Oldham, J., and Russakoff, L. M. (1987). The Personality Disorder Examination: a preliminary report. *Journal of Personality Disorders* 1:1–13.

Malinow, K. (1981). Passive-aggressive personality. In *Personality Disorders: Diagnosis and Management*, ed. J. Lion, 2nd ed., pp. 121–132. Baltimore: Williams & Wilkins.

Mellsop, G., Varghese, F., Joshua, S., and Hicks, A. (1982). The reliability of Axis II of DSM-III. *American Journal of Psychiatry* 139:1360–1361.

Michels, R. (1987). How should the criteria for personality disorders be formulated? *Journal of Personality Disorders* 1:95–99.

Millon, T. (1981). *Disorders of Personality: DSM-III: Axis II*. New York: Wiley.

Millon, T., and Kotik, D. (1985). The relationship of depression to disorders of personality. In *Handbook of Depression*, ed. E. Beckham and W. Leber, pp. 700–744. Homewood, IL: Dorsey.

Morey, L., and Ochoa, E. (1987). *An investigation of influences upon misdiagnosis: borderline and antisocial personality*. Paper presented at the 95th annual meeting of the American Psychological Association, New York, August.

Pfohl, B., Coryell, W., Zimmerman, M., and Stangl, D. (1986). DSM-III personality disorders: diagnostic overlap and internal consistency of individual DSM-III criteria. *Comprehensive Psychiatry* 27:21–34.

Reich, J., Noyes, R., Hirschfeld, R., et al. (1987). State and personality in depressed and panic patients. *American Journal of Psychiatry* 144:181–187.

Rosewater, L. (1987). A critical analysis of the proposed self-defeating personality disorder. *Journal of Personality Disorders* 1:190–195.

Sacco, W., and Beck, A. (1985). Cognitive therapy of depression. In *Handbook of Depression*, ed. E. Beckham and W. Leber, pp. 3–38. Homewood, IL: Dorsey.

Shrauger, J., and Osberg, T. (1981). The relative accuracy of self-predictions and judgments by others in psychological assessment. *Psychological Bulletin* 90:322–351.

Siever, L., and Klar, H. (1986). A review of DSM-III criteria for the personality disorders. In *Psychiatry Update: American Psychiatric Association Annual Review*, vol. 5, ed. A. Frances and R. Hales, pp. 279–314. Washington, DC: American Psychiatric Press.

Simons, R. (1987). Self-defeating and sadistic personality disorders: needed additions to the diagnostic nomenclature. *Journal of Personality Disorders* 1:161–167.

Spitzer, R., and Williams, J. (1985). Classification of mental disorders. In *Comprehensive Textbook of Psychiatry*, vol. 1, ed. H. Kaplan and B. Sadock, 4th ed., pp. 592–613. Baltimore: Williams & Wilkins.

Spitzer, R., Williams, J., and Gibbon, M. (1985). *Instruction Manual for the Structured Clinical Interview for DSM-III-R (SCID, 7/1/85 Revision)*. New York: New York State Psychiatric Institute.

Spitzer, R., Williams, J., and Skodol, A. (1980). DSM-III: the major achievements and an overview. *American Journal of Psychiatry* 137:151–164.

Stangl, D., Pfohl, B., Zimmerman, M., et al. (1985). A structured interview for the DSM-III personality disorders. *Archives of General Psychiatry* 42:35–46.

Walker, L. (1987). Inadequacies of the masochistic personality disorder diagnosis for women. *Journal of Personality Disorders* 1:183–189.

Widiger, T. (1987). *Personality interview questions II.* Unpublished manuscript, University of Kentucky, Lexington.

Widiger, T., and Frances, A. (1985a). Axis II personality disorders: diagnostic and treatment issues. *Hospital and Community Psychiatry* 36:619–627.

——— (1985b). The DSM-III personality disorders: perspectives from psychology. *Archives of General Psychiatry* 42:615–623.

——— (1987a). *Comorbidity of personality and Axis I disorders.* Paper presented at the 140th annual meeting of the American Psychiatric Association, Chicago, IL, May.

——— (1987b). Definitions and diagnoses: a brief response to Morey and McNamara. *Journal of Abnormal Psychology* 96:286–287.

——— (1987c). Interviews and inventories for the measurement of personality disorders. *Clinical Psychology Review* 7:49–75.

——— (in press). Controversies concerning the self-defeating personality disorders. In *Self-Defeating Behaviors: Experimental Research and Practical Implications*, ed. R. Curtis. New York: Plenum.

Widiger, T., Hurt, S., Frances, A., et al. (1984). Diagnostic efficiency and DSM-III. *Archives of General Psychiatry* 41:1005–1012.

Widiger, T., and Hyler, S. (1987). Axis I/Axis II interactions. In *Psychiatry*, ed. J. Cavenar, R. Michels, and A. Cooper, pp. 1–10. Philadelphia: J. B. Lippincott.

Widiger, T., and Trull, T. (1987). Behavioral indicators, hypothetical constructs, and personality disorders. *Journal of Personality Disorders* 1:82–87.

Widiger, T., Trull, T., and Frances, A. (1987). *Controversies about avoidant personality disorder.* Paper presented at the 140th annual meeting of the American Psychiatric Association, Chicago, IL, May.

Wiggins, J. (1982). Circumplex models of interpersonal behavior in clinical psychology. In *Handbook of Research Methods in Clinical Psychology*, ed. P. Kendall and J. Butcher, pp. 183–221. New York: Wiley.

Williams, J. (1985). The multiaxial system of DSM-III: where did it come from and where should it go? I: Its origins and critiques. *Archives of General Psychiatry* 42:175–180.

Williams, J., and Spitzer, R. (1983). The issue of sex bias in DSM-III: a critique of "A woman's view of DSM-III" by Marcie Kaplan. *American Psychologist* 38:793–798.

Wrobel, T., and Lachar, D. (1982). Validity of the Weiner subtle and obvious scales for the MMPI: another example of the importance of inventory-item content. *Journal of Consulting and Clinical Psychology* 50:469–470.

Zimmerman, M., Pfohl, B., Stangl, D., and Corenthal, C. (1986). Assessment of DSM-III personality disorders: the importance of interviewing an informant. *Journal of Clinical Psychiatry* 47:261–263.

13

Child and Adolescent Abuse

TIMOTHY J. WOLF, Ph.D.

The investigation of child and adolescent abuse and neglect has not always been the sophisticated and specialized process it is today. Beginning with the 1875 organization of the New York County Society for the Prevention of Cruelty to Children, voluntary societies began to take responsibility for the protection of children. These voluntary, nonpublic organizations were gradually replaced by public welfare agencies. Today, child social workers have broadened the scope of child abuse intervention to include not only the legal protection of the child but also the rehabilitation of the family. In the 1960s, beginning with Kempe's (1962) published report of the "battered child syndrome," physicians, psychiatrists, and psychologists began to call attention to the special conditions surrounding physical abuse, neglect, and sexual abuse of children. Concurrently, legal developments have paved the way for greater professional involvement. The Federal Child Abuse Prevention and Treatment Act was passed in 1974, and by 1978 most states provided protective services and reporting laws for physical, sexual, and emotional child abuse and neglect.*

The developing fields of child psychiatry and child psychology during the last 30 years have shed light on child abuse in terms of child development, child sexuality, and family dynamics. In that same period, the view of the credibility of children who report abuse has significantly changed. Until the 1960s, most perpetrators, especially if they were parents, were believed over the accusations of the child. In the case of sexual abuse, it was more likely that the child would be seen as inventing the allegation or encouraging the sexual abuse. During the 1960s and 1970s, it was believed that children rarely reported abuse unless it had actually occurred. This shift reflected the research in child development rather than reliance on Freudian theory. More recently, a middle ground seems to be emerging in which each case is judged individually, without presupposition. This may be partly due to a growing number of abuse

---

* Unless otherwise noted, the information in this chapter applies to adolescents as well as children.

accusations in custody cases that are being documented as false (Benedek and Schetky 1985) in order to obtain custody or to terminate the accused parent's rights. Since there is often little evidence to document the cases of neglect or emotional or sexual abuse, and no reliable research indicates what percentage of child accusations are true, the clinical judgment of the therapist often becomes the critical criterion for the determination of circumstances.

Not only the clinical interviewer or team, but a virtual army of professionals are involved in the investigation of child abuse. It is therefore vital that the therapist or team conducting the interview and assessment of the child have both an understanding of the process of child abuse reporting and specialized skills in investigation, as well as a knowledge of the available treatment network. A sensitivity to other professionals involved may also be important to the success of the investigation and treatment. When this focus is maintained, psychiatrists, psychologists, pediatricians, social workers, marriage, family and child counselors, child protective service workers, teachers, police, and attorneys can maintain cooperation and professionalism and can work together successfully to support both the child or adolescent and the family.

GOALS FOR EVALUATION

Before proceeding with any evaluation, the therapist should have specific goals. These goals should be determined by reviewing information already obtained in the investigation process, clarifying who is asking for the evaluation, and being cognizant of how the evaluation results will be used.

The interviewer must consider the following questions: What has happened to the child prior to the clinical interview? Has the child been through a medical examination or legal investigation, or both? Has the child been removed from the home? Or is the interviewer in the position of being the person to initiate a suspected abuse report?

Second, what are the dynamics of the allegations, and who is referring the child for evaluation? The court? One parent, or both? A lawyer? Who are the other professionals with whom cooperation and exchange of information is necessary?

Third, who will use the information and for what purpose? Is there consideration of removing the child from the home? Is this a dispute about physical or legal custody? Who will see this child for psychotherapy? To what extent will the results be used in court, and will you be called upon to testify as an expert witness? To what extent is a family unification treatment plan necessary?

When these kinds of questions are answered, the therapist can begin to formulate a direction for the interview. Since many professionals may be involved in each case, the interviewer will want to make his evaluation complement the information previously compiled, so that the assessment is as comprehensive as possible. Each clinician should strive to serve the best interests of both the child and the family with the least amount of trauma.

ESTABLISHING RAPPORT

Special attention should be given to establishing rapport with the child. This is especially critical for abused children who have experienced frequent violations of trust with adult figures. The therapist should not hurry the child, yet at the same time a specific agenda should be maintained. If a child should inquire, it is important to be honest with the child about the clinician's role and about how the information obtained will be used and with whom it will be shared.

Establishing rapport means entering the world of the child. I am reminded of a professional with whom I studied who would sit with legs crossed in a chair while the child played on the floor. It was not surprising that this professional did not elicit the information requested since he was so out of sync with his patients.

The best way to enter the world of a child is to mirror the child. *Mirroring* is matching the child's behavior, including body posture, specific gestures, breathing rhythms, facial expressions, activity levels, and voice tone and tempo (Cameron-Bandler 1985). Mirroring enhances the child's trust in the therapist. Once this trust has been established, honest responses and significant information can be expected, and the credibility of the child is enhanced. For example, if the child's activity level is high, the therapist begins by mirroring the activity level, by sitting forward, playing on the floor, fingering an object. Once the child and therapist are in sync, the therapist can begin to slow down or alter his pace. This technique can be used to gain the child's confidence. Since parents who batter their children are usually out of sync or rhythm with them, teaching parents similar techniques will be an important part of later therapy.

RECOGNITION OF PHYSICAL AND SEXUAL ABUSE

The therapist should incorporate questions about physical and sexual abuse and neglect into all interviews with children, using the child's frame of reference and language that is age appropriate. Such questions might include the following: How did you learn about sex? Do parts of your body trouble you? Do you know other children who have been hurt by others? Have you ever been touched by others in ways that made you feel bad?

Before beginning the interview, therapists must honestly assess whether their own discomfort with sexual or physical abuse investigation or reporting will interfere with their advocacy in behalf of the child. The child is not likely to volunteer the information, and unless the therapist is comfortably sensitive to the issues, the child may face additional trauma, miss the opportunity to work through past trauma, or withhold information.

An immense volume of literature has been generated in the past decade regarding child and adolescent sexual abuse. Clinicians should familiarize themselves with current information as part of their continuing education. Federal, state, and local laws and guidelines cover the definition, reporting, and investigation of child abuse. These laws and guidelines vary from state to state, so we cannot address them specifically here. Any clinician who sees children is obliged to keep abreast of these changing laws and guidelines.

Within the context of evaluation and later psychotherapeutic treatment of the child, physical and sexual abuse is always an interactive process between adults and children. In cases of physical abuse, there is, (1) the perpetrator, who may have some predisposition to act aggressively toward the child, (2) the child, who may be behaving in a way that triggers the perpetrator's aggressive feeling, and (3) a stressful context that aggravates the adversive feelings of the perpetrator (Kadushin and Mortin 1981). The research on physical abuse somewhat consistently identifies the perpetrator as having a history of childhood abuse or rejection; low self-esteem; a rigid, domineering, impulsive personality; social isolation; a history of inadequate coping; poor interpersonal relationships; high unrealistic expectations of children; and a lack of empathy (Kadushin and Mortin 1981). In addition to these characteristics, the perpetrator in sexual abuse is more likely to have a personality disorder associated with sexual deviation (Shetky and Green 1988).

In studies of the family dynamics of physical abuse, the parent–child interaction is less positive, less child-centered, and less tolerant, with more reliance on physical punishment for discipline than in nonabusive families (Kadushin and Mortin 1981). The incestuous family has been described as rigid, patriarchal, and prone to secrecy, with the father maintaining his dominant, coercive position (Herman 1981, Meiselman 1978, Swanson and Biaggio 1985). The marital relationship suffers from unmet dependency needs, with the mother often delegating marital and homemaking responsibilities to the daughter. The father may assume a nurturing role, which he enacts in a sexual context (Meiselman 1978, Mrazch et al. 1981).

While clinicians should have a thorough knowledge of the foregoing research, they should also be cautious when evaluating a child from this perspective. There are few controlled studies that substantiate the universality of any of these hypotheses, including the concept of intergenerational abuse (Kadushin and Mortin 1981). The therapist should strain to see each child and family within its own unique interactional context.

CLINICAL ASSESSMENT

During the assessment process, every effort must be made to avoid further traumatizing the child. Many children are more traumatized by parental reaction and medical, legal, and psychological intrusion than by the initial alleged incident of abuse. The clinician is in the unique position of being able to minimize further trauma while at the same time obtaining a detailed body of information. Care should be taken to avoid placing the dynamics of family pressures and the demands of other professionals ahead of the needs of the child. Further, child abuse cases are often highly emotionally charged, and therapists should be careful not to allow the demands or pressures of family members and of legal, medical, or child protective workers to cloud their objectivity or sensitivity to the child.

ELEMENTS OF ASSESSMENT

Ideally, the clinical assessment of the child should include interviews with the child, the perpetrator, and other family or care-taking persons; a developmental history; and standardized measures. Assessment of the child includes cognitive, social, physical, and emotional information as well as assessment of abuse.

Cognitive

In the cognitive assessment, special attention should be paid to questions of cognitive development that validate the child's verbal report. First, the child must be able to understand the concepts of who, where, and what. The clinician can determine the child's level of understanding by asking simple questions based on the child's developmental age: What is your name? Where do you live? For what reason are you here today? Second, the therapist must determine whether the child has a concept of a true statement versus a lie. Again, simple questions should be geared to the child's developmental level. Young children might be asked simple questions like, If you ate a candy bar and said you didn't, would that be a lie?

When asking questions, the clinician must consider the child's developmental level. Questions for the preschooler should reflect the home environment and times and circumstances with which the child is familiar; questions to school-age children, on the other hand, may reflect a more standardized developmental model. The therapist must be very careful to avoid leading the child with questions that prejudice the answers or verbally or nonverbally rewarding the child for answers. The cognitive information in the interview may be compared to the information from the intellectual assessment for a more complete picture.

Emotional

The therapist should assess how the child is feeling about himself. This assessment may include questions about the kinds of nurturing he perceives based on his parents' or caretaker's touch, feeding, time, and attention. What is the strength of attachments to various members of the family or outside caretakers? Does the child play a particular role in the family or outside of the family? Projective instruments can be used to add validity to many of the child's perceptions.

Social

An examination of the child's social relationships will provide the therapist with many clues to his interaction in the world. Does the child have friends? Are they older, younger, or the same age? Is the child engaging in age-appropriate play? What characterizes the child's interactions with adults? Teachers and childcare workers are an important source of social information since children often spend a significant part of each day with these persons.

Physical

Physical indicators are an important part of understanding the child. Is the child small or large for his age? How does he perceive his physical size or physical development? Are fine or gross motor skills developmentally appropriate? Are there soft neurological signs that may indicate sensory motor problems, or attentional deficits, or minimal brain damage as a result of abuse? If the child has not had a medical examination, is it necessary? Or is it necessary to reduce trauma from a medical examination that has already been performed?

In the case of sexual abuse in which a medical exam is necessary, special attention should be paid to the child's anxiety and fear. There may be a tendency for the child to interpret the physical exam as another aspect of physical intrusion or as punishment. Young children may be able to work through this difficulty by acting it out using a doctor's play kit, in combination with the clinician's carefully prepared words of support and encouragement. For the child who has not been physically examined, this play will pave the way for a less frightening experience. For older childen, discussion of the medical examination in terms of their bodies and blossoming sexuality will help to lessen their fear and anxiety. Tedesco and Schnell (1987) suggest using a research-proven presurgical model in which parents are involved in preparing the child for the examination, thereby reducing anxiety for both children and parents.

CONTENT AREAS

The following questions should be included in the assessment of abuse:

1. What was the child's relationship with the perpetrator? Was the perpetrator a parent, relative, neighbor, or a complete stranger?
2. What was the duration of the abuse? Was the abuse an isolated incident, or did it occur over a long period or a short extended period?
3. How was the child violated? In the case of sexual abuse, was there penetration or fondling? In the case of physical abuse, how was the child hurt? In cases of neglect, what were the physical manifestations?
4. What kind of power did the perpetrator exercise? To what extent was there violence or manipulation of the child? (If the child is extremely withdrawn, the clinician may suspect that extreme violence has occurred.)

5. How long did the child keep the secret? Is this something that the child has been carrying around for years, or did the child go straight to his parents?

6. What is the level of the child's ego strength? Is the child well nurtured, independent, and psychologically healthy? Or is the child passive, dependent, undernurtured, and psychologically repressed?

These factors may be related to the length of time in treatment for sexually abused children (Hewitt and McNought 1985). If the answers to the questions indicate severe abuse, a longer period of treatment may be necessary, and the prognosis may be more limited.

A standard developmental history should be obtained, including the child's cognitive, social, emotional, and physical development since birth. The clinician may wish to use a standardized developmental form that the parent can complete while the clinician is interviewing the child.

STANDARDIZED MEASURES

The following are standardized tests that the clinician may find useful for gathering more information and validating findings:

Cognitive
Wechsler Intelligence Scale for Children, revised
Emotional
Children's Apperception Test
Roberts Apperception Test (for older children)
Draw-A-Person Test
Kinetic Family Drawing
Rorschach (for older children and adolescents)
Sentence Completion Test
Social
Personality Inventory for Children
Burks' Rating Scales
Family
Minnesota Child Development Inventory
Benet-Anthony Test of Family Relations

INTERVIEWING OTHERS

A complete evaluation includes data obtained from the perpetrator (whether from within or outside the family), from the parents, and from siblings, teachers and childcare workers. Information obtained from the police report, medical examiner, child protective service worker, and attorney (if applicable) should also be reviewed in order to complete the evaluation.

In interviewing perpetrators, the clinician should focus on their interaction with the child. When the parents are involved in the abuse, it is usually helpful to observe the perpetrator and spouse interacting with the child. Attention should be paid to the perpetrator's family and psychosocial history; the system of psychological defense; the ability to abstractly or concretely react to the situation; the ability to assume responsibility; personality, thought, or mood disorders; drug or alcohol abuse; parenting skills (if the perpetrator is a parent); and personality strengths. If possible, such information should be validated with a standardized psychological instrument like the Minnesota Multiphasic Personality Inventory.

When the abuse has occurred within the family, information about and observation of family dynamics will give the clinician a great deal of insight about evolution, prognosis, and treatment. The spouse of the perpetrator should be interviewed to assess his or her role of support, denial, anger, or protection. The spouse's psychiatric and social history as well as current psychological functioning should be evaluated, along with substance abuse history and parenting skills. If the abuse has occurred outside of the family, the clinician should deal with the family's anxiety and anger.

Siblings will also provide important, and often untarnished, information about the abuse and about family dynamics. It is important to rule out the possibility that siblings have been involved in the abuse.

Often overlooked are teachers and childcare workers. Since children often spend more significant time in these settings than in interaction with their parents, these persons become important evaluators of children's cognitive, social, emotional, and physical health.

INTERVIEW AIDS

Anatomically Correct Dolls

Anatomically correct dolls have become widely used for evaluation of physical and especially sexual abuse. Therapists who use these dolls should be cautioned about their validity. While White and colleagues (1986) and Jampole and Weber (1987) found that abused children displayed more sexually related behaviors than nonabused children, Jensen and associates (1986) and Gabriel (1985) reported that in their samples, abused and nonabused children could not necessarily be discriminated. A California court has disallowed evidence obtained using anatomically correct dolls (in Amber B. & Tella B. 1987 191 Calif 3rd 682; in Christine C. & Michael C. 1987 191 Calif App. 3rd 676).

On the basis of these conflicting findings, it may be useful to adopt an objective procedure for the use of anatomically correct dolls such as that developed by White and her colleagues (1986). Schetky (1988) suggests that the dolls should not be used without guidelines or to contaminate the interview by teaching, coaching, or suggesting to the child what has happened. The dolls should also be visually pleasing to the child and should be integrated in a relaxed manner into the play interview. Children under the age of 3 appear to be confused by the family of dolls and should be given only the doll who represents the perpetrator.

Drawings

The Draw-A-Person test and the Kinetic Family Drawing may give the clinician some clues as to the extent or dynamics of abuse. According to Di Leo (1973), children do not usually draw genitalia or nude figures, and such drawings may be indicators of possible aggression or emotional disturbance (Koppitz 1968). Hibbard and colleagues (1987) also found that sexually abused children were more likely to draw genitalia than were control subjects.

In addition to these more standardized drawings, time should be given to children to draw pictures of themselves, their families, or the abuse situation. Sgroi (1984) outlines a procedure in which the child draws a picture of the abuse situation, an activity which appears to help the child to describe the details of the abuse. Information can be obtained by having children talk about their pictures or answer questions about the kinds of touch they have experienced on various body parts. Older children who are reluctant to draw detailed pictures may be more comfortable starting with a drawing of their room or the floor plan of the house (Goodwin 1982).

Videotaping

There are numerous advantages and disadvantages to videotaping an interview with a child. The most obvious reason for videotaping is for courtroom procedures, yet videotapes are seldom admissible in trials (MacFarlane 1985). Another reason for videotaping has been to minimize the frequency with which children must tell their story, thus saving them emotional trauma and preserving the affective content of the story, which may diminish with repetition. Tedesco and Schnell (1987) reported that children become more negative in reaction to the investigative process as a direct correlation to the number of interviews. Hauggard and Repucci (1988) also point out that when a child initially denies that abuse occurred and later changes his story, the videotape may provide evidence that the clinician did not encourage this change. The videotape may also be used as a therapeutic resource for the nonoffending parent or as an educational tool for the therapist. Videotaping often forces the clinician to begin the interview with a thorough case background and a structured strategy of assessment.

The disadvantages of videotaping are also numerous. In order for the videotape to be a professional product, technical and comfort factors must be optimal. Videotaping is not suggested for the novice. An unprofessional videotape will not serve the best interests of the child.

Another disadvantage of videotaping concerns confidentiality. The defendant who is charged and the attorney have rights to all evidence related to the case. This may include the videotaped interview. The videotape can become public and may be used out of context. Parents who are made aware of these confidentiality issues may refuse to permit videotaping. Last, if the clinician videotapes only part of the assessment, he must be able to support his selection of the portions chosen. Ideally, the clinician should videotape all of the assessment interview or none of it.

It is suggested that videotaping decisions be made on a case-by-case basis in consultation with the assessment team and with legal professionals. Videotaping should also be used only when the clinician is skilled in and comfortable with the process.

Hypnosis

Although hypnosis for psychotherapeutic intervention is becoming increasingly accepted, its use remains somewhat controversial, especially in courts of law. It is usually not necessary to employ formal hypnosis during the initial child abuse evaluation. Children spend a great deal of their time in natural trance states, especially in play. If the therapist establishes an optimal rapport, children will use their natural trance states to answer questions or to interact in a comfortable, consistent, and candid manner.

ADOLESCENTS

Special attention should be paid to establishing rapport with adolescents. Adolescents are especially sensitive to the boundaries of social acceptability. Mirroring techniques are important, with special emphasis on language. With the adolescent who uses slang, the therapist may evoke a more honest response by asking, "What happens when the shit hits the fan at home?" rather than "What happens when you get in trouble?" Clinicians who are not entirely comfortable with such language should not risk alienating the adolescent by using it.

Adolescents may be particularly sensitive about confidentiality. A frank discussion about confidentiality issues within the context of the requirements imposed by the evaluation will set the stage for a respectful relationship. I can remember my own experience as a young therapist with an adolescent boy who offhandedly related that he was suicidal shortly after I explained confidentiality, neglecting to tell him the limits of a confidential relationship. It took about a year to win back this patient's trust. Fortunately, he allowed the opportunity and time.

It is also helpful if the therapist is comfortable talking to adolescents about their bodies and their sexuality. The therapist's comfort with this subject can help abused adolescents to gain or regain confidence in their physical and sexual selves. Adolescents may need reassurance that others have experienced and successfully conquered their fears and anxieties about the abuse.

GOING NOWHERE?

Despite the best plans and execution, there may be times when the clinician is failing to receive the information necessary to complete the evaluation. The first question the clinician should ask is whether rapport has been established so that the child can address the questions being asked. Or is the clinician hurrying, or using developmentally inappropriate language? If so, the clinician may attempt to re-establish rapport by re-entering the child's world.

If the therapist fails to obtain an answer to a particular question, he can incorporate it into a later phase of the assessment or schedule a later assessment time. The therapist can use questions or statements that bounce the issues back to the child, such as "I'm just trying to figure out what really happened," or "I don't understand," or "I'm curious about that."

If the clinician has exhausted these techniques without success, he must consider the possibility that the child is developmentally or traumatically unable to furnish detailed information. In this case, simply reporting this assessment may fulfill an important aspect of the evaluation.

In conclusion, the professional evaluation of child abuse and neglect requires a knowledge of the syndrome's manifestations in the major spheres of functioning (intrapsychic, interpersonal, behavioral, and social). The detection of and therapeutic intervention into such abuse can forestall many of the deleterious consequences of abuse that could develop later in life.

REFERENCES

Benedek, E. P., and Shetky, D. H. (1985). Allegations of sexual abuse in child custody and visitation disputes. In *Emerging Issues in Child Psychiatry and the Law*, ed. D. H. Shetky and E. P. Benedek, pp. 98–133. New York: Brunner/Mazel.

Cameron-Bandler, L. (1985). *Solutions.* San Rafael, CA: Future Press.

DiLeo, J. (1973). *Children's Drawings as Diagnostic Aids.* New York: Brunner/Mazel.

Gabriel, R. M. (1985). Anatomically correct dolls in the diagnosis of sexual abuse of children. *Journal of the Melanie Klein Society* 3:41–49.

Goodwin, J. (1982). The use of drawings in incest cases. In *Sexual Abuse: Incest Victims and Their Families*, ed. J. Goodwin, pp. 268–334. Boston: John Wright.

Hall, E. T. (1983). *The Dance of Life.* Garden City, NY: Doubleday.

Hauggard, J. J., and Repucci, N. D. (1988). *The Sexual Abuse of Children.* San Francisco: Jossey-Bass.

Herman, J. (1981). *Father–Daughter Incest.* Cambridge: Harvard University Press.

Hewitt, S., and McNought, J. (1985). *Program in Human Sexuality*. University of Minnesota, Minneapolis.

Hibbard, R. A., Roghmann, K., and Hoekelman, R. A. (1987). Genitalia in children's drawings: an association with sexual abuse. *Pediatrics* 79:129–137.

Jampole, L., and Weber, M. K. (1987). An assessment of the behavior of sexually abused children with anatomically correct dolls. *Child Abuse and Neglect* 11:187–192.

Jensen, J. B., Realmuto, G. M., Wescoe, M. D., and Garfinkel, B. D. (1986). *Are there differences in the play with anatomically complete dolls: abused versus non-abused children.* Paper presented at the annual meeting of the American Academy of Child and Adolescent Psychiatry, Los Angeles, October.

Kadushin, A., and Mortin, J. (1981). *Child Abuse: An Interactional Event*. New York: Columbia University Press.

Kempe, R., and Kempe, C. (1978). *Child Abuse*. Cambridge: Harvard University Press.

Koppitz, E. M. (1968). *Psychological Evaluation of Children's Human Figure Drawings*. New York: Grune and Stratton.

MacFarlane, K. (1985). Diagnostic evaluations and the use of videotapes in child sexual abuse cases. *University of Miami Law Review* 40:136–165.

Meiselman, K. (1978). *Incest: A Psychological Study of Causes and Effects with Treatment Recommendations*. San Francisco: Jossey-Bass.

Mrazch, P., Lynch, M., and Bentovim, A. (1981). Recognition of child sexual abuse in the United Kingdom. In *Sexually Abused Children and Their Families*, ed. P. Mrazch and H. Kempe. New York: Pergamon.

Sgroi, S. (1984). Validation of sexual abuse. In *Handbook of Clinical Intervention in Child Sexual Abuse*, ed. S. Sgroi. Lexington, MA: Lexington Books.

Shetky, D. H. (1988). The clinical evaluation of child sexual abuse. In *Child Sexual Abuse*, ed. D. H. Shetky and A. H. Green, pp. 57–81. New York: Brunner/Mazel.

Shetky, D. H., and Green, A. H. (1988). *Child Sexual Abuse*. New York: Brunner/Mazel.

Swanson, L., and Biaggio, M. (1985). Therapeutic perspectives on father–daughter incest. *American Journal of Psychiatry* 142:667–674.

Tedesco, J. F., and Schnell, S. V. (1987). Children's reactions to sex abuse investigation and litigation. *Child Abuse and Neglect* 11:267–272.

White, S., Strom, G., Santilli, G., and Halpin, B. (1986). Interviewing young sexual abuse victims with anatomically correct dolls. *Child Abuse and Neglect* 10:519–529.

14
Attention Deficit Disorder

THOMAS W. PHELAN, Ph.D.

The problem of attention deficit disorder (ADD) has recently been receiving tremendous attention. Much of this has been due to the controversy over drug treatment, but the issue of ADD is quite important in its own right. Many authors, such as Barkley (1981), believe that ADD is the most common cause of initial referrals to child guidance clinics across the country, and that it may generate as much as 40 percent of these first contacts. Estimates of the prevalence of ADD generally range from 5 to 10 percent of the school-age population; the vast majority of patients are boys (Ross and Ross 1982).

HISTORICAL OVERVIEW

A brief historical overview will shed light on some of the diagnostic dilemmas that complicate the evaluation of ADD. One of the earliest investigators, Still (1902), used the term "brain damage syndrome" to describe children with demonstrable lesions. He also noted that some of these children showed signs of hyperactivity. The connection between hyperactivity and brain damage was further reinforced in 1918 when, after an outbreak of encephalitis, many investigators noted that some afflicted children had later become hyperactive and had developed learning problems (Hohman 1922).

Later, writers such as Strauss and Lehtinen (1947) further developed the notion, and in the 1950s the term "minimal brain damage" was commonly used. This had the unfortunate consequence of frightening many parents, who imagined that their children had some kind of irreparable tissue damage. The term was later modified to "minimal brain dysfunction," but it was not until the late 1970s (Rutter 1977) that two rather obvious facts were realized: (1) less than 5 percent of hyperactive children show any hard evidence of physical brain damage, and (2) most children who do show structural damage are not hyperactive.

Even before Rutter's work, there was a trend in labeling from guesses about causality to symptomatic descriptions, with the primary focus being on overactivity. In the 1968 DSM, the American Psychiatric

Association used the label "hyperkinetic reaction of childhood." In the 1970s, research, such as that carried out by Douglas (1972) at McGill University, began to focus more on the concentrational difficulties that hyperactive childen experienced. Thus in 1980, in the DSM-III, the problem was renamed attention deficit disorder. There were three types: (1) ADD with hyperactivity, (2) ADD without hyperactivity, and (3) ADD, residual type (referring to an adolescent or adult who had outgrown the hyperactivity but not all the other ADD symptoms). In the DSM-III-R, the label was again changed, this time to attention-deficit hyperactivity disorder (ADHD), a change which many workers in the field consider to be awkward, unfortunate, and unnecessary.

PRIMARY SYMPTOMS AND CORRELATES OF ADD

The DSM-III defined fairly simple criteria for ADD with hyperactivity. These criteria included age-inappropriate inattention, impulsivity, and hyperactivity. It was also required that the onset of the problem be before age 7, that the problem be of at least six months' duration, and that schizophrenia, affective disorder, and severe or profound mental retardation be ruled out.

Many writers (Barkley 1981, Ross and Ross 1982, Goldstein and Goldstein 1985) have elaborated on this symptom list, adding other common symptoms and mentioning a number of correlates of the disorder. To the basic symptom list are often added difficulty delaying gratification, emotional overarousal, and noncompliance. Frequently associated with ADD are social problems, school underachievement, coordination problems, allergies, learning disabilities (LDs), and mild physical anomalies.

A brief description of each of the basic symptoms follows.

INATTENTION

The ADD child has an inappropriate attention span for his age. He cannot sustain concentration on an activity, especially if he sees it as even slightly boring. As a result, school is usually very difficult for the child. Another way of looking at this "core" symptom is to think of it as distractibility. The ADD child is too easily taken off task by visual, auditory, somatic, and fantasy distractors. If the child next to him is tapping his pencil on his desk, for example, it may render the ADD child incapable of concentrating on his assignment.

IMPULSIVITY

Children with attention deficit often act and speak without thinking. They seem to be unable to anticipate consequences. Douglas (1972) said they cannot "stop, look, and listen" long enough, when entering a situation, to be able to respond appropriately; they just act. They often speak out of turn in the classroom, in an attempt to offer correct answers as well as to clown around.

HYPERACTIVITY

Most, but not all, ADD children are also hyperactive, especially when they are younger. They seem to their parents as if they are "driven by a motor"; they are always on the go. In free play situations, it is harder to distinguish ADD children from normal children, but in situations in which concentration and restraint are in order, the ADD child's hyperactivity and restlessness often become much more obvious. ADD girls generally tend to be less active than ADD boys.

DIFFICULTY DELAYING GRATIFICATION

ADD children are usually very impatient; they want what they want when they want it. Their frustration tolerance is poor, and when they do not get what they want they often incessantly badger their parents or have a fit of temper. Their impatience also causes them to be sloppy and disorganized at home and at school, and they frequently scribble their schoolwork in order to get it over with as quickly as possible.

EMOTIONAL OVERAROUSAL

Many ADD children tend toward very intense feelings, whether positive or negative. If they are happy, they may get into a "hyper-silly" routine, especially in groups. Although everyone else may appreciate how ridiculous and overdone their behavior is, ADD children do not seem to realize this themselves. If they are angry, on the other hand, they may throw temper tantrums that many parents describe as almost insane.

NONCOMPLIANCE

Barkley (1981) suggested that this characteristic of ADD children be added to the list of primary symptoms. The ADD child often has difficulty following rules and complying with adult requests. This is due to their general forgetfulness and disorganization, but it also can be related to their impulsivity and often strong oppositional tendencies. Therefore, both messiness and defiance are common.

There is some disagreement in the literature as to whether or not these symptoms constitute a "syndrome"; in other words, if the patient has one, does he have to have them all? A simple, common-sense response to this question is, sometimes yes and sometimes no. There are many ADD children who show all of the symptoms just listed, yet there are also many who present only some. We know, for example, that ADD girls tend to be less hyperactive than ADD boys (Wender 1987). Many investigators also believe that the DSM-III category of ADD without hyperactivity is still a valid subtype. A child with this diagnosis will not only be less hyperactive, but will also often show less impulsivity, emotional overarousal, and aggressive noncompliance.

The ADD child who has most or all of the symptoms just listed will tend to have pervasive problems that will seriously affect his performance at school, at home, and socially. Since diagnosis must involve evaluation of these three areas, it will be useful to describe how the ADD child performs in each.

SCHOOL

The ADD child is often a significant and obvious negative force in the classroom. Because of the requirements to both sit still and concentrate, the child will be restless and distractible, will not finish work, and will sometimes bother other childen. The child will have difficulty with rules, especially when they change and especially when going from a less structured to a more structured situation, such as moving from gym or recess to social studies. The teacher's efforts at control will often be met with resistance and oppositional behavior. This leads to greater efforts at control, more opposition, and eventually to a vicious circle that worsens as the year progresses.

Although most ADD children are probably of normal intelligence, the ADD symptoms render them unable to use all of their ability. To make matters worse, many ADD children also have learning disabilities. The incidence of combined ADD and LD is a matter of dispute, but estimates have ranged as high as 85 percent (Silver 1984). This obviously can worsen underachievement as well as behavioral problems.

The ADD child can also be amazingly inconsistent. They can have very good and very bad hours, days, weeks, and sometimes even years. This inconsistency confounds teachers and parents, who often conclude that these children simply refuse to perform to their potential; they are just "lazy." The real reasons for the inconsistencies usually have to do with a particular subject's interest to the child and with the child's sensitivity to his relationship with the teacher.

HOME

The hyperactive child can be an enigma to his parents and a source of constant disruption. He is disorganized and has difficulty with rules and following through with activities like chores and homework. He is noisy and often produces a great deal of sibling friction. ADD children who have no siblings are often much easier for their parents to manage. Most of the interactions with parents and siblings are likely to be negative, which can be extremely destructive to the self-esteem of all involved. Many parents of an ADD child, especially if it is their first, feel devastated by their inability to parent effectively, and this can produce depression, especially in the mothers, who usually have to spend more time with the child in the early years. Most parents of ADD children have also encountered noncompliance problems in public, which can result in extreme embarrassment.

SOCIAL

The same basic ADD symptoms will produce serious social problems for the child. Playing even simple games with others requires restraint and cooperation, and the ADD child in a social situation tends to be overly aggressive. He is often a poor loser, and his low frustration tolerance can result in cheating, arguments, and refusal to complete games. If he does quit and go home, his account of the problem to his parent almost always involves placing total blame on the other children. The ADD child can be extremely naive and insensitive to normal verbal and nonverbal social cues, such as facial expressions.

The result of these difficulties is that the ADD child often winds up isolated and is sometimes blatantly ostracized. Alternatively the ADD child may wind up playing with younger mates, who will tolerate the bossiness and who may even find the hyperactivity stimulating and enjoyable.

MISCONCEPTIONS ABOUT ADD

Several misconceptions about ADD persist. Because they often lead to misdiagnosis and mistreatment, they must be clarified.

1. ADD children are always hyperactive.

Many people believe that the ADD child never stops moving and cannot pay attention to anything for more than a few seconds. This is not the case. As previously mentioned, in *situations that are characterized by one-to-one interaction or that are novel, interesting, or intimidating, the ADD child can often sit still and concentrate.* Nevertheless, many pediatricians, for example, will ask the distressed mother of an ADD child whether the child can sit still while watching television. If the response is yes, the conclusion is that the child is not hyperactive and that the problem must be something other than ADD. Often the child's behavior in the physician's office will be exemplary and will unfortunately reinforce this conclusion. Too many professionals do not realize that approximately 80 percent of hyperactive children will sit still in a doctor's office (Sleator and Ullman 1981).

2. ADD will be outgrown.

A second misconception, and fortunately one that seems to be rapidly disappearing, is that hyperactivity or ADD will be outgrown. Although the specific symptom of gross-motor restlessness usually does disappear or moderate quite a bit by adolescence, other symptoms, such as distractibility, impulsivity, and emotional overarousal, can persist into adulthood. Researchers began to recognize this in the 1970s (Bellak 1979), with the result that DSM-III included the diagnosis of ADD, residual type. Weiss and Hechtman (1984) have described the continuation of ADD symptoms into adulthood in a 25-year follow-up study of children previously diagnosed as having ADD. Wender (1987) has also described the expected residual symptoms of adult ADD.

3. ADD is caused by faulty parenting.

It is probably still true that most teachers, pediatricians, and mental health professionals believe that ADD is caused by the parents' behavior. As a result, most parents adopt this belief, which produces a tremendous amount of guilt and a keen sense of helplessness. Barkley (1981), on the other hand, presents a number of compelling arguments against the psychogenic viewpoint. Many writers are now leaning toward the belief that an inherited, biochemical deficiency produces ADD (Goldstein and Goldstein 1985, Wender 1987).

4. A final misconception that can confound the diagnostic process has to do with the use of stimulant medications, which are often employed in the treatment of ADD. For many years it was believed that ADD children would have a positive response to these medications, but that normal children would become aroused and overstimulated by them. Thus the therapeutic response to drugs such as methylphenidate (Ritalin) was considered paradoxical, meaning that the stimulant had the odd effect of calming, rather than exciting, the ADD child. Stimulant medication may reduce hyperactive behavior without improving concentration or school performance.

A corollary of this belief was that a positive response to stimulants could be considered diagnostic of ADD. A number of studies, culminating in the work of Rapoport and colleagues (1978), contradicted this notion. Rapoport and her co-workers demonstrated that moderate doses of stimulant medications have *similar*—rather than opposite—effects on children with ADD and on normal children. When medication was administered to the normal groups, they also responded with increased alertness and decreased motor activity. Thus a medication trial cannot produce a definitive diagnosis. When a child does show a dramatic change in behavior while on medication, however, it is very difficult for a therapist not to take it as confirmation of the diagnosis, especially when other diagnostic criteria for ADD are positive.

THE DIAGNOSTIC PROCESS

The diagnosis of ADD is often difficult. The main reason for this is that, oddly enough, the *direct observation of the patient in the office is one of the least helpful parts of the evaluation process.* There are probably two reasons for this. The first has to do with Sleator and Ullman's (1981) finding that 80 percent of ADD children will not evidence symptoms in a doctor's office. The second reason is that many ADD children are simply poor historians; they cannot accurately recall or describe their past experiences. Others can recall but are defensive and initially unwilling to admit problems.

The result is that the diagnostic process depends upon information collected from sources other than the child. Of course the child must be seen, but what is needed primarily is qualitative and quantitative information about the child's school, home, and social functioning, gathered from multiple sources.

Any *trained* mental health professional or physician can competently conduct an evaluation for ADD. Contrary to Wender's (1987) claims, a medical consult is not always essential. A physician's participation becomes necessary if stimulant medication is considered, just as a psychologist's participation would be necessary if psychological testing were indicated.

The evaluation process should involve the following:

1. An interview with the parents to cover the presenting problems, developmental history, and family history, and to set up the rest of the diagnostic format. However, children who are 13 years of age or older are usually seen first because many adolescents believe that their parents will prejudice the evaluator against them.
2. An interview with the child to obtain as much information as he is willing to provide about home, school, and social functioning, and to rule out other diagnoses such as psychosis or depression.
3. Some type of rating scale, such as the Conners Questionnaires, which describe home and school functioning and which can be scored using quantitative age and sex norms.
4. Home and school situations questionnaires.
5. The collection of other school information, such as grades, achievement test scores, and current placement.
6. Psychological testing for IQ and LD screening, unless it has already been carried out.

Interview with the Parents

The child's parents are usually the most vital source of information. They must be approached with a nonjudgmental attitude; thus the evaluator must keep in mind that it is unlikely, if the child has ADD, that the cause is faulty parenting.

For three reasons, it is not always easy to keep this in mind. First, many parents are so stressed by the child's behavior that they may make a poor impression on the diagnostician. They can come across as angry, hysterical, depressed, or worse, and therapists who lean toward family dynamic theory will often conclude, "No wonder the kid's having such a rough time—anybody would with parents like these!" However, many parents will accurately report that they were not anxious and considered themselves fairly normal before the child arrived on the scene. As long ago as the 1960s, Bell (1968) argued that some evidence for the deleterious effects of parents on children should be interpreted in exactly the opposite direction.

Second, there is evidence that the biological parents of hyperactive children as a group show a higher incidence of certain other psychiatric disorders (Cantwell 1972), including alcoholism, depression, hysteria, sociopathy, and psychosis. Further, since ADD is often hereditary and since it is found predominantly in males, the fathers themselves will often present with residual ADD symptoms. In an interview they often seem fidgety and very intense, frequently interrupting the interviewer.

Third, the couple is likely to disagree and argue during the interview about the child as well as about other issues. Indeed, there is a higher incidence of marital dissatisfaction, separation, and divorce in families in which there is an ADD child (Barkley 1981). If only one parent is willing to come to the session, it will almost always be the mother, and she may show the effects of the stress of living with not only one but *two* ADD sufferers—her son and her husband.

The therapist must first determine what prompted the parents to schedule the interview. A general question about the presenting problems should be asked first. Then, if ADD is suspected, the therapist should ask more specifically about other symptoms that might not have been spontaneously mentioned, such as emotional overarousal or difficulty delaying gratification. Parents usually begin by focusing on school underachievement and misbehavior and on the domestic difficulties that are part of living with the child. The usual interviewing skills, such as active listening, are, of course, essential.

Following a detailed analysis of the presenting problems, a developmental history should be taken. For ADD screenings this should involve more than just notation of the usual developmental milestones. Since many writers believe that ADD symptoms can appear in 60 to 70 percent of hyperactive kids around the age of 2 (Goldstein and Goldstein 1985), the interviewer should specifically inquire about the onset of the ADD symptoms listed before, such as impulsivity, hyperactivity, impatience, emotional overarousal, noncompliance, and social aggressiveness. It should be noted that few parents will report a problem with short attention span in a 2-year-old, since 2-year-olds are expected to have short attention spans. The interviewer should focus on age-inappropriate behavior. This is not easy, especially when the ADD child is a firstborn and the parents may have little perspective on what is normal for various ages.

Information about pregnancy, labor, and delivery is sometimes relevant, since there is a possibility that prenatal insults may produce ADD (Ross and Ross 1982). Infant characteristics are not reliable predictors, but Goldstein and Goldstein (1985) do suggest some mild correlations between ADD and infants with temperaments that are characterized by negative responses to change or to new situations, more time spent in a negative mood (including colic), and exaggerated emotional responsiveness. After 3 to 6 months, they also suggest, the list of ADD infancy correlates can include resistance to cuddling, high activity level, sleep and feeding disturbances, and monotonous, ongoing vocalizations or crying.

After taking the develomental history, the therapist should obtain a family history due to the possibility of genetic predisposition to ADD. Because this disorder affects a greater number of males than females, the father is usually asked first about his performance in grammar school. The focus here is often limited to parameters like concentration, grades, and misbehavior, because it is often difficult for adults to recall this early period. The mother is then asked similar questions. It is usually a good idea to explain to the parents why these questions are being asked. For many parents, this will be the first exposure to the notion that their child's problems may be genetic and biological rather than a result of faulty parenting.

Next, inquiries about other relatives, including siblings, are often helpful. The interviewer is looking for signs of ADD or residual ADD, especially in uncles, as well as symptoms of depression, alcoholism, hysteria, sociopathy, and psychosis. In very large families, reports of a few relatives with these problems should initially be taken with a grain of salt.

Finally, the initial interview with the parents should conclude with a joint planning of the rest of the evaluation and, if ADD is suspected, some means for the parents to learn more about the disorder. The parents should be given the Conners Questionnaires and Situations Questionnaires to fill out and to take to the child's teachers. They should also be asked to obtain additional information from the school, which will be described later.

For educational purposes, parents are asked to attend a three-hour workshop that I present on ADD, or to purchase a video- or audiotape or book. This is a very helpful part of the diagnostic process, because many parents will almost be able to make the diagnosis themselves after hearing more about the common problems and typical developmental course of untreated ADD. In addition, many of the fathers—and a few of the mothers—will recognize themselves in the descriptions. This may lead to the possibility of treatment for them for adult ADD.

Interview with the Child

As previously mentioned, the therapist should not expect the child to manifest hyperactive symptoms during the initial interview. Although there are some children who cannot sit still and who will constantly move and chatter, only about 20 percent of patients will present this way.

The goals of the initial interview are to rule out more serious disorders, such as psychosis; to assess the child's willingness to talk; to get as much information as possible about how the child feels about his school, home, and social life; and to begin to build a therapeutic relationship.

It is often best to begin by acknowledging that the child might have been reluctant to attend the session—perhaps by saying in a matter-of-fact way something like, "I assume it wasn't your idea to come here." Most children do not want to see a physician, and this lets them know that it is not unusual to feel that way. They will then usually talk much more freely. Most children will talk, though with widely varying degrees of accuracy and candor. It is important that the interviewer not be overly friendly; ADD children will frequently become very suspicious in response to an excessively solicitous adult.

Older children can sit and talk for 45 minutes to an hour, and many will be quite self-disclosing in response to an adult who is sincerely trying to understand them. They are often so accustomed to criticism that such an interaction is a refreshing experience. Younger children may be more verbal if they can draw or play while they talk. They may be more tolerant of a short session, perhaps limited to a half hour.

When a child is too defensive to be able to tolerate sitting and talking about problems, there are several options. One is to talk about enjoyable topics or to focus on strengths for a while. Other children are quite interested in the school records that have been collected, such as their old report cards or achievement test scores, and these can be shown to them and often discussed very fruitfully. The Cancellation of Rapidly Recurring Target Figures test (Rudel et al. 1978) is also useful; it is like a game to many children and is also a rough measure of visual concentration.

Another useful instrument which can yield helpful information and provide for a kind of structured interview is Loney's (1974a) Teacher Approval–Disapproval Scale (TADS). This scale actually gives the child a chance to evaluate his teacher, a task which some children relish, and it provides valuable information about the child's attitude toward school.

Toward the end of the session, the child is told, as are the parents, just what the rest of the diagnostic process will involve. Some children, for example, resist completing the Conners Questionnaire for school because they do not want their classmates to know that they are seeing a "shrink." Other children may willingly participate in psychological testing if it might reveal some of their strengths. Older children can be involved in the design of the assessment process, thereby reducing resistance.

The Conners Rating Scales

A number of rating scales are available for ADD, but the Conners scales are probably the most widely recognized. The parents questionnaire has been revised to include 48 items that describe children's behaviors or characteristics. Ten of these are scored on a scale from 0 to 3, with 3 indicating that that item is "very much" a problem for the child. Therefore the best score is a 0 and the worst score is a 30.

Although some writers use a simple cutoff score of 15 or above as a positive indication for ADD, I prefer the age and sex norms provided by Goyette and colleagues (1978). These norms recognize that ADD is defined as age-inappropriate behavior, and also that girls with ADD are usually less hyperactive than boys with ADD. Goyette and Conners' numerical criterion, therefore, varies with age and sex, and scoring above it, according to their normative data, places the child 2 standard deviations above the mean for normal behavior. This means, in a sense, that the child is showing more ADD type behavior than 97 percent of the children of his own age and sex.

When using the Conners parent scale, it is often useful to have the mother and father fill out separate scales, or make separate markings for their ratings on the same scale. The reason for this is that ADD children often behave much better with their fathers, who are often more intimidating and less familiar. When this difference in behavior with parents occurs, it is helpful to be aware of it in one's future work with the family.

The Conners teacher questionnaire has been revised to include 28 items. Ten of these are also scored on a scale from 0 to 3, and Goyette and colleagues (1978) provide age and sex cutoff norms for this scale.

Home and School Situations Questionnaires

Barkley (1981) has developed two rating scales that approach the problem from a somewhat different angle. The Home Situations Questionnaire, filled out by the parents, lists 16 different situations, such as "when at meals . . ." or "when playing with other children. . . ." The parents indicate whether each situation is a problem by indicating yes or no, and, if yes, its severity on a scale from 1 to 9. The suggested indicator for ADD is simply more than 50 percent affirmative responses. The severity ratings are used only to provide more clinical information. As with the Conners questionnaire, it is often useful to have mothers and fathers provide separate responses.

The School Situations Questionnaire includes 12 items, such as "when arriving at school . . ." and "during individual task work. . . ." The response format and scoring are the same as the parents' form. The School Situations Questionnaire is very useful but has one limitation: It can be used only before the child reaches junior high school, usually the sixth grade. The reason for this is that when a child has many teachers, as in junior high or high school, no one teacher has access to all the information necessary to complete the form.

Other School Information

The collection of other school information, in addition to the current teachers' impressions, is critical to the diagnostic process. ADD is a condition that has an early onset, so most of the children seen will have had school problems for a long time, many even during the preschool years.

The therapist should try to obtain the child's report cards, all the way back to kindergarten if possible. Many parents save them, and they are of interest not only for the grades themselves, but also for the teachers' comments. With ADD children, comments related to the basic symptoms are frequent and reappear year after year. Such comments may include "always wandering around," "bothers others," "blurts out answers," and "easily distracted."

The grades of ADD children are often variable. These children may, on the same report card, receive every possible grade, from A to F. This often reflects the child's sensitivity to the teacher and to the subject; the ADD child can often function well if he likes the teacher and the subject. The child's grades can also vary widely for the same subject for the four quarters of the school year. In addition, since underachievement is a hallmark of the ADD child, the grades will usually fall below the child's estimated level of ability.

Achievement test scores are also gathered, going back as far as possible. These scores can be somewhat difficult to interpret. Achievement tests are group-administered, and ADD children usually perform better in a one-to-one situation than in a group. With many ADD children, therefore, achievement test scores will not be consistent with actual ability. With other children, however, achievement test scores may not only be better than the child's grades for the same subject, but may actually match the IQ. This may be due to the fact that some of these children see this type of testing as intimidating or perhaps novel. This seemingly odd occurrence may also be related to the disappointing observation (Barkley 1981, McDaniel 1988) that achievement test scores do not improve after several years of medication therapy, even though grades do.

Achievement scores, therefore, are more useful for clinical information than for discriminating ADD, despite the striking inconsistencies often noted. I usually take the achievement scores to be a minimum estimate of the child's actual achievement as well as ability, assuming that IQ and achievement correlate reasonably well.

The child's current placement in school is also noted. If the child is in special education, psychological testing and staffing information should also be collected. This may make further intelligence testing and LD screening unnecessary.

Psychological Testing

The intellectual potential of the ADD child and the possibility of LD in addition to the attentional problems should be evaluated. I concur with Gittelman Klein (1988) that projective tests are not worth the time they take and are not effective in discriminating ADD anyway. Vague comments about low self-esteem or hostility toward authority figues are not especially helpful.

INTELLIGENCE

The intelligence tests usually used are the Stanford-Binet; the Wechsler Intelligence Scale for Children, revised; or the Wechsler Adult Intelligence Scale, revised, for older adolescents. A knowledge of the child's intellectual ability is important for several reasons:

1. The IQ tells us what we can reasonably expect from the child and to what extent he is underachieving.
2. The IQ is a necessary part of the definition of LD.
3. IQ is a major prognostic indicator with ADD.
4. Higher IQ levels can modify the ADD symptom picture in some children by inhibiting hyperactive behavior at school.

Kaufman (1979) has suggested that Wechsler scores may contain a "distractibility factor" that is reflected in the arithmetic, digit span, and coding subtests. Such a factor, if it exists, would certainly be important in evaluating the ADD child. While this trio of subtests is deserving of note, they do not powerfully discriminate ADD children from those who do not suffer from ADD. Kaufman admits that although these three subtests do cluster in factor analytic studies, the reason for deficits in these scores does not necessarily reflect an attentional problem in all children.

LEARNING DISABILITIES

Since 50 percent or more of the children with ADD may also be classified as LD, these diagnoses should be separately evaluated. Difficulties with visual and auditory perception or memory, as well as expressive language difficulties, are common. Handwriting problems are frequently encountered with ADD children, although it is initially difficult to determine whether these are due to the child's impatience with schoolwork or to a fine visual-motor coordination problem.

As Keogh (1988) points out, the LD field "is an important component of American education, but it continues to be a service category characterized by inconsistency and disagreement." The model I use to define the presence of LD is the standard score model, wherein LD is said to exist when there is a variation of more than 1 standard deviation, 15 points, between an IQ test score and two other standard test scores: (1) an individually administered achievement test score, and (2) a *related* processing score from an individually administered test. The scores must all be standard scores, with a mean of 100 and a standard deviation of 15. For example, a child with a WISC IQ of 103 who scores 78 on a reading decoding test and 75 on a test of auditory memory would be classified as LD.

The individually administered achievement tests include the Wide-Range Achievement Test, the Peabody Individual Achievement Tests, or the Woodcock-Johnson Psychoeducational Battery. Tests of processing abilities, such as perception, sequencing, and memory, include the Detroit Tests of Learning Aptitude and the Illinois Test of Psycholinguistic Abilities.

A unique problem arises when we consider testing ADD children: To what extent will the ADD itself artificially lower the tests scores? When it comes to testing, it seems that there are two types of ADD children. The first type is capable of responding well enough in a one-to-one situation—in which feedback of some sort comes every few seconds—that their scores are accurate. The second type of ADD child retains symptoms, such as distractibility and impulsivity, even in the testing situation, so that the scores become suspect. Although a competent examiner can observe these interfering behaviors during testing, it is difficult to predict which children will show them, and one runs the risk of the testing time being wasted.

There are solutions to this problem. Children who have a history of retaining their ADD symptoms even in one-to-one, novel, interesting, or intimidating situations may not be able to be tested immediately. Instead, as Kinsbourne (1988) notes, if medication is to be considered, it should be titrated carefully and administered before testing is done. Children who can maintain their self-control in these situations might be tested without medication, although this still might carry some risk.

PHYSICAL AND NEUROLOGICAL EXAMINATIONS

It is certainly important to know whether or not a child is in good health and whether or not his sensory apparatus is intact. Beyond this, the physical and neurological examinations usually contribute much less than might be expected to the diagnosis of ADD. The role of the physician can be to exclude other possible physical causes of the symptoms, such as lead poisoning or thyroid pathology, and to recommend other tests that might be helpful.

A neurological exam is not usually essential, although many clinicians who still tend to think in terms of the "minimal brain damage" idea often believe that a referral to a neurologist is indicated. The neurologist can often pick up what are called "soft" neurological signs, such as fine-motor coordination problems, motor overflow, or perseverative behaviors. However, these symptoms are only occasional correlates of ADD and can also appear in normal children as well, so their discriminative value in the diagnosis of ADD is limited. The same is true of the electroencephalogram (EEG). Although some children with ADD will show some EEG abnormalities, such as an increase in slow-wave activity, many ADD children have normal EEGs, so the test is not definitive. The EEG should not be a routine part of ADD evaluations unless other problems, such as a seizure disorder, are also suspected or unless the child complains of chronic, severe headaches.

INTEGRATION

Since ADD is not an all-or-nothing disorder—there are varying degrees of severity—and since there is no one definitive diagnostic procedure or test, the final assessment must rely on an integration of all the data collected. The following procedure is suggested for making sense out of the information collected; the therapist should strive to develop a profile of strengths and weaknesses in addition to a statement about the presence or absence of ADD.

STEP 1:

Is the presenting problem consistent with the ADD symptoms previously listed (short attention span, impulsivity, hyperactivity, difficulty delaying gratification, emotional overarousal, and noncompliance)? School underachievement and social problems that usually involve overaggressiveness should also be noted. Correlates of ADD are also examined, such as allergies, fine- and gross-motor coordination problems, and minor physical anomalies.

STEP 2:

Is the developmental history consistent with the typical course of untreated ADD? The therapist should note the presence of the symptoms just listed, but with a focus on how the picture changes with age. Early hyperactivity, for example, will often be outgrown. Self-esteem and depression do not usually become significant until after age 7 or so. Retention in school is common in the early years, but has been known to occur with ADD children as late as junior high school.

STEP 3:

Does the family history indicate a predisposition to ADD? The single most frequent indicator is the "chip-off-the-old-block syndrome." If the father, especially, says that he was very similar to the child when he was in school, and says this without much doubt or hesitation, it should be considered strong evidence for genetic transmission. A previously diagnosed ADD sibling is also a strong indicator, because it increases the chances of ADD in the child being evaluated from approximately 5 percent to approximately 30 percent (Barkley 1981).

STEP 4:

Is the information from the child consistent with the usual ADD symptoms? Consistency here can mean two things. Some ADD children can and do describe *in their own words* typical symptoms. The symptoms most often described include distractibility and sometimes emotional intensity; the others are mentioned less frequently because the child sees them as weaknesses. Other children manifest ADD symptoms indirectly, through other types of comments, such as saying that they "hate school because of the work" or consistently blaming others—teachers, playmates, parents—for their problems. It is important to keep in mind that approximately 20 percent of these children *will* show hyperactive behavior in the office, such as fidgeting, interrupting, and being distracted by objects in the room.

STEP 5:

Does the child score above the cut-offs for the Conners Questionnaires according to the age and sex norms?

STEP 6:

Are more than 50 percent of the situations on the Home and School Situations questionnaires checked as problems?

STEP 7:

Do the school records and testing information support the notion that the child is not working to capacity, and to what extent is LD accounting for this underachievement if it exists?

STEP 8:

Do the parents, after attending the ADD workshop or watching an educational videotape, believe that their child has ADD? Most of the parents who say "That's my kid!" are correct.

Many children will "test positive" for ADD according to all eight steps. The diagnosis is then made, and treatment planning proceeds according to the child's specific strengths and weaknesses. In other cases, the diagnosis will clearly not be ADD, or the picture will be more ambiguous. Several factors can substantially change the typical symptom pattern and may at times cause the diagnosis to be missed in a child who actually does suffer from ADD. These factors include the following:

GOOD SOCIAL SKILLS

A significant number of ADD children will get along well with their peers. They will have friends, not be particularly aggressive, and may not show the usual low frustration tolerance in competitive situations. In some of these children, some of the ADD symptoms are moderated just enough to become social assets. Bossiness, for example, becomes leadership, or excessive energy makes the child the "life of the party."

HIGH IQ

ADD children who are intelligent enough can not only succeed in school, but may also actually enjoy it. Because of their academic success and the reinforcement they may receive from parents and teachers, their inappropriate behavior may be inhibited while they are at school. However, the symptoms may become immediately apparent once they arrive home.

SHYNESS

From the earlier descriptions of ADD children, they sound anything but shy. Instead they seem socially boorish and uncaring about how others see them. However, some children with ADD are socially reticent and are extremely concerned about the opinions of others. They consequently inhibit their hyperactive behavior in public, but, like the high-IQ child, they will usually manifest ADD symptoms at home. Some of these children have become quite shy because of coordination or speech difficulties that in their earlier years made them the targets for ridicule from peers.

ONE-TO-ONE PRESCHOOL SITUATION WITH PARENTS

In a few children who are hyperactive, their problems will not appear until they begin to attend school. The developmental history described by the parents does not include reports of extreme hyperactivity, impulsivity, or overarousal. This may occasionally be due to the lack of siblings at home during these years. Apparently the lack of competition, combined with the presence of competent, attentive parents, can produce fairly normal behavior, at least for awhile.

ADD WITHOUT HYPERACTIVITY

Although this category has been eliminated in DSM-III-R, it may still be legitimate. When hyperactivity is not a problem in the child's early years, many of the other symptoms also tend to be moderated. In such a case, the diagnosis must focus heavily on the existence of the concentrational deficit itself, and differentiating ADD and LD becomes much more difficult.

This last diagnostic problem—the difficulty discriminating ADD from LD—merits further explanation. These two categories often overlap, but some children have one handicap and not the other. There are several characteristics that help to differentiate ADD from LD. The first is the developmental history. Most children with LD will not manifest at age 2 or 3 the ADD symptoms of hyperactivity, impulsivity, emotional overarousal, social aggressiveness, and so on. Second, if the child's IQ and achievement are not discrepant and the tests or other measures are considered valid, LD can be ruled out by definition. Third, if there are consistent comments about distractibility and short attention span from the early school years on, then the diagnosis of ADD is more likely to apply. Finally, a medication trial can often eliminate many ADD symptoms. If the child, once medicated, manifests age-appropriate behavior and shows no academic handicaps or underachievement, then the problem is probably ADD.

With proper assessment and evaluation, and with early intervention that attends to the educational, social, and psychological needs of the child and which involves the parents as active participants in the process, we can reduce the manifestation of the ADD syndrome, and improve long-term outcome.

REFERENCES

American Psychiatric Association (1968). *Diagnostic and Statistical Manual of Mental Disorders*, 2nd ed. Washington, DC: APA.

American Psychiatric Association (1980). *Diagnostic and Statistical Manual of Mental Disorders*, 3rd ed. Washington, DC: APA.

American Psychiatric Association (1987). *Diagnostic and Statistical Manual of Mental Disorders*, 3rd ed., rev. Washington, DC: APA.

Barkley, R. (1981). *Hyperactive Children: A Handbook for Diagnosis and Treatment.* New York: Guilford.

Bell, R. Q. (1968). A reinterpretation of the direction of effects in studies of socialization. *Psychological Review* 75:81–95.

Bellak, L., ed. (1979). *Psychiatric Aspects of Minimal Brain Dysfunction in Adults.* New York: Grune & Stratton.

Cantwell, D. P. (1972). Psychiatric illness in the families of hyperactive children. *Archives of General Psychiatry* 27:414–417.

Douglas, V. I. (1972). Stop, look and listen: the problem of sustained attention and impulse control in hyperactive and normal children. *Canadian Journal of Behavioural Sciences* 4:259–282.

Gittelman Klein, R. (1988). Questioning the clinical usefulnesss of projective tests for children. In *Annual Progress in Child Psychiatry and Child Development 1987*, ed. S. Chess, A. Thomas, and M. Hertzig, pp. 451–461. New York: Brunner/Mazel.

Goldstein, M., and Goldstein, S. (1985). *The multidisciplinary evaluation and treatment of children with attention deficit disorders.* Private workshop conducted in Chicago, May.

Goyette, C. H., Conners, C. K., and Ulrick, R. P. (1978). Normative data on revised Conners parent and teacher rating scales. *Journal of Abnormal Child Psychology* 6:221–236.

Hohman, L. B. (1922). Postencephalitic behavior disorder in children. *Johns Hopkins Hospital Bulletin* 33:372–375.

Kaufman, A. S. (1979). *Intelligent Testing with the WISC-R.* New York: Wiley.

Keogh, B. K. (1988). Future of the LD field: research and practice. In *Annual Progress in Child Psychiatry and Child Development 1987*, ed. S. Chess, A. Thomas, and M. Hertzig, pp. 207–219. New York: Brunner/Mazel.

Kinsbourne, M. (1988). *Attention deficit disorders.* Private workshop conducted in Milwaukee, March.

Loney, J. (1974a). *The Teacher Approval-Disapproval Scale.* University of Iowa.

McDaniel, K. D. (1988). Pharmacologic treatment of psychiatric and neurodevelopmental disorders in children and adolescents. In *Annual Progress in Child Psychiatry and Child Development 1987*, ed. S. Chess, A. Thomas, and M. Hertzig, pp. 462–493. New York: Brunner/Mazel.

Rapoport, J. L., Buchsbaum, M. S., Zahn, T. P., et al. (1978). Dextroamphetamine: cognitive and behavioral effects in normal prepubertal boys. *Science* 199:560–563.

Ross, D. M., and Ross, S. A. (1982). *Hyperactivity: Current Issues, Research, and Theory.* New York: Wiley.

Rudel, R. G., Denckla, M. B., and Broman, M. (1978). Rapid silent response to repeated target symbols by dyslexic and nondyslexic children. *Brain and Language* 6:52–62.

Rutter, M. (1977). Brain damage syndromes in childhood: concepts and findings. *Journal of Child Psychology and Psychiatry* 18:1–21.

Silver, L. B. (1984). *The Misunderstood Child.* New York: McGraw-Hill.

Sleator, E. K., and Ullman, R. K. (1981). Can the physician diagnose hyperactivity in the office? *Pediatrics* 67:13–17.

Still, G. F. (1902). The Coulstonian Lectures on some abnormal physical conditions in children. *Lancet* 1:1008–1012, 1077–1082, 1163–1168.

Strauss, A. A., and Lehtinen, L. E. (1947). *Psychopathology and Education of the Brain-Injured Child.* New York: Grune & Stratton.

Weiss, G., and Hechtman, L. T. (1986). *Hyperactive Children Grown Up.* New York: Guilford.

Wender, P. H. (1987). *The Hyperactive Child, Adolescent, and Adult.* New York: Oxford University Press.

PART IV

Focused Interviews

15
The Mental Status Examination

ELIEZER SCHWARTZ, Ph.D.

The phenomenological approach to the diagnosis of mental illness reached a credible position through the work of Emil Kraepelin (1856–1926). A compulsive and skilled observer, Kraepelin integrated findings of experimental psychology with confirmed observations to develop a psychiatric nosology. His systematized observations presented an accurate, sensitive picture of human suffering. The descriptions of manic-depressive patients that he presented to his students in the lecture hall are still valid today.

Kraepelin's classic work was the genesis of a psychiatric nosology based on descriptive phenomena. These phenomena, which are sufficiently objective to allow easy and clear clinical inferences, include a variety of signs and symptoms presented by patients. Specific constellations of *signs* (observable behaviors) and *symptoms* (subjective experiences reported by a patient), with a particular and identifiable natural history (age of onset, life course, complications, and prognosis) ultimately define clinical entities (Spitzer 1976). Consequently, the psychiatric diagnosis presents the psychopathology of the patient through its etiology, pathogenesis, and current behavioral manifestations.

Generations of psychiatrists, following in Kraepelin's footsteps, have maintained a tradition of assessment based on a diagnostic interview conducted rigidly and in a planned fashion:

> The student or physician who approaches the case without a definite plan in mind is certain to overlook important facts or permit the patient to lead too much in the examination, often with the result that the time is not spent to the best advantage or that he is misled into drawing false conclusions. [Lewis 1934, p. 11]

The emphasis on preselected topics considered crucial for accurate diagnosis makes the traditional psychiatric interview follow explicit, a priori guidelines, actively directed by the clinician and without regard for any demonstration of initiative on the part of the patient (Pope 1979). Such initiative is considered irrelevant and quite disruptive, and the clinician might prefer to disregard the information presented by a verbose, undisciplined, and noncompliant patient in favor of the desired data obtained from relatives and friends.

Descriptive psychiatry, which has dominated European psychiatry from the beginning of the century to the present, suffered in the United States from the growing popularity and competition of a variety of psychological approaches to psychopathology and mental illness. For many decades, the descriptive approach to mental illness, which emphasized the *what* of observable behavior, was considered too narrow and at times too shallow in providing the necessary information toward a well-prognosticated treatment plan. However, the psychological approaches, with their focus on the *how* and *why* of inferred dynamic forces and functions of personality structures, offered more attractive (and at times more seductive) promises for the diagnosis and treatment of human pathology.

The introduction in 1980 of the third official psychiatric nomenclature for the United States, the DSM-III, formally revived the descriptive approach as a serious foundation for diagnostic work. Many factors participated in this Kraepelinian revival and in the emergence of the DSM-III (Maxmen 1986). Social and economic forces joined therapists' dissatisfaction with the biased and unreliable theoretical positions on mental health and illness, and gave license to both psychiatrists and psychologists to at least recognize each other's approaches as viable alternative modes of diagnosis and treatment. Further, the emergence of specialties integrating and bridging medical and psychological processes (such as health psychology and neuropsychology), along with the increasing significance and use of psychotropic drugs, forced the proponents of traditional psychological approaches to study and use descriptive techniques in the investigation of psychopathological conditions. Consequently, psychologists have learned to use the DSM-III-R and have come to appreciate the value that behaviors and complaints presented by patients during interview situations add to the latent content of their verbalizations.

MENTAL STATUS EXAMINATION

Spitzer (1976) discusses two main purposes for diagnostic work. The first is to *define clinical entities*, and the second is to *determine treatment.* Clinical entities are diagnostic classifications based on recognizable behavioral characteristics and enduring functional patterns. When a group of individuals present similar symptoms and signs, and their emotional and cognitive distress is the result of a similar natural history, they are diagnosed as suffering from the same pathological condition, and they are considered candidates for the same form of treatment:

> How a diagnosis will define a disorder and guide treatment depends on its validity and reliability. When a diagnostic category represents a genuine entity—that is, when patients with the same diagnosis have similar clinical

features, natural histories, etiologies, pathogenesis, and responses to treatment—the category is said to have *high validity*. The more clinicians agree on a diagnosis when examining the same patient, the greater its (*interrater*) *reliability*. [Maxmen 1986, p. 4]

The formulation of a treatment plan follows a formalized diagnosis and prognosis, which in turn are based on data systematically collected from a variety of sources. Psychological tests, laboratory findings, behavioral observations, and interviews with the patient and others provide valuable information for diagnostic formulations. However, the formal descriptive assessment process considers the initial patient interview the most significant source of diagnostic data (Maxmen 1986).

Levenson (1981) distinguishes between *subjective* and *objective* parts of an interview. The subjective component consists of information offered by the patient, but unwitnessed by the therapist. Such information typically includes psychosocial background and the events leading to the patient's current mental state. The objective component is that part of the interview that allows the therapist to observe (directly and indirectly) the signs and symptoms of the patient's present mental state. When therapists observe the behaviors emitted by the patient (Nelson and Barlow 1981) and categorize them toward a diagnostic definition of a clinical entity, they are engaged in a mental status examination (MSE).

The relative independence of MSE data from the verbalized content of the interview and the therapist's ability to observe and recognize known indicators of pathological entities allow for the validity and reliability of this process as a diagnostic tool. The MSE is not necessarily a standardized test with rigidly planned guidelines, and its validity and reliability are based not on its psychometric features, but on its simplicity and on the inherent ability of this tool to identify with clarity specific behaviors that are diagnostically significant and prognostically possible objectives for treatment. The MSE does not require a specific setting or the use of standardized questions. It can be a part of a diagnostic session, as well as part of a therapeutic one. It can be part of any event that requires observation and study of a patient's overt behaviors in interaction with another. The MSE is an ongoing process performed by clinicians and laypersons alike, as long as they observe interacting individuals (Nelson and Barlow 1981).

The MSE is used by therapists in need of information about specific behavioral targets for treatment. The ability of the MSE to identify relevant objectives for intervention allows clinicians from different theoretical and therapeutic orientations to adapt this diagnostic mode for their own purposes. Traditional phenomenologists observe the flat affect of the individual suffering from depression, regardless of the presence or absence of verbalized morbid thoughts (Wing et al. 1974). Pharmacotherapists are sensitive to loose associations or clang associations as pharmacologically responsive states, targets for major tranquilizers, independent of a patient's reported delusions or hallucinations (Levenson 1981). Neuropsychologists pay attention to the patient's effort in speech production and speed of body mobility to differentiate between anterior and posterior cortical insults, without the administration of more structured and standardized tests (Strub and Black 1977). The operational criteria of major clinical entities presented by the DSM-III makes the MSE, a symptomatic diagnostic process, a useful instrument in the hands of behavioral psychologists. Nathan (1981) describes the relationship between behavioral assessment and the DSM-III, and the significant contribution of the DSM-III toward increased accountability for assessment procedures. He concludes that behavioral assessment and symptomatic diagnosis now have about the same level of reliability and utility, indicating the need for behavioral psychologists to learn how to use both.

CATEGORIES OF BEHAVIORAL OBSERVATIONS

Many writers have described and discussed the MSE, providing guidelines for the interview process and outlines to categorize the behavioral observations collected during such an examination (Freedman et al. 1975, Maxmen 1986, Noyes and Kolb 1963, Rosenthal and Akiskal 1985, Slater and Roth 1969, Taylor 1981). The Present State Exam, a very detailed and elaborate standardized extension of the MSE, was published by Wing and colleagues (1974), with sample questions and data on reliability. The following categories of behavioral observations of a MSE are not as detailed, but they provide an adequate outline of this assessment procedure.

General Appearance

Taylor (1981) considers appearance the first topic to be addressed by the examiner. The patient's age, sex, race, body type, and quality of nutrition, health, and personal grooming are essential. Initiating a report of MSE findings with a paragraph describing the patient's appearance allows the reader to have a visual perception of the patient. These observations enable the reader to distinguish the patient being interviewed from others of the same age, economic background, and educational level.

This behavioral category also includes an assessment of the patient's *state of consciousness.* Consciousness is assessed on a continuum from *alertness* to *coma.* States of consciousness have important implications for the patient's ability to respond to environmental stimuli. In addition, the examination of general appearance includes an assessment of *manner* and *attitude*, which is based on the quality of the interaction with the examiner. Assessment of these parameters requires no specific inquiry, as the needed information is available to the observer throughout the interview period. Even seasoned clinicians are not immune to hostile feelings toward manipulative patients who endeavor to humiliate them; on the other hand, cooperative and grateful patients successfully reinforce examiners' self-perceptions of being caring and competent.

Behavior

This category of observation refers to the patient's overall profile of motor activities. The examiner concentrates on the patient's gait, frequency and speed of movement, rhythm or coordination, and the presence or absence of abnormal movements (Taylor 1981).

The process of greeting the patient outside the office, shaking hands, and walking together allows the clinician to observe gait and overall coordination. Noted abnormalities (such as tics, twitches, favoring a foot, and so on) alert the examiner to points of inquiry and specific questions to be addressed to the patient. The patient's awareness of the abnormality is clinically significant. For example, it is expected that an individual with a vascular brain lesion within the right hemisphere will exhibit denial of left-sided motor losses. Without an etiology of an insult to the brain, however, such denial is indicative of strong psychological defensiveness.

Intense mood is usually expressed motorically through increased frequency of motor behavior. States of anxiety, depression, or anger result in such agitated behavior as pacing, foot tapping, restlessness, or jerky shifts of the body while sitting. On the other hand, the increased frequency of activities (unlike agitation, which is reflected through frequency of motor behavior) is called *hyperactivity*, while the decrease in frequency of activity is termed *hypoactivity*. The hypoactive patient who sits dejected in a corner, lethargic and rarely moving, might suffer from depression; but the patient who exhibits extreme hyperactivity or hypoactivity (excitement or stupor) might be exhibiting signs of catatonia.

Behavioral stereotypes (repetitive and nongoal-directed actions), frequently observed with catatonic patients, are often confused with obsessive–compulsiveness. The clinician's knowledge of psychopathological syndromes is demonstrated in the capacity to differentiate between the catatonic patient, with stereotypic behaviors but without the insight of the "ridiculousness" of such actions, and the obsessive–compulsive individual, who knows how ridiculous and senseless repetitive behaviors are but is compelled to perform them to find relief from extreme anxiety.

Affect and Mood

The emotional coloration underlying the behavior of the patient during the MSE is called *affect*. Taylor (1981) discusses affect in terms of range, amplitude, stability, appropriateness and quality of mood, and relatedness. Rosenthal and Akiskal (1985) suggest that *affect* is the emotional tone as observed by the clinician, while *mood* is the self-reported and subjectively felt experience of the patient. Consequently, mood and affect are not always in congruence with each other. For example, a patient may appear excited and joyful, but report being chronically depressed for over a long period of time.

Subjective emotions are expressed in terms of sadness, happiness, anxiety, anger, or apathy (Taylor 1981). These various types of affective messages indicate the *quality* of mood. The *amplitude* of emotions is measured by the patient's intensity in expressing a particular mood, while the variability of these expressions over a period of time—in this case throughout the MSE—is the *range* of affect. Normal expression of affect is expected to vary appropriately, according to the content of the diagnostic dialogue. *Inappropriateness* of mood (for example, laughing when reporting a recent death in the family), *constriction* in range of affect (when the interview is dominated by the expression of a single mood), or *lability* of affect (instability expressed in rapid and inappropriate shifts in mood) are signs of psychopathology.

The patient's *relatedness* during the interview is not only an important subject of investigation but also a difficult dimension of affect to measure and describe. Relatedness involves the patient's capacity to interact emotionally, to establish rapport with the examiner, and to express warmth toward the examiner (Taylor 1981). The unrelated patient appears blunt, cold, or labile. Clinicians often experience an unrelated patient as a machine or an object. Individuals suffering from a schizophrenic disorder are known to respond to examiners in an unfeeling manner, frequently leaving the impression of talking to a computer or a mechanical voice.

Speech and Thought

Thought disorders, which are communications based on pathological thinking processes, hold a central role in understanding and evaluating severe forms of mental illness. However, the term *thought disorder* is not favored by the DSM-III-R because of the nonspecificity and failure to offer operationalized descriptions of pathological thinking. Consequently, Maxmen (1986) suggests four categories of observations, each dealing with a distinct aspect of thought processes, and each sufficiently tangible to allow for descriptive specificity.

THE QUANTITY OF THOUGHT

1. The *quantity of thought* is also referred to as *stream of thought.* For example, the patient whose speech pattern is slow and who utters very few words is exhibiting *poverty of speech*, a characteristic typical of depressed individuals or of those suffering from an organic impairment.

THE QUALITY OF ASSOCIATION

2. The *quality of association* between ideas communicated by the patient is referred to as *continuity of thought.* Disturbed associations manifest themselves in a variety of verbal idiosyncrasies, such as word salad, perseveration, neologisms, word approximations, paraphasia, echolalia, and clang associations. In addition, disturbed linkages between words and phrases (such as looseness of associations, flight of ideas, blocking, and so on), which are frequently indicative of psychopathology, are observed and inferentially assessed. The examiner must be sensitive to the difference between disturbances resulting from psychopathology of thought and the temporary consequences of humor, sarcasm, sickness, fatigue, intense

affect, differences in language and culture, and impoverished education or intelligence.

THE CONTENT OF THOUGHT

3. The *content of thought* refers to the patient's verbal expressions of experiences, thoughts, perceptions, and feelings. Pathology of thought content is evident in delusions, illogical or magical thinking, overvalued ideas, incomprehensible speech, and obsessions.

Delusions are belief systems without cultural, social, or religious foundation. They present the person as disowning his inner experiences (thoughts, feelings, perceptions), which at times are considered externally imposed, mobilizing the patient to act as though against his will. The grandiosity evidenced in a paranoid patient's delusion that he is William Shakespeare is also an example of *illogical thinking* when in defense of this belief he states "We both are English." Persistent and disturbing thoughts that constitute an *obsession*, are the ideational basis of compulsive behaviors, which are stereotypic and repetitive actions. Therefore, the presence of compulsions (when recognized by the patient as senseless) should alert the examiner to inquire about obsessions.

ABSTRACTION

4. *Abstraction* is the ability to think symbolically and to conceptualize and generalize. Organically impaired patients and those suffering from psychosis have impoverished abstractive abilities. Disturbed abstractive capacity is identified by the examiner through specific requests to interpret proverbs and identify similarities. Pathology is manifested as concrete or bizarre responses to these requests. For example, questions like "What is the similarity between an eagle and a parrot?" are answered in the abstract with "They are birds." A concrete answer would be "Both have feathers," while a bizarre response would be "Both attack green-eyed women." A concrete interpretation of the proverb "One swallow does not make a summer" would be "One swallow cannot bring the summer; you need more swallows." A bizarre interpretation would be "In the summer you drink a lot."

Maxmen (1986) includes *abstraction* as a dimension of inquiry into thought processes. However, many writers consider abstraction a parameter of *intellectual functioning*, a category discussed later in this chapter. For the interested reader, an elaborate and detailed presentation of observable characteristics of speech and thought is presented by Taylor (1981).

Rosenthal and Akiskal (1985) discuss the need for every reported MSE to contain a statement about the presence *or* absence of *suicidal ideas* during the interview. Contrary to the popular belief that direct inquiry about suicide might aggravate or exacerbate a vulnerable emotional state, they advocate direct questioning about suicidal thoughts. They also indicate that failure to address suicidal ideation is frequently more dangerous than the remote risk involved in "putting ideas into the patient's head." The gravity and seriousness of suicide potential must be assessed and, if necessary, treated immediately. Only direct and tactful questioning can provide the examiner with the diagnostic information necessary for proper intervention. Rosenthal and Akiskal (1985) also note that *homicidal thoughts*, if they emerge during the MSE, necessitate direct inquiry, proper documentation, and appropriate intervention.

Perceptual Disorders

The impaired reality testing of patients who suffer from severe personality disorders, neurological pathology, or psychosis is also manifested in sensory and perceptual disturbances. These phenomena may also occur *temporarily* in normal people in states of physical illness, fatigue, expectancy, or emotional arousal. However, persistent perceptual distortions and errors of sensation are pathognomonic.

Hallucinations are perceptions without external stimuli, while *illusions* are distorted perceptions of actual stimuli. Hallucinations and illusions can involve all sensory modalities. Auditory hallucinations (hearing voices or commands) are the most common perceptual disturbances found in schizophrenic disorders. They are also characteristic of neurological impairment, major affective disorders, and intoxication. Visual hallucinations, more commonly found in transient psychotic states and in depressive conditions, may occur together with auditory hallucinations in deliriums, and frequently are quite frightening.

Haptic illusions and hallucinations (such as sensations of bugs crawling on the body) are experienced during delirium or drug-induced psychosis. Patients with delirium tremens or psychosis induced by psychotomimetic drugs can experience "flying" or vestibular hallucinations. In some organic conditions, such as epilepsy, patients can also experience olfactory hallucinations.

Depersonalization, *derealization*, and *déjà vu* are perceptual disorders found in both organic conditions and intense affective states. For example, "out-of-body" experiences, distorted perceptions of physical distances from others, or the misperception of depth are common in postsurgical periods as manifestations of masked depression.

Orientation

The patient's capacity to orient himself is measured by most clinicians in three spheres: *person*, *time*, and *place*. Rosenthal and Akiskal (1985) add a fourth sphere: orientation to *situation*. Strub and Black (1977) include *geographic* orientation as a significant fifth sphere requiring diagnostic scrutiny.

Specific questions about the identity of the interviewer and the patient (such as, What is your name? Who am I?) provide an indication of orientation to *person*. Asking the patient to identify the day of the week, the full date (day, month, year), and the time of day assesses orientation to *time*. An inquiry regarding the patient's address and the location of the interview gives clues to orientation to *place*. The patient is considered disoriented to *situation* when he fails to recall or know the purpose of being in the examiner's office. Orientation to *space* (geographic orientation) can be observed in the patient's ability to orient himself in a new environment. The patient's failure to recognize his ward, or the inability to recall the location of the washroom, are pathognomonic for organic disorders.

Patients with neurological deficiencies are usually disoriented in one or more spheres. Similarly, drug intoxication and acute psychoses are characterized by failures of orientation. However, most individuals suffering from schizophrenia or affective disorders are well oriented in all spheres, indicating clear sensorium.

Attention and Concentration

Once the patient is found to be fully alert, the examiner has to observe the patient's ability to attend to a stimulus and to concentrate. The capacity to attend selectively and to concentrate on a task over time without being distracted by other environmental stimuli is a prerequisite to more complex capabilities. Therefore, the examiner cannot evaluate functions of memory, learning, language, or thinking without first establishing that the patient has attention and concentration skills.

Both neurological/physiological and emotional disorders can impair attention and concentration. Careful observation and sensitivity are needed to differentiate between attentional deficiency and oppositional behavior. The former is involuntary, while the latter is a conscious, and possibly purposeful, attempt to manipulate the interview process.

Memory

Mnestic deficiencies are categorized as *immediate*, *recent*, and *remote.* Immediate memory refers to the patient's capacity to recall information within seconds or minutes following its presentation. Often, failure of short-term (immediate) memory is mistaken for the distractibility resulting from attention or concentration difficulties. The distractible patient tends to appear preoccupied, confused, and anxious, and is unable to follow goal-directed tasks (Luria 1973). The patient deficient in immediate memory might be anxious, but is also aware of the problem and will try to perform to capacity (Taylor 1981).

Recent memory refers to the ability to recall events from the past several days, weeks, or months, while remote memory involves events from many years ago.

Simple tasks, such as asking the patient to repeat numbers (forward and/or backward) presented by the examiner, allow for the assessment of concentration and immediate memory. In addition, the examiner might assess immediate memory by presenting a few cards with simple geometric configurations for the patient's visual inspection; the examiner then removes the cards and, following a delay of a few seconds, asks the patient to reproduce these configurations (Strub and Black 1977).

Inquiry into the patient's past allows for the assessment of recent and remote memory. Confabulations (recollections of imaginary events) indicate that the patient has memory deficits. The availability of documents or data collected from interviews with family members (or close friends) may provide verification of the patient's recollections.

Remote memory seems to be the most resilient in the face of neurological insult, while concentration and immediate memory are affected by even mild trauma to the central nervous system. Individuals suffering from chronic schizophrenia might exhibit severe remote memory losses, while recent and immediate memory deficiencies are less pronounced (Mendel 1976).

Intellectual Functioning

Intellectual functioning refers to complex processes that are based on the integrity and the interaction of more basic skills (such as selective attention, perception, memory, language, and motor abilities). Many neurological and psychological deficiencies are manifested through impoverished intellectual capacity, while the more basic skills remain intact.

The MSE evaluates intelligence through observations and assessment of the patient's vocabulary, general fund of knowledge, use of previously learned information, and abstract thinking. Most writers (Rosenthal and Akiskal 1985, Taylor 1981, Wing et al. 1974), unlike Maxmen (1986), who evaluates *abstraction* toward an understanding of *thought processes*, consider *abstract thinking* an important ingredient in the assessment of intellectual functioning.

In assessing intelligence, the examiner must consider the patient's level of education, past experiences, and access to resources. Such information allows the examiner to develop a set of expectations. An academician would be expected to have a rich lexical stock, while a high school dropout would probably be limited in the abstract use of language. The socially exposed, well-travelled person is most likely quite informed, with a broad fund of general information. In comparison, the life-long ghetto resident who rarely leaves the neighborhood is probably more limited in his knowledge of world affairs. Therefore, intelligence is measured relative to the patient's premorbid life experiences. Consequently, the examiner must be able to differentiate between inability and lack of opportunity. For example, a limited use of low-frequency words is usually the result of lack of education and not intellectual deficiency. On the other hand, a patient with only an elementary education who demonstrates good abstractive skills is most likely very intelligent.

The therapist's dialogue with the patient is often a sufficient basis on which to assess the patient's vocabulary, use of words, and fund of knowledge. When the therapist is in doubt, or when the patient is not adequately verbal, a few specific questions (for example, Who is the governor of this state? What is the capital of Brazil? How far is it from Los Angeles to New York?) can provide a reasonable estimate of the patient's knowledge.

Use of previously learned material is ordinarily tested through basic arithmetic calculations or problem-solving exercises. Completion of a conceptual series, a verbal abstraction exercise requiring the ability to solve unfamiliar problems, allows assessment of the patient's ability to abstract. For example, the patient is asked to complete a series of numbers (1, 2, 1, 4, 1, 8, 1, __) or a series of letters (A, C, E, G, I, __) by adding one number or letter, respectively.

Reliability

Throughout the diagnostic session, the examiner is also assessing the patient's prognosis. The value of diagnostic work is measured by its capacity to predict the outcome of therapeutic intervention. Therefore, clinical diagnosis must provide sufficient information on both pathology and prospects for treatment. The prognosis is based on, among other variables, the *reliability* of the patient's presentation. Many ingredients of the patient's presentation contribute to reliability. General intelligence, clarity and chronology of background information presented by the patient, and the availability of alternative sources of information to validate the accuracy of presented material are significant. The confabulations of the chronic alcoholic with memory deficits, the confusion of the patient in an acute psychotic state, or the intentionally exaggerated and distorted report of the individual with antisocial tendencies are examples of unreliable presentations. The prognostic meanings of these situations are based on the patient's capacity for *insight* and *judgment.*

When the patient is aware of his problems and exhibits an understanding of the causes and the development of these problems, *insight* is considered good. Adequate intelligence is usually a prerequisite for insight, but intelligence does not ensure insight. Highly intelligent patients often surprise clinicians with their extreme lack of insight. Like insight, *judgment* is based on intellectual adequacy, but intelligence alone is not sufficient to ensure good judgment. The patient's ability to adjust to social demands and to deal appropriately with social encounters is a good indicator of judgment. The examiner observes the patient's behavior during the MSE and assesses the appropriateness of his actions. In addition, the examiner asks questions that require the patient to relate to common social situations and to present an understanding of social cause-and-effect relationships. Hypothetical situations are presented to assess the patient's comprehension of the consequences of particular social actions. For example, the examiner might ask, "What would you do if you were the first person to see smoke in a movie theater?" or "What would you do if you lost a book that you had borrowed from a friend?"

USE OF THE MSE

The act of clinical diagnosis is, by definition, an act of expert decision making. Such an act is usually entrusted to the hands of professionals—

individuals considered knowledgeable and able to use their knowledge to determine the nature of a clinical entity and the most profitable treatment approach. The knowledge in the field of mental health is very broad, based on a number of disciplines, a multitude of perspectives, and a variety of approaches to the understanding of human behavior. Consequently, a diagnostician not only considers the patient's presenting complaints, but actively searches for a particular constellation of symptoms and signs that validate specific a priori assumptions about human behavior and psychopathology. These a priori assumptions are theoretically based; therefore, each diagnostician, regardless of the tools of investigation, is guided by a theoretical orientation and a philosophical bias.

The value of the MSE is demonstrated in its adaptability as a diagnostic tool in the hands of clinicians from various theoretical perspectives. Next we will review some of the uses of the MSE, along with brief clinical examples to demonstrate features that are unique to each of these approaches.

Toward a DSM-III Diagnosis

The phenomenological approach to diagnosis considers, differentially, questions of etiology and description of a clinical entity. Traditionally, the etiological question differentiates between organic and functional conditions (Levenson 1981), while the descriptive question differentiates among known syndromes or recognizable constellations of signs and symptoms. Maxmen (1986) discusses the DSM-III approach as stressing two fundamental principles: *parsimony* and *hierarchy*. The first principle, that of parsimony, directs the diagnostician to look for "the single most elegant, economical, and efficient diagnosis that accounts for all the available data" (p. 40); if one diagnosis does not explain *all* the available information, the clinician is directed to seek the fewest diagnostic possibilities. The second principle, of hierarchy, "is that mental disorders generally exist on a hierarchy of syndromes, which tend to decline in severity from top to bottom" (p. 40). All DSM-III diagnoses are grouped in general syndromes presented in a hierarchy of declining severity as follows: organic, psychotic, affective, anxiety, somatic, psychosexual, personality disorders, adjustment disorders, and conditions not attributed to mental disorders. When both principles operate together, as is the case when an individual presents symptoms indicative of several disorders, the most parsimonious decision is to diagnose the person as having the most severe syndrome.

Nelson and Barlow (1981) recognize several factors involved in deciding upon an appropriate diagnosis. First, the diagnostician needs a solid base of knowledge in abnormal psychology, and has to know the "response covariations" for clinical entity (a list of responses, cognitions, and emotions that tend to occur together and are distinctive features of a given pathological condition). For example, some of the typical signs of schizophrenia are delusions, auditory hallucinations, illogical thinking, inappropriate affect, and loosening of associations; however, the presence of these signs *together* with significant intellectual impoverishment might indicate an organic condition. Second, the diagnostician has to have the skills to elicit in the patient sufficient responses to allow a decision as to which of the known "response covariations" are present in this particular individual. Third, the diagnostician must be familiar with the specific diagnostic criteria of the DSM-III.

The MSE does not address etiological questions but provides the necessary data for the description of a syndrome. The hierarchical structure of the disorders and their specific diagnostic criteria provided guide the clinician toward an agenda for inquiry and a logic for diagnostic decisions. The authors of the DSM-III-R suggest the use of *decision trees*—flow charts that allow for a systematic review of obtained diagnostic data.

The examiner actively elicits material designed to enable him to determine whether the patient's signs and symptoms meet the DSM-III-R criteria for particular diagnoses. For example, criterion B for the diagnosis of obsessive-compulsive disorder states: "The obsessions or compulsions cause marked distress, are time-consuming . . . or significantly interfere with the person's normal routine, occupational functioning, or usual social activities or relationships with others" (1987, p. 247). Therefore, the examiner must question the patient to determine his level of insight into the link between the distress he experiences as a result of his obsessions or compulsions and the disturbance in his social functioning. The hierarchical structure of the DSM-III-R directs the clinician to compare the presenting clinical picture with each possible syndrome, starting with the most severe. Therefore, the therapist must structure the interview so as to provide the data necessary for hierarchical diagnostic decision making. For example, reported delusions, which are typically considered indicative of a schizophrenic disorder, require an examination for possible signs of organicity, because delusions are also predominant characteristics of organic delusional syndrome.

CASE HISTORY

Ms. E. was a 36-year-old white divorced mother of two teenagers, who live with her. She reported that she and her children "have regular and friendly contacts" with her ex-husband. Ms. E., who had been partially hearing impaired since early childhood, had been unemployed for the last 20 months, following a car accident in which she sustained head injuries. She was amnesic for the accident details but recalled driving the car away from an unsuccessful job interview. Relatively recent medical and neuropsychological tests found her physically and cognitively fully recovered from the accident, without any evidence of lasting brain dysfunction. She was referred by the rehabilitation services department for assessment of the possible cause of her failure to find a job. The MSE was recorded as follows:

Ms. E. was slim and petite. Her bright complexion was porcelainlike, giving her attractive facial features an aura of fragility and coldness. A noticeable small scar under her chin seemed like an intrusion to the symmetry and perfection of her facial lines (Ms. E. later explained that this scar, which "always reminds me how close I was to God," resulted from the car accident). Her well-styled hair and casual attire, along with her informal but haughty manner of relating, initially made the examiner somewhat uneasy and apprehensive. Ms. E. was an alert, compliant (but not quite cooperative), and seemingly open person, whose guardedness was manifested in her careful choice of words and frequent silent pauses. She sat rigidly in her chair, often "picking" nervously on her fingernails, the only significant bodily sign of tension. Her eye contact with the examiner seemed forced, giving the impression of a continuous "tug of war" with him; the examiner felt annoyed at times, when her penetrating eyes seemed to look not at him but through him.

Ms. E. was oriented to time, place, and person. Her intelligence, language skills, and ability to abstract were above average, commensurate with her college education. She spoke of her early childhood, her family, and her marital difficulties in organized, chronological order. She related her history in a matter-of-fact tone of voice, typifying the constricted range of affect which dominated the entire interview. Her vocal tone, along with her forceful and calculated verbal expression, alerted the examiner to consider her apathy a mask for underlying anxiety and anger. Similarly, the functional rapport established with Ms. E. was nothing more than a facade of cordiality, hiding a sense of seclusiveness and coldness. Ms. E.'s thought expression was characterized by a slow and at times hesitant rate of speech, which became somewhat pressured when she responded to questions probing emotionally laden information.

She admitted having had periods of depression prior to the car accident, relating these feelings to specific difficulties she had had with her ex-husband. She impressed the examiner with her attentiveness, with the clarity and logic of her answers, and with her excellent memory. The intellectualized style of her presentation, her excellent command of the language, and the goal-directedness of her answers seemed paradoxical to her claim to have "psychic powers." With the exception of this statement, there was no evidence for disturbed language functions or thought disorder. When asked to elaborate, Ms. E. claimed that she was able to communicate with dead relatives and to heal the sick. She also stated that the car accident was "God's way of granting me life" so that she could continue her "life's mission." Such divine intervention was needed, according to Ms. E., because prior to the accident she had been lonely and desperate and had felt useless, particularly as a mother. When questioned about suicidal ideation, however, she smiled (as if amused at such a ridiculous thought) and said, "It's against my faith; I wouldn't even think about such a cop-out." Ms. E. admitted having difficulty falling asleep. When asked about her failure to find a job, she said, "I don't know . . . it's hard to find something in my neighborhood." Later she said, "I don't want to drive anymore." She rejected the examiner's suggestion that the car accident had made her fearful of driving, but she admitted that prior to the accident she had had no such inhibitions.

Ms. E. was a reliable interviewee in her ability to provide factual information. However, her judgment and insight were limited. When told that she would be referred for psychological testing, she seemed confused and surprised, stating, "I need a job. I don't understand why everybody thinks that something is wrong with me."

This MSE is interesting because of the differential diagnostic possibilities and because the examiner's obvious countertransference reactions cast doubt on the objectivity of some of the observations. DSM-III-R criteria guide the examiner to consider posttraumatic stress disorder on Axis I, together with premorbid possibilities of psychotic or affective nature. More information should be gathered to support possible personality disorders on Axis II.

Neuropsychological Evaluation

Traditional psychiatry and neurology have failed to provide sufficient understanding of the cognitive and emotional consequences of brain injury. The general label of organic brain syndrome was used to differentiate these conditions from other clinical entities, without sufficient diagnostic specificity or pragmatic recommendations for treatment. The field of neuropsychology provided the knowledge necessary for the development of assessment techniques and specific guidelines for management. The last decade has witnessed a growing body of neuropsychological literature, which established the diagnosis and treatment of many neurobehavioral disorders in both outpatient and hospital settings.

The MSE, with its sensitivity to pathognomonic signs and symptoms, has become a natural component of the comprehensive neuropsychological evaluation. Many writers consider the MSE a necessary addition to both neurological and psychiatric diagnostic assessments (Berg et al. 1987, Strub and Black 1977). The trained clinician, knowledgeable about brain function and the characteristics of neurological disorders, can depend on the MSE findings to help determine the need for and direction of a more elaborate neuropsychological assessment.

Theories of brain function present the central nervous system as a functional organ system, controlling interacting processes in hierarchical fashion. The integrity of more complex functions (such as thinking and social judgment) is based on the integrity of simpler processes (such as movement, perception, and speech). Therefore, the MSE is conducted in a systematic and orderly fashion, starting with basic brain functions and working up to more integrative cognitive operations. For example, if a patient consistently fails to understand simple questions like "Did you eat breakfast today?" or "Is it day or night now?" then a request for proverb interpretation is unnecessary.

The behavioral categories most commonly observed in the neuropsychological MSE are as follows, in order of assessment: level of consciousness, attention, language skills, amnestic abilities, constructional abilities (drawing or working with three-dimensional configurations), higher cognitive functions. An elaborate discussion of the MSE and its use in neurology and neuropsychology is presented in Berg and colleagues (1987) and in Strub and Black (1977).

CASE HISTORY

A 27-year-old male with a short history of unusual behavior was brought to a local hospital by his roommate. Five days prior to the hospitalization, while intoxicated in a bar, the patient was involved in a brawl. In the days that followed he seemed increasingly strange. He was confused, talked "differently," and seemed unable to relate appropriately to others. Routine medical and neurological exams found him healthy. When initially interviewed, he was found to be disoriented and alert, but not attentive. He manifested a number of signs of disturbed thought processes. His flat affect, inappropriate speech, and withdrawn manner led the medical staff to consult with a psychiatrist. The patient was admitted to a psychiatric unit, with a provisional diagnosis of schizophreniform disorder. Following several days without improvement, a neuropsychological assessment was ordered. The MSE report stated the following:

> This right-handed young male was awake and alert. He failed digit-repetition tasks, but seemed attentive, vigilant, and goal-oriented while copying geometric figures. His speech was fluent but tangential, with many paraphasic distortions. His comprehension was very limited: Simple verbal instructions were not followed; he recognized very few common objects when asked to point to them; and he failed to repeat words or sentences. While he seemed to understand a few simple instructions, he had word-finding difficulties. Upon further observation, he was found to be quite efficient with constructional tasks, particularly when instructions were given nonverbally, and he relied on mimicking or following the examiner's gestures.

The presence of many aphasic signs, as the single, most obvious cluster of disabilities, persuaded the examiner to direct further diagnostic efforts toward the left temporal lobe. More extensive neurological tests (including arteriography and a computerized tomography scan) identified a left posterior temporal mass. Surgery confirmed a large subdural hematoma, consistent with an injury resulting from a violent blow.

Psychiatric Evaluation for Pharmacotherapy

In certain conditions, pharmacotherapy is the only therapeutic option that will bring relief from distress. By now, regardless of theoretical and philosophical biases, most mental health practitioners accept psychoactive drugs as an undeniable reality. Therefore, nonmedical mental health workers must recognize the need to enhance their knowledge of psychopharmacology.

Levenson (1981) identifies the main objective for drug treatment as the remission of specific distressing states. He emphasizes that such intervention is not a cure. Alone or together with psychotherapy and environmental changes, drug treatment can help sufferers improve the quality of their lives. Levenson discusses the variables involved in the decision to use drugs and the choice of the most appropriate drug and dosage: (1) the knowledge and experience of the physician, (2) a physical and laboratory examination to assess the patient's physiological status, (3) the patient's history, and (4) "a working knowledge of psychopharmacologically responsive psychopathology" (1981, p. viii). This working knowledge includes the ability to recognize signs and symptoms of psychiatric states that are responsive to drug treatment, and the capacity to assess these syndromes in a relatively rapid fashion.

Levenson describes the Rapid Psychiatric Assessment (used to determine both initial and follow-up clinical dispositions) as an interview consisting of a subjective and an objective component. In the subjective component, the examiner uses specific questions to guide the patient to describe past psychiatric history (including effectiveness of specific drugs) and recent or current symptoms (such as sleep disturbances or specific feelings or thoughts). The objective component consists of the examiner's observations of signs, which together with the presenting symptoms can indicate the presence of a drug-responsive syndrome. This objective component is a set of observations made by the examiner, based on a priori expectations that certain abnormalities (in state of consciousness, motor activity, affect, thought processes, and thought content) are indicative of possible larger symptoms for drug treatment.

Functional and organic disorders often present similar symptoms. Organic disorders, particularly acute states of brain trauma (such as intoxication or lowered level of consciousness immediately following head trauma), are often contraindicative to drug treatment. Therefore, the differential diagnosis between functional and organic conditions is crucial to pharmacotherapists. Consequently, the MSE includes questions and observations geared toward assessment of the possibility of a neurological disorder. Questions that test recent memory capacity and the ability to perform simple calculations can help to differentiate manifestations of psychosis from signs of recent brain trauma. For example, thought blocking (sudden cessation of verbal production) and paraphasia (idiosyncratic production of word sounds) can be signs of a psychotic process. When the patient also demonstrates partial loss of recent memory, impaired intellectual functions, and an intact capacity to repeat digits forward but serious impairment in backward repetition, blocking and paraphasia are understood as aphasic reactions to brain trauma.

CASE HISTORY

A 32-year-old male, recently admitted to a psychiatric inpatient unit, is examined by a psychiatrist, who records the following clinical profile:

Based on information from relatives, the patient has no psychiatric history. His wife recalls recent complaints (for the last 7 to 8 weeks) of sleep difficulties, periods of agitation, and irritability. She also reluctantly admitted being annoyed with the increased frequency of her husband's sexual advances. Physical and laboratory parameters were within normal limits. The review of symptoms found him somewhat concerned about initial and intermittent sleep disturbances, but he insisted that he has a positive outlook toward the future. He stated, "Doc, actually I feel great . . . never felt so energized in my life." The MSE found him alert, somewhat distractible, and quite euphoric, with an overall hypermotility. His speech was slightly pressured and at times incoherent, and his accelerated thought production included flight of ideas. There were no signs of organicity.

This patient was diagnosed as having an acute hypomanic reaction, and he was judged a good candidate for pharmacotherapy with the drug of choice lithium carbonate. The observed agitation and hypermotility indicated the need to prescribe a major tranquilizer along with the lithium.

This chapter introduced the MSE as part of an initial diagnostic interview and as one of the most significant sources of data toward the formal description of a clinical diagnosis. The MSE was described as a set of systematic behavioral observations in pursuit of known manifestations of pathological conditions. The categories of behavioral observations collected during the MSE were outlined and discussed. The value of the MSE as a diagnostic tool was presented in terms of its adaptability to various theoretical perspectives. Case examples were presented to demonstrate the uses of the MSE by psychologists, psychiatrists, neuropsychologists, and pharmacotherapists.

REFERENCES

American Psychiatric Association (1968). *Diagnostic and Statistical Manual of Mental Disorders*, 2nd ed. Washington, DC: APA.

American Psychiatric Association (1980). *Diagnostic and Statistical Manual of Mental Disorders*, 3rd ed. Washington, DC: APA.

American Psychiatric Association (1987). *Diagnostic and Statistical Manual of Mental Disorders*, 3rd ed., rev. Washington, DC: APA.

Berg, R., Franzen, M., and Wedding, D. (1987). *Screening for Brain Impairment: A Manual for Mental Health Practice.* New York: Springer.

Freedman, A. M., Kaplan, H. I., and Sadock, B. J. (1975). *Comprehensive Textbook of Psychiatry*, vol. 1. Baltimore: Williams & Wilkins.

Levenson, A. J. (1981). *Basic Psychopharmacology.* New York: Springer.

Lewis, N. D. C. (1934). *Outlines for Psychiatric Examinations.* Albany: New York State Department of Mental Hygiene.

Luria, A. (1973). *The Working Brain.* New York: Basic Books.

Maxmen, J. S. (1986). *Essential Psychopathology.* New York: W. W. Norton.

Mendel, W. M. (1976). *Schizophrenia: The Experience and its Treatment.* San Francisco: Jossey-Bass.

Nathan, P. E. (1981). Symptomatic diagnosis and behavioral assessment: a synthesis? In *Behavioral Assessment of Adult Disorders*, ed. D. H. Barlow, pp. 13–43. New York: Guilford.

Nelson, R. O., and Barlow, D. H. (1981). Behavioral assessment: basic strategies and initial procedures. In *Behavioral Assessment of Adult Disorders*, ed. D. H. Barlow, pp. 13–39. New York: Guilford.

Noyes, A. P., and Kolb, L. C. (1963). *Modern Clinical Psychiatry*, 6th ed. Philadelphia: W. B. Saunders.

Pope, B. (1979). *The Mental Health Interview: Research and Application.* New York: Pergamon.

Rosenthal, R. H., and Akiskal, H. S. (1985). Mental status examination. In *Diagnostic Interviewing*, ed. M. Hersen and S. M. Turner, pp. 25–52. New York: Plenum.

Slater, E., and Roth, M. (1969). *Clinical Psychiatry*, 3rd ed. Baltimore: Williams & Wilkins.

Spitzer, R. L. (1976). More on pseudoscience in science and the case for psychiatric diagnosis: a critique of D. L. Rosenhan's "On being sane in insane places" and "The contextual nature of psychiatric diagnosis." *Archives of General Psychiatry* 33:459–470.

Strub, R. L., and Black, F. W. (1977). *The Mental Status Examination in Neurology.* Philadelphia: F. A. Davis.

Taylor, M. A. (1981). *The Neuropsychiatric Mental Status Examination.* New York: Spectrum.

Wing, J. K., Cooper, J. E., and Sartorius, N. (1974). *The Measurement and Classification of Psychiatric Symptoms.* Cambridge, England: Cambridge University Press.

Wolpert, E. A. (1977). *Manic-Depressive Illness: History of a Syndrome.* New York: International Universities Press.

16
Assessment of Suicide Potential

ROBERT I. YUFIT, Ph.D.

The evaluation of suicide potential is one of the most difficult tasks in the field of psychological diagnostic assessment. A primary reason for this difficulty is the multi-intentionality of the patient's behavior and the accompanying ambivalence that can distort intention. Does the suicide-prone patient want attention via his actions? Does he want to hurt or punish himself, or does he want to shame someone else? Or does he really want to die? Can we call a person suicidal whose intent is self-harm or attention?

There is considerable ambivalence in almost all suicidal behavior, at all levels of intention (Beck et al. 1979, Menninger 1938, Neuringer 1974). Many persons are simply not certain what they want the outcome of their action to be, but they *do* know that they want to do *something* to themselves—or to *communicate* something to someone else. Thus we don't always know whether we are evaluating an attempt at communication or an act geared toward actual self-destruction (Dorpat and Ripley 1967).

Some suicidal patients' intentions are clearly manipulative. They may want to elicit sympathy from the evaluator (or from a neglectful loved one). They may have meant to take into account the myriad variables related to suicidal behavior. The precipitating factors and the person's ability to handle change need careful exploration. These variables (objective and subjective) must be explored to see whether they are present (this is *screening*), and some kind of assessment of the current *degree* or *intensity* of these variables must be made.

In other words, the interview should be quantified so that the degree of lethality of any present suicide potential can be determined. Such an assessment often helps to determine actual intention—whether the patient's wish is to harm himself, or others, or to gain attention from inattentive others, or to actually end his life. Some overt behaviors are very obvious in their self-harm or self-destructive intent. Others are more indirect, and may be disguised as accident-proneness or as an abusive life-style (overeating, excessive drinking, smoking, illicit drug use and overwork are examples).

THE QUANTIFIED FOCUSED INTERVIEW

In order to explore the important variables, a *Quantified Focused Interview (QFI)* format has been developed. The interview covers specific variables considered to be correlated with high suicide potential which are quantified by 13 rating scales. A total score can be derived to provide an index of suicide potentiality. The goal is not to try to predict suicidal behavior as a specific act, but to establish some guidelines for assessing suicide potential or risk.

The task of suicide screening and assessment can be divided into two broad evaluation areas:

1. Is the person suicidal? (screening task)
2. If so, what is the *degree* of *lethality* that a suicide attempt may carry? (assessment task)

Will the suicide attempt be a bid for attention, or to create shame, or do limited self-harm? Or will the behavior be aimed at a level of lethality so high that death is the most likely outcome? A defined plan must be assessed in terms of its likely outcome. Some plans are definitely aimed at survival, not death. Of course, the survival plan may be based on a miscalculation (medication dosage, hoped-for rescue), and death may result. Many completed suicides happen this way.

The major indices of lethality are defined by the actual suicide behavior, the likelihood that the plan that is being considered will be carried out, the degree of ambivalence based on intention (unconscious versus conscious), the probability that the result will be death, and the method(s) available and finally chosen.

Degree of lethality in the former case of actual behavior is based on:

1. Degree of reversibility of the act (for example, jumping from a high place versus superficial wrist cutting)
2. Probability of rescue (Was the timing of the attempt geared to coincide with being discovered?)
3. Method chosen in light of methods available (for example, taking several pills from a bottle of 100 while at home in a 10th-floor apartment)
4. Degree of medical injury resulting from the behavior (The more serious the injury, the greater the likelihood that lethality intent was high. The patient's physical health and intellect must be considered.)

In assessing patients who are reporting suicidal ideation but who have not yet acted, the *plan* can be evaluated in similar terms. How reversible is the method being considered? What is the risk for rescue? How lethal is the method compared to those available?

Establishing the patient's *intention* along with the method chosen will allow for a measurement of *ambivalence*; both parameters are critical to evaluating the intensity of the patient's motivation (Beck et al. 1975, Dorpat and Ripley 1967, Tuckman and Youngman 1968). An "accidental overdose" is rare. If intentions are explored in detail, it often becomes clear that unconscious desires have played a vital role in outcome.

While the QFI can be more useful than the more subjective nonfocused interview by providing some structure, the use of specific assessment scales direct the clinician's attention to exploring the intensity of suicidal ideation, by requiring the clinician to give weight in the rating of these relevant areas. The total score of the summed weighted ratings will indicate the degree of lethality of the patient's intentions.

SUICIDE SCREENING CHECKLIST

Very few suicide screening or assessment scales have been universally accepted, mainly because most have a poor record of establishing acceptable validity and reliability (Lester 1970). Follow-up studies have generally been inadequate. They are few in number and often poorly designed. There is the added problem that effective treatment may "contaminate" the development of future suicidal ideation or acting out. Yet how are we to know whether a patient evaluated to have high suicide potential is actually suicidal unless we have short-term and long-term follow-up?

This problem also brings up the issue of evaluating a patient for short-term risk—that is, the likelihood that suicidal behavior will occur within the next 24 to 48 hours. Longer-term suicide risk (that is, the risk that the patient will attempt suicide within the next 30 days or longer) may be indicated by particular characterological patterns, although I do not believe that there is a specific "suicidal personality." However, vulnerability to stress induced by loss and by change will give indications of long-term risk.

Definition of the anatomy of these vulnerabilities is a core task for suicide assessment research. We should also explore and define those coping skills that enable "healthy" persons to deal with loss and change so that we can use therapeutic intervention to develop these skills in our suicidal patients.

Some persons are chronically suicidal and have made many attempts, usually of low lethality. The therapist should consider *all* suicide attempts serious, regardless of their lethality. Multiple suicide attempts reflect the inadequacy of coping and adaptive skills for dealing with stress, sometimes even minor stress. There is no such thing as a nonserious suicide attempt. Many completed suicides occur because the patient has miscalculated the degree of lethality, or has combined two minimally lethal means into a high-risk method.

Objective suicide screening and assessment techniques, which are often structured in the form of scales or questionnaires, should be used to supplement the interview. Clinical judgment, usually based on extensive clinical experience, must be given considerable weight when the results of the assessment procedures conflict with one's clinical judgment.

In some instances, the clinical judgment of the experienced clinician should supercede the results of an assessment technique that has low validity or reliability. Such assessment techniques should be improved, replaced, or supplemented by serial assessment, or an assessment battery. More on that later.

A useful procedure for establishing the utility of suicidal screening and assessment procedures is to develop such a procedure based on empirically established variables. Such variables are really correlates of suicidal behavior. If they are present, suicidal behavior can be considered more likely. Correlates can be presented in the form of a *checklist*, which can then be used to categorize interview data. The checklist instrument can be constructed around these empirical clusters of variables and can enable the clinician to do a more comprehensive assessment.

Such an instrument, called the Suicide Screening Checklist (SSC), has been developed (Yufit and Benziss 1973) but has not yet been sufficiently piloted to determine its validity (Figure 16–1). The SSC allows the interview data to be categorized based on empirical research. Such an assessment procedure is an abbreviation of the task posed by the more detailed clinical assessment by interview, the QFI. The SSC consists of 60 items, many of them numerically weighted on the basis of empirical evidence from formal research studies, and from the accumulated "hands-on" knowledge of clinicians who have had extensive experience evaluating suicidal patients.

The SSC usually can be scored in about 20 minutes by the experienced clinician after asking the necessary questions, or it can be applied to the existing data. The SSC is scored on basis of presence (Yes) or absence (No) of data and by summing the separate item weighted scores. The total SSC score will provide an index to suicide potential, as indicated on the form. These ranges have not yet been validated. The SSC can be considered a checklist interview, focused on significant variables. A disadvantage is that such an interview can become "mechanical" and can lack the richness of a more intensive exploration. The QFI, which is more loosely structured, allows more data to be gathered than that which is required for the rating scales. Genuine rapport between the patient and the clinician should be established before inquiries into these variables are made. Emergency room personnel find this format useful, as do school counselors.

THE TIME QUESTIONNAIRE

Another dimension quite relevant to suicide screening and assessment is time perspective. The Time Questionnaire (TQ) has been developed to provide a time profile (Yufit and Benziss 1973, 1979). The TQ consists of four sections: present, future, past, and an information sheet. Each section contains individual items, which are scored according to a scoring manual. The future section asks the respondents to select a future year and then answer a series of items as if they were living in that future year

Figure 16-1. Suicide Screening Checklist (SSC)

Directions: On the basis of interview and other available data, score each item, using the weights in parentheses, when so listed. Use only one weight for each item listed, unless otherwise indicated.

Suicide history (Max. = 18):	*Yes*	*No*	*Uncertain*
1. Prior attempt			
2. Two or more prior attempts in past year (highly lethal = × 2)			
3. Prior suicide threats, ideation			
4. Suicide attempts in family (× 2)			
5. Completed attempts in family (× 3)			
6. Current suicide preoccupation, threats, attempt (× 2); detailed highly lethal 1 plan (× 2); access to weapon, medication in home (× 4); all three "yes" = 8			
7. Preoccupation with death			
Psychiatric history (Max. = 11):			
8. Psychosis and hospitalization (× 3)			
9. Any psychiatric diagnosis (× 2); diagnosis of schizophrenia or manic depressive (× 3)			
10. Alcoholism or other drug abuse (current = × 3; past = × 2)			
11. Poor impulse control; explosive rage episodes (indicate chronic, single recent, single past)			
12. Accident-proneness (list frequency, examples)			
School/Job (Max. = 9):			
13. School failure, work failure			
14. Rejection			
15. Poor social relations			
16. On probation, dropped out of school, or fired from job (× 2)			
17. Disciplinary crisis (× 2)			
18. Anticipation of severe punishment, serious criticism			
19. Unwanted change of school or job			
Family (Max. = 25):			
20. Recent major negative change, usually a loss (death, divorce, serious health problem) (irreversible loss = × 3; divorce = × 3; both "yes" = × 6)			
21. Lack of emotional support; estrangement from significant others			
22. Loss of employment (parent or self)			

FIGURE 16-1. (*continued*)

Family (Max. = 25):	*Yes*	*No*	*Uncertain*
23. Major depression in parent, sibling (× 2)			
24. Alcoholism in family member (× 2)			
25. Psychiatric illness in family member (× 2); (23–25 "yes" = 6 × 2)			
26. History of sexual abuse			
Society (Max. = 6):			
27. "Contagion" suicide episode (× 3)			
28. Economic downshift in community			
29. Loss of major support system (group, job, career problems) "High lethality" defined as method with low degree of reversibility, poor potential for rescue, substantial medical injury			
Personality and behavior; cognitive style (Max. = 54):			
30. Anger, rage (unexpressed = × 3)			
31. Depression (intense depression = × 2; agitated depression = × 4)			
32. Hopelessness (× 2); (30, 31, 32 all "yes" = 9, then 9 × 2 = 18)			
33. Mistrust (paranoia = × 2)			
34. Disgust, despair			
35. Withdrawal, isolation			
36. Poor "future" perspective (× 2)			
37. High "past" orientation (× 2); ("yes" on 36, 37 = 4 × 2)			
38. Rigidity, perfectionism (× 4)			
39. Lack of sense of belonging			
40. Indifference, lack of motivation (boredom = × 2)			
41. Worthlessness, feeling that no one cares			
42. Shame or guilt (both = × 2)			
43. Helplessness			
44. Inability to have fun (× 2)			
45. Extreme mood or energy fluctuation (both = × 2)			
46. Giving away valuables			
Physical (Max. = 14):			
47. Male (× 3); white (× 2); both "yes" = 5			
48. Significantly delayed puberty (after age 16)			
49. Recent physical injury resulting in deformity, impairment (permanent = × 2)			
50. Marked obesity (+20% standard given by height-and-weight tables)			
51. Marked recent underweight or anorexia (−15% of standard; over 20% = × 3)			

FIGURE 16-1. *(continued)*

Physical (Max. = 14):	*Yes*	*No*	*Uncertain*
52. Sleep disturbed (onset, middle, early-morning awakening)			
53. Ongoing physical pain			
Interview behavior (Max. = 10):			
54. Noncommunicative, encapsulated			
55. Negative reaction of patient to interviewer (× 2)			
56. Negative reaction of interviewer to patient			
57. Increasing emotional "distance" during interview			
58. Increasing hostility, lack of cooperation			
59. Highly self-critical, self-pitying (× 2)			
60. Discusses death, suicide (× 2)			

Suicide Potential range risk guidelines: (Tentative ranges - to be evaluated by additional field testing.)

Total score = ____________
(Max. = 144)
Severe .... (100 to 144)
Moderate .... (60 to 99)
Low .... (below 60)

Confidence level: High Low
Reasons for low confidence rating:

now. A total score is derived from the summed individual and section scores. A "lie scale" is used to detect attempts to distort in either direction—to "look bad" or to "look good."

The suicidal patient appears to have a unique time profile, different from that of the nonsuicidal person. Most suicide-prone patients have a minimal involvement in the future, as might be expected. The involvement in the present is also minimal and usually quite negative in tone. The bulk of the suicidal patient's time perspective is in the past. This preoccupation with the past usually takes two forms. One is the nostalgia for the "good old days" that cannot be recaptured, which results in frustration, considerable psychological pain, and depression. There is often a key person from the past or a more coveted environment which appears to be (or may actually be) permanently lost in the present, and difficult or impossible to re-establish in the future.

The second orientation to the past characterizing the suicidal patient is less of a regression, but more of an obsession. The obsession usually takes the form of a preoccupation with a poor decision made in the past, and the apparent irreversibility of that decision in the present (examples include a poor career or job choice, or the selection of an incompatible marital partner). The patient wishes to go back and relive the past, in order to undo the present dilemma. Time-profile tests on over 1,000 patients who had considered or attempted suicide demonstrated a very strong preoccupation with the past, and rarely more than a one-year projection into the future.

The time perspective of most (nonsuicidal) Americans is focused in the future and, to a slightly lesser degree, in the present, with minimal involvement in the past. In our study, several hundred subjects, grouped in matched "control" populations, reflected this characteristic profile of time perspective. Use of the TQ on some European and Asian suicide-prone populations (Belgians, Germans, and Japanese) reveals a time-profile pattern identical to that of suicide-prone Americans, except that the European and Asian control subjects were somewhat more focused on the present than on the future. The time profiles of suicide-prone persons versus nonsuicidal persons are presented in Table 16–1.

These time profiles were consistent in five years of field testing of several matched populations of clinical and nonclinical samples totaling over 1,600 persons (Yufit and Benziss 1973). Time perspective is a useful indicator, but it is too narrow in scope to be used by itself, and a supplemental interview is recommended. The TQ is best used serially, or in combination with other assessment procedures, to more clearly encompass the need for comprehensiveness in the evaluation of suicide potential.

COGNITIVE STYLE

It has been found that there is a particular cognitive style that characterizes suicidal patients. First, their thinking tends to be rigid (Neuringer 1964). Suicide-prone patients do not easily develop alternative solutions to problems. They are unable to "roll with the punches." They lack resiliency and perspective. Their rigidity leads to the use of a word that suicidologists dislike hearing: only. "It is the *only* way out, the *only* thing to do."

When rigidity is accompanied by two other commonly found feeling states among suicide-prone persons—*hopelessness* and *helplessness*—there is cause for even greater concern about suicide risk. Hopelessness implies a lack of trust and a diminished expectation that future desires and goals can be attained. It implies a lack of optimism that bad situations will improve, or that losses can be replaced. Vulnerability to suicide attempts

Table 16-1. Time-Perspective Profiles

	Suicide-prone	Nonsuicidal	
Focus on	Most cultures	American	European/Asian
Past:	High	Minimal	Minimal
Present:	Low and/or negative	Moderately high	High
Future:	Minimal or none	Very high	Moderately high

has been a key concept for a number of authors (Beck et al. 1975, Menninger 1938, Shneidman and Farberow 1957). Helplessness often indicates a deficiency of internal assets, a lack of confidence, underdeveloped autonomy, a poor self-image, overdependency on nongiving others, and doubt regarding one's ability to influence or control one's future. The result is usually a low achievement drive and inadequate energy levels, which can lead to fear, anxiety, stagnation, and depression. Consequent failure to attain desired goals adds to feelings of helplessness, creating a downward spiral.

Frustration often builds when these feelings of hopelessness and helplessness persist and predominate. The rigidity minimizes any shift in thinking and thwarts efforts to find alternative solutions. When the resulting psychological pain is too great, suicide can become the "only" way out, often to lessen the pain—a need that may be experienced as more critical than the wish to die. Identification and assessment of this pain is critical to timely intervention.

Excessive expectations can also increase the likelihood of failure and feelings of helplessness. Perfectionism frequently accompanies rigidity and is a characteristic commonly found in achievement-oriented young people who exhibit suicidal behavior.

Anger is a frequent result of continued feelings of helplessness and hopelessness. Because passivity is often a function of rigidity and helplessness, anger may not be overtly expressed.

Anger turned inward is probably one of the major psychodynamics that pulls the trigger of the suicidal impulse, wrote Menninger (1938) in his classic book *Man Against Himself*. The suicidal person may turn his anger on himself, after other outlets for his anger have been blocked by loss of control and by fear of the unknown response of the actual target of the anger, and "self-murder" can result. Danger to others is an additional concern, as the anger may not be entirely displaced toward the self.

The existence of a sudden, unexpected loss or failure requires considerable coping and adaptation after a variable period of mourning. A rigid person often lacks the adaptive skills necessary to cope and to adapt to change, or the resiliency to view the trauma in proper perspective. The uncovering of feelings of hopelessness, helplessness, and suppressed or repressed anger following sudden negative (and sometimes even positive) life changes is important in evaluating suicide potential. Guilt and shame can accompany these feelings and may create intolerable psychological pain (Shneidman and Farberow 1957).

Another critical area for assessment is the *nature of the patient's support system.* Are there close friends available who can be trusted? What is the nature of the interpersonal relationships? Are previously nurturing persons now gone? Are current relationships fulfilling and providing meaningful experiences? Isolation and alienation are ominous contexts that are often found in suicidal persons. The resulting loneliness often magnifies the loss and further distorts perspective. A good relationship with the self becomes critical.

Does the patient have a sense of *belonging*—to someone, or to some place, or to a career or a leisure-time pursuit? Does the patient feel a sense of belonging to himself? Can he enjoy being by himself? Is there intimacy with himself, with significant others, and with enjoyed activities? Intimate relationships with valued others are especially important in helping patients to cope with sudden negative life changes (Beck et al. 1979, Dorpat and Ripley 1967). Such intimacy intensifies a sense of belonging. Feelings of belonging and intimacy are rarely found in suicidal persons. Their absence often precipitates emptiness, loneliness, and feelings of deprivation. Stagnation, boredom, and despair can result.

When internal resources are minimal, external support systems are crucial. When they are also absent, or worse yet, when support systems are experienced as hostile and withholding, the vulnerability of the isolated person increases exponentially. Suicidal behavior becomes a desperate means of finding a way out, again, often to end the psychological pain of rejection.

While cognitive rigidity is an ominous trait, the opposite extreme—manic behavior—can be of equal concern, as impulse control and thought regulation become loose or nonexistent. Bipolar disorders are associated with one of the highest suicide rates of any psychiatric diagnostic category, along with schizophrenia (Pokorny 1964). The poor impulse control of the manic patient minimizes the deliberation and reasoning necessary for effective problem solving. A thought flashes through the manic patient's mind—and why not act on it? Meditation and thinking through are not part of the problem-solving process. Do it, act fast; the impulsivity becomes a part of being. When these characteristics are noted in an assessment of personality and behavior, the patient should be considered a high suicide risk. Such impulsivity tends to compel quick and dramatic solutions, usually to distract from psychological pain by inflicting injury (self-harm behavior) or to end the pain permanently (suicide).

Depression is important in considering suicide potential, but some recent studies have indicated that as many as one-third of persons who completed suicide were not significantly depressed immediately prior to their suicide (Beck et al. 1979, Pokorny 1964). Of course, any *psychotically* depressed patient should be considered a potential suicide threat, but the absence of a clinical depression does not, in itself, mean that suicidal behavior is unlikely. I would rank suppressed anger and hopelessness, both common precursors of depression, as more critical to the evaluation of suicide potential than depression per se.

How important is a suicidal history? Very important. Despite some conflicting data in a recent study, most research demonstrates that even a series of low-lethality suicide attempts are to be considered as an ominous forerunner to the likelihood of further suicidal behavior. The nature and frequency of the previous attempts, the methods used, an increasing gradient of lethality in recent attempts, an existing life stress (or absence of stress) at the time all must be carefully explored and categorized during the clinical interview so that some estimate of the patient's vulnerability or coping skills can be made. Vulnerability is directly related to suicide risk when coping abilities are minimal.

The therapist must also note whether there is a progressive pattern in the suicide attempts. Have the physical injuries in a series of attempts been progressively more, or less, life threatening? Is there a seasonal pattern to the series of prior attempts? Are there significant anniversary reactions relating to prior attempts? Is there a common precipitating stress component to the previous attempts? Since the rate of completed suicides is so much higher for males, and the attempt rate is much higher for females, should we consider different factors to evaluate for suicidal risk based on gender? Any one of the variables may give important clues to what has happened in the past, and may allow a more comprehensive accounting of all current factors that must be considered in evaluating immediate risk as well as long-term risk.

On the other hand, a long history of suicidal ideation, and no overt suicidal behavior, can be of equal concern. When an attempt *is* made, will it be of such magnitude that it will be fatal? Or is the pattern one of attention-seeking, such as that represented by the dramatic behavior patterns of the hysteric. This may suggest low lethality. Some have argued that such patients should *not* be considered suicidal, even though their behavior may clearly be classified as attempts at suicide (Dorpat and Ripley 1967, Tuckman and Youngman 1968). Such advice may be dangerous. These patients *should* be considered suicidal.

From a clinician's point of view, the semantics are not important. Patients who make a suicidal gesture may miscalculate the lethality of the next attempt and may die by accident, even though death was not the intent. Terms such as *suicidal gesture* in reference to a low-lethality attempt, should be avoided, as they imply a lack of seriousness by the attempter and can result in an overly casual response in the plan of treatment.

RECOMMENDATIONS

Each suicidal patient is a unique individual, but the rules of assessment are standard and should be applied to all:

1. Listen with intensity and care. Developing a good rapport quickly is critical to obtaining genuine responses. Involved interaction reflects the capacity for intimacy. A good interview experience also helps to create a positive attitude toward subsequent psychotherapy and the establishment of an effective therapeutic alliance.
2. Observe body movement and posturing as well as voice tone and facial expressions. Appropriate, animated responses are usually a better sign than flat, emotionless, remote responses.
3. Be compassionate and empathic in probing for information. Develop a "flow" by asking open-ended questions that also allow a chance to evaluate thinking, reasoning, and judgment.

4. Try to "reach" the patient behind the facade of defenses without destroying the protective covering.

5. Use other informants (or previously existing valid data) for information to corroborate questionable data, or when the patient appears to be manipulating.

6. Assess the critical correlates cited in the QFI and SSC.

7. Derive a quantitative score to reflect the degree of suicide proneness, as well as a qualitative sense of the vital balance between the patient's assets (coping skills) and deficiencies (vulnerability).

8. Note the changes that occur during the course of the interview, especially increasing or decreasing cooperation and closeness in the interview diad.

9. Be aware of countertransference reactions.

CASE HISTORY

Karen is a divorced 45-year-old employed woman who sought help following the suicide of her only son, an 18-year-old high school senior. She lives with her only other child, a single, 20-year-old employed daughter. Their relationship is poor, and the suicide made for considerably more tension and isolation around the house. The loss drove a further wedge between mother and daughter, even though they both professed love for him.

The presenting complaint was Karen's anger at what her son had done, anguish at why she hadn't been more aware of his problems, and her own suicidal ideation, which was affecting her sleep and eating patterns. She was suffering from insomnia and anorexia, and had lost several pounds.

Karen had made a suicide attempt several years earlier, following her husband's desertion, but she had led an uneventful life since then, being troubled only by her children's presumed drug use and by constant financial pressure.

Karen had dated, but she had been wary of men since her divorce and doubted that she would remarry. She overindulged in alcohol about once a month. Her work associates liked her, and she performed adequately at her job.

Karen was evaluated using a battery of assessment techniques, including the previously cited instruments. She was considered to be at moderately high risk for suicide. She scored fairly high on the TQ, with the cited characteristic time profile. She had considerable involvement in the past, the time when her son was alive, but she also had some hope for the future. Her QFI demonstrated high scores on anger and hopelessness, and the total score was moderately high, as was her score on the SSC. Her drinking behavior was of particular concern, as was the history of a family suicide and her limited social support network.

Karen was verbal and very expressive in the opening individual therapy sessions. She was not clinically depressed, but she expressed doubts that anything could go right, and she was both angry and guilt-ridden about her son's suicide, his second attempt. She was eating well but sleeping poorly.

As mentioned, her scores on the QFI and the SSC were in the moderately high range, and despite the added stress of the quarrelsome relationship with her daughter, which created an isolated home environment, it was decided to treat her on an outpatient basis, in twice-weekly individual psychotherapy. Medication was not prescribed.

A good rapport developed rapidly but unevenly, and this pattern was maintained throughout the early sessions, although Karen felt that therapy was "for the birds" and that it would not bring her son back. She was given optimal opportunity to express her anger and was offered much support to dilute her guilt feelings and reduce her shame and remorse over her son's suicide. Trust developed slowly but steadily.

Her suicidal ideation was addressed openly, and the effects of her son's suicide and her own potential suicide on her daughter's life were extensively discussed. We discussed the lost opportunities to do some good things for herself in the future if she carried out her suicide threats. Efforts were made to set attainable future goals, increase her earning capacity and income level, and develop more effective communication with her daughter; the latter was the most difficult task.

She was encouraged to recognize her assets and to develop her social life, and after a year of therapy she ambivalently began to date a man regularly. She received a substantial salary increase at her job and developed some leisure-time pursuits to curb her frequent drinking. With my strong urging, she also joined a support group of survivors and developed some good relationships with other survivors, with whom she felt she had much in common. She had finally found a group to which to belong.

While her early improvement in therapy had been very uneven, she began to explore herself more intensively, and she gained some important insights and understanding that the traumatic events in her life were not her punishments for being bad, and that she had some assets that she could develop to her future advantage. Her responses to individual items in the TQ and SSC served as useful guides to areas of exploration.

Karen became quite depressed on the first anniversary of her son's suicide, but her own suicidal ideation had been reduced markedly by her new insights and the slow development of some future goals. Her anger was also diminished, but she continued to have communication problems with her daughter. She terminated therapy after two years, markedly improved, especially in handling her anger, and controlling her shame and guilt.

Reduced financial pressures, resulting from another salary increase, allowed more leisure and a more rewarding life-style, and while she had dissolved the relationship with her boyfriend, she looked forward to a more involved social life in the future. Some men were not so bad (our paternalistic transference relationship helped considerably), and some fulfilling relationships continued with some female peers in the survivor's group.

A six-month follow-up revealed that Karen had attained a slightly improved level of functioning and a reasonable resolution of her son's death, which she finally admitted was his choice and not her doing. While Karen remains a somewhat higher-than-usual suicide risk, the therapeutic strategies worked reasonably well, and she is still working on a number of additional goals.

> She was less vulnerable to suicidal ideation at termination than she had been at the onset of treatment, and she had learned to use her long-lost intellectual skills to improve her coping abilities and to adapt more realistically to the very difficult irreversible loss of a child.

Effective assessment procedures not only serve to provide a picture of the patients' current balance of coping ability and vulnerability, but the response patterns can also be useful in governing the areas of focus for the treatment process.

Probably the most efficient technique to evaluate suicide potential will depend on the development of a suicide assessment battery. Several assessment techniques can be used, either concurrently to provide a measure of construct validity, or serially over several days, to provide a mini-longitudinal approach to assessing the balance between coping and vulnerability. Shifts in intention and degree of ambivalence can be evaluated in this manner. A funnel approach, to help focus and pin-point areas of concern for treatment, can be performed by using such a suicide assessment battery including the clinical interview. Special training for clinicians would be imperative, to aid in this kind of optimal comprehensive assessment procedure.

We are working on the development of these forms of assessment techniques, which will center around the major suicide correlates discussed in this chapter.

The use of these techniques will greatly enhance the accurate assessment of suicide potential by providing a structured, quantified supplement to the usual clinical interview, and should allow for more valid and reliable clinicial decisions regarding management and treatment plans for suicidal patients.

REFERENCES

Beck, A. T., Kovacs, M., and Weissman, A. (1975). Hopelessness and suicidal behavior: an overview. *Journal of the American Medical Association* 234:1146–1149.

Beck, A. T., Resnik, H. L., and Lettieri, D. J., eds. (1979). *The Prediction of Suicide.* Bowie, MD: Charles Press.

Dorpat, T. L., and Ripley, H. S. (1967). The relationship between attempted suicide and committed suicide. *Comprehensive Psychiatry* 8:74–79.

Lester, D. (1978). Attempts to predict suicidal risk using psychological tests. *Psychological Bulletin* 74:1–17.

Menninger, K. A. (1938). *Man Against Himself.* New York: Harcourt, Brace, and World.

Neuringer, C. (1964). Rigid thinking in suicidal individuals. *Journal of Consulting and Clinical Psychology* 28:54–58.

—— (1974). Problems of assessing suicidal risk. In *Psychological Assessment of Suicidal Risk*, ed. C. Neuringer, pp. 3–17. Springfield, IL: Charles C Thomas.

Pokorny, A. D. (1964). Suicide rates in various psychiatric disorders. *Journal of Nervous and Mental Disease* 139:499–506.

Shneidman, E. S., and Farberow, N. C. (1957). *Clues to Suicide*. New York: McGraw-Hill.

Tuckman, N., and Youngman, W. F. (1968). Assessment of suicide risk in attempted suicides. In *Suicidal Behavior: Diagnosis and Management*, ed. H. L. P. Resnick, pp. 190–197. Boston: Little, Brown.

Wilson, M. (1981). Suicidal behavior: toward an exploration of differences in female and male roles. *Suicide and Life Threatening Behavior* 11:131–140.

Yufit, R. I. (in press). *The Suicide Screening Checklist*. Atlanta: Center for Disease Control.

Yufit, R. I., and Benziss, B. (1973). Assessing suicide potential by time perspective. *Journal of Suicide and Life-threatening Behavior* 3:270–280.

—— (1979). *The Time Questionnaire and Scoring Manual*. Palo Alto, CA: Consulting Psychologists Press.

17
Diagnostic Assessment of Children

NELL LOGAN, Ph.D.

Children of all ages are referred to mental health professionals in schools, medical center clinics, other outpatient and inpatient facilities, and private practice for psychological evaluation and intervention. Most are 5 years of age and older, but children under 5 years old, including infants, are also being seen. Children are referred for a variety of problems, including speech dysfunctions, learning difficulties, fears, nervousness, depression, unhappiness, overactivity, disobedience, fighting, temper tantrums, withdrawal, eating problems, tics, difficulty making friends, fire setting, stealing, lying, school truancy, excessive and unusual use of fantasy, and failure to reach developmental milestones.

The purpose of an assessment of a child is to arrive at an understanding of the child's presenting problems and the factors contributing to the difficulties. Problems may be manifestations of any number of physiological, psychological, or sociocultural variables. The assessment must include an understanding of specific characteristics of the child, his physiological status, the sociocultural background of the family, psychological characteristics of other family members, structure and dynamics of the family, other life circumstances, and the severity of the problem in the context of the child's age and these other contributing variables (Eissler et al. 1977, Kessler 1966, McDonald 1965, Mishne 1983, Noshpitz 1979a, Werkman 1965, Witmer 1964).

This chapter will summarize important aspects of the diagnostic assessment of children. It will discuss diagnostic classification, assessment guidelines and format, work with parents, individual interviews with children, specialized evaluations, formulation of the problems, and treatment planning. The focus is on interviewing and observing children.

DIAGNOSTIC CLASSIFICATION OF CHILDHOOD DISORDERS

Most evaluations of children are conducted within the framework of a diagnostic classification system. The primary classification system currently in use for work with children is DSM-III-R. This manual contains a section entitled "Disorders Usually First Evident in Infancy, Childhood, or Adolescence." Any other categories in DSM-III-R that are applicable to adults may also be applied to children. The sections entitled "Affective Disorders," "Schizophrenic Disorders," and "Adjustment Disorders" in particular are fairly frequently applied to children.

A number of authors (Mishne 1983, Noshpitz 1979b, Sperling 1982) still rely on more traditional categories. Mishne (1983), for example, has used the following categories: mental retardation, autism and psychosis, preoedipal disorders, and psychoneurosis. Preoedipal disorders include the borderline syndrome, narcissistic personality disorder, and character disorder. The psychoneuroses include anxiety states, phobias, and hysteria.

ASSESSMENT GUIDELINES

Children seldom approach someone outside the family about their problems, although occasionally this happens, especially if the child has known someone who has received help in this way. A physician, teacher, other professional, parent, relative, or friend of the family is more often the one who initiates the referral. The parents usually bring the child for the evaluation.

Although evaluations occasionally occur in settings where it is difficult or impossible to obtain the cooperation of parents, it is important if possible to work closely with parents or guardians in order to establish rapport with them and to obtain information. When parents feel that the atmosphere is respectful and supportive, they are more likely to ally themselves with the interviewer, reveal important aspects of themselves and their child, keep appointments, and support the child's involvement in the process. One evaluator may work with parents, child, and other members of the family. In some settings, one therapist interviews the child; another interviews the parents, and sometimes even a third person sees the family as a whole. All interviewers then collaborate closely.

An interviewer will achieve a deeper understanding of the problems by carefully listening to family members' communications, by noting the types of questions raised and the topics pursued, and by reflecting what is being said. *The interviewer wants to gain a sense of what it is like to be these parents with this child in this family and what it is like to be this child with these parents in this family.* The relationship between interviewer and family members develops as the interviewer tries to help them to clarify the nature of the difficulties. Family members should feel that they have been successful in communicating with the interviewer, have gained some new understanding, and have been validated as worthwhile people.

An important aspect of a child evaluation is to *place the problems within the context of the child's age and life circumstances* (Eissler et al. 1977, Goodman and Sours 1967, McDonald 1965). Childhood problems may reflect appropriate child developmental issues; common, transitory reactions to specific life circumstances; or more severe difficulties. Tantrums or clinginess in a 2-year-old, for example, even after a relatively calm period in which the child seems cooperative and independent, are common developmental phenomena. Frequent crying in a 5-year-old following the divorce of parents or a death of a parent is a common reaction in children of this age to this trauma. However, these same behaviors may reflect more severe difficulties, for example, if they are unusually intense or persist for a relatively long period of time. In assessing the severity of the problems, an evaluator especially looks at the extent to which the disturbances are interfering in important ways with play, learning, and interpersonal relationships and are slowing or impeding the development of important capacities.

Children are very involved in their families, and they trigger and react to many aspects of their families and of individuals within the family. However, they also have their own individual ways of coping with people and situations. It is useful to begin to assess the contribution of their individual characteristics as well as the contribution of the characteristics of other family members and the family as a whole to the problems. A child with severe asthma, for example, may have an intense fear of death, which partially arises from frequently being near death. However, this fear may have been exacerbated by anxieties, overprotectiveness, or underprotectiveness of other family members. It may also have been exacerbated by the child's anger, depression, or loneliness.

Interviewer Reactions

Children frequently act on their impulses, thus vividly manifesting their problems. They may be angry, destructive, sexually provocative, demanding, clinging, silly, passive, withdrawn, or inhibited. Parents also react intensely to their children's problems with anxiety, anger, rage, shame, humiliation, guilt, demanding and controlling behavior, self-criticism, helplessness, and withdrawal. Such reactions may trigger strong responses in an interviewer.

A major hazard for interviewers is the somewhat common tendency to empathize with the perspective of either a child or a parent and then to side with that person. One may feel either that the child has been treated very badly by the parents or that the parents have been stuck with a very difficult child.

An interviewer's reactions can provide important clues to the child's specific characteristics as well as suggest reactions that parents and others have to that child. An interviewer's reactions to a parent can also suggest reactions that a child or other parent may have to that particular parent. Remaining aware of and carefully thinking about one's own reactions is very important. An outside consultation is sometimes useful in coping with very intense reactions.

EVALUATION FORMAT

Types of Data

The literature on child assessment suggests that it is useful to obtain data on presenting problems, other aspects of a child's current functioning, developmental history, significant events in the child's life, highest level of functioning at any time prior to the current difficulties, and characteristics of the family as a whole and of specific family members in order to understand factors that may be triggering and maintaining the current problems (Eissler et al. 1977, Goodman and Sours 1967, Greenspan 1981, Kessler 1966, McDonald 1965, Mishne 1983, Noshpitz 1979, Werkman 1965). Following is a list of types of data to gather. Some evaluations will be briefer than others and will thus obtain less information.

1. Identifying information
   a. Child's age, birthdate, grade in school, sex, race
   b. Parents' ages, birthdates, occupations, educational backgrounds, socioeconomic backgrounds
   c. Ages and relationship to child of siblings and others who live in the home
2. Referral information and presenting problems
   a. Referral source and nature of referral
   b. Description of presenting problems, with examples
   c. First appearance and history of problems
   d. Major precipitating factors
3. Description of child, parents, and other family members during interview
4. Current psychological status of child, including strengths and weaknesses
   a. Physiological status
      Physical appearance
      Vision and hearing
      Speech
      Overall health
      Physical difficulties
   b. Wishes, needs, and affects
      Predominant mood during interview
      Important wishes or needs
      Frustration tolerance
      Sources of anxiety
      Internal conflicts
      Other specific affects
      Methods of coping and defenses

Conscience
Values
c. Interpersonal relationships
Quality and style of interaction with parents, siblings, teachers, peers
Perceptions of these other people
Specific conflicts with other people and methods of coping with conflicts
Communication patterns
Activities with others
Empathy for others
d. Perceptions of self and identity
Dependence and autonomy
Gender identity
Sociocultural and religious identity
Interests
Aptitudes
Self-confidence and self-esteem
e. Cognitive functions
Thought processes
Perceptual processes
Perceptual-motor skills
Overall intellectual capacities
School achievement
Specific problems
f. Overall level of organization, integration, and rigidity
5. Developmental history
6. Parents and family
a. Personality functioning of each parent and siblings
b. Family structure and processes
c. Specific events in the life of the family
7. Other life circumstances
8. Formulation of problems
9. Treatment plan

Interview with Parents and Family

Therapists frequently interview parents before seeing a child individually in order to obtain data on the presenting problems, history of the problems, past methods of coping with the problems, strengths of the child, significant events in the life of the child, such as moves or a death, and physical problems or illnesses. It can also be useful at some point during an evaluation to gather information on discipline, supports for the child, history of the parents' relationship, sources of conflict within the family, ways of coping with conflict, strengths and weaknesses of each parent, and characteristics of other members of the family. Observation of the parents during contacts with them will reveal information about the nature of the parents' interaction, roles played by each, sources of conflict, ways of handling conflict, attitudes toward each other and toward the child, and the nature of supports for each other and for the child. It may be useful to interview each parent separately, especially if there is some indication that a parent is having difficulty talking openly in the presence of the other parent.

The first interview or interviews may suggest that the family difficulties are as important as the child's specific problems or that data on the family as a whole will enrich significantly the evaluation. In these cases an interview may be held with the entire family, including parents, children, and sometimes others living in the home or relatives outside the home. An interviewer may ask specific questions about the presenting problems, strengths and weaknesses of the family, roles of individuals in the family, nature and sources of conflict, ways of handling conflict, patterns of communication, support styles, and family activities. The interviewer will also observe actual interaction during the interview.

Preparing a Child for an Evaluation

Children are usually at least somewhat anxious about an evaluation. This anxiety may be enhanced by a vivid imagination about possible dangers. If the problems are urgent, such as in the case of a suicide attempt, there may be little time for preparation. However, at least some preparation can help to reduce anxiety to more tolerable levels. Therapists can help parents think about ways of preparing a child for the evaluation.

Understanding a child's ambivalence about obtaining help can be useful in talking to a child. Children are at least somewhat aware that certain aspects of their lives are not going well for them. They may, for example, be fearful, worry a lot, feel rejected by others, or be criticized for school work. They usually are aware that some aspects of their lives concern their parents or teachers. Obtaining help may provide some relief. However, the idea of receiving help may also be frightening. They may imagine that physical pain or increased psychological pain, such as rejection or criticism, will result.

Some parents and children discuss their concerns openly with each other. Parents sometimes sense a child's unhappiness and talk about it with the child. At other times a child may talk to a parent, for example, about being teased and left out by other children. In some families, conversations about problems lead to heated arguments, criticisms, or angry outbursts. In other families, issues are not discussed openly.

In any of these cases, discussion of the problems and ideas about seeking help should be presented as calmly as possible in language that is comfortable for a child. For the younger child, the ideas may be very concrete or simple, such as "You have been getting into a lot of fights" or "We feel bad that you are so unhappy so often." It is easier for young children when the discussions do not occur too far ahead of the actual appointment. A few days to a couple of weeks ahead is usually sufficient. Discussions with older children may be more complex and may occur over a longer period of time. Parents may try to obtain their child's interest in an evaluation, or they may decide to state firmly that they plan to go with their child for help.

Confidentiality

Whether the same therapist or different therapists interview the child and other members of the family, the issue of confidentiality must be considered. The child may wonder what has been told to the parents about him and about what he has said or done, and parents may wonder how much has been told to the child. When two or more interviewers work with the family, some discussion of confidential information occurs between them. Parents also usually want some feedback on the nature of their child's problems, and most mental health professionals believe that parents in most situations are entitled to some feedback. The most general guideline is to *provide parents with a summary of the major problems and dynamics of the problems within the context of the child's strengths without divulging specific pieces of information.* An interviewer can state this guideline to both parents and child. Many interviewers also state briefly to the child the major ideas that will be presented to parents.

It is possible to base discussions with parents upon the nature of information that they provide, using interviews with the child primarily as general guides both to the types of information to elicit from parents and to the nature of the child's problems. Parents frequently can describe a child's behavior, including conversations with the child, in enough detail so that the interviewer can use that detail as the basis for raising questions and providing feedback to the parents about the nature of the problems. Careful interviewing is important here. A parent, for example, may describe specific behaviors of a child that indicate depression; then describe significant strengths, such as good work in school, a close friendship, or specific hobbies; and then discuss some significant events, such as the recent death of a grandparent to whom the child was very close and several past family moves. Such information may provide enough information to parents to enhance their understanding of the problems. An interviewer in this case, for example, might state that the child is doing very well in many respects but is experiencing a rather severe depression following the death of the grandmother; he has had rather severe difficulties recovering from this separation because of several past separations and because of his tendency to react with depression following disappointments and separations.

It is frequently useful to obtain information from teachers, physicians, and others who have previously worked with a child. It may also be important to provide information about the evaluation to people who will be involved with whatever treatment is pursued. Most interviewers discuss this issue carefully with parents and children. States, communities, and agencies have laws or policies governing such release of information and specific guidelines for what must be stated on forms. Parents must sign a statement granting permission for this transfer of information to occur. It is now common and sometimes legally required that children be asked to sign these statements along with parents. When children refuse to sign, the therapist and parents can usually sign the form and release information if they believe that it is in the best interest of the child.

INDIVIDUAL INTERVIEWS WITH CHILDREN

General Philosophy and Style

Since it may be difficult or impossible to converse directly with a child, especially a very young child, the term *interview* is used broadly in work with children to refer to interactions with and observations of children (Glenn 1978, Greenspan 1981, Haworth 1964, Mishne 1983). The interactions may or may not include conversation. The purpose of such interviews is to learn as much as possible about the internal world and interactions of the child.

Sullivan's (1954) idea that the activity of the interviewer is "participant observation" is very relevant to work with children. As a participant, the interviewer must be aware of the child's potential and actual reactions to the interviewer and to the interview situation, respond in terms of these reactions, and help the child to feel comfortable, safe, and acceptable enough to reveal some important aspects of himself. The interviewer as a participant also experiences what it is like to be with this child and, in a limited way, what it is to be this child.

It is very important for an interviewer to know about communication styles and thought patterns of children of different ages with different cognitive capacities. Goodman and Sours (1967) recommend slow, concise, simple speech without too much direct questioning. They suggest statements such as the following: "All children are sometimes afraid; I wonder what things frighten you" or "Suppose someone were eating dinner in the evening with your family; what would he see?"

Some people change their tone of voice when talking to a very young child. This is not necessary and may sound patronizing or condescending to a child. Therapists must respect children in the same manner as they respect peers and convey this respect in the same way. Most interviewers of children keep some toys and drawing materials in the interview room. This equipment may be used primarily in the context of an unstructured play interview or may be available in more structured interviews in the event that a child feels more comfortable with the interviewer while using them.

Advantages and disadvantages of structured and unstructured interviews have been discussed at some length in the liteature (Goodman and Sours 1967, Greenspan 1981, Haworth 1964, McDonald 1965, Mishne 1983). In structured interviews, the interviewer provides specific stimuli. For younger children the stimuli may include concrete tasks with specific instructions, such as designs to be copied, paper and markers with which to draw a person or family, and puzzles and games. The structured stimuli for older and younger children may be specific questions. The idea behind unstructured interviews is that the less the therapist intrudes into or structures a situation, the more a child will project personal modes of action, feelings, and thoughts onto the situation, thus structuring the situation in a personal manner. Many interviews contain both structured and unstructured features.

Children's Fantasies about Assessment Interviews

Young children in particular, but all children in some ways, view adults and other aspects of the adult world as large, powerful, omniscient, unpredictable, and magical. They may view themselves as strong or weak, intelligent or stupid, controlling or controlled, vulnerable or invulnerable. They also in general view themselves, others, and the world as good or bad without making the kinds of more subtle discriminations that are made by many adults. These views all contribute to anxiety, worry, ambivalence, and hesitation about interviews.

Some children are especially afraid that the therapist will read their minds, find out about their weaknesses, and then attempt to control them. Other children are afraid that they are crazy, will be made to feel crazy, or will be driven crazy. Still other children are afraid of revealing "secrets" of either one or both parents or the family, about, for example, physical or sexual abuse, alcoholism, gambling, or psychiatric illnesses.

Probably the most intense and pervasive fears are of the exposure of personal weaknesses or "badness" and the resulting anxiety, embarrassment, shame, humiliation, guilt, criticism, punishment, anger, disapproval, and rejection. Young children in particular, but also many older children, react with very intense, unmodulated affects; sudden mood swings; and sudden drops in self-esteem during interviews. Such reactions may be "normal" responses in children, especially young children, to specific unpleasant stimuli, and may also occur in children with relatively minor as well as more severe problems.

Play Interviews

Interviews with children 10 years of age and younger frequently are conducted as play interviews. Play interviews may be very unstructured, with children using the play materials in their own way with only occasional comments or questions by the interviewer. Play interviews may also be partially unstructured and partially structured. Such interviews frequently begin in a totally unstructured manner, with the child allowed fairly free use of the materials. The interviewer then gradually begins to ask questions about worries, fears, dreams, friends, parents, siblings, school. Some of these questions can be woven into ongoing play, while other questions may be related very little if at all to the play but are raised during the play with the idea that the child may be more comfortable answering questions while occupied with more pleasant activities.

Some therapists watch the child but do not become involved in the actual play. Others follow the child's wishes and may or may not become involved in enacting stories or helping the child, depending on the child's wishes. Children vary in the amount and kind of talking that they do during play sessions. Their speech may be focused on the play or on other topics. Play equipment need not be elaborate but may include some or all of the following: wooden kindergarten blocks; small, flexible dolls used sometimes in dollhouses, consisting of mother, father, boy, girl, and baby, a baby doll, perhaps with anatomically correct genitalia; small cars and trucks; toy soldiers, cowboys and Indians; puppets; modeling clay; small toy guns; paper and markers.

The major idea underlying the use of play interviews is that children will project their key issues into the content of the play and into the ways in which they use the play materials. Children frequently do not have the language, concepts, or introspective capacity to put their feelings and thoughts into words, and they may hesitate to discuss their problems or more actively resist such discussions. However, children often use play to master their concerns. They may indirectly reveal fears, sources of anger, sexual concerns, guilt, and conflicts with parents through their play. Such capacities as intelligence, creativity, spontaneity, defenses, perceptual-motor skills, thought processes, organization, perceptions of self and others, and nature of interactional processes can be assessed through observation of play.

Conversational Interviews

Some children, especially those over 10 years of age but also some younger children, prefer conversation to play and will discuss a variety of topics with the interviewer. They may especially enjoy talking about pleasant, safe topics. Topics considered nonthreatening will vary with the child but may include play activities, interests, friends, classes in which they do well, and family outings.

Some children will discuss their problems, or some aspects of the problems, fairly spontaneously without direct questioning, especially if these problems have been discussed with parents in a relatively safe manner. Other children will provide clues about the problems in the context of talking about comfortable topics. The therapist can then begin raising questions about the problems in the context of the safer topics.

Many children have difficulty discussing specific aspects of the problems for which they have been referred because of embarrassment, shame, humiliation, guilt, specific fears, or more generalized anxiety. Aspects of the conversation or interaction with a child may provide enough clues about the nature of the problem so that direct questioning may be unnecessary. It is frequently useful, however, to probe gently into the subjects that evoke more intense anxiety.

Children through the ages of at least 10 or 12 years are not very introspective and do not engage in the type of abstract thought that is a basic part of psychological understanding. They may be able to label some feelings, describe dreams or play sequences, or tell about activities of friends and family members. Such discussions are often very concrete, with specific descriptions of activities or statements of simple feelings rather than more complex elaborations of feelings or thoughts. In giving feedback, it is useful to present simple, concrete thoughts, reflecting the child's words or thoughts as much as possible.

Interview Process

Some children accompany the therapist to the interview room fairly readily without a parent. Other children, especially very young children, are very hesitant about or resistant to parting from their parents. When this happens, the usual procedure is to talk to the child for a while in the waiting room and then invite the child again to go into the interview room. If the child remains very reluctant to leave the parent, most interviewers invite the parent to accompany the child to the interview room. The parent may leave the room at some point or may remain throughout the interview.

Some children easily initiate play, conversation, or other interaction with the therapist. When this happens, the therapist then decides how much, when, and in what ways to structure the interview. Other children are very inhibited in thought and action with the therapist and may say or do little. The therapist may remain quiet for a while. It then can be helpful to make a simple comment such as "I would like to get to know you a little bit in here" or "It is difficult to know what to do with this situation." Sometimes a simple statement about what is already known about the child from the parents or teacher or a simple question about what the child knows about why he is there will help to initiate interaction.

The therapist then usually follows the child's lead. The therapist may remain silent, make comments, or raise questions, keeping in mind the presenting problems and data obtained from other sources. The specific data that emerge will provide clues about the child's strengths and weaknesses and the nature of the problems. The interviewer should guide the interview enough to communicate some understanding, acceptance, and respect and to obtain a deeper understanding of the problems than the child or parent has.

One of the major questions raised by interviewers is how much freedom to allow a child during an interview. Interviewers may trigger intense affect, and many children act upon impulses quite freely. The most common guideline is to allow quite a bit of freedom but to stop behavior that is destructive of property; physically hurtful to the child, interviewer, or another person; evokes an abundance of anxiety in the child; or interferes with the rights of others. The control of such behavior may involve physically restraining a child or terminating an interview. However, a sensitive interviewer will often note signs of possible escalation of behavior before it occurs and will attempt to offer some calming comments.

Some children, on the other hand, are very inhibited during interviews. Sometimes it is possible with a few brief comments to help a child feel more comfortable. The child may remain very constricted, however. Even when a child says or does little in the examination room, there are clues about many facets of the child in his way of being with the therapist from the time of the first meeting to the end of the interview. Nonverbal behavior as well as brief verbal communications are important data. The establishment of a relationship is also more important than the amount of data gathered.

Since children have a different sense of time than adults and have difficulty with separations, it can be useful five to ten minutes before the end of an interview to mention the limited time available. Most therapists also request the child's help in picking up play equipment, although allowing the child some freedom to decline. At the end of the interview some therapists offer feedback to the child. Most therapists also briefly discuss the nature of further contacts with the child and parents.

Adjuncts to Play and Conversation

Drawings can be a rich source of data on a child. Many children spontaneously draw pictures during an interview. Other children readily draw when an examiner requests this. Koppitz (1968) and DiLeo (1973) have discussed ways in which drawings reveal information on intellectual capacities, personality characteristics, family relationships, social attitudes and behaviors, attitudes toward physical impairments, and specific perceptual-motor and other learning problems.

Beiser (1979) has discussed ways in which playing games with children can provide data on attitudes toward rules, ways of coping with winning and losing, impulsivity, dependent and independent behaviors, willingness to be taught, learning styles, risk-taking behavior, initiation of interaction, styles of interaction, and attitudes toward competition. Other techniques, such as the "mutual story-telling technique" (Gardner 1977) and the "squiggle game" (Winnicott 1971), have been described in the clinical literature. Such techniques may be especially useful in engaging more inhibited or resistant children.

Specialized Assessments

In the course of the evaluation, an interviewer may decide that more specialized evaluations or psychological testing will help in understanding problems more thoroughly. Referrals may then be made for evaluations of speech, language, perceptual-motor development, intellectual functioning, specific school problems, or physical disorders. Some evaluators will do psychological testing themselves; others refer the child to another psychologist for testing.

Infant Assessment

The body of literature on normal and pathological development in infancy and on infant assessment has been increasing in the past fifteen years (Brazelton 1973, 1980, Fraiberg 1980, Greenspan and Lieberman 1980, Noshpitz 1979c). Therapists typically rely heavily on interviews with parents in these assessments, but they also interact with and observe the infant. Such structured devices as the Brazelton Neonatal Behavioral Assessment (Brazelton 1973, 1980), the Bayley Scales of Infant Development, and the assessment categories developed by Greenspan and Lieberman (1980) provide structured techniques for assessing various aspects of infant development. Many interviewers also conduct more unstructured observations, based upon their interactions with the infant, the parent's caregiving and play activities with her infant, and the infant's use of various objects, including play equipment. The interviewer notes affects, social interaction, use of play equipment, initiation of activities, response to people and objects, use of sounds, feeding behavior, and perceptual-motor behavior.

Behavioral Assessment

Although much of the past literature on child assessment developed out of psychodynamic thought, behavioral assessment has been discussed more frequently over the past fifteen years (Mash and Terdal 1976, Patterson 1977, Ross and Ross 1976, Ross 1988). These assessments primarily focus on observable behavior but also include inferences about anxiety, fear, anger, interests, and standards of right and wrong. An evaluator may observe behavior in natural settings where it is a problem, such as school or home or in an office or clinic, using specific categories for observation.

Ross (1980) recommends that the assessment primarily involve parents. He uses an interview with parents but may also ask parents to use checklists or rating scales for assessing amounts and kinds of behavior in various situations. Ross also notes that interviews with a child can provide additional information. He does not advocate the use of a play interview, however, because it requires too many inferences. Interviews with teachers and teachers' use of checklist and rating scales are also part of the assessment.

FORMULATION OF PROBLEM AND TREATMENT PLANNING

Information from the evaluation must be interpreted and integrated to provide a deeper understanding of the presenting problems. This formulation should include statements about specific personality assets and deficits and ways in which they are related to the problems; severity of the problems; physiological, psychological, family, and sociocultural variables contributing to the development and maintenance of the problems; consequences of the problems for the child and family; and current means of coping with the problems.

The nature of the recommendations should flow from the formulation of the problems. Such recommendations might include one or more of the following: special classroom placement; remediation of specific learning problems; individual, group, parent, and/or family therapy; treatment of physical problems; hospitalization; and residential treatment.

It is important to provide adequate feedback to parents and child and to work with them around obtaining treatment. Some parents quickly understand and accept feedback and treatment recommendations and follow through with intervention on their own or with some help from the evaluator. It can be helpful with other parents to provide several interviews to describe the problems and treatment recommendations in a way that they can gradually understand and accept and to work more closely over an extended period of time with them in obtaining appropriate interventions.

CASE HISTORY

A 5-year-old boy was referred for a thorough evaluation after a month in a kindergarten class. The teacher described poor use of language, silly behavior, angry verbal outbursts and hitting, inability to sit still for more than a few minutes, refusal to do any work in the classroom, refusal to cooperate in other ways such as playing games on the playground or picking up after himself, and inappropriate interactions with other children. The parents reported similar problems at home as well. They said that he had been slow to develop from birth and had begun having temper tantrums very early. They had not had success in getting much cooperation from him. They thought he would outgrow some of this behavior. The parents were also concerned about birth defects, especially since he had been conceived when they were using contraceptive measures. Their pediatrician, however, had found no specific physical problems.

A speech and language evaluation revealed moderate difficulties in understanding language and more severe problems in using language. Psychological testing showed overall intellectual functioning in the low-average range, with verbal skills well below average and perceptual-motor skills above average.

Psychological testing and interviews suggested that this child felt very dependent upon his parents; became very anxious at being alone, in new situations, meeting expectations, or taking initiative; showed very disorganized thought processes; was easily angered; and acted readily on his angry impulses. He was able to get attention, avoid being alone, and evade expectations through silliness, clinginess, and angry, resistant, uncooperative behavior.

The parents had not wanted this child and were very unhappy about being "stuck" with a "defective" child. They alternated being extremely protective and gratifying and being very depriving and punitive. The parents also were experiencing intense marital conflicts, which frequently erupted into shouting matches in their son's presence.

The recommendations for this child included the following: placement in a special classroom for children with emotional problems and learning disabilities, speech therapy, individual play therapy, parent counseling, and marital therapy. The evaluator was able to work with the parents to obtain the school placement, with speech therapy to be conducted at the school. The child began play therapy with one therapist, who also occasionally met with the parents for parent counseling. The parents began marital therapy and parent counseling with another therapist. The two therapists coordinated their work with each other and with the teacher and therapist at the school.

Interviewing children is certainly different from interviewing adolescents or adults. Children think about, perceive, react to, and speak about themselves and the work in unique ways that may seem strange and unfamiliar to many adults, especially those who do not remember much about their own childhood or who have had little experience with children.

Children are usually brought for evaluation by others and thus frequently do not choose such an evaluation. Their anxiety and wishes to avoid the situation are frequently stronger than their wishes for help and may lead to withdrawal, inhibition, or aggressive actions that are strong resistances and may be difficult to surmount. When such actions are viewed as coping mechanisms for situations that evoke anxiety, however, rather than as resistances, they are easier to understand, tolerate, and handle in ways that have been suggested in this chapter. Mutual cooperation may develop slowly, however.

Children are quite influenced by their environments, especially home, school, and neighborhood. It is frequently difficult to understand and have an impact on the child unless work with the child is coordinated with work with the parents or family and sometimes also with the school or other groups that affect that particular child. Such work complicates therapeutic intervention.

Since issues in work with children differ from those in work with adults, it is important for clinicians to obtain specialized training in such work. It has been traditional in the past for most training programs to emphasize work with adults and to provide training for work with children as a subspecialty. In more recent years, some training programs are providing opportunities for study about and work with children that goes hand in hand with training for work with adults. It is also becoming more common for therapists to train primarily for work with children from the beginning of their studies.

Although work with children may be complex and difficult, it can also be very rewarding. Many children themselves are eager for a good relationship with an adult, especially when they begin to trust the adult, and may be relatively flexible, which enables them to change in important ways. It is gratifying to the therapist when these children go on to lead more meaningful lives than they might have without clinical intervention.

REFERENCES

American Psychiatric Association, Task Force on Nomenclature & Statistics (1980). *Diagnostic and Statistical Manual of Mental Disorders*, DSM III, 3rd ed. Washington, DC: APA.

Beiser, H. R. (1979). Formal games in diagnosis and therapy. *Journal of the American Academy of Child Psychiatry* 18:480–491.

Brazelton, T. B. (1973). *Neonatal behavioral assessment, National Spastic Society Monographs, Clinics in Developmental Medicine #50.* London: William Heinemann & Sons.

——— (1980). Neonatal assessment. In *The Course of Life: Psychoanalytic Contributions toward Understanding Personality Development: Infancy and Early Childhood*, vol. 1, ed. S. I. Greenspan and G. H. Pollock, pp. 203–233. Adelphi, MD: National Institute of Mental Health.

DiLeo, J. H. (1973). *Children's Drawings as Diagnostic Aids.* New York: Brunner/Mazel.

Eissler, R. S., Freud, A., Kris, M., and Solnit, A. J., eds. (1977). *An Anthology of the Psychoanalytic Study of the Child, Psychoanalytic Assessment: The Diagnostic Profile.* New Haven: Yale University Press.

Fraiberg, S. (1980). *Clinical Studies in Infant Mental Health.* New York: Basic Books.

Gardner, R. A. (1977). Mutual storytelling technique. In *Psychiatric Treatment of Children*, ed. J. F. McDermott and S. I. Harrison, pp. 187–200. New York: Jason Aronson.

Glenn, J., ed. (1978). *Child Analysis and Therapy.* New York: Jason Aronson.

Goodman, J. D., and Sours, J. A. (1967). *The Child Mental Status Examination.* New York: Basic Books.

Greenspan, S. I. (1981). *The Clinical Interview of the Child.* New York: McGraw-Hill.

Greenspan, S. I., and Lieberman, A. (1980). Infants, mothers, and their interaction: a quantitative clinical approach to developmental assessment. In *The Course of Life: Psychoanalytic Contributions toward Understanding Personality Development: Infancy and Early Childhood*, vol. 1, ed. S. I. Greenspan and G. H. Pollock, pp. 271–312. Adelphi, MD: National Institute of Mental Health.

Harrison, S. I., and McDermott, J. F., eds. (1980). *New Directions in Childhood Psychopathology: Developmental Considerations*, vol. 1. New York: International Universities Press.

Haworth, M. R., ed. (1964). *Child Psychotherapy.* New York: Basic Books.

Kessler, J. (1966). *Psychopathology of Childhood.* Englewood Cliffs, NJ: Prentice-Hall.

Koppitz, E. M. (1968). *Psychological Evaluations of Children's Human Figure Drawings.* New York: Grune & Stratton.

Mash, E. J., and Terdal, L. G., eds. (1976). *Behavior Therapy Assessment: Diagnosis, Design, and Evaluation.* New York: Springer.

McDonald, M. (1965). The psychiatric evaluation of children. *Journal of the American Academy of Child Psychiatry* 4:569–612.

Mishne, J. M. (1983). *Clinical Work with Children.* New York: The Free Press.

Noshpitz, J. D., ed. (1979a). *Basic Handbook of Child Psychiatry: Development,* vol. 1. New York: Basic Books.

——— (1979b). *Basic Handbook of Child Psychiatry: Disturbances in Development,* vol. 2. New York: Basic Books.

——— (1979c). *Basic Handbook of Child Psychiatry: Therapeutic Interventions,* vol. 3. New York: Basic Books.

Patterson, G. R. (1977). Naturalistic observation in clinical assessment. *Journal of Abnormal Child Psychology* 5:309–322.

Ross, A. O. (1980). *Psychological Disorders of Children.* New York: McGraw-Hill.

Ross, D. M., and Ross, S. A. (1976). *Hyperactivity: Research, Theory, and Action.* New York: Wiley.

Sperling, M. (1982). *The Major Neuroses and Behavior Disorders in Children.* New York: Jason Aronson.

Sullivan, H. S. (1954). *The Psychiatric Interview.* New York: W. W. Norton.

Werkman, S. L. (1965). The psychiatric diagnostic interview with children. *American Journal of Orthopsychiatry* 35:764–771.

Winnicott, D. W. (1971). *Therapeutic Consultations in Child Psychiatry.* New York: Basic Books.

Witmer, H. L., ed. (1964). *Psychiatric Interviews with Children.* New York: Commonwealth Fund.

18
The Forensic Interview

J. REID MELOY, Ph.D.

In 1924, the lord chancellor of England said, "Psychology is a most dangerous science to apply to practical affairs" (Overholser 1953, p. 109). Nowhere is this more apparent than in the forensic arena, through which the psychologist walks an invited, but not necessarily sanctified, guest. The dangers to the professional, moreover, in such an adversarial and public system are legion, yet the opportunities are challenging and exciting; a colleague of mine called forensic psychology the only true "contact sport" in the behavioral sciences.

The heart of forensic psychology is the forensic interview: a clinical interview conducted in the context of a legal process, or pertaining to a psychologal question. This chapter will present the six distinguishing characteristics of the forensic interview. A focus on the core dimensions of the forensic interview naturally leads to thoughts about specific knowledge, skills, attitudes, approaches, and techniques that the psychologist can apply to the forensic interview to make the final product worthy of his and others' approbation.

THE COERCIVE CONTEXT

The term *forensic* is derived from the Latin *forensis*, meaning "the forum" (Webster 1977). The forum is commonly understood as a public, or legal, forum; hence the application of the term to describe those professionals who practice in a legal context, whether they be psychologists, psychiatrists, or even dentists—so-called forensic odontologists. Inherent in this forensic context is the element of coercion, the first core characteristic that distinguishes forensic interviews from other interviews. Complete voluntariness should never be assumed. Rather, it should be assumed that the interviewee is being either partially or completely forced to do something against his will.

The element of coercion is often obvious. A criminal defendant's attorney recognizes that his client can neither cooperate with him nor understand the nature of the proceedings against him. The attorney therefore enters a motion for his client to be evaluated to determine whether he is competent to stand trial (*Dusky* v. *United States*). The defendant, by virtue of the case and statutory law surrounding procedures to determine competency to stand trial, can refuse the evaluation only if he is willing to risk being held in contempt of court (Melton et al. 1987). Yet his Fifth Amendment right against compulsory self-incrimination is also protected if he should give evidence during the competency evaluation that further incriminates him. Even though a competency motion granted by the court usually benefits the defense due to a complete suspension of the criminal proceedings, a seriously mentally disordered defendant, perhaps with a paranoid delusional system, would probably irrationally, but strenuously, resist answering questions in a forthright manner. One defendant who was brought to me for a competency evaluation while in custody angrily accused me of being a "schoolworm." Intrigued by his neologism, I asked him what it meant. He replied, "an educated person trying to worm his way into my mind." He was clearly schizophrenic, but he was also right.

A more subtle form of coercion may be present in a civil custody dispute. A mother of a 4-year-old daughter accuses her ex-husband of violating certain visitation terms in the divorce decree. A psychologist is appointed by the court to evaluate the situation and make recommendations to the court. The forensic psychologist, seasoned to the inherent distortions that occur in custody disputes, insists that he evaluate each member of the psychological family, both individually and as a unit, including the individual parents' new live-in companions. The mother, who initiated the new proceedings through her attorney in the hope of reducing her ex-husband's visitation, is now in the uncomfortable position of being interviewed by a psychologist and probably completing certain psychological tests. To her relief, she is initially asked only about her parenting attitudes and beliefs, but she suddenly feels coerced and invaded when the psychologist, with little introduction, presents her with an ambiguous inkblot and asks her, "What might this be?" She consequently produces an invalid Rorschach protocol—too few responses and too many pure F responses.

Coercion may also be an internally perceived process, such as the case of the paranoid schizophrenic who is compelled by his command hallucinations to confess a murder. Such intrapsychic coercion, although recently not recognized by the US Supreme Court as a legal basis for compulsory self-incrimination (*Colorado* v. *Connelly*), may still be quite clinically salient to the forensic interview.

How should the forensic interviewer respond to this ubiquitous core characteristic? First, this question should be considered prior to the evaluation: What are the legal and clinical factors in this particular interview that could be perceived as coercive? Second, once these factors are identified, the clinician should consider the ways in which coercion will affect the interview. One of the major ways is through malingering or dissembling (concealment) of symptoms, a separate core characteristic which I will consider later. Third, the clinician should tailor the interview to minimize the impact of the coercive factors: (1) Conduct the interview in a neutral setting if at all possible—evaluations in custody settings *must* be done in a private soundproof interview room, although security personnel may insist, for good reason, that they be able to visually observe the interview; (2) ask that the interviewee not be physically restrained during the interview unless there is an imminent risk to your safety, which there may be; (3) inquire about the reasons for restraints before requesting their removal; and (4) discuss your speculations about the coercive elements of the interview directly and empathically with the interviewee. This brief, but frank, discussion will help establish rapport without misleading the interviewee, and should predict the extent to which the evaluation will be reliable and valid.

> A female superior court judge had been verbally threatened by a defendant, now in custody, and asked me to evaluate him. Supported by civil and case law (*Tarasoff* v. *Regents of Univ. of California*), I agreed.
>
> The defendant was brought to me while in custody. He sat and glowered at me, remaining mute. I explained to him the nature of my interview and made several empathic statements concerning the obvious coercion he must be feeling. He stared at me. I then asked him that if he understood my statements but was voluntarily choosing not to answer me, he should nod his head. He did. I then told him that if he wanted to end our brief encounter, he should nod his head. He did. The deputy escorted him, at my request, back to his cell.

All criminal defendants should be allowed an opportunity to consult with counsel before they participate in a forensic psychological interview. This protects the defendant's Sixth Amendment right to counsel, it shields the psychologist from inadvertently giving legal "advice" concerning the defendant's choice to participate in the interview, and it may attenuate the felt coercion during the interview. In civil proceedings, such as personal injury and custody cases, a right to consult with counsel is usually a moot issue since no criminal process is involved and both parties have usually retained their own counsel prior to any request for a psychological interview.

THE ABSENCE OF PRIVILEGE

Mental health professionals are ethically trained to value and protect the confidentiality of patient care and its written products. The legal correlate of confidentiality—privileged communication—is also considered an essential right held by the patient. In forensic interviews, however, there is virtually always a partial or complete waiver of privilege. This is often quite unsettling to the clinician first entering the forensic arena because it jostles his heretofore sanctified belief in the inviolate nature of the patient–therapist relationship. It also brings with it a "fishbowl effect": The professional's behavior with patients is no longer as insulated as he would like it to be. Forensic interviewing is no place for narcissistically sensitive clinicians who feel entitled to privacy in their work.

The nature and degree of waivers of privilege are quite variable. Criminal defendants entering a plea of not guilty by reason of insanity (NGRI) automatically waive all privilege since they are introducing their mental state at the time of the alleged crime as a complete defense. The court forces a partial waiver of privilege when it finds a reasonable doubt that a criminal defendant is competent to stand trial, even if the prosecution enters the motion; yet the forensic examination is limited to evaluation of the defendant's psychological processes relevant only to his competency, and incriminating evidence uncovered during the examination is protected. Depending on the jurisdiction, clinicians retained by the defense in a criminal trial and then subsequently not used as experts may or may not be called as witnesses by the prosecution (*United States ex. rel. Edney* v. *Smith*; *United States* v. *Alvarez*). The judicial rule of thumb in most criminal litigation is a balancing of the individual's rights to privileged communication and the public safety.

In civil litigation, waiver of privilege is often carefully controlled by the court. California, for example, established a constitutional basis for privileged communication between therapist and patient when it wrote, in part,

> We believe that a patient's interest in keeping such confidential revelations from public purview, in retaining this substantial privacy, has deeper roots than the California statute and draws sustenance from our constitutional heritage. . . . [U]nder a properly limited interpretation, the litigant–patient exception to the psychotherapist–patient privilege . . . does not unconstitutionally infringe the constitutional rights of privacy of either psychotherapists or psychotherapeutic patients. . . . [W]e point out, however, because of the potential invasion of patients' constitutional interests, trial courts should properly and carefully control compelled disclosures in this area in light of accepted principles [*In re Lifschutz*].

How should the forensic interviewer respond to this core characteristic? First, therapists should be thoroughly familiar with their jurisdiction's penal code, civil code, and evidence code concerning privileged communication. There may be contradictions among these codes, and subsequent case law may have been written to clarify or delineate the nature and extent of privilege in certain representative cases.

Second, the clinician should be quite familiar with his profession's code of ethics, and should ponder potential areas of conflict in a particular case between his profession's ethical principles and his jurisdiction's settled law. For example, the American Psychological Association states that psychologists have an ethical responsibility to "avoid undue invasion of privacy" (principle 5, American Psychological Association 1981). However, ethical principles generally carry little weight in court.

Third, the legal context of a particular case, and its impact upon privilege, should be thoroughly assessed and understood before the forensic interview. A legal consultation with an attorney *knowledgeable in this area of law* may be quite propitious.

Fourth, at the beginning of the interview, forensic clinicians should spend as much time as needed to explain to the interviewee *who* they are, *what* they are doing, *why* they are doing it, *how* they are going to do it, *what* will be produced, and *where* the product will be used. The interviewee must be fully informed. I might conduct this portion of the interview as follows:

> Hello, Mr. Smith. My name is Doctor Reid Meloy. I am a psychologist hired by your attorney [who] to meet with you this afternoon. I am here to learn as much as I can about you, and the crime you are charged with [what]. As you know, the reason I am here is that you and your attorney are considering an insanity defense. This means that because of a mental disorder at the time of the crime, you were not responsible for your behavior [why]. Any questions?
>
> I will be talking with you and asking you lots of questions. You do not have to answer any of them, and can ask me to repeat or clarify any questions you don't understand. I'll also be asking you to fill out some questionnaires, and I may ask you to respond to certain objects, drawings, or pictures that I'll show you [how]. Any questions?
>
> When we're finished, I will be thinking about everything you've told me and studying all the other information I've received from your attorney. Then I will write a report [what]. This report, which I expect to have finished one week from today, will be sent only to your attorney. But if you do plead insanity, my report will go to the court, the judge, and the district attorney, the prosecutor [where]. I can then be forced to testify truthfully and completely about anything you've told me or any opinions that I've formed. Any questions? Do you understand? Can you tell me briefly what I've told you so I know you understand?

The disclosure of such information, although it appears tedious, is generally expected behavior in forensic interviews. It is consonant with ethical principle 6, wherein psychologists must "fully inform consumers as to the purpose and nature of an evaluative . . . procedure" (American Psychological Association 1981), and with recent case law (*Estelle* v. *Smith*).

The doctrine of informed consent is not as germane to a forensic interview as it is to treatment, since most forensic evaluations are court-ordered. However, the clinician should be sensitive to the possible need for informed consent prior to a forensic interview, and should seek it in writing if necessary. Three elements are considered to determine whether informed consent has been obtained: (1) the adequacy of disclosure from both the clinician's and the patient's perspective, (2) the patient's competency to give consent, and (3) the voluntariness of the consent (*Salgo* v. *Leland Stanford Jr. Univ. Bd. of Trustees*; Grisso 1986). Informed consent is more likely to be a requirement in civil work (personal injury, family, and custody cases) than in criminal work.

A LAY COMMUNICATION TOOL

Unlike other mental health interviews, the forensic interview is essentially a means to gather information that can then be communicated to non–mental health professionals. The product of the forensic interview, whether it be a written report or an oral testimony, is only valuable if it is understandable to educated lay professionals, usually attorneys and judges. The clarity, simplicity, and thoroughness of the work product will not only determine its usefulness in a particular case, but will either enhance or discredit the forensic clinician's reputation. In no other mental health specialty is one's "paper trail" more important to professional standing in the community. Even if the report does not become a matter of public record, it may be exhumed years later in another legal matter concerning the same individual. The forensic report, and to a lesser degree forensic testimony, is the legacy of the forensic psychologist.

Clarity means that written and oral communication about the forensic interview is free of technical jargon, or, if technical terms are necessary, that they be carefully defined throughout the report or testimony. For instance, hallucinations are consistently defined as "false sensations" and delusions are defined as "fixed and false beliefs."

Simplicity means that any individual of average intelligence can understand what the report means. This is a measure of external validity, or utility. It is the mandate that one must expose one's ideas and opinions to their reflections in the variously shaped mirrors of others (Gill 1967). Projection as a psychological defense, for instance, can be simply understood as the attribution of one's thoughts and feelings to others. If the psychological concept is too esoteric or complex, it is useless in the forensic context. It may be ambiguous to begin with, or it just may need to be further analyzed, or broken down, for intelligible consumption. Forensic communication requires disciplined and analytic thought, often anathema to clinicians who are trained only to be synthetic and empathic.

Thoroughness means that every issue is explored if it is relevant to the forensic issue being addressed. Forensic interviewing usually requires additional corroboration of the data gleaned from the interview. Nothing discredits a forensic clinician more than the mere regurgitation of the interviewee's perspective in the report or through testimony. It is evidence of the clinician's laziness and naivete, and may be very embarrassing if easily contradicted by information that was available but was not sought.

How should the forensic psychologist manage the forensic interview as a means of lay communication? First, the forensic interviewer's writing and oratory skills should be reasonably good. Close attention may need to be paid to enhancing one's writing skills; much can be gained from reading Strunk and White's *Elements of Style* (1979). Second, forensic report writing should be addressed as a specialized skill through some excellent available texts (Blau 1984, Curran et al. 1986, Melton et al. 1987, Rogers 1986, Shapiro 1984). Most forensic reports, regardless of legal context, should include the following content, in this sequence:

1. Legal reason for evaluation
2. Complete database used in the evaluation
3. History of defendant/patient
4. Clinical observations during interview(s)
5. Mental status examination

6. Interpretation of psychological testing
7. DSM-III-R diagnosis
8. Clinical findings
9. Clinical opinion
10. Recommendations

Third, note taking during the forensic interview should be sufficient to ensure the reliability and validity of the interview, and may be protected as the clinician's "work product." Test protocols and answer sheets may be sought by attorneys for either side, however, despite the clinician's ethical obligation to protect such data (principle 8, American Psychological Association 1981). Although case law in this specific area has not developed, the forensic psychologist should refuse to turn over any "raw data," such as test answer sheets, protocols, and the like, except to another qualified individual, usually a clinician retained by the other side. Psychiatrists are generally not qualified to interpret raw psychological test data unless they have specialized training, and may be functioning outside their areas of competency by attempting to do so. It has been my experience that if the court orders the raw data to be produced through *subpoena duces tecum*, a letter to the court accompanying the data, explaining the ethical violation of such conduct on the part of the psychologist and requesting that the court turn over the data to another qualified psychologist retained by the other side, will suffice in protecting this important professional privilege (*People* v. *Laws*).

If this argument fails, it may be useful to distinguish for the court the difference between the psychologist's "work product" (notes, scoring, interpretations) and the interviewee's "raw psychological test data" (answer sheets, drawings, projective responses). Dr. Sherry Skidmore (personal communication) has suggested that a set of *unscored* answer sheets and responses sent to the opposing psychologist can be a useful way of demarcating "work product" from "raw data," since a *scored* Rorschach protocol, for example, is a combination of both raw data from the patient and "work" done by the psychologist. Unscored and uninterpreted data also protect the patient (ethical principle 8, American Psychological Association 1981).

Fourth, the forensic interviewer should strive to be both an empiricist and a humanist in his communication to others concerning a particular case: The presentation, whether oral testimony or formal report, should be a complete behavioral science document, but should also communicate an *experiential feel* for the interviewee. This is the science *and* the art of forensic psychological communication.

DISTORTION

The fourth core characteristic of the forensic interview is the conscious distortion of information provided during the evaluation. This is a direct outgrowth of the first core characteristic, coercion, but is also spawned by the general presence of external factors that would be considered "secondary gain" in most forensic settings, such as monetary settlements, movement to a less restrictive level of care (prison to hospital), or mitigation of a criminal offense.

Although there are a wide variety of forms of distortion, I will limit this discussion to conscious, willful distortion by the interviewee. Other forms of distortion that have more symbolic and unconscious meanings, such as factitious disorder, must be clinically ruled out in forensic evaluations, but they are not as prevalent as intentional distortion. This core characteristic *must be assumed to exist* in all forensic interviews until it is disproven.

Distortion in the interview usually takes one of two forms: *simulation* (malingering), which is the feigning of symptoms that do not exist; and *dissimulation* (dissembling), which is the concealment or minimization of symptoms that actually do exist. Other combinations are possible. Garner (1965) defined pure malingering as the feigning of disease where none exists; partial malingering as the conscious exaggeration of symptoms that do exist; and false imputation as the ascribing of actual symptoms to a cause consciously recognized as having no relationship to the symptoms.

Although dissimulation is not mentioned in DSM-III-R, simulation is termed *malingering*, and is defined as "the intentional production of false or grossly exaggerated physical or psychological symptoms, motivated by external incentives . . ." (p. 360). It should be strongly suspected in any medicolegal setting if any combination of the following are noted: marked discrepancy between claimed symptoms and objective findings, lack of cooperation during the diagnostic evaluation, and a diagnosis of antisocial personality disorder. This "suspicion index" would also apply to dissimulation.

How should the forensic clinician respond to the core characteristic of distortion? Prior to any forensic evaluation, whether civil or criminal, one should construct the hypothesis that *distortion will be present in this evaluation.* Once this particular perspective is taken, *disproving* this hypothesis then becomes the clinical task. In order to accomplish this task, the clinician must be familiar with the research literature on simulation and dissimulation (Adelman and Howard 1984, Gorman 1984, Resnick 1984, Rogers 1984a). Rogers (1984a) constructed both heuristic and empirical models of malingering and deception, and I have adapted and combined them in Table 18–1.

All indicators have heuristic support among a group of experienced forensic clinicians that Rogers (1984a) surveyed. This table also covers the three data sources for the clinician to consider in determining whether an interviewee is distorting: the clinical interview, psychological testing, and independent corroborative information. A judgment of distortion should not be made without consideration of all three data sources, if available.

The clinical interview's contribution to the distortion hypothesis can be viewed from the dual perspective of observation and intervention.

Table 18-1. Clinical Indicators of Distortion

Indicators	Response styles		
	Reliable	Simulated	Dissimulated
1. Severity of symptoms	variable	severe	minimal
2. Selectivity of reporting symptoms	selective	overendorsement	underendorsement
3. Consistency of self-report	consistent	consistent	consistent
4. Contradictory symptoms	unlikely	likely	unlikely
5. Rare symptoms	unlikely	likely	unlikely
6. Sequence of symptoms	consistent with diagnosis	inconsistent	inconsistent
7. Obvious v. subtle symptoms	balanced	more obvious	more subtle
8. Appearance of symptoms	gradual onset and resolution	sudden onset	sudden resolution
9. Memory of past psychological problems	normal memory	heightened memory of impairment	heightened memory of adjustment
10. Potentially self-damaging statements	likely	unlikely	unlikely
11. Random response pattern	no	unlikely	no
12. Self-report inconsistent with clinical observation	no	unlikely	likely
13. Endorsement of highly specified symptoms	unlikely	likely	unlikely

Adapted by permission of Van Nostrand Reinhold, from Rogers, 1984a. Underlines denote indicators that are empirically supported in the literature (a five-year search of Psych Abstracts, PsyInfo, and NCMHI databases).

Observations of an individual attempting to distort or deceive find direction in the following research conclusions: Increased body movements and postural shifts are more indicative of deception than is facial expression (Ekman and Friesen 1969, McClintock and Hunt 1975, Rogers 1984a); visual clues serve more as a distraction than as a facilitation in the detection of deception (Littlepage and Pineault 1978, Rogers 1984a); verbal content is a primary determinant in the detection of deception (Maier and Thurber 1968, Rogers 1984a); intuitive assumptions concerning an individual's veracity may lead to misjudgments in the face of actual honesty or dishonesty (Zuckerman et al. 1979); and clinical research of distortion in psychiatric populations is extremely important, but very limited (Rogers 1984a).

Interventions during the clinical interview to ferret out distortion include: purposeful lengthening of the interview to induce fatigue; varying the pace and speed of questioning; confrontation of the interviewee with the suspicion that he is distorting; repeat questioning with sufficient time and interference to increase the difficulty of remembering prior deceptions; suggesting the need for 24-hour hospitalization to thoroughly assess the clinical situation (and sometimes carrying out the suggestion); in criminal settings, evaluating the defendant as soon as possible after the crime was committed; avoidance of leading or suggestible questions about symptoms; using open-ended questions to inquire about symptoms (for example, "Can you describe to me what it's like to be depressed?"); intentionally mixing symptoms from various diagnostic categories that are usually mutually excludable (for example, "Do you ever have auditory or visual hallucinations right after you've had a drink of alcohol?"); linking preposterous or fantastic symptoms to complaints ("Have you noticed a change in your hat or glove size since you started hearing the voices?"); purposefully inducing stress ("I don't want you to be anxious about what I'm going to ask next"); and expanding on details at random without following a detectable order or sequence. I always try to present myself as an "ambiguous stimulus" to the interviewee, especially at the beginning of the evaluation, after the initial legal and ethical introductions. This minimizes clues to which the interviewee can consciously adapt if he is planning a distortion strategy. If he is not planning to distort, his initial presentation should be quite reliable and valid without needing me to provide the antecedents for his behavior.

Thorough knowledge of the nature and expression of certain commonly feigned symptoms is also very important. Hallucinations, for instance, are a troublesome symptom in a forensic setting because they cannot be absolutely disproved or objectively measured. Yet clinical research has given the clinician a wealth of information about hallucinations, particularly in schizophrenia: Command hallucinations are experienced by only a small proportion (less than 20 percent of schizophrenic patients (Hellerstein et al. 1987) and are successfully resisted by most patients who hear them (Goodwin et al. 1971). Command hallucinations do not significantly increase the risk of inpatient violence (Hellerstein et al. 1987). Hallucinations are usually accompanied by delusions, and are usually related to some psychic purpose (Resnick 1984). Voices speaking directly to the patient or commenting on his behavior are characteristic of schizophrenia, but are less easily discussed than alcohol-induced hallucinations (Alpert and Silvers 1970, Resnick 1984). Schizophrenic hallucinations are usually intermittent, and rarely continous (Goodwin et al. 1971). The majority of schizophrenic patients, when asked if their hallucinations could be a product of their imagination, will say yes (Goodwin et al. 1971). Most auditory hallucinations will be heard "outside" the head and will contain both male and female voices (Goodwin et al. 1971). The message is usually clear, and is accusatory about one-third of the time (Goodwin et al. 1971). Hallucinating patients should also be asked what they do to make the voices go away. Common coping strategies include specific activities, changes in posture, seeking out others, or taking medication (Resnick 1984).

> Patient A complained of continuous auditory hallucinations telling him to kill his sister. He was absolutely sure that the voices were a product of his schizophrenia, which he gladly talked about with any clinician. He said that they were always "inside" his head, especially when one of the clinicians suggested that this location of hallucinations was "much more serious" than if they occurred "outside" his head. He had not thought of any strategies to alleviate the "voices." The clinical staff concluded that he was malingering (simulating) the symptom of auditory hallucinations, and his motivation to deceive became a focus of treatment.

The use of psychological tests to ferret out distortions in a forensic setting is the second source of data to be considered by the clinician. It is beyond the scope of this chapter to review all of the psychological tests commonly used to detect distortion, so instead I will briefly comment on two of the most widely used tests: the Minnesota Multiphasic Personality Inventory (MMPI) and the Rorschach.

Self-report measures in criminal populations are inherently unreliable (Hare 1985a). Yet the MMPI should be considered the clinician's "workhorse" in adult forensic interviews due to the enormous amount of research available concerning its clinical use, and the sensitivity of its various indicators of distortion.

The most commonly used indicator of distortion, whether simulation (fake bad) or dissimulation (fake good) is the configuration of the validity scales L, F, and K. Since the early work of Hunt (1948) and Gough (1950), the F-K index has been confirmed as a reliable indicator of distortion (Greene 1980, Osborne et al. 1986, Rogers 1984a).

The Wiener (1948) Subtle-Obvious items on five scales of the MMPI also appear to be especially useful in forensic settings. A difference of greater than 1 standard deviation between the subtle and obvious items on any one of the scales should alert the clinician to the possibility of simulation or dissimulation around the particular symptom complex measured by the scale, depending on the direction of the difference (subtle items greater than obvious items suggests dissimulation; obvious items greater than subtle items suggests simulation). Rogers (1983) noted, however, that specific indicators of randomness should be measured before distortion conclusions are drawn from the Wiener-Harmon subscales. He suggested the use of the Carelessness Scale (Greene 1978) and the Test-Retest Scale (Buechley and Ball 1952) to rule out random responding.

The Rorschach remains the second most widely used psychological test (Piotrowski et al. 1985) by members of the Society for Personality Assessment (SPA), and it is popular with other clinicians as well (Lubin et al. 1984). The Comprehensive Scoring System (Exner 1986) is gaining in use and was preferred by more than one-third of the SPA members who responded to Piotrowski and colleagues' (1985) survey.

Controversy surrounds the vulnerability of the Rorschach to distortion. Albert and co-workers (1980) found that a group of untrained subjects could successfully simulate paranoid schizophrenia and fool a group of expert clinicians who were given their Rorschachs. This study has been critiqued, however, for its small sample size (six subjects in each group), blind analyses, and unknown methods of scoring (Exner 1978, Ziskin 1984). Exner (1978) and others (Seamons et al. 1981) found that standardized administration and scoring of Rorschach protocols did allow for respectable discrimination between faked and genuinely psychotic Rorschach protocols. Albert and colleagues' (1980) study has yet to be replicated using Exner's (1986) Comprehensive System of scoring.

The heart of Rorschach distortion appears to lie in the difference between content and structural analysis. Both Exner (1978) and Seamons and associates (1981) noted that the layperson's idea of "faking psychosis" is to give dramatic and fantastic content responses. Blind content analysis of such data would be misleading in the absence of other behavioral data. Structural analysis of the same protocol would probably yield nonpsychotic indices, however, since these would be much more difficult to compute and distort, even with prior knowledge of their meaning. In the Exner (1986) system, such indices as X+%, X−%, and Special Scores, as indicators of reality convergence, reality distortion, and cognitive slippage, respectively, would be very difficult to intentionally distort.

I would suggest that interpretation of the Rorschach in a forensic setting begin with the Comprehensive System (Exner 1986) to determine whether the protocol is valid, with a particular focus upon number of responses and lambda (see Meloy 1988 for Rorschach criteria with psychopathic individuals). The Exner (1986) scoring is also the most defensible in court due to the extensive empirical studies that have been done. Once validity has been established, content analysis of the Rorschach can then proceed so that certain object relational and psychodynamic patterns are fully apprehended. I think this multidimensional analysis of the Rorschach is most revealing and useful in forensic settings (Meloy 1988). My clinical experience suggests that the best way to "beat" the Rorschach is to refuse to take the test, but this behavior is also diagnostically and behaviorally revealing.

The third source of data to be considered in distortion is collaborative information on the individual. This source is crucial to disproving the distortion hypothesis and should be aggressively pursued by the forensic examiner. One very useful forensic instrument, the Hare Psychopathy Checklist (Hare 1980), a trait measure of psychopathic disturbance completed by the forensic clinician, has *greater* reliability and validity when based upon only corroborative information than when based upon only the clinical interview (Hare 1985b).

The following behaviors are useful in increasing the amount of available corroborative information: Obtain all records on the patient (school, medical, psychiatric, psychological, criminal history, arrest, prosecution, defense, archival court, and so on) and read them before the examination; meet with the patient at least twice, and consider administering some tests twice, to measure temporal reliability; audio- or videotape the evaluation, always with the patient's permission, and review it later; conduct collateral interviews, using the efficiency of the telephone to do so; and gather data on the patient in as "naturalistic" a manner as possible. The latter method might include observing the patient approaching and leaving the office; observing the patient's interactions with others; asking the secretary about the individual's behavior in the waiting room; or visiting the individual's home (or jail module) for a portion of the evaluation. It can also be useful at the end of the evaluation for the clinician to lay paper and pencil down, sit back, and ask the patient, "Now, is there anything else you'd like to tell me?" The obvious nonverbal clues here suggest to the patient that the clinician may be receptive to some "off the record" comments, without his actually saying so. It is a misleading, and some would consider deceptive, gesture, but it may yield important new information.

When evaluating for criminal responsibility, it is especially important to talk to individuals who observed the defendant just prior to, during, or right after the offense. The reconstruction of an offense is central to the task of inferring the defendant's state of mind, and therefore criminal responsibility, in all insanity evaluations (Rogers 1986).

DISAGREEMENT AND SCRUTINY

Regardless of the clarity, simplicity, and thoroughness of the work product of the forensic interview (oral testimony or written report), it will usually be disliked and disparaged by half of the individuals privy to it. This is the nature of the adversarial system wherein the two sides of any legal question advocate as strongly as possible for their opposite positions. The judicial hope is that the trier of fact, whether judge or jury, will then be better able to discern the truth.

The forensic clinician must steel herself to this adversarial reality, being careful not to personalize and feel narcissistically insulted by disagreements from "the other side." It is less usual to have both legal counsels stipulate to (accept) the forensic "work product," and this most commonly happens when the forensic psychologist is appointed as *amicus curiae* (friend of the court) to conduct the evaluation. Such consensual gifts are the exception, not the rule.

Disagreement by opposing counsel is therefore accompanied by careful scrutiny of the work product to ferret out mistakes; such errors of omission or commission during the forensic interview then serve as points of attack during cross-examination if the case goes to trial.

Such disagreement and scrutiny is the fifth distinguishing core characteristic of the forensic interview. How should the forensic clinician prepare for this core characteristic? *Most fundamentally, forensic clinicians should advocate for their data and interpretations based only upon sound scientific reasoning.* This should take precedence over all personal philosophy, political views, social reformist ideals, and therapeutic goals for the patient. The forensic interview is not the place to develop a social advocacy or psychotherapy treatment plan for the interviewee. This principle is most easily followed when the clinician is appointed by the court, but it presents major difficulties when he is retained by counsel and the forensic interview findings are not what counsel wants. He will likely seek another examiner, reluctantly pay the clinician's bill, and not call him again. This may be quite economically damaging in the short run, but in the long run will build the clinician's reputation among attorneys and judges as a professional that *cannot be bought.* It takes great integrity and resolve to maintain a neutral, behaviorally scientific position in an adversarial system that is continuously attempting to distort the facts and findings of every scientific investigator and may initially punish by not referring more cases.

Moreover, the ability to successfully advocate for a forensic database depends upon the reliability and validity of the content of the database. Certain steps can be taken to ensure that the forensic interview is both reliable and valid.

First, attorneys should be excluded from observing or participating in most forensic interviews. The one exception may be during an evaluation for competency to stand trial, when the interactions between the attorney and his client are crucial behavioral samples to correctly answer the legal question. This exclusionary position finds case law support at both the federal and state level for both criminal and civil evaluations. Despite the opposing Sixth Amendment right to counsel, most courts have deferred to the request of the clinician that attorneys be excluded in both civil and criminal proceedings when the examiner is court appointed (*United States* v. *Byers*, *Durst* v. *Superior Court*, *Tarantino* v. *Superior Court*, *In re Spencer*, *Rollerson* v. *United States*, *Edwards* v. *Superior Court*, *Vinson* v. *Superior Court*). The American Bar Association (1984) also supports the exclusion of counsel from clinical interviews in most cases. However, attorneys do not like to be excluded from anything. Such a clinical position may raise the ire of counsel, particularly opposing counsel, but when faced with such a demand it is very important not to capitulate. The clinician should allow the attorney to take his demand to court in the form of a motion and let the court rule on the appropriateness of his presence.

Second, it is most wise to use structured interview formats when conducting forensic interviews. Such formats demonstrate to anyone who scrutinizes clinicians' work that they do have a "standard of care" and are interested in their own clinical reliability. It also ensures that crucial areas to be probed will not be overlooked because of momentary anxiety or distraction.

Structured interview formats may range from the clinician's own list of questions that he repeatedly uses when he addresses a certain psycholegal question, to much more formalized structured interviews that have both reliability and validity in the larger scientific community.

One such instrument, the Rogers Criminal Responsibility Assessment Scales (R-CRAS), is an excellent example of a structured interview for evaluating insanity at the time of the criminal offense (Rogers 1984b). The R-CRAS is a systematic and criterion-based instrument modeled after the Schedule of Affective Disorders and Schizophrenia. It consists of a 15-page examination booklet that is organized into two parts. Part 1 consists of 25 assessment criteria that are each quantified into four to six gradations of increasing severity. They address patient reliability, organicity, psychopathology, cognitive control, and behavioral control. Part 2 consists of three decision models that operationalize the American Law Institute (ALI), Guilty But Mentally Ill (GBMI), and McNaghten standards of criminal responsibility. The structured instrument has a moderate degree of internal consistency and a high degree of interjudge reliability (Meloy 1986).

A second example of a structured interview, this time used to assess competency to stand trial, is the Interdisciplinary Fitness Interview (IFI) by Golding and colleagues (1984). Ideally used in a joint interview by both a mental health professional and an attorney, the IFI covers the joint domains of psychopathology and law from an explicitly functional perspective. It consists of three sections: legal items (for example, "quality of relationship with one's current attorney"); psychopathological items (for example, "delusional processes"); and overall evaluation ("overall fitness judgment").

Interjudge agreement yielded a kappa coefficient of 0.93 in one study (Golding et al. 1984). It appears to have both a low false positive and a low false negative rate, and many fewer false positive errors than the older Competency Screening Test (McGarry et al. 1973). Further validity studies are needed, however (Meloy 1985).

A third example of structured interviewing, although not standardized, is the "structural interview" developed by Kernberg. In Kernberg's (1984) own words,

> The structural diagnostic interview . . . combines a psychoanalytic focus on the patient–interviewer interaction with a psychoanalytic technique for interpreting conflictual issues and defensive operations in this interaction in

> order to highlight simultaneously the classical anchoring symptoms of descriptive psychopathology and the underlying personality structure. [p. 30]

Kernberg's interview begins in a traditional manner with a history taking and mental status examination, but then probes more deeply into the patient's personality by focusing on questions that are bound to elicit certain transference and countertransference reactions: emotions perceived by the examiner that may be crucial to identifying underlying Axis II disorders that are endemic in forensic settings. Kernberg begins his investigation of pathological character traits with the following questions: "You have told me about your difficulties, and I would now like to hear more about you as a person. Could you describe yourself, your personality, what you think is important for me to know so that I can get a real feeling for you as a person?" (p. 33). Such a structured interview that combines both descriptive-symptomatic and object relational areas of inquiry can be particularly useful in assessing psychopathically disturbed individuals (Meloy 1988).

A third method to ensure the reliability and validity of the forensic interview is always to address the psycholegal question—nothing more and nothing less. The design of the forensic interview should be a logical outgrowth of the psycholegal question to be answered, and the database produced by the interview should build inferences that logically answer the psycholegal question. Anyone scrutinizing the forensic clinician's work should not be surprised by the interview methods or tests chosen to address a particular question, and subsequently should not be taken aback by the conclusions drawn from the accrued database.

I am always amazed at the frequency with which this seemingly simple and direct proposition is not followed by forensic clinicians. One way this commonly occurs is by what I call the "Oh, no!" technique (rather than the "Ah ha!" experience). One is carefully reading a forensic evaluation that appears to be accumulating more and more information supporting a particular legal opinion (for example, the individual did not know the difference between right and wrong at the time of the offense). Suddenly, on the last page,the evaluator renders the *exact opposite* opinion, and the reader is left feeling surprised and confused. Reasons for such Aristotelean failures abound, but the essential problem is that the logical progression has been negated and reversed.

Another common way this occurs is by what I call the "leap-before-you-look" technique. One begins reading a forensic evaluation that is supposedly addressing a psycholegal question. As the report proceeds, the reader waits expectantly, and more impatiently, for the forensic interviewer to *do* something or *say* something that is relevant to the psycholegal question. Then the report is finished with an opinion and a recommendation.

Something has been lost; the structure of the interview, the questions asked, the tests administered, the database collected, and the resultant conclusions *had nothing to do with the psycholegal question.* I have read reports that addressed competency to stand trial when the psycholegal question was insanity at the time of the offense. I have seen clinicians attempt to diagnose organic brain syndrome using the Rorschach. I have seen psychiatrists render opinions of dangerousness based solely upon a diagnosis of schizophrenia. Absolute reliability may occur in the face of absolutely zero validity. The forensic interview must be scientifically relevant and therefore a valid measure of the psycholegal question.

The courts have long recognized the importance of reliability and validity in expert testimony, and the admonition set forth in *Frye* v. *United States* (D.C. Circuit 1923) is also applicable to the structuring of the forensic interview:

> Just when a scientific principle or discovery crosses the line between the experimental and demonstrable stages is difficult to define. Somewhere in this twilight zone the evidential force of the principle must be recognized, and while courts will go a long way in admitting expert testimony deduced from a well-recognized scientific principle or discovery, the thing from which the deduction is made *must be sufficiently established to have gained general acceptance in the particular field in which it belongs.* [italics mine, 293 F. 1013]

This admonition, known as the "Frye test," is usually understood to mean that the particular scientific technique in question must be accepted by a majority of the profession, usually through authoritative scientific writings and other judicial citations.

The mental status examination, for example, would successfully pass the Frye test because it is used by most clinicians in conducting diagnostic evaluations. In fact, the *absence* of a mental status examination during a diagnostic evaluation could call into question the interviewer's competence. On the other hand, forensic clinicians using the Piotrowski method for interpreting the Rorschach could be seriously challenged using the Frye test since only 5 percent of survey respondents espouse this method of Rorschach interpretation (Piotrowski et al. 1985). The Exner Comprehensive System is rapidly gaining acceptance among clinicians (35 percent of survey respondents espoused this method) and may soon be the only Rorschach interpretive method that will pass the Frye test.

In California, *People* v. *Kelly* established a two-prong test for admissibility of new scientific technique: The reliability of the method must be established, usually by expert testimony; and the witness so testifying must be properly qualified as an expert to give an opinion on the subject. The court also noted, however, that this "Kelly-Frye rule" applied to novel devices or processes, not to expert medical testimony: "Such a diagnosis need not be based on certainty, but may be based on probability; the lack of absolute scientific certainty does not deprive the opinion of evidentiary value . . ." (*People* v. *Mendibles* at 557).

One can therefore conclude that the forensic interview should be conducted in a manner and with certain assessment techniques that would be accepted by a majority of the forensic psychology community.

The opinion rendered on the basis of the forensic interview would not have to be accepted by a majority of the professional community to have evidentiary value, however. Such planning should ensure the reliability and validity of the forensic interview and should protect the forensic clinician, who continually faces scrutiny and disagreement.

FORENSIC PSYCHOLOGICAL INVESTIGATION

The final distinguishing core characteristic of the forensic interview is the attitude and expectation of the interviewer. Forensic interviews compel the forensic clinician to assume the role of a *forensic psychological investigator.* The attitude is one of impartiality and objectivity. The expectation is that data will accumulate that will eventually answer the psycholegal question that prompted the evaluation. The "client" may be a government agency, a private attorney, a referring professional, or the judiciary. It is rarely the interviewee. Monahan (1980) has edited an excellent compilation of papers about the ethics of psychological intervention in the criminal justice system.

The role of the forensic psychological investigator precludes certain other expectations that are often deeply embedded in the clinician's professional training; the role of healer, therapist, "helper," and patient advocate *must be abdicated* if forensic psychological investigation is to occur in a reliable and valid manner. This does *not* mean, however, that respect for the dignity and worth of the individual, protection of his civil rights, protection of his welfare, or awareness of his legal rights should be ignored. In fact, these ethical imperatives must be vigilantly pursued, since forensic investigation, by its nature, may tempt the clinician to violate or compromise them.

The role of the forensic psychological investigator is fully consonant with the psychologist's ethics. Nothing in the ethical principles implies that all professional interactions must be "therapeutic" or "helping." There are limits, however, to psychological investigation:

> While demanding for themselves freedom of inquiry and communication, psychologists accept the responsibility this freedom requires: competence, objectivity in the application of skills, and concern for the best interests of clients, colleagues, students, research participants, and society. [Preamble, American Psychological Association 1981]

I have occasionally seen such role confusion lead to contrived ethical conflicts for the clinician and, in some cases, defensive and angry posturing under cross-examination. When this happens, the clinician's credibility as an expert witness is usually lost, and the courtroom experience becomes an unpleasant, if not painful, emotional memory.

How does the clinician prepare to assume the role of a forensic psychological investigator? First, the clinician must be comfortable with the goal of understanding, rather than changing, human behavior. If this is not the case, and the clinician's primary identification is with the role of therapist or "healer," he should not undertake the role of forensic psychological investigator.

Second, careful thought must be given to potential ethical problems that may arise with each forensic case. The ethical caveat concerning dual relationships (American Psychological Association 1981) is most germane to this consideration. For instance, if at all possible, a clinician should avoid conducting a forensic psychological investigation of a patient he has seen in psychotherapy, regardless of whether the treatment has ended. Sometimes a court order will make this virtually impossible, but the clinician is ethically obligated to inform the court of his professional imperative to avoid such dual relationships (principle 6, American Psychological Association 1981). Clinicians should avoid serving as experts for attorneys who are also friends or social acquaintances. This can be particularly difficult in small communities, but would be considered a violation of the dual-relationship clause if ethically challenged. The assessment of competency for execution is another area of professional concern that raises profound ethical problems for clinicians who believe in the primacy of individual life (Heilbrun 1987). Such an evaluation may violate the preamble, principle 3, and principle 6 of the psychologist's ethical principles (American Psychological Association 1981).

And third, clinicians should be knowledgeable about the other core characteristics that I have outlined and should prepare themselves with the requisite skills, attitudes, approaches, and techniques that I have suggested accompany each characteristic: the coercive context, the absence of privilege, a lay communication tool, the presence of distortion, and disagreement and scrutiny.

Such preparation for the forensic interview should foreshadow success in the forensic arena. After all, it would be a shame if the forensic clinician suddenly realized that his self-perceived "good reputation" was only a symptom of *pronoia*: the delusional belief that others are saying nice things about him behind his back.

REFERENCES

Adelman, R., and Howard, A. (1984). Expert testimony on malingering: the admissibility of clinical procedures for the detection of deception. *Behavioral Sciences and the Law* 2:5–20.

American Bar Association (1984). *Criminal Justice Mental Health Standards.* Chicago: author.

Albert, S., Fox, H., and Kahn, M. (1980). Faking psychosis on the Rorschach: can expert judges detect malingering? *Journal of Personality Assessment* 44:115–119.

Alpert, M., and Silvers, K. (1970). Perceptual characteristics distinguishing auditory hallucinations in schizophrenia and acute alcoholic psychoses. *American Journal of Psychiatry* 127:298–302.

American Psychiatric Association (1987). *Diagnostic and Statistical Manual of Mental Disorders*, 3rd ed., rev. Washington, DC: APA.

American Psychological Association (1981). Ethical principles of psychologists. *American Psychologist* 36:633.

Blau, T. (1984). *The Psychologist as Expert Witness.* New York: Wiley.

Buechley, R., and Ball, M. (1952). A new test of "test validity" for the group MMPI. *Journal of Consulting Psychology* 16:299–301.

Colorado v. *Connelly*, 107 S. Ct. 515 (1986).

Curran, W., McGarry, L., and Shah, S. (1986). *Forensic Psychiatry and Psychology.* Philadephia: F. A. Davis.

Durst v. *Superior Court*, 35 Cal. Rptr. 143 (1964).

Dusky v. *United States*, 362 U.S. 402 (1960).

Edwards v. *Superior Court*, 16 Cal. 3d 906 (1976).

Ekman, P., and Friesen, W. (1969). Nonverbal leakage and clues to deception. *Psychiatry* 32:88–106.

Estelle v. *Smith*, 451 U.S. 454 (1981).

Exner, J. (1978). *The Rorschach Comprehensive System: Current Research and Advanced Interpretation*, vol. 2. New York: Wiley.

——— (1986). *The Rorschach: A Comprehensive System: Foundations*, vol. 1, 2nd ed. New York: Wiley.

Frye v. *United States*, 293 F. 1013 (D.C. Cir. 1923).

Garner, H. (1965). Malingering. *Illinois Medical Journal* 128:318–319.

Gill, M., ed. (1967). *The Collected Papers of David Rapaport.* New York: Basic Books.

Golding, S., Roesch, R., and Schreiber, J. (1984). Assessment and conceptualization of competency to stand trial. *Law and Human Behavior* 8:321–334.

Goodwin, D., Alderson, P., and Rosenthal, R. (1971). Clinical significance of hallucinations in psychiatric disorders: a study of 116 hallucinatory patients. *Archives of General Psychiatry* 24:76–80.

Gorman, W. (1984). Neurological malingering. *Behavioral Sciences and the Law* 2:67–74.

Gough, H. (1950). The F-K dissimulation index for the Minnesota Multiphasic Personality Inventory. *Journal of Consulting Psychology* 14:408–413.

Greene, R. (1978). An empirically derived MMPI carelessness scale. *Journal of Clinical Psychology* 34:407–409.

——— (1980). *MMPI: An Interpretative Manual.* New York: Grune & Stratton.

Grisso, T. (1986). *Evaluating Competencies.* New York: Plenum.

Hare, R. (1980). A research scale for the assessment of psychopathy in criminal populations. *Personality and Individual Differences* 1:111–119.

——— (1985a). Comparison of procedures for the assessment of psychopathy. *Journal of Consulting and Clinical Psychology* 53:7–16.

——— (1985b). *The Psychopathy Checklist.* Vancouver, Canada: University Press of British Columbia.

Heilbrun, K. S. (1987). The assessment of competency for execution: an overview. *Behavioral Sciences and the Law* 5:383–396.

Hellerstein, D., Frosch, W., and Koenigsberg, H. (1987). The clinicial significance of command hallucinations. *American Journal of Psychiatry* 144:219–221.

Hunt, H. (1948). The effects of deceit deception on the Minnesota Multiphasic Personality Inventory performance. *Journal of Consulting Psychology* 12:396–402.

In re Lifschutz, 2 Cal. 3d 415, 85 Cal. Rptr. 829, 467 P. 2d 557 (1985). In *Law and the Mental Health System*, ed. R. Reisner, pp. 249–251. St. Paul: West.

In re Spencer, 63 C. 2d 400 (1964).

Kernberg, O. (1984). *Severe Personality Disorders: Psychotherapeutic Strategies.* New Haven: Yale University Press.

Littlepage, G., and Pineault, T. (1978). Verbal, facial, and paralinguistic cues to the detection of truth and lying. *Personality and Social Psychology Bulletin* 4:461–464.

Lubin, B., Larsen, R., and Matarazzo, J. (1984). Patterns of psychological test usage in the United States, 1935–1982. *American Psychologist* 39:451–454.

Maier, N., and Thurber, J. (1968). Accuracy of judgment of deception when an interviewer is watched, heard, and read. *Personnel Psychology* 21:23–30.

McClintock, C., and Hunt, R. (1975). Nonverbal indicators of affect and deception in an interview setting. *Journal of Applied Social Psychology* 5:54–67.

McGarry, A. L., Curran, N. J., Lipsitt, P. D., et al. (1973). *Competency to Stand Trial and Mental Illness.* Washington, DC: US Government Printing Office.

Meloy, R. (1985). *The Fitness Interview Test*, by R. Roesch, C. Webster, and D. Eaves (book review). *Bulletin of the American Academy of Psychiatry and the Law* 13:419–420.

——— (1986). *Rogers Criminal Responsibility Assessment Scales*, by R. Rogers (book review). *Bulletin of the American Academy of Psychiatry and the Law* 14:99.

——— (1988). *The Psychopathic Mind: Origins, Dynamics, and Treatment.* Northvale, NJ: Jason Aronson.

Melton, G., Petrila, J., Poythress, N., and Slobogin, C. (1987). *Pyschological Evaluations for the Courts.* New York: Guilford.

Monahan, J., ed. (1980). *Who is the Client?* Washington, DC: American Psychological Association.

Osborne, D., Colligan, R., and Offord, K. (1986). Normative tables for the F-K Index of the MMPI based on a contemporary normal sample. *Journal of Clinical Psychology* 42:593–595.

Overholser, W. (1953). *The Psychiatrist and the Law*, p. 109. New York: Harcourt Brace.

People v. *Kelly*, 17 Ca. 3d 24 (1976).

People v. *Laws*, San Diego County Superior Court, MH 74987, The Honorable J. Perry Langford, June 17, 1987.

People v. *Mendibles*, 245 Cal. Rptr. 553 (1988).

Piotrowski, C., Sherry, D., and Keller, J. (1985). Psychodiagnostic test usage: a survey of the Society for Personality Assessment. *Journal of Personality Assessment* 49:115–119.

Resnick, P. (1984). The detection of malingered mental illness. *Behavioral Sciences and the Law* 2:21–38.

Rogers, R. (1983). Malingering or random? A research note on obvious vs. subtle subscales of the MMPI. *Journal of Consulting and Clinical Psychology* 39:257–258.

——— (1984a). Towards an empirical model of malingering and deception. *Behavioral Sciences and the Law* 2:93–112.

——— (1984b). *Rogers Criminal Responsibility Assessment Scales.* Odessa, FL: Psychological Assessment Resources.

——— (1986). *Conducting Insanity Evaluations.* New York: Van Nostrand Reinhold.

Rollerson v. *United States*, 343 F. 2d 274 (1964).

Salgo v. *Leland Stanford Jr. Univ. Bd. of Trustees*, 317 P. 2d 170 (1957).

Seamons, D., Howell, R., Carlisle, A., and Roe, A. (1981). Rorschach simulation of mental illness and normality by psychotic and nonpsychotic legal offenders. *Journal of Personality Assessment* 45:130–135.

Shapiro, D. (1984). *Psychological Evaluation and Expert Testimony.* New York: Van Nostrand Reinhold.

Strunk, W., Jr., and White, E. (1979). *The Elements of Style, 3rd ed.* New York: Macmillan.

Tarantino v. *Superior Court*, 48 C.A. 3d 465 (1975).

Tarasoff v. *Regents of the University of California*, 118 Cal. Rptr. 129, 529 P. 2d 553 (1974); 17 Cal. 3d 425, 551 P. 2d 334 (1976).

United States v. *Alvarez*, 519 F. 2d 1036 (1975).

United States v. *Byers*, 740 F. 2d 1104 (1984).

United States ex. rel. Edney v. *Smith*, 425 F. Supp. 1038 (1976); affirmed 556 F. 2d 556 (1977).

Vinson v. *Superior Court*, 43 Cal. 3d 833 (1987).

Webster, N. (1977). *The Living Webster Encyclopedic Dictionary.* Chicago: The English Language Institute of America.

Wiener, D. N. (1948). Subtle and obvious keys for the Minnesota Multiphasic Personality Inventory. *Journal of Consulting Psychology* 12:164–170.

Ziskin, J. (1984). Malingering of psychological disorders. *Behavioral Sciences and the Law* 2:39–50.

Zuckerman, M., Larrance, D., Hall, J., et al. (1979). Posed and spontaneous communication of emotion via facial and vocal cues. *Journal of Personality* 47:712–733.

INDEX